A Cognitive Neuropsychological Approach to Assessment and Intervention in Aphasia

A clinician's guide

Second edition

Anne Whitworth, Janet Webster and David Howard

Psychology Press
Taylor & Francis Group
LONDON AND NEW YORK

Second edition published 2014
by Psychology Press
27 Church Road, Hove, East Sussex BN3 2FA

and by Psychology Press
711 Third Avenue, New York, NY 10017

Psychology Press is an imprint of the Taylor & Francis Group, an informa business

First edition published by Psychology Press 2005

British Library Cataloguing in Publication Data
A catalogue record for this book is available from the British Library

Library of Congress Cataloging in Publication Data
A catalog record for this title has been requested

ISBN: 978–1–84872–097–8 (hbk)
ISBN: 978–1–84872–142–5 (pbk)
ISBN: 978–1–315–85244–7 (ebk)

Typeset in Times New Roman
by Swales & Willis Ltd, Exeter, Devon

MIX
Paper from
responsible sources
FSC   FSC® C013056
www.fsc.org

Printed and bound in Great Britain by
TJ International Ltd, Padstow, Cornwall

No method of treatment is better than the principles on which it is based, and the search for principles should concern us no less than the immediate clinical situation.

(Zangwill, 1947, p. 7)

Contents

Preface

The first edition of this book evolved from the activity of a group of speech and language therapists in Newcastle-upon-Tyne, UK, who met, and still meet, regularly to evaluate new developments in aphasia, explore new assessment tools and approaches, exchange views on management strategies, encourage clinical research and generally swap stories of working with people with aphasia. Steeped within a strong cognitive neuropsychological tradition, we decided, in the early 2000s, to tackle the frustration that arose from the lack of accessible literature in this area for the working clinician and try to draw together what it was that we did in our daily practice. Our project benefited us all, evolving into an ambition to make it more comprehensive and accessible to a wider group of clinicians and students working with people with aphasia; this saw the publication of the first edition of this volume. Following the success of this book as a significant resource for clinicians, students and researchers alike in many different countries, and with the continued support and input of the Newcastle Aphasia Study Group, this second edition continues the original aim of making sense of this vast area of aphasia research for the practising clinician. In doing so, it is intended to benefit directly the clients we work with, to advance our own skills in creating and using the evidence, and to contribute to the interface between cognitive neuropsychology and aphasia therapy. Members of the Newcastle Aphasia Study Group who contributed to lively discussions throughout this process are, in alphabetical order, Deborah Annis, Jennifer Bell, Helen Bird, Jessica Bristowe, Kirsty Bramley, Frauke Buerk, Ros Emerson, Gill Everson, Louise Ferguson, Catherine Fishwick, Jane Giles, Liz Green, Ruth Hall, Amanda Harris, Pat Heaney, Rose Hilton, Fiona Hinshelwood, Lisa Hirst, David Howard, Louise Kelly, Louise Kellett, Anne-Marie Laverty, Rachael Leisk, Amy Lewis, Christine Lucas, Jenny Malone, Selena Mathie, Aileen McDonald, Janet McWilliam, Fiona Menger, Laura Mizzi, Jennie Morgan, Julie Morris, Kath Mumby, Helen Nazlie, Chris Plant, Laura Quietch, Josie Roy, Jennifer Scott, Lucy Skelton, Lucinda Sommerset, Bryony Stevens, Fiona Stewart, Susan Stewart, Jill Summersall, Clare Telford, Julie Trimble, Sonja Turner, Jennifer Vigouroux, Julia Wade, Heather Waldron, Vicki Watts, Janet Webster, Anne Whitworth and Sheila Wight. Our many thanks to the group members for their efforts and support that allowed this book, and its predecessor, to see the light of day, and their continued enthusiasm for discussing and evaluating their work with aphasia that permeates our lively meetings. A special thanks also to Jenny Crinion for her helpful insights into recent neurological developments in aphasia. In addition, we would like to continue to offer our thanks to Lyndsey Nickels, Sue Franklin and Lisa Perkins for their contributions to the original volume.

Anne Whitworth, Janet Webster and David Howard

Introduction

While a cognitive neuropsychological approach is widely used in aphasia clinics throughout the UK and other countries to assess and treat people with aphasia, there is relatively little published information that is accessible to the speech and language therapist (or speech language pathologist) that explores the application of this approach. A small number of published assessment tools, for example the Psycholinguistic Assessments of Language Processing in Aphasia (Kay, Lesser & Coltheart, 1992) and the Comprehensive Aphasia Test (Swinburn, Porter & Howard, 2005), while widely used, are not supported by accessible literature to assist the working clinician in selecting the appropriate test to use, interpreting the results and identifying intact and impaired processing systems. These are, we would argue, crucial steps in devising therapy that is, as Hatfield and Shewell (1983) put it, both rational and specific; rational in the sense that it is based on a coherent account of impaired and intact processes, and specific in that it is targeted towards the effects of the impairments for an individual.

Therapeutic application of cognitive neuropsychology also remains difficult to digest. While there is a developing literature on therapy for people with aphasia that uses therapy approaches grounded within a cognitive neuropsychological perspective, these case reports are presented in various forms that differ in their accessibility to clinicians and transparency with the theoretical models used. This book aims to link theory and practice within a cognitive neuropsychological framework, presenting the theoretical literature and relating it directly to available assessment tools and reported therapy techniques. It is intended to provide both a theoretical and practical reference for the working clinician. It does not aim to be prescriptive; it is anticipated that it will provide information that will help clinicians to use cognitive neuropsychological knowledge in the assessment and treatment of people with aphasia.

As service provision to people with aphasia often occurs within the context of healthcare systems, the terms 'person with aphasia' and 'client' are used interchangeably throughout the book. Further, the terms 'clinician' and 'therapist' are used interchangeably to refer to speech and language therapist or speech–language pathologist.

The person with aphasia and the broader clinical context

Before embarking on our exploration of this approach, we wish, as clinicians, to state the obvious. Investigation and interpretation of communication impairments using this approach is only one facet in the holistic approach to working with people with aphasia. This approach should, we believe, only be used within a total communication framework, with the person with aphasia being central and his or her personal circumstances and partners in communication being integral to the entire process. The importance of looking at areas other than deficits, of viewing the person with aphasia as an autonomous human being, of considering communication in context and of looking outside traditional modes of service delivery, are assumed to be obvious elements of any coherent holistic approach to working with people with aphasia.

We do not, therefore, wish to imply that this approach should be used in isolation from the broader context of the person with aphasia's real-life circumstances, but we do believe that a comprehensive analysis of his or her language-processing system often forms a necessary and vital part in understanding the nature of the difficulties encountered by the person with aphasia and in directing and informing subsequent management.

Structure of the book

This volume is divided into three discrete but interconnected sections. Part 1 sets out the cognitive neuropsychological approach used within the current management of people with aphasia, placing it within both an historical and contemporary framework.

Part 2 provides a working explanation of the theoretical model, outlining the deficits that may arise from impairment to each stage of the model and discussing assessment for each stage. The areas of spoken and written word comprehension, spoken and written word production, and object recognition are then explored in Chapters 4 to 8. While strictly outside the domain of language, object and picture recognition have been included because many assessments employ picture materials; as a result, these impairments may impact on performance on language assessments. In the chapters of Part 2, we seek to provide an accessible guide to the use of assessment tools in identifying underlying impairments. This is supported by brief case studies illustrating various patterns of impairment. Developments in this second edition of this volume include the addition of new assessments onto the market, in particular, the Comprehensive Aphasia Test (CAT) (Swinburn *et al.*, 2005), the removal of previously reported assessments where they are no longer available and/or widely used, and the inclusion of assessments that focus on the comprehension and production of verbs. The attention given to verbs reflects the growing interest in verbs more generally in aphasia, both in furthering our understanding of how we process different word classes and how we can intervene to have the greatest impact on communication.

Part 3 provides a selective review of the therapy literature, with detailed summaries of the therapy used. An introductory chapter to therapy sets out the principles of using a cognitive neuropsychological approach in intervention in aphasia, along with an overview of the methods used and practical suggestions for designing therapy studies in clinical practice. The role of the clinician researcher in both applying the evidence reported in the literature and testing out new hypotheses with clients is highlighted, as is the reciprocal contribution our activity can make to the theory of aphasia and normal processing. The therapy studies, set out in Chapters 10 to 14, have been systematically reviewed to provide information on the therapy procedures employed in each study, including, for example, tasks, materials and feedback given to the client, alongside brief details of the client and the outcome of therapy. A synthesis of the therapy literature is provided for auditory comprehension, word retrieval, reading and writing, summarising what has been gained, to date, from clinical research using a cognitive neuropsychological approach to manage communication impairment in people with aphasia. As with the assessment chapters, the chapters focusing on intervention have been expanded to include those studies targeting verb retrieval. For ease of reading, therapies aimed at noun production and verb production are presented in two separate chapters. Those studies that have sought to explore the relative impacts of employing the same therapies with both nouns and verbs are explored in the second of these chapters. The literature reviewed here is not exhaustive, and the studies discussed are neither necessarily methodologically ideal nor are described taking the exact theoretical position of the authors of this volume. We believe, however, that they are representative of the research in the area and allow us to shed light on the utility of the theoretical models many clinicians and researchers have been applying to the management of aphasia. In doing so, we trust that engaging with this literature will have a direct benefit for people with aphasia and their families.

Part 1

Theory and principles

1 A cognitive neuropsychological approach
Theories and models

An historical perspective

Cognitive neuropsychology first emerged as a coherent discipline in the 1970s as a reaction to the then dominant approach in neuropsychology. This earlier approach to neuropsychology (the 'classical approach') sought to characterise the performance of people with aphasia by defining them in terms of their localisation of lesion (see Shallice, 1988, for further discussion of this approach). The aim here was to understand the psychological functions of parts of the cortex by investigating the patterns of deficits shown by individuals with lesions in these areas, and identify syndromes defined in terms of deficits that frequently co-occurred. Over the last 30 years, in the UK at least, cognitive neuropsychology has expanded to become the dominant approach in neuropsychology. Part of the reason is that it moved neuropsychology from being of interest only to those concerned with brain behaviour relationships to a major source of evidence on the nature of normal processing. Another reason is that good cognitive neuropsychology pays real attention to providing accounts that address how individual people with brain lesions behave, often using sophisticated experimental methods to investigate the determinants of their performance.

The origins of cognitive neuropsychology lay in two papers on people with reading disorders by Marshall and Newcombe (1966, 1973). There were two critical features. First, Marshall and Newcombe realised that individual people with reading disorders could show qualitatively different patterns of impairment that would have been obscured by treating them as a group. They described two people who made semantic errors in single-word reading (e.g. NEPHEW → 'cousin', CITY → 'town'; a difficulty described as 'deep dyslexia'), two people who made regularisation errors (e.g. LISTEN → 'liston', ISLAND → 'izland'; 'surface dyslexia'), and two people who made primarily visually related errors (e.g. EASEL → 'aerial', PAMPER → 'paper'; 'visual dyslexia'). The second feature was that the nature of the individual's problems could be understood in terms of an information-processing model developed to account for the performance of normal individuals, in this case the 'dual-route' model of reading. Three of the essential features of cognitive neuropsychology that were to define the approach were evident here: (1) the realisation that the performance of the individual, not the average of a group, was the important evidence; (2) that the nature of errors was informative; and (3) that the explanations of individuals' performance were to be couched in terms of information models of normal language processing and not in terms of brain lesions.

The approach developed from an initial focus on reading disorders to encompass a variety of other domains. These include, in a vaguely chronological order, spelling disorders, memory impairments (including both long- and short-term memory), semantic disorders, disorders of word retrieval, disorders of object and picture recognition, word-comprehension impairments, disorders of action, executive disorders, sentence-processing impairments, number processing, and calculation. The initial focus, in terms of the people whose disorders were investigated, was on adults with acquired brain lesions, typically following stroke, head injury or, more rarely, brain infections such as herpes simplex encephalitis. The focus has now broadened to encompass developmental disorders, and those disorders found in progressive brain diseases, most prominently the dementias.

Methods have also shown a gradual change. While the early studies were in-depth investigations of single individuals, there has been an increasing use of case series designs where a series of people are investigated using the same set of tasks. The data are not, however, analysed in terms of groups, but rather the focus is on accounting for the patterns of performance of a group of people analysed individually. Here, both differences and similarities between individuals constitute the relevant evidence. Theoretical models have also evolved. While box and arrow models of cognitive architecture remain a major source of explanatory concepts, there has been increasing use of computational models, usually confined to specific domains such as reading, word retrieval or comprehension.

Finally, there has been, since 1987 – when effective functional imaging of language was first developed – and particularly in the last 15 years, a resurgence of interest in localisation of cognitive functions in the brain. This has been fuelled by the development of imaging methods such as positron emission tomography (PET) and functional magnetic resonance imaging (fMRI) that can be used to measure changes in regional blood flow (reflecting local synaptic activity) in the brain while people are engaged in cognitive tasks. These methods have allowed people to explore how and where the information-processing modules are represented in the brain (e.g. Price *et al.*, 2003; Price, 2012).

Cognitive neuropsychology as a working theoretical model

With the abandonment of theories that drew direct links between localising lesions in the brain and characterising deficits in speech and language, the replacement model drew on the components involved in processing information and the interconnections between such components. These were first illustrated in Morton and Patterson's (1980) version of the logogen model. Morton and Patterson (1980) revised and articulated earlier versions of the logogen model (which date back to Morton, 1969) to account for both the types of errors and the factors influencing reading performance (e.g. word imageability; part of speech) in people with deep dyslexia. This model was a quintessential 'box and arrow' processing diagram that specified a number of component processes (the boxes) and how they interrelate (the arrows). The model referred to in this book is illustrated in Figure 1.1 and is (loosely) based on Patterson and Shewell's (1987) adaptation of the earlier logogen models.

While a model of this kind may appear complex, each of these components appears to be necessary to account for the processing of single words. As Coltheart, Rastle, Perry, Langdon and Ziegler (2001) argued: 'All the complexities of the model are motivated. If any box or arrow were deleted from it, the result would be a system that would fail in at least one language-processing task at which humans succeed' (p. 211).

If different modules and connections (boxes and arrows) in this model can be independently impaired, a very large number of possible patterns of performance may result from a lesion. Given this large number, one clearly cannot assume that any two people will necessarily have the same pattern of performance. The idea, therefore, that aphasia can be grouped into a limited number of identifiable and homogeneous 'syndromes' must

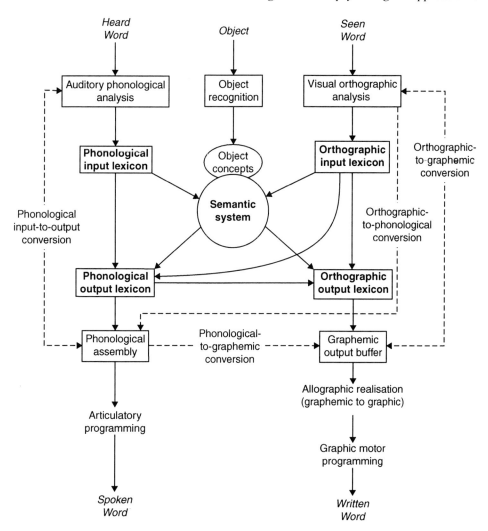

Figure 1.1 Language-processing model for single words, based on Patterson and Shewell's (1987) logogen model

necessarily fail. This does not, of course, mean that there will not be resemblances between the performances of different people with aphasia; to the extent that they have the same components damaged, this is precisely what we would predict. Nor does it mean that some combinations of symptoms do not appear more frequently than others. It simply means that one cannot group data from people with aphasia together as the differences between individuals are important (Shallice, 1988). Analysis of data from single individuals is the necessary consequence.

Using this kind of model to explain patterns of performance with people with aphasia involves making several assumptions, described and defended in detail by, among others, Caramazza (1986), Shallice (1988) and Coltheart (2001). Coltheart (2001) describes four assumptions:

1   *Functional modularity.* Some, at least, of the components of the cognitive system are modular, meaning that they operate independently, or relatively independently, of other components.

2   *Anatomical modularity.* Some, at least, of the modules of the cognitive system are localised in different parts of the brain. As a result, brain lesions can result in selective information-processing deficits, either by destroying the tissue responsible for particular modules or by disconnecting them. Functional modularity does not necessarily entail anatomical modularity.

3   *Universality of cognitive systems.* This simplifying assumption is that all normal people have the same cognitive systems. This is a plausible assumption for language processing, for example, but is clearly not directly applicable in domains of which some people have no experience, for example music. Note that it is not claimed here that all people will have equal experience and facility in all aspects of their cognitive system, rather that different people do not have radically different cognitive architectures for the same processes.

4   *Subtractivity.* The result of a brain lesion is to destroy, damage or impair one or more components of the normal cognitive system. Damage does not result in new information-processing systems. On the other hand, a person with brain damage may rely on different sources of information to perform a task, but these use processing systems that were available pre-morbidly. For example, a person with a severe face recognition impairment (prosopagnosia) may come to rely on a person's dress or voice to recognise them. While normal individuals may not rely on these strategies to recognise people, they can do so when necessary.

Models like that in Figure 1.1 are, in this form, radically underspecified. The diagram says nothing about how the processing in the boxes is achieved. Each of the cognitive modules will necessarily have structure and may comprise a whole set of component processes. For example, Figure 1.1 has a box called 'phonological assembly'. Levelt, Roelofs and Meyer (1999) argue that there are a number of separable processes involved in phonological assembly, including separate spell out of both the segmental and metrical structure. There is evidence that there can be separable impairments of these component processes (Nickels & Howard, 2000).

A working assumption is that any of the modules in the diagram can be lost or damaged as a result of cortical lesions. An individual with aphasia might have damage to one or several modules or the mappings between them. Because of the functional architecture of the brain, some patterns of deficits will be more frequent than others, but because lesions vary both in their precise cortical locations and in the cutting of sub-cortical white matter fibre tracts, identical patterns of deficit in any two people are unlikely. One objective in assessment can be to identify which of the modules and mappings (boxes and arrows) are damaged and which are intact, yielding a concise explanation of the pattern of performance across a range of tasks and materials.

In Chapters 4–8 we describe, in outline only, the nature of the processing in many of the components of the model. We are aware, of course, that we are not putting forward a complete, or even necessarily accurate, model of language processing even just for single words. Our fundamental claim, in the context of this book, is much more modest. It is that the model in Figure 1.1 provides a usable working model of language processing. It provides a level of description that can be used to guide a process of assessment that can identify levels of breakdown and intact and impaired processes in people with aphasia.

Competing models

There are many models of single-word processing that can be, and have been, used to account for patterns of language breakdown as well as normal processing. Many of these are task-specific, dealing, for example, with spoken word production (e.g. Foygel & Dell, 2000; Levelt *et al.*, 1999; Rapp & Goldrick, 2000, Oppenheim, Dell & Schwartz, 2010), spoken language comprehension (e.g. Marslen-Wilson, 1987), or semantic representation (e.g. Tyler, Moss, Durrant-Peatfield & Levy, 2000). Evaluation of such models is beyond the scope of what this book aims to achieve. However, while these models do attempt to provide detailed accounts of representations and processes involved in particular tasks, they provide little information on how different tasks relate to each other. For example, the phonological assembly module in the lexical model of Figure 1.1 is a common output process shared by picture naming, word reading and word repetition. Impairment at this level should result in qualitatively similar patterns of impairment across all three tasks (some quantitative differences may be due to the differing nature of the input to the module). This is the pattern found in many people with phonological deficits in speech production (e.g. Caplan, Vanier & Baker, 1986; Franklin, Buerk & Howard, 2002).

Some models do, however, highlight the shared nature of processes and aim to account for patterns of performance across different tasks. In 1979, motivated by patterns of cross-modal repetition priming, Morton had revised the original 1969 logogen model that had a single lexicon for spoken word recognition, spoken word production, written word recognition and written word production, to have the four separate lexicons shown in Figure 1.1 (Morton, 1979a). Allport and Funnell (1981) pointed out that Morton's priming data only motivated a separation of orthographic and phonological lexicons, and, arguing against the need for the separation into input and output lexicons, suggested that a single phonological lexicon was used for both spoken word recognition and production, and a single orthographic lexicon was used for written word recognition and writing (see also Allport, 1985). There have been discussions about the explanatory adequacy of this proposal centring on a number of issues (see Howard & Franklin, 1988; Monsell, 1987). For example, there are people with deficits apparently at a lexical level in word retrieval with unimpaired recognition of the same words in spoken form (e.g. Howard, 1995) and, conversely, those with a lexical level of deficit in spoken word recognition with relatively unimpaired spoken naming (Howard & Franklin, 1988). This dissociation seems to imply separate input and output phonological lexicons. On the other hand, there have been reports of item-specific difficulties in reading and spelling that may be most easily captured by proposing impairment to a common orthographic lexicon (Behrmann & Bub, 1992).

A computational interactive activation model that also incorporated a single lexicon for word recognition and production was developed by Martin, Dell and their colleagues (Martin, Dell, Saffran & Schwartz, 1994; Schwartz, Dell, Martin & Saffran, 1994). In the original form of the model, word comprehension depended on exactly the same components as in word production operating in reverse. They used this to model the pattern of errors in repetition and naming in a single person who made semantic errors in repetition. However, when Dell, Schwartz, Martin, Saffran and Gagnon (1997) tried to use this model to account for the pattern of errors in naming and repetition in a group of further people with aphasia, they found that lesions that captured, with reasonable accuracy, the individuals' patterns of errors in naming, typically radically underestimated their repetition accuracy. Coupled with demonstrations that the model, in its unlesioned form, was only able to comprehend two-thirds of words correctly, was unable to repeat nonwords, and could not account for the relationships between accuracy in comprehension and production found in people with aphasia (Nickels & Howard, 1995b), Dell *et al.* (1997) abandoned this as a model of comprehension. Even its ability to account for the patterns of errors found in naming with people with aphasia has been challenged (Ruml & Caramazza, 2000). As a result of these problems, the 2000 version of this model by Foygel and Dell (2000) restricts its aims simply to accounting for patterns of errors in picture naming. Nozari, Kittreddge, Dell & Schwartz (2010) developed the model to account for word repetition, developing a sub-lexical route in addition to account for their data. Dell, Nozari and Oppenheim (in press) give an elegant summary of their view. There have been a variety of papers on therapy inspired by this model.

Finally, we need to consider the 'triangle model' developed by McClelland, Plaut, Seidenberg, Patterson and their colleagues (Plaut, McClelland, Seidenberg & Patterson, 1996; Seidenberg & McClelland, 1989). This is a computational model of lexical processing that, like that of Allport and Funnell (1981), has only a single phonological system serving both production and comprehension of spoken words and a single orthographic system for both written input and output. The radical innovation in this model, however, is that there is no lexical representation. A set of units in phonological space, for example, encodes any possible phonological string whether word or nonword. Mappings from phonology to semantics or orthography will have been learned, using a real word vocabulary. During the process of learning, the weights in the connections between the input units and hidden units, and those between hidden units and orthography and semantics, will have been adjusted so that they achieve the correct mappings for the words used to train the model (see Plaut *et al.*, 1996, for a detailed description of this model). Knowledge of the mappings for individual words are not localised in a lexicon, but distributed across all the weights in all the connections between the domains.

The triangle model has been in development since Seidenberg and McClellands' (1989) proposal. There are two particularly notable achievements that have resulted. Plaut and Shallice (1993) showed that, at least with a limited vocabulary, a model mapping from orthography via semantics to phonology can account for most of the features found in people with deep dyslexia. Plaut *et al.* (1996) and Plaut (1999) have developed a model of the direct mapping from orthography to phonology for single-syllable words. With the right representations in both the orthographic and phonological domains, this model has enjoyed considerable success in accounting for the phenomena of normal reading and the patterns of deficit found in people with surface and phonological dyslexia. Most radically, the model shows that a single computational mechanism, trained only on a real word vocabulary, is able to generate the correct phonology for both irregular words (e.g. YACHT, PINT) and nonwords (e.g. THORK, SLINT). Rogers, Lambon Ralph, Garrard *et al.* (2004) developed this to account for a range of semantic tasks for people with semantic dementia.

Computational models of these kinds present a very interesting new way of understanding how mappings between domains might be implemented. It is important to realise, however, that the capabilities of these models depend critically on how the representations in the input and output domains are coded, as well as features of the architecture of the model such as the numbers of hidden units, and how they are connected. Models of this kind generally find it much easier to learn mappings between domains that are mostly systematic and generalisable, as in the mapping from orthography to phonology (where, for instance, the letter M at input almost always relates to a phoneme /m/ in output). This is because it finds it easiest to learn mappings where similar inputs result in similar outputs (see Plaut & Shallice, 1993). Where, as in the mapping from orthography to semantics, there is no systematicity of this kind, the connectionist model finds this difficult to learn, although, eventually, it can succeed. Children, on the other hand, learn the mapping between new words and their meanings with extraordinary rapidity (Clark, 1993).

These models are currently limited in scope. Most of the implemented models have only feed-forward connections (that is, they use only one-directional connections between levels), although the overarching triangle model always uses bidirectional connections between domains. Since we know that the architecture of the models is critically important for how they behave, we do not know whether a model that could deal with both writing to dictation and reading aloud would behave in the same way in reading as the existing model that incorporates only connections in one direction.

One problem with connectionist models of this kind is that the way they behave is not clear until they are implemented. Given that, in the existing models, only reading aloud has been implemented, how they might extend to other tasks, such as word and nonword repetition, spoken word retrieval or writing, remains unclear. One result is that they cannot, in their present form, address the interesting associations and dissociations between tasks that are easily accommodated within the lexical model of Figure 1.1. An example of this is the fact that every person who is unable to repeat nonwords is also unable to write nonwords to dictation, but may be reasonably good at nonword reading (see Howard & Franklin, 1988, for discussion). In contrast, there are people who can repeat nonwords accurately and read them but are unable to write them to dictation (Shallice, 1981). For these reasons, at its current state of development, the triangle model's utility to the practising clinician in guiding assessment and identifying underlying deficits remains limited. There is, nevertheless, huge potential for using computational models in understanding how language can break down in aphasia.

2 Identifying and characterising impairments
Principles and evidence

As we have argued, cognitive neuropsychology is based on the assumption that, as a result of a lesion, the language system can be impaired to produce identifiable patterns of impairment that can be interpreted in terms of a processing model. This is now more than an assumption; over the last 30 years, a substantial volume of research has shown the utility and productivity of the approach. The goal of assessment, both for the researcher and the practising clinician, is to identify the processes that are intact and those that are impaired, and to show how these interact to produce the observed patterns of behaviour. The skill of assessment lies in the selection of the tasks and the interpretation of the data that will allow this goal to be achieved both revealingly and economically.

Looking for the evidence

The assessment process used in identifying impairments is one of forming and testing hypotheses; the focus of these hypotheses is on testing the relative intactness of specific components of the model. In assessing the different levels of breakdown using this model, use is usually made of three kinds of evidence. A first source of evidence is the effect of different variables (such as word length, imageability and so on) on performance. This is what Shallice (1988) describes as the 'critical variable approach' that 'seeks to establish the variables that affect the probability that a task will be correctly performed' (Nickels & Howard, 1995a, p. 1281) by a client. A second source of evidence is the nature of the errors made in different tasks. Where the tasks involve written and spoken word production, errors are made overtly, and can be classified. In comprehension tasks, the nature of possible errors is constrained by the design of the task. For example, in spoken word-to-picture matching, errors in word recognition at a lexical or pre-lexical level that result in misrecognition of a word as another phonologically related word will not be detected when the stimuli use only semantically related distractors. They would, on the other hand, be detected in word-to-picture matching using phonologically related distractors, or in a spoken word definition task.

While errors are revealing, their interpretation is not necessarily straightforward. For example, almost all clients who make semantic errors (e.g. UNCLE → 'nephew') in single-word reading ('deep dyslexics') also make visual errors (e.g. SCANDAL → 'sandal'). The obvious interpretation of these visual errors is that there is impairment in letter recognition or in the orthographic input lexicon. But, as Patterson (1979) has shown, this explanation cannot be correct (see also Coltheart, 1980; Morton & Patterson, 1980) (see the SANDAL–SCANDAL–SMANDAL paradox illustrated in Box 2.1). In general, errors of a particular kind suggest that there is an impairment at the level at which their defining feature is

Box 2.1 The SANDAL–SCANDAL–SMANDAL paradox

PW was a man with deep dyslexia and aphasia described by Patterson and her colleagues (Morton & Patterson, 1980; Patterson, 1978, 1979; Patterson & Marcel, 1977). PW made many semantic errors in single-word reading (e.g. SHADOW → 'dark'; SHOULDER → 'arms'; SEPULCHRE → 'tomb') – the defining symptom of deep dyslexia. Like other people with deep dyslexia, PW also made 'visual' errors in reading (e.g. TYING → 'typing'; SMOULDER → 'boulders'; APPRAISE → 'arise'). The obvious hypotheses to entertain to account for these visual errors are: (i) that there is impairment in letter recognition at the level of visual orthographic analysis; or (ii) that there is impairment to the orthographic input lexicon so that words are sometimes misrecognised as other words. Both of these hypotheses predict that: (i) performance should be poor in visual lexical decision – that is, deciding if a letter string is a real word or not; (ii) nonwords should be misrecognised as real words and so real word errors will be made in reading nonwords; and (iii) visual errors should be equally likely on high- and low-imageability words (as imageability, a semantic variable, is not relevant to lexical and pre-lexical processing).

The results described by Patterson (1979) showed that these hypotheses had to be rejected. PW was able to perform at normal levels in lexical decision, where a person has to decide if a letter string is a real word or a nonword. Given SCANDAL, he would classify it as a word, and would judge SMANDAL to be a nonword. And, given nonwords such as SMANDAL to read, he did not say 'sandal', but 'it's not a word, I can't read it'. And, as Morton and Patterson (1980) discuss, visual errors tend to occur on lower imageability targets and the errors tend to be higher in imageability than the targets; so, for instance, PW read SCANDAL as 'sandal'. This is sometimes called the SANDAL–SCANDAL–SMANDAL paradox. It shows clearly that the visual reading error cannot be ascribed to a difficulty in word recognition or letter perception. The semantic effects on visual errors are evidence for post-lexical levels of processing being involved.

The solution to the paradox Morton and Patterson (1980) offer is as follows:

SCANDAL activates the correct entry in the orthographic input lexicon but, because of an impairment to abstract word semantics (for which there is independent evidence), cannot activate a semantic representation. Then, the threshold on the orthographic input lexicon is reduced so that the next most active entry – SANDAL – can retrieve its (concrete) semantic representation and drive a response that results in the 'visual' error. This explanation, which relies, as in Morton's (1969, 1979a) logogen model, on lexical entries that have to reach a threshold level before they can pass activation on to other modules, might be reformulated in terms of models that allow for the cascade of information between levels, such as Coltheart and colleagues' (Coltheart, Curtis, Atkins & Haller, 1993; Coltheart, Langdon & Haller, 1996; Coltheart *et al.*, 2001) DRC (dual-route cascade) model. At a lexical level, SCANDAL is the most activated entry and its level of activation is sufficient to produce a correct lexical decision response. However, SANDAL also, because of its very high similarity, has a high level of activation. All of the units active in the visual input lexicon send activation to the semantic system. Because the semantics of abstract words are impaired, the semantic representation of SANDAL is more highly activated than the semantics of SCANDAL, and so the semantics of SANDAL drives the retrieval of a spoken reading response.

relevant, but as this example shows, this is not necessarily the case. Further evidence from the effects of variables and performance in related tasks is normally required.

The third way of investigating the underlying impairment is to contrast performance on tasks that share some of their processing components. For example, in the case of PW, described in Box 2.1, normal performance in visual lexical decision requires, at least, letter recognition and lexical access. This finding immediately eliminates an account for visual errors at a lexical or pre-lexical level. The assumption that it reflects a central impairment to the semantic representations of abstract words predicts that PW will perform poorly in other tasks not involving visual word recognition but that do involve abstract word meaning. This can be tested using synonym judgements on spoken words. On these, as predicted, PW performs poorly with abstract words (Howard, 1985).

There are, then, three principal sources of evidence from the performance of people with aphasia that can be used to identify the nature of their underlying impairments: (1) the effects of critical variables, (2) the nature of errors and (3) convergent evidence from different tasks that use common processing components. On their own, the evidence from none of these is conclusive. Together, however, they can provide very strong evidence that allows the clinician to identify impaired processes. For this, of course, the specification of the relationships between tasks that is captured by the 'box and arrow' model in Figure 1.1 is critical.

Critical variables affecting performance

There are many factors that can be manipulated to provide information in the process of assessment. These variables give rise to error patterns from which certain assumptions can be drawn. Here we simply list some of the most commonly used variables. Others are discussed where they are relevant in Chapters 2–6.

Word frequency

Word frequency estimates derive from counting the number of occurrences of individual words. The most commonly used count is that of Kučera and Francis (1967) based on a million written words of American English of the 1960s. More recently, the CELEX database makes available much more extensive counts of British English, Dutch and German (Baayen, Piepenbrock & Gulikers, 1995). The English count is of 16.3 million words of printed texts and 1.6 million words from spoken corpora gathered during the 1980s. This much larger corpus gives more reliable frequency counts than those provided by Kučera and Francis.

When testing for *frequency effects*, the usual method is to compare performance on a set of high-frequency words and a set of low-frequency words, matching the sets for other variables such as length, phonological complexity, imageability, and so on. When using these sets, it is important to remember that the terms high and low frequency are relative and not absolute. Across different experiments, the mean frequency of a set of high-frequency words can vary from 500 words per million (wpm) to 30 wpm, and low-frequency words from 50 to 1 wpm; one researcher's low-frequency word is another researcher's high-frequency word. This partly reflects the task used. While any high-frequency word can be used in reading, there are very few words with a frequency of more than 200 wpm that can be used in a picture-naming task.

Word frequency is strongly associated with age of acquisition (i.e. the age at which a word is likely to have been acquired) and it is difficult, although not impossible, to vary these factors independently. It has been argued that apparent word-frequency effects are really effects of age of acquisition (Ellis & Morrison, 1998). Word frequency is also very strongly related to rated familiarity. This is not surprising, as familiarity is rated in terms of how frequently a word is encountered or used.[1] There is a strong argument that rated familiarity may capture frequency differences among very low-frequency words more accurately than word-frequency counts that are rather unreliable for words that occur very infrequently in the corpus (Gernsbacher, 1984).

The locus of word-frequency effects on accuracy in the model after damage is not totally clear. In almost all tasks with normal people, reaction times are shorter for high-frequency words. This has generally been attributed to either faster mapping between representations for high-frequency words (e.g. McCann & Besner, 1987; McCann, Besner & Davelaar, 1988; the effect is in the arrows) or more accessible lexical representations (e.g. Morton, 1979b; i.e. the effect is in the boxes). In the event of impaired processing, frequency effects on accuracy have often been taken to indicate a lexical level of impairment (e.g. Lesser & Milroy, 1993). However, in semantic dementia, where the primary difficulty seems to be on a semantic level, there are very substantial frequency effects, suggesting that semantic representations corresponding to low-frequency words are more susceptible to damage (Lambon Ralph, Graham, Ellis & Hodges, 1998). It is likely that frequency effects on accuracy with people who have language impairments may arise at lexical or semantic levels or in the mappings between them.

Imageability

When people are asked to rate words for imageability (how easily the word evokes a visual or auditory image), some words get high ratings (e.g. cat, book) and other more abstract words are judged to have low imageability (e.g. happiness, idea). Such words are used to determine the presence of an imageability effect. Imageability is closely related to concreteness (the concrete–abstract dimension) and, indeed, these dimensions may be impossible to distinguish (though see Marcel & Patterson, 1978, for evidence that imageability may be the determining factor). It has been suggested that imageability effects may reflect the richness of semantic representations with more imageable, concrete words having more semantic features than less imageable, abstract words (Plaut & Shallice, 1993). Another proposal is that high-imageability words have much more clearly defined and consistent meanings than low-imageability words, which tend to have meanings that are dependent on their linguistic context (Breedin, Saffran & Coslett, 1994).

There is agreement that imageability effects occur at a semantic level. Better performance with high-imageability words than low-imageability words is a very frequent feature of aphasia (Franklin, 1989). The effects may occur at a semantic level, or in the processes of input and output from semantics (Franklin, Howard & Patterson, 1994, 1995; Franklin, Turner, Lambon Ralph, Morris & Bailey, 1996). There are, however, occasional people with aphasia or with progressive disorders who show the reverse effect – that is, better performance with abstract, low-imageability words than concrete, high-imageability words (e.g. Breedin *et al.*, 1994; Marshall, Chiat, Robson & Pring, 1996; Warrington, 1975, 1981). This suggests that there may be partially independent representation of semantics for high- and low-imageability words.

Word length

Words and nonwords can be varied in their length (e.g. one-, two-, three-syllable words), while controlling for other variables such as frequency and imageability. Sets of these words are used to determine the presence of a length effect, where longer words and/or nonwords are repeated or accessed less accurately.

Seeking the roots of length effects is not straightforward. As words with more syllables have more phonemes, is the length effect due to the number of syllables or the number of phonemes? The obvious test is to use words that differ in their number of syllables but keeping the number of phonemes constant, for example comparing performance on four-phoneme, one-syllable words (e.g. 'trout') with four-phoneme, two-syllable words (e.g. 'poppy'). However, these words differ in their number of consonant clusters. The result is that the effects of phoneme length, syllable length and the number of clusters in a word can be very difficult to disentangle. Based on nine people who made phonological errors in production, Nickels and Howard (2004) present data that suggest that the number of phonemes is the only important factor. In contrast, Romani and Calabrese (1998) argue that phonological complexity is the determining factor for the person in their study.

With visually presented stimuli, the situation is even more complex. While in general the number of letters in a word is strongly related to the number of phonemes, this relationship is much less than perfect. For instance, ACHE has four letters but only two phonemes, whereas FLAX, also with four letters, has five phonemes. Similarly, some one-syllable words and three-syllable words have the same number of letters (e.g. PRINCE and BANANA).

These disputes may be of less importance for the clinician; in general, better performance with words with fewer phonemes suggests a problem in phonological output, most likely in the processes of phonological assembly. The rare individuals who are better at producing long words than short words (Best, 1995; Lambon Ralph & Howard, 2000) are more difficult to explain, but are most probably accounted for by a difficulty in accessing output phonology (because longer words, with fewer neighbours, are more distinctive in their phonological representations).

Word-length effects in spoken word recognition have not often been reported, perhaps because they have rarely been investigated. There are indications that people with impairments at the level of the phonological input lexicon or in access to semantics from the lexicon are better at understanding *longer* words (Franklin *et al.*, 1996; Howard & Franklin, 1988). This is probably because longer words are more distinctive in phonological space, and activate fewer similar competitors during the process of lexical access.

Word regularity

Word regularity involves comparing performance among matched sets of words with predictable or regular spelling-to-sound correspondences (e.g. MINT, RAVE) and words with less predictable spelling-to-sound correspondences (e.g. PINT, HAVE). These words are used to determine the presence of a regularity effect in reading, where regular words are read better than irregular words.

In English, the relationship between sound and spelling is much less predictable than the relationship of spelling to sound. For example, /pil/ can be correctly spelled as PEAL, PEEL or PELE (as in Pele Tower – a form of fortified late mediaeval farmhouse found in the North of England). But each of these can only plausibly be pronounced as /pil/. Whereas in reading most single-syllable words are regular in their spelling-to-sound correspondences (e.g. WHALE, CAUSE, FLAME), in spelling it is difficult to find many words (such as BANK, HILL, PANT) that can only be spelled in one way. When people with aphasia are better at reading or spelling regular words than irregular words, this suggests that they are using sublexical correspondences for the task. The implication is that lexical processing mechanisms are impaired at some point.

Lexicality

The model has processing systems that depend on lexical access; for example, reading via the orthographic input lexicon will only be possible for real words, because only familiar, known words are represented within that system. Nonwords can only be processed using routines that incorporate general rules for mapping between the input and output domains (for example, nonword reading requires the use of the process of 'orthographic-to-phonological conversion' that may depend on rules relating graphemes to phonemes).

Real words can be processed by the same procedure; generally this will result in correct performance, except where they are exceptions to the rules. So, for instance, all real words would be repeated correctly using 'phonological input-to-output conversion', as this mapping is completely consistent and without exceptions. In reading, in contrast, any real word with exceptional spelling-to-sound relationships (e.g. HAVE, BEAR, PINT) would be misread ('regularised') when its output is generated by the sub-lexical conversion procedure.

Comparisons of performance with real words and nonwords matched for length and phonological complexity can therefore provide useful information about how a task is performed. A *lexicality effect* is seen when performance with real words is better than with matched nonwords. Two conclusions then follow: first, that there is an impairment at some point in the sub-lexical procedure; second, lexical procedures are involved in real word processing. Better performance with nonwords than real words is a much less likely outcome but can occur, for instance, in 'surface dysgraphia' (Behrmann & Bub, 1992; Weekes, Davies, Parris & Robinson, 2003). This means that there is an impairment at some point to the lexical procedure and thus the person is relying on sub-lexical procedures. For example, in writing to dictation, a person who relies on sub-lexical procedures will produce plausible (and therefore correct) spellings for nonwords. Real words will very often be incorrectly but plausibly spelled (e.g. spelling TRAIN as TRANE).

Word grammatical categories

These usually involve nouns, verbs, adjectives and function words, and are used to determine the presence of a grammatical class effect. There are systematic differences in word imageability across word classes. Nouns are typically rated as being much more imageable than verbs; adjectives are usually somewhere in between. Function words are both much less imageable and much more frequent than content words. They are also often shorter. The question of whether word class effects are real or are reducible to the effects of confounding variables such as imageability has often been raised. Allport and Funnell (1981) showed that differences between nouns and verbs in reading could disappear when word imageability was controlled. Disputes on whether all differences between nouns and verbs can be reduced to imageability differences continue (e.g. Berndt, Haendiges, Burton & Mitchum, 2002; Bird, Howard & Franklin, 2000). Wider reviews of noun and verb differences can be seen in Conroy, Sage and Lambon Ralph (2006), Mätzig, Druks, Masterson and Vigliocco (2009), and Vigliocco, Vinson, Druks, Barber and Cappa (2011).

With the contrast between content words and function words, the question of whether differences found are due to confounds with imageability or frequency is even less easily determined. Certainly, differences between content words and function words can disappear when lists matched for frequency and imageability are used (Bird, Franklin & Howard, 2002; Howard & Franklin, 1988). One problem is that when matched lists are used for this, both the content words (very high frequency and very low imageability for content words) and the function words (very high imageability and very low frequency for function words) are atypical.

The nature of errors

In addition to these manipulated error patterns, the nature of the errors is a further source of information that may be used in seeking convergent information to identify the intact and impaired performance in processing. At a first approximation, errors suggest that there is an impairment at the level at which their defining feature is relevant. Semantic errors, for example, suggest that the underlying deficit lies in semantic representations or in the process of input to semantics or output from it. Similarly, phonological errors in production are consistent with impairment at the level of the phonological output lexicon or in more peripheral levels in phonological output. The nature of errors can never, however, by itself, be conclusive evidence of the level of underlying impairment. We have already highlighted in the SANDAL–SCANDAL–SMANDAL paradox (see Box 2.1) that, in the case of PW, a person with deep dyslexia, visual errors in reading cannot be attributed to any difficulty in letter or word recognition.

There are several cautions to be noted. In many comprehension tasks, the possibility of errors is limited by the distractors used. Phonological or visual errors in word recognition will only be noticed when phonological or visual distractors are used. Similarly, semantic errors will only be made when semantically related distractors are used. Additionally, the opportunities for these errors relate directly to the number of distractors used in the relevant domain. For example, in word-to-picture matching, the rate of semantic errors will be very different if four semantically related distractors are available than if there is only one semantic distractor. Semantic error rates may also be different when a more limited range of distractors is used in word–picture verification, where the person being assessed needs to decide whether the presented word is the name of a picture, comparing the presented name with all possible names. In comprehension, the opportunity for making diverse errors is maximised when the client is asked to define a presented word. The clinician must, therefore, select assessments carefully based on the hypotheses about the client's impairment as well as interpret performance within the context of task requirements.

In production, it is relatively straightforward to classify responses into (i) semantic errors, (ii) phonological errors and (iii) unrelated errors. Within phonological and unrelated errors, one can distinguish between real word and nonword responses. None of these classifications, however, are without their problems. For instance, how closely related does an error need to be to call the result semantically related? As there is no independent metric of semantic relatedness, the borderline is, essentially, a matter of choice. Martin *et al.* (1994) describe ATTITUDE → 'everybody has one of those days' as a semantic error. Howard and Franklin (1988) classify SHIRT → 'iron' as being unrelated.

Similarly, the degree of phonological relatedness required to classify an error as phonologically related varies radically between studies. Adopting a criterion inherited from Morton and Patterson (1980), Nickels and Howard (1995b) recognise responses as phonologically related when they share at least 50% of their phonemes with the target in approximately the same order. Martin *et al.* (1994) adopt a very much less stringent criterion – that is, a response that shares just one phoneme with the target (except for schwa) is counted as phonologically related! How errors are to be classified is, to a considerable extent, a matter of judgement. There are no correct answers that can be identified in advance. This is one reason why, in our view, errors constitute just one source of evidence about levels of breakdown. Strong conclusions about intact and impaired processes for any individual person with aphasia can only be drawn from converging evidence from the effects of critical variables and perform-ance in related tasks together with the nature of errors made.[2]

It is also important to realise that, as Cutler (1981) pointed out, errors are multiply deter-mined. In other words, an error can have more than one source. So, for instance, semantic errors in production may occur either when semantics are impaired or when the lexical form of the target word is unavailable (Caramazza & Hillis, 1990).

Comparisons across tasks

The comparison of performance on different tasks, where these different tasks share infor-mation-processing components, is the final critical source of evidence for identifying the locus of impairment. Much of the content of Chapters 4–8 deals with ways of making such comparisons. There are many possible ways in which this can be done, all of which depend on a task analysis that determines the processes necessary for performing a particular task. Useful comparisons are set out below.

Comparisons across modalities

Comparisons of the same tasks in spoken and written word comprehension are often used to identify whether the difficulties a person with aphasia shows are at a level common to the two modalities (when a similar level of performance, a similar distribution of errors and simi-lar effects of psycholinguistic variables on performance should be found in the two modali-ties) or are specific to a single modality. Similar comparisons can be made between spoken and written naming (both necessarily involving semantic processing), or between naming, reading aloud and word repetition (all involving phonological assembly).

Comparisons of tasks tapping different levels within a modality

Franklin (1989) showed how a set of tasks that tap access to different levels of representation can be used to determine the level of breakdown in auditory word comprehension. She used: (i) nonword minimal pairs, which require access only to the output of auditory phonological analysis; (ii) auditory lexical decision, which requires access to the phonological input lexi-con; and (iii) word comprehension tasks, including word-to-picture matching and synonym judgements (requiring access to semantics). Franklin argued that, if the model of Figure 1.1 is correct in the stages it postulates in spoken word comprehension, they would form a hierarchy such that impaired performance at any one level would result in impairment in all tasks tapping subsequent levels (see Table 2.1). This was the pattern she found (see client summaries in Chapter 4). This study demonstrates how careful thinking about tasks and the levels of representation that they tap can allow levels of impairment to be identified.

In word production, tasks that tap different levels without requiring processing at subse-quent levels are less easily identified, although there are some comparisons of this kind that can be useful. For example, homophone judgements on pairs of written words (e.g. do SEW and SO sound the same?) require access to phonological representations without spoken out-put. Good performance on homophone judgements and poor oral reading of the correspond-ing words suggests that the reading difficulty lies in the output processes of phonological assembly or articulatory programming. Conversely, if performance in both is impaired, it shows that the reading process is impaired at some earlier level, common to both reading aloud and homophone judgements.

Table 2.1 The relationship between levels of impairment in spoken word comprehension and patterns of impairment in tasks tapping different levels in the processes involved (Franklin, 1989)

Task	Level of impairment			
	Auditory phono-logical analysis	Phonological input lexicon	Access to semantics from the phonological input lexicon	Semantic representations
Nonword minimal pairs	✗	✓	✓	✓
Auditory lexical decision	✗	✗	✓	✓
Spoken word comprehension	✗	✗	✗	✗
Written word comprehension	✓	✓	✓	✗

Comparison of disparate tasks that share a common processing level

This point is best illustrated by example. A first example is seen in the instance of phonological assembly where, in the model of Figure 1.1, this is a process shared by picture naming, word and nonword repetition, and word and nonword reading. Where there are similar patterns of impairment across all these tasks (e.g. worse performance with words of greater phoneme length), similar errors (phonological errors identified primarily by phoneme omissions and substitutions) and similar levels of accuracy, there is strong evidence that the person's deficit is located in the processes of phonological assembly.

A second example is seen in the process of sub-lexical orthographic-to-phonological conversion being required for nonword reading. This process is also needed for nonword homophone judgements (e.g. deciding that PHAIP and FAPE are homophones) and for phonological lexical decision (deciding that KRAIT would sound like a real word when pronounced, but BRAIT would not). Similar deficits in all three tasks suggest a deficit in their common process of sub-lexical orthographic-to-phonological conversion.

A third example is apparent where, again in the model of Figure 1.1, semantic processing is required for a number of processes, including spoken and written word comprehension, and spoken and written picture naming. A common deficit in all of these tasks, with similar characteristics, suggests impairment at a semantic level (Hillis, Rapp, Romani & Caramazza, 1990; Howard & Orchard-Lisle, 1984). It should be remembered, however, that when making a comparison between input and output tasks (comprehension and naming, in this instance), performance in the comprehension tasks may be less affected because the opportunity to make errors is limited by the distractors used.

Notes

1 Familiarity in the MRC Psycholinguistic Database (Coltheart, 1981) is derived from a subjective rating of the frequency of use of a word. In the Snodgrass and Vanderwart (1980) norms, it is a rating of the concept familiarity. These are not the same.

2 While we think converging evidence across these domains is critical for identifying intact and impaired processes, there are some who do not accept this. For example, Dell and his colleagues (Dell *et al.*, 1997; Foygel & Dell, 2000; Schwartz *et al.*, 1994; Nozari *et al.*, 2010; Dell, Nozari & Oppenheim, in press) offer a model that aims to account for the pattern of errors in picture naming, but does not specify anything about the effects of psycholinguistic variables apart from word frequency or performance in tasks other than picture naming or word repetition. Their model has nothing to say about such effects.

Part 2
Deficits and assessment

3   Introduction to assessment

The following five chapters explore the model across five key domains, those of spoken word comprehension, spoken word production, reading, writing, and object and picture recognition. Each chapter focuses on a single domain, setting out the model as it relates to that aspect of the language-processing system and the deficits that may arise from disruption within that domain. Assessment is then addressed for each area, identifying:

- factors to exclude in assessment;
- general issues related to word types and effects to observe;
- indicators of impairment for each module or process within the domain;
- key areas of assessment;
- available assessment methods and tools, setting out the response types involved;
- additional assessment options;
- interpretation of the findings; and
- examples of case studies from the literature that exemplify the deficit patterns.

While each of these areas provides information for the clinician to apply throughout the assessment, the clinician needs to be strategic in his or her approach to this process.

Hypothesis testing and selectivity of tests

A hypothesis-testing approach should be taken in the assessment process, resulting in a rationalised selection of assessments (see Nickels, 2008, for a comprehensive discussion). The aim of the hypothesis-testing approach is to determine the underlying cause or causes of the disruption in communication abilities – that is, which components of the model are impaired, and how these relative impairments influence each other. The clinician must be selective in deciding which assessments to use to distinguish between performance (or relative performance) on tasks contributed to by the different processing components. A clinician would not, then, attempt to assess all components of the model with the view to obtaining a fully comprehensive picture of performance, but would aim to identify the most defining assessments for a particular client.

Drawing on observations of communication

When setting up initial hypotheses, the clinician should take into account individual information obtained on the client from initial conversational contact, such as apparent difficulties in understanding questions or clear lexical retrieval difficulties, as well as self or carer report.

Consideration should also be given to observing sensory deficits, such as with vision or hearing, as these may influence the person's performance in assessment.

Refining the level of assessment

Whether the focus is on input or output processing, the whole route should be looked at initially before assessing specific processing components and refining the level of breakdown. Spoken word comprehension should be assessed, in the first instance, by tapping comprehension of a word (using a spoken word–picture matching task, for example). If this is intact, then the processes of identifying speech sounds (requiring auditory phonological analysis) and word recognition (drawing on the phonological input lexicon) can be considered to be intact. If the client has difficulty, then the component processes should be tested to establish the reasons underpinning the breakdown. That is, is auditory phonological analysis impaired? Is the phonological input lexicon impaired? Or, is it due to impairment at the semantic level?

Similarly, spoken word production should be assessed initially on a naming task that can assess the whole output route. Here, the client is required to draw on semantic representations, lexical representations, processes involved in phonological planning and assembly, as well as articulatory programming. Again, if naming is successful, assumptions can be made as to the intact nature of the component processes. If difficulties arise, the component processes can be selectively targeted for further assessment. In a naming task, the analysis of error types and the critical variables affecting performance would help to narrow down the hypotheses.

Tasks that require a more fine-tuned level of functioning may be selected first when assessing a particular processing component. For example, discrimination of minimally contrasted pairs of words may be used initially to assess a person's auditory phonological analysis skills, rather than words that have maximal contrasts. If performance is poor, it would be reasonable to then progress to maximally contrasted words to identify the level at which performance breaks down. If, however, performance was good, then it can be assumed that performance on the easier task would also be good.

Similarly, when assessing the integrity of the semantic system from auditory input, a task requiring the manipulation of heard synonyms would be more taxing than selecting from a choice of pictures in response to a heard word. Success at the former would imply success at the latter, so long as the client did not have additional difficulties related to pictorial material. Beginning with a task such as synonym judgement, however, would need to be balanced with predicted success. Where a client has semantic impairment, a word–picture matching task may expose him or her to less failure initially (while also providing an important baseline of performance); a synonym judgement task may be too high a level at which to commence assessment.

Number of test items

A further factor to consider in selecting and administering assessments is the number of items used to measure performance. A smaller number of test items may be used as the assessment process refines to establish a diagnosis; the assessor must, however, recognise that the ability of a test to detect an effect of a variable is a function of the number of items in a test (more precisely, the size of an effect that is likely to be detected depends on the square root of the number of items). Where it is important to establish whether or not a variable has an effect, a sufficiently large number of items should be used. Once component processes are identified as being impaired, however, assessment should be carried out using a sufficiently large number of items that will enable any change (or lack of it) from pre- to post-therapy to be detected (this is explored further in Chapter 9). A distinction may therefore be drawn by the clinician in assessment to reach a diagnosis and assessment to monitor change following treatment.

Assessments

Two key assessments are referred to in the subsequent chapters, the Comprehensive Aphasia Test (CAT; Swinburn, Porter & Howard, 2005) and the Psycholinguistic Assessment of Language Processing in Aphasia (PALPA: Kay, Lesser & Coltheart, 1992); these draw directly on the cognitive neuropsychological theory set out in Chapter 1 and cover input and output modalities. The other assessments listed focus on particular aspects of language, e.g. auditory comprehension or word retrieval.

The CAT is an aphasia battery designed to provide a summary profile of performance across a range of tasks. The CAT consists of three parts:

(a) A cognitive screen designed to identify deficits in visual processing, semantic and episodic memory, acalculia and ideomotor/ideational apraxia. These are deficits known to co-occur with aphasia and can impact a person's ability to respond to therapy.
(b) A language assessment covering auditory comprehension, written comprehension, repetition, oral reading, verbal and written expression. The sub-tests are designed to look at the effects of critical variables within a very limited number of items; the degree of impairment across sub-tests can be compared, enabling relative strengths and weaknesses to be determined.
(c) A disability questionnaire designed to assess the person with aphasia's perception of their difficulties, the emotional consequences of the aphasia and the impact of those difficulties on daily life.

The CAT is standardised, providing the opportunity to compare the performance of an individual with that of normal participants and with a normative sample of people with aphasia. The test has good reliability and validity. Assessment with the CAT takes between 1 and 2 hours to complete and it is, therefore feasible, to use the test in its entirety. Extensive information about test design, use and interpretation can be found in the assessment manual and in Howard, Swinburn & Porter *et al.* (2010). The manual also gives data on the amount of change in each sub-test needed to be statistically significant.

The PALPA allows a more detailed examination of discrete sub-components of language. The battery consists of 60 sub-tests, grouped into four main sections: (1) auditory processing, (2) reading and spelling, (3) picture and word semantics and (4) sentence comprehension. The authors make it clear that 'PALPA is not designed to be given in its entirety to an individual – rather the assessments should be tailored to those that are appropriate to the hypothesis under investigation' (p. 2–3). Given the larger number of items in the PALPA sub-tests compared to the CAT, results from CAT sub-tests can be used to determine areas of language that then warrant further detailed assessment, beginning an iterative process of hypothesis testing. While normative data is available for specific PALPA sub-tests, the full battery is not standardised; robust measures of validity and reliability are also not provided.

Other assessment batteries have been developed using similar principles but are not detailed here due to their less frequent use within clinical practice. These include the Psycholinguistic Assessment of Aphasia (PAL) (Caplan & Bub, 1990) and the more recent adaptation, the Alberta Language Function Assessment Battery (Westbury, 2007). In using batteries with similar sub-tests, it is important to consider the extent to which sub-tests are controlled for psycholinguistic variables. Adaptations of the PALPA and the CAT for other languages have also been developed that, while identifying component language processes, recognise particular features of the different language. Adaptations have been developed for Spanish (EPLA; Valle & Cuetos, 1995), Dutch (PALPA Dutch; Bastiaanse, Bosje & Visch-Brink, 1995) and Portugese (PALPA-P; Castro, Caló & Gomes, 2007), while the SALA (Fujibayashi *et al.*, 2004) was developed in Japan following a systematic scrutiny of the principles for the Japanese language, and culminating in 40 sub-tests. The different degree of transparency, for example, in the orthography of Spanish where regular grapheme to phoneme conversion is high will contrast to the explicit attention required for the various scripts found in Japanese orthography. Similarly, the CAT can be found translated, to date, into Dutch/Flemish (Visch-Brink, Smet, Vandenborre & Mariën, in press), Egyptian (Abou El-Ella *et al.*, 2013) and soon to appear in Chilean Spanish and Saudi Arabian.

4   Auditory comprehension of spoken words

Model of auditory comprehension of spoken words

Figure 4.1 shows the processes involved in the auditory comprehension of words. There are three stages involved in listening for meaning: auditory phonological analysis, the phonological input lexicon and the semantic system.

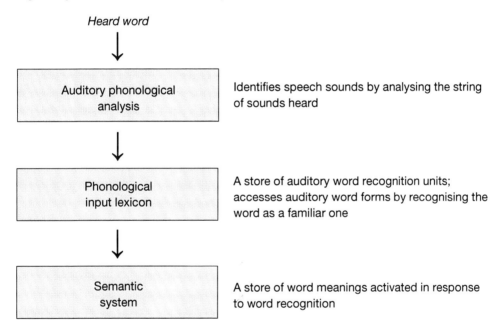

Phonological input-to-output conversion is also relevant here. This links auditory phonological analysis to phonological assembly. As this route bypasses the lexicons, it allows repetition of nonwords while also contributing to real word repetition.

Deficits of auditory comprehension of spoken words

Auditory phonological analysis

A deficit in auditory phonological analysis has been referred to as 'word sound deafness' (Franklin, 1989). Impairment at this level will have a profound effect on auditory comprehension,

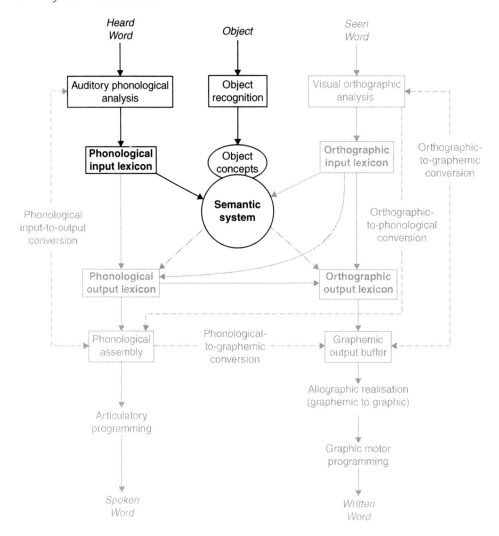

Figure 4.1 Auditory comprehension of words

as it affects all stages of auditory verbal comprehension. It will not, however, affect the ability to discriminate between non-verbal sounds (e.g. bells) or the ability to match characteristic sounds to pictures.

As access is subsequently impaired to the phonological input lexicon, the ability to repeat real words is reduced (repetition of real words uses this route). Semantic information may, however, assist the repetition of real words by providing semantic support. As the direct route from phonological analysis to phonological assembly cannot be used, repetition of nonwords will also be impaired. Repetition of both real and nonwords may be assisted by lip-reading.

Shorter words may be harder to understand than longer words because they have more phonological neighbours with which they can be confused (Luce & Large, 2001; Luce, Pisoni & Goldinger, 1990). 'Phonological neighbours' are other real words differing by a single phoneme. Single-syllable words usually have several, and often many, neighbours. For example, *cat* has neighbours that include *hat, rat, sat, cap, cad, can, cot, cut, kit*, and so on. Three-syllable words have many fewer neighbours: *crocodile* has none and *elephant* just two – *element* and *elegant*.

Semantics may still be accessed via reading. Comprehension may be aided by: (a) slowed speech; (b) lip-reading (which provides a visual source of phonetic information); and (c) context.

Phonological input lexicon

A deficit in the phonological input lexicon, or access to it, has been referred to as 'word form deafness' (Franklin, 1989). As access to the lexicon (or auditory word forms) is impaired, a string of phonemes will not be recognised as a real word. Real words will be repeated as if they were nonwords. Words and nonwords can still be repeated via the direct route from phonological analysis to phonological assembly.

Frequency effects may be present – that is, high-frequency words are easier to comprehend than low-frequency words. Lexical deficits are possible, however, without frequency effects in lexical decision or auditory word comprehension (Howard & Franklin, 1988), and frequency effects do not only result from impairments at the lexical level (frequency effects have also been attributed to semantic deficits, e.g. Garrard & Hodges, 1999).

Semantics may still be accessed via reading. Reading comprehension is not affected by a deficit of the phonological input lexicon.

There is a heavy reliance on context to aid comprehension. Word recognition (in both lexical decision and naming to definition) may be better for longer words, which have fewer neighbours, than short words (e.g. Howard & Franklin, 1988).

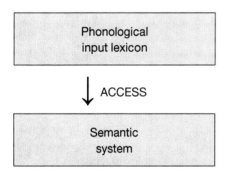

A deficit in accessing the semantic system from the phonological input lexicon has been referred to as 'word meaning deafness' (Franklin, 1989). As access to semantics is damaged, auditory comprehension is poor. Comprehension may be better for longer words than shorter words, because access to semantics is supported by more distinctive representations at a lexical level (Franklin *et al.*, 1996).

A string of phonemes is recognised as a word but not understood – that is, performance on lexical decision is good. Words and nonwords can still be repeated.

Semantics may still be accessed via reading. Again, reading comprehension is not implicated by a deficit accessing semantics from the phonological input lexicon.

Semantic system

Comprehension of both the auditory and written input modalities is impaired. All output modalities are also impaired (i.e. spoken and written production). Semantics is usually 'degraded' (and partially impaired) rather than totally inaccessible or destroyed.

Imageability effects are typically present – that is, words that are highly imageable (e.g. cat, book) are easier to understand than words with low imageability (e.g. happiness, idea). Reverse imageability effects with better understanding of abstract, low-imageability words than concrete, high-imageability words can occur, though rarely so.

Some people with central semantic deficits can show category effects. The most common is more impaired comprehension of words referring to animate categories – animals, plants, fruits and vegetables – than artefacts (objects) (e.g. Participant JBR, Warrington & Shallice, 1984). The reverse pattern also occurs, although more rarely (e.g. Participant CW, Sacchett & Humphreys, 1992). In addition, a variety of more selective deficits has been reported, including: selective impairment for animals with other animate categories together with objects relatively well-preserved; relative preservation of names referring to geographical features; a particular difficulty with body part names, or with proper names (e.g. Participant PC, Semenza & Zettin, 1988). Such deficits appear to be relatively uncommon, but even when they occur they may not be noticed.

People with intact object concepts but with a lexical semantic impairment will perform poorly in tasks involving words, but may perform well in non-verbal semantic tasks – for example, three-picture Pyramids and Palm Trees (Howard & Patterson, 1992; see Nickels, 2001, for discussion).

Assessments of auditory comprehension of spoken words

Exclude deficits of auditory acuity and higher level auditory analysis through:

- A hearing test
- Tests using environmental sounds

General notes on assessment

Mild auditory comprehension deficits are not always evident in conversation because of the extensive use of context. Observing interaction is not therefore sufficient to rule out an auditory comprehension deficit. When assessing auditory comprehension, tests that consider the complete process (e.g. spoken word–picture matching with a variety of distractors) are a useful starting point. If performance is impaired, investigate the pattern of errors and allow this to direct further assessment. Impairment to peripheral processes (auditory phonological analysis and the phonological input lexicon) will affect subsequent processing for meaning. If performance on spoken word–picture matching is retained but comprehension deficits are still suspected, then assessment on more difficult tasks with words of lower imageability and frequency would be recommended. It is also important to note that reading comprehension and spoken and written naming can be intact in the presence of impaired auditory comprehension, so long as the semantic system is intact. A discrepancy between spoken and written comprehension would be a key clinical indicator of auditory comprehension difficulties before the level at which semantics becomes involved. Some clinicians may have access to the ADA Comprehension Battery (Franklin, Turner and Ellis, 1992) but this is no longer commercially available. The battery consists of a range of well-designed and carefully controlled assessments similar to the PALPA tests and is particularly useful as all tests have data on normal performance.

Word types

In assessing auditory comprehension of spoken words, four types of word contrasts are useful:

1   Words with contrasting phonology, for example minimal pairs (where one phoneme in two words differs on only one distinctive feature, e.g. bat/pat) and maximal pairs (where one phoneme has a maximal number of contrastive features across two words, e.g. bat/sat).
2   Nonwords, matched in length and phonological complexity to real words.
3   Long and short words.
4   High- and low-imageability words.

Analysis of performance on these variables allows conclusions to be drawn about three effects:

(a)   A lexicality effect in minimal pair discrimination. Where nonwords are discriminated less accurately than real words of equivalent difficulty, this may imply impairment to auditory phonological analysis. Real word minimal pair discrimination can be supported by information at the lexical or semantic level.
(b)   A reverse length effect where there is more accurate comprehension of long words than short words. This can result from lexical impairment (Howard & Franklin, 1988) or problems in access to semantics (Franklin *et al.*, 1996).
(c)   An imageability effect. Where there is more accurate comprehension of more highly imageable words than low-imageability words, this suggests impairment to the semantic system or in access to it.

   Lip-reading can improve access to phonetic information and therefore may support the client's comprehension.

```
┌─────────────────────────────────┐
│     Auditory phonological       │
│            analysis             │
└─────────────────────────────────┘
```

Indicators of impairment

•   Reduced discrimination between phonemes.

General notes on assessment

The following tasks can be performed with and without lip-reading to determine whether visual information can supplement auditory information.

Key assessment areas and available methods

Area of assessment	Examples of available assessment tools	Response type
Auditory discrimination of nonword minimal pairs	PALPA 1 [a]: Same/different discrimination using nonword minimal pairs	Same/different
Auditory discrimination of real word minimal pairs	PALPA 2: Same/different discrimination using word minimal pairs	Same/different
	PALPA 3: Minimal pair discrimination requiring written word selection	Written word selection
	PALPA 4. Minimal pair discrimination requiring picture selection	Picture selection
Auditory discrimination of real word maximal pairs	Maximal pairs (Morris *et al.*, 1996)	Same/different
a Psycholinguistic Assessment of Language Processing in Aphasia (Kay *et al.*, 1992).		

Additional assessment options

Area of assessment	Examples of available assessment tools	Response type
Repetition of nonwords	CAT[b] 14: Repetition of nonwords	Repetition
	PALPA 8: Repetition: nonwords	Repetition
Repetition of words	CAT 12: Repetition of words	Repetition
	PALPA 7: Repetition: syllable length	Repetition
	PALPA 9: Repetition: imageability × frequency	Repetition
b Comprehensive Aphasia Test (Swinburn *et al.*, 2005)		

Interpretation

✓   Good discrimination of words and nonwords implies that auditory phonological analysis is intact.

✗   Reduced discrimination of words and nonwords implies that auditory phonological analysis may be impaired.

✗   Reduced discrimination of nonwords relative to words (lexicality effect) implies a deficit in auditory phonological analysis with relatively intact lexical and semantic processing.

✗   Repetition of nonwords and words would also be impaired if auditory phonological analysis is implicated. Performance is characterised by phonologically related errors.

✗ Reduced performance in discriminating between minimal pairs relative to maximal pairs may provide an indication of severity.

✗ Better performance on minimal pair discrimination using written response choices (PALPA 3) than when using auditory stimuli (PALPA 1 and 2) may indicate short-term memory impairment.

Box 4.1 A case of impairment to auditory phonological analysis (word sound deafness): Client ES (Franklin, 1989)

ES was a 74-year-old male who was 3 years post-onset at the time of testing. He was an estate agent before his retirement. His aphasia resulted from a CVA. ES had fluent speech and impaired auditory comprehension. On testing, he presented with a severe phoneme discrimination deficit. His performance was characterised by severely impaired minimal pair discrimination, auditory lexical decision and auditory synonym matching. Real word repetition was as poor as nonword repetition. In terms of the discrimination of CVC words, his errors followed no pattern in terms of site or type of features contrasted. Franklin suggests that this may reflect the severity of the impairment or may be an artefact of the high number of false–positive responses on the test. ES performed significantly better on written lexical decision and written synonym matching tests than on auditory tasks.

Phonological input
lexicon

Indicators of impairment

• Reduced ability to recognise a word as a real word and to reject a nonword.
• Possible frequency effects (high-frequency words easier than low-frequency words).

General notes on assessment

Impaired auditory phonological analysis will impair performance on assessments of the phonological input lexicon. Consideration of performance on, for example, minimal pair tasks discussed above will be essential in determining the contribution of any impairment in auditory phonological analysis to the integrity of the phonological input lexicon.

Key assessment areas and available methods

Area of assessment	Examples of available assessment tools	Response type
Auditory lexical decision	PALPA 5: Auditory lexical decision: Imageability and frequency	Yes/no response

Additional assessment options

Area of assessment	Examples of available assessment tools	Response type
Repetition of real words if unable to repeat nonwords	CAT 12: Repetition of words	Repetition
	PALPA 9: Imageability and frequency repetition	Repetition
Identification of spoken words using phonological distractors (written and picture response modalities)	PALPA 3: Minimal pair discrimination requiring written word selection	Written word selection
	PALPA 4: Minimal pair discrimination requiring picture selection	Picture selection
	CAT 7: Comprehension of spoken words (phonological distracters)	Picture selection
Picture verification of words (phonological real word and nonword distractors)	Picture–word decision test (Howard & Franklin, 1988)	Yes/no response

Interpretation

✓   Good performance on lexical decision tasks implies that the phonological input lexicon is intact.

✗   Reduced performance on lexical decision tasks implies impairment of the phonological input lexicon.

✗   Reduced performance on picture-matching tasks and picture-verification tasks with the selection of phonological distractors may imply impairment of the phonological input lexicon.

✗   Reduced performance with low-frequency words relative to high-frequency words (frequency effect) may suggest impairment of the phonological input lexicon, but is not a necessary feature of impairment at this level.

✗   Reduced performance with low-imageability words relative to high-imageability words (imageability effect) may imply that the person is drawing on an impaired semantic system.

Box 4.2 A case of impairment to the phonological input lexicon (word form deafness): Client MK (Franklin, 1989; Howard and Franklin, 1988)

MK was a 69-year-old man who was 2 years post-onset at the time of testing. He was a consultant for an oil company. His aphasia resulted from a CVA. He had fluent speech and impaired auditory comprehension. MK was able to discriminate phonemes as well as normal controls, indicating no impairment at the level of auditory phonological analysis. He showed a mild deficit in auditory lexical decision and a moderate impairment in auditory synonym matching. His performance in written synonym matching was significantly better than his performance on the auditory version. MK made errors on a word–picture matching task with phonological distractors. He defined words he heard with definitions appropriate to phonologically related words; for example, when given the word 'pardon', he gave a definition appropriate to 'garden'. MK was unable to repeat nonwords due to an impairment in phonological input-to-output conversion. He was better, although still impaired at, repeating real words with imageability predicting performance; this would suggest the use of a semantically mediated route for repetition (Franklin, 1989)

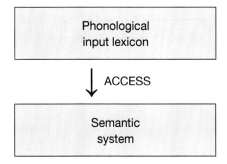

Indicators of impairment

- Ability to recognise a word as a real word but not know its meaning.
- Good access to semantics via the written modality but impaired via the auditory modality.

General notes on assessment

Impairment to auditory phonological analysis or the phonological input lexicon will also affect access to semantics. Consideration of performance on tasks assessing these components will be essential in determining any contribution that impairment in these may play in accessing semantics from the phonological input lexicon.

Key assessment areas and available methods

Area of assessment	Examples of available assessment tools	Response type
Assess semantic system	See next section	
Compare written and auditory comprehension of words	CAT 7 and 8: Comprehension of spoken and written words (with semantic distractors)	Picture selection
	PALPA 47 and 48: Spoken and written word–picture matching (with semantic distractors)	Picture selection

Additional assessment options

Area of assessment	Examples of available assessment tools	Response type
Repetition followed by spoken definition of words, with comparison to written semantic access	Informal (as described in Franklin *et al.*, 1996)	Repetition and spoken definitions, with comparison to reading comprehension and spoken definitions

Interpretation

✓   Comparable auditory performance and written performance implies input from the phonological input lexicon to semantics is intact.

✗   Reduced auditory performance relative to written performance implies input from the phonological input lexicon to semantics is impaired.

Box 4.3 A case of impairment of input to semantics from the phonological input lexicon (word meaning deafness): Client DRB (Franklin, 1989; Franklin *et al.*, 1994)

DRB was a 55-year-old man who was 2 years post-onset at the time of testing. He was a travel agent before his CVA. He had fluent speech and impaired auditory comprehension. On formal testing, he showed no impairment on minimal pair discrimination and auditory lexical decision tasks. His performance on written lexical decision was also equivalent to that of normal individuals. He showed a severe impairment on auditory synonym matching but significantly better performance on written synonym matching. He showed a significant imageability effect on the spoken version of the task but was able to access semantic information about low-imageability words from the visual word form. DRB was unable to repeat nonwords due to an impairment in phonological input-to-output conversion but was able to repeat some real words. His real word repetition was characterised by an imageability effect and some semantic errors (suggesting the use of a semantically mediated route.

Semantic system

(comprehension)

Indicators of impairment

•   If a semantic impairment, the person will have:

(a) impaired comprehension for both the auditory and written input modalities and

(b) semantic errors in both spoken and written output (but semantic errors may also indicate impairment at other levels).

•   Imageability effects in all tasks requiring semantic processing.

General notes on assessment

Need to assess auditory *and* written comprehension, and spoken *and* written production, but consider effects of peripheral impairments in each modality.

Key assessment areas and available methods

Area of assessment	Examples of available assessment tools	Response type
Comprehension of spoken words – high-imageability nouns	CAT 7: Comprehension of spoken words	Picture selection
	PALPA 47: Spoken word–picture matching	Picture selection
Comprehension of written words – high-imageability nouns	CAT 8: Comprehension of written words	Picture selection
	PALPA 48: Written word–picture matching	Picture selection
Comprehension of spoken words – high- and low-imageability nouns	PALPA 49: Auditory synonym judgements	Same/different
Comprehension of written words – high- and low-imageability nouns	PALPA 50: Written synonym judgements	Same/different
Comprehension of spoken words – verbs	VAST [a] Verb comprehension	Picture selection
	NAVS [b] Verb comprehension	Picture selection
	Informal assessment of verb comprehension in Webster, Morris, Whitworth & Howard (2009)	Picture selection
Comprehension of written words – verbs	Informal assessment of verb comprehension in Webster, *et al. (2009)*	Picture selection
Comparison across modalities	PALPA 53: Picture Naming/ Written Naming/Repetition/Oral Reading/ Written Spelling	Spoken and written naming, repetition, oral reading, writing
Semantic association/ real world knowledge – nouns	CAT 2: Semantic memory	Picture selection
	Pyramids and palm trees (picture and written versions) (Howard & Patterson, 1992)	Picture selection, written word selection
	Camel and cactus test (Adlam *et al.,* 2010)	Picture selection

	PALPA 51: Word semantic association	Written word selection
Semantic association – verbs	Kissing and dancing test (picture and written versions) (Bak & Hodges, 2003)	Picture selection, written word selection
Access to semantics where avoidance of pictures is necessary; comparison with single modality (spoken and written word comprehension)	PALPA 52: Spoken word– written word matching	Written word selection

a The Verb and Sentence Test (Bastiaanse, Edwards & Rispens, 2002)
b The Northwestern Assessment of Verbs and Sentences (Thompson, 2011)

Additional assessment options

Assessments that control for imageability investigate the use of the route through the semantic system. Imageability effects in tasks imply the use of semantic mediation in those tasks.

Area of assessment	Examples of available assessment tools	Response type
Imageability effect in other modalities	CAT 12: Repetition of words	Repetition
Convergent and divergent semantic tasks e.g. Providing definitions and naming to definition	PALPA 9: Repetition: imageability × frequency	Repetition
Providing super-ordinate categorical information and naming from this	PALPA 25: Visual lexical decision: imageability × frequency	Written word selection
Generative category naming (i.e. category fluency) Sorting/categorisation tasks	PALPA 31: Oral Reading: imageability × frequency See Chapey, 1981	Oral reading Varied
Semantic associations	Semantic links (Bigland & 1992)	Picture selection

Interpretation

✓ Retained performance on spoken and written picture-matching and synonym judgement tasks implies an intact semantic system.

✗ Semantic errors on spoken and written picture-matching tasks alongside impaired word retrieval imply a semantic impairment.

✗ The choice of distant semantic errors on picture-matching tasks implies a more severe semantic deficit.

✗ Visually similar errors may imply a visual perceptual element.

✗ An even spread of errors may imply either (a) lack of attention or (b) severe semantic impairment.

✗ Errors on low-imageability words in spoken and written tasks but with retained performance on high-imageability words may imply a semantic impairment for low-imageability items.

Box 4.4 A case of impairment to the semantic system: Client KE (Hillis *et al.*, 1990)

KE was a 52-year-old, right-handed man. He was working as a manager in a large corporation before his CVA. A CT scan showed an infarct in the left fronto-parietal region. He was 6 months post-onset at the time of testing. KE's spontaneous speech consisted of over-learned phrases, single nouns and frequent semantic errors. In auditory comprehension, he made errors at both single word and sentence level. KE had a very limited ability to read aloud, producing mainly no responses in the reading of words and nonwords. His errors in word reading were semantically related errors (e.g. HUNGRY → 'starve') and some morphologically related errors (e.g. BUY → 'bought'). There was no evidence that orthographic-to-phonological conversion was contributing to his reading. He was at chance at matching auditory to written words. KE was able to spell some concrete nouns. His errors in writing to dictation consisted of semantic errors and mixed errors (e.g. SCREWDRIVER → 'screwswitch'). He was unable to write nonwords and his writing showed no evidence of the use of non-lexical spelling procedures. KE was tested on the same items across oral and written picture naming, oral reading, writing to dictation and auditory and written word–picture matching. Detailed analysis of his performance showed very similar error rates and types of errors, regardless of the modality of stimulus or response. In each task, he produced a high percentage of semantic errors. There was a high degree of item consistency across modalities and in test–retest scores. There were significant differences in semantic error rates across different semantic categories that were consistent across modalities and were not predicted by frequency. The authors interpret KE's performance as evidence of selective damage to a unitary, modality-independent semantic system.

5   Spoken word production

Model of spoken word production

Figure 5.1 shows the processes involved in spoken word production during picture/object naming. There are four main stages involved in retrieving words from the semantic system (as in picture naming): the semantic system, the phonological output lexicon, phonological assembly and articulatory programming.

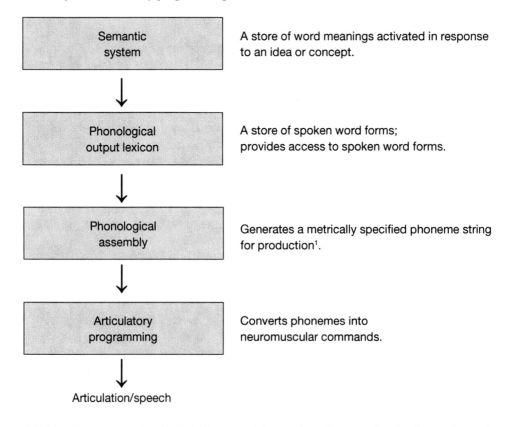

Semantic system	A store of word meanings activated in response to an idea or concept.
Phonological output lexicon	A store of spoken word forms; provides access to spoken word forms.
Phonological assembly	Generates a metrically specified phoneme string for production[1].
Articulatory programming	Converts phonemes into neuromuscular commands.

Articulation/speech

Additional processes involved during repetition and reading words aloud are shown in Figure 5.2.

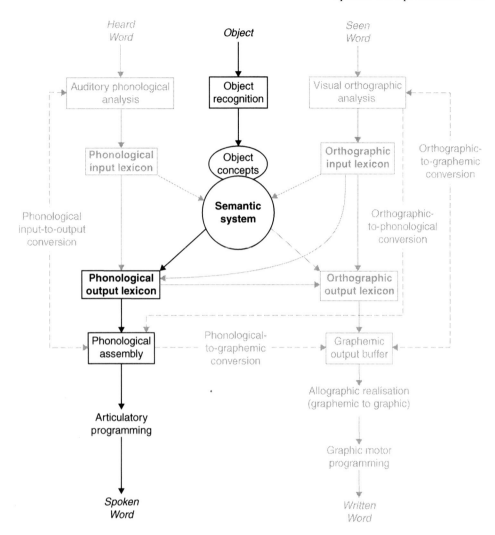

Figure 5.1 Spoken naming

Deficits of spoken word production

Semantic system

The production of both spoken and written words is impaired, together with impaired comprehension of both the auditory and written input modalities. Semantics is usually degraded rather than totally inaccessible or destroyed. Imageability effects are typically present – that is, words that are highly imageable (e.g. cat, book) are easier to produce than words with low imageability (e.g. happiness, idea). Reverse imageability effects – better production of abstract, low-imageability words than concrete, high-imageability words – can occur, although rarely.

The production of spoken words is characterised by anomia with both failures and delays in word retrieval. Semantic errors are produced in both spoken and written naming.

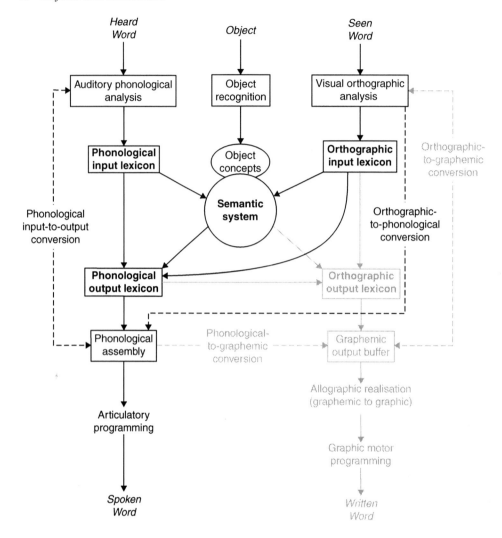

Figure 5.2 Spoken naming with reading and repetition

When cued by a phonemic cue for a semantic associate (phonemic miscueing), clients with naming disorders arising from a semantic impairment may produce a semantic associate (Howard & Orchard-Lisle, 1984). For example, when given a picture of a lion and the phoneme /t/ they produce 'tiger'.

Phonological output lexicon (and access to the lexicon from the semantic system)

An impairment at this level results in impaired word retrieval in spoken naming but written word retrieval may be intact. Spoken and written comprehension are intact. Spoken production is characterised by features which may include:

1   delays and failures in word retrieval;
2   circumlocutions;

3   semantic errors (Caramazza & Hillis, 1989);
4   phonological errors or the production of word fragments;
5   a frequency effect may be present.[2]

If the problem is degradation of the representations within the mental lexicon itself, there may be a consistent difficulty in retrieving the same items (Howard, 1995). Retrieval may be more inconsistent if the problem is in accessing the lexicon from the semantic system. In this case, retrieval of the word in repetition and/or reading aloud may be less impaired than in naming (Kay & Ellis, 1987).

Phonological assembly

An impairment in phonological assembly impacts all spoken production tasks (naming, reading aloud and repetition). Comprehension and written word retrieval are intact.

Spoken production is characterised by the production of phonological errors and neologisms. Clients may produce *conduite d'approche* (repeated attempts at the target word that often result in a closer approximation to the target word).

Length effects may be present, with shorter words being easier to produce than longer words.

Articulatory programming

A deficit in articulatory programming, seen in apraxia of speech, results in an impairment to all spoken production tasks with the production of phonetic errors. Written word retrieval is intact.

Articulation/speech

Articulation difficulties result in dysarthria.

Assessments of spoken word production

Exclude deficits of motor speech and visual object recognition through:

- Tests for motor speech disorders to assess dysarthria and apraxia of speech
- Tests for object recognition (see Chapter 8)

General notes on assessment

As word-retrieval deficits are usually evident in spontaneous speech, observation of spontaneous output will provide an important first opportunity to observe presenting patterns. If a person has difficulty with verb retrieval, particularly as a consequence of a semantic impairment, their sentence production may be very restricted with a reliance on single phrases and/or high frequency, semantically light verbs (Berndt, Haendiges, Mitchum & Sandson, 1997). When assessing spoken word production, picture-naming assessments are a useful starting point. Tests that control for a variety of contrasts (e.g. imageability and frequency) can provide some information about the possible level of any impairment. Investigations of the error types and the client's response to semantic and phonemic cues provide additional support for the diagnosis. Finally, comprehension tests and other tests of spoken word production (e.g. reading aloud and repetition) should be carried out. If performance on picture naming is not impaired but word-retrieval difficulties are evident in spontaneous speech, consider carrying out tests of word retrieval that do not use picture stimuli (e.g. naming to definition, category fluency).

Word types

In assessing spoken production, three types of word contrasts are useful:

1   High- and low-imageability words
2   High and low frequency words
3   Words that vary in number of phonemes/syllables.

Analysis of performance on these three variables allows conclusions to be drawn about three effects:

(a)   An imageability effect. Where more highly imageable words are accessed and produced more easily than low-imageability words, this may imply impairment to the semantic system or output from the semantic system to the phonological output lexicon.
(b)   A frequency effect. Where more frequent words are accessed and produced more easily than less frequent words, this may imply impairment at the level of the phonological output lexicon. Frequency effects do not only, however, result from impairments at the lexical level.[2]
(c)   A length effect. Where shorter words are accessed and produced more easily than longer words, this may imply impairment in the processes of phonological assembly or articulation.

Error types

The second source of available evidence is the nature of the errors made in spoken production. These can be classified, for example, into the following categories:

1   A delay or failure to retrieve a word.
2   Semantic errors: responses that are semantically related to the target, e.g. NAIL → 'screw'.
3   Phonological errors: errors that are similar to the target in phonological form. A common criterion for phonological similarity is that at least 50% of the phonemes in the stimulus occur in the error response in approximately the same order, e.g. NAIL → /nəɪk/. They can be words or nonwords.
4   Neologisms: nonword responses that do not share sufficient phonemes to be classified as phonological errors.
5   Semantically related circumlocutions are responses that indicate access to some intact semantic information in the absence of a phonological representation, e.g. NAIL → 'you bang it into wood'.

Key assessments of word retrieval

Naming assessment	Factors manipulated
CAT 17: Naming objects	Assesses noun retrieval. Word frequency, animacy, imageability and length varied. High and low frequency words matched for length and imageability. High- and low-imageability words matched for length and frequency. One and three syllable words matched for frequency and imageability.
CAT 18: Naming actions	Assesses verb retrieval.
PALPA 53: Picture naming × oral reading, repetition & written spelling	Assesses noun retrieval. Regular and irregular words matched for word frequency, familiarity, concreteness, age of acquisition, letter length, and number of syllables.
PALPA 54: Picture naming × word frequency	Assesses noun retrieval. Word frequency varied and words matched for number of syllables, letters and name agreement.
Nickels' Naming Test (described in Nickels & Howard, 1994)	Assesses noun retrieval. Word frequency and length varied, high and low frequency words matched for length. One, two and three syllable words matched for frequency.
Boston Naming Test (Kaplan, Goodglass & Weintraub, 2001)	Assesses noun retrieval. Difficulty graded.
Graded Naming Test (McKenna & Warrington, 1983)	Assesses noun retrieval. Difficulty graded.
Action naming in The Verb and Sentence Test (VAST) (Bastiaanse *et al.*, 2002)	Assesses verb retrieval. Syntactic structure (transitive or intransitive verbs) and frequency and name relatedness with a noun varied.
Verb naming test in the Northwestern Assessment of Verbs and Sentences (NAVS) (Thompson, 2011)	Assesses verb retrieval. Argument structure (obligatory one, two and three argument verbs and optional two and three argument verbs).
An Object and Action Naming Battery (Druks & Masterson, 2000)	Assesses verb and noun retrieval. Word frequency, familiarity, length, age of acquisition, imageability and visual complexity varied. Matched lists which investigate frequency and age of acquisition, familiarity. Conroy, Sage & Lambon Ralph (2009c) provide a set of 20 nouns and 20 verbs from this battery matched for imageability, frequency, age of acquisition and visual complexity.
Verb and Noun Test (Webster & Bird, 2000)	Assesses verb and noun retrieval. Word frequency, imageability and length varied. Nouns and verbs matched for frequency and length. Within nouns and verbs, high and low frequency words matched for imageability and length, high- and low-imageability words matched for frequency and length and short and long words matched for imageability and frequency.

Additional resources for assessment of word retrieval

There are also picture resources which may be used in the assessment of and treatment for word-retrieval difficulties. The Snodgrass pictures (Snodgrass & Vanderwart, 1980) depict objects, with information provided on name agreement, familiarity and visual complexity. A set of very similar line drawings, though of much better quality, can be found at: http://wiki. cnbc.cmu.edu/Objects with similar normative data (Rossion & Pourtois, 2004). As part of the International Picture Naming project, a large corpus of both objects (520 line drawings) and actions (275) are available at: http://crl.ucsd.edu/experiments/ipnp/ ; alongside the black-and-white drawings, subjective ratings of age of acquisition, word frequency, familiarity, visual complexity and goodness of depiction are provided for a range of languages. A set of photo stimuli can be found at: http://wiki.cnbc.cmu.edu/BOSS; this set of 480 object photographs have been normalised for name, category, familiarity, visual complexity, object agreement, viewpoint agreement and manipulability (Brodeur, Dionne-Dostie, Montreuil & Lepage, 2010). A set of action pictures, with an informal assessment of naming, can be found in the therapy resources developed by Webster *et al.* (2009).

Additional assessments of word retrieval

FAS verbal fluency (Spreen & Benton, 1977)
Verb and noun naming in categories (described in Bird, Howard & Franklin, 2003)
Naming to definition (as described by Chapey, 1981)
Noun production to verb, verb production to noun and generation of verb in response to verbal scenario (as described in Marshall, Pring & Chiat, 1998)

Semantic system	(production)

Indicators of impairment

- If a semantic impairment, the person will have:

  (a) impaired comprehension for both the auditory and written input modalities; and
  (b) semantic errors in both spoken and written output (but semantic errors may also indicate impairment at other levels).

- Imageability effects in all tasks requiring semantic processing.

General notes on assessment

Need to assess spoken and written production and auditory and written comprehension but consider effects of peripheral impairments in each modality. Assess the effects of semantic cueing, phonemic cueing and phonemic miscueing.

Key assessment areas and available methods

Area of assessment	Examples of available assessment tools	Response type
Comparison across modalities	PALPA 53: Picture naming × oral reading, repetition & written spelling (See assessment of input modalities in Chapters 4 and 6)	Spoken and written naming
Error analysis of naming	As above	Picture naming

Interpretation (for the semantic system)

✓ Retained word retrieval alongside intact auditory and written comprehension implies an intact semantic system.
✗ An impairment of the semantic system is implied when a deficit is present in spoken naming in the presence of intact repetition and reading and impaired comprehension. Picture naming requires the semantic system, whereas repetition and oral reading do not necessarily involve semantic mediation.
✗ An impairment of the semantic system is implied when similar errors and severity of errors are present in written and spoken naming.
✗ Naming is characterised by semantic errors together with delays and failures in word retrieval, and clients may produce semantic errors in response to phonemic miscues.

See Box 4.4 in Chapter 4 describing client KE.

| Phonological output lexicon |

(and access to the lexicon from the semantic system)

Indicators of impairment

• Impaired word retrieval characterised by:

(a) delays and failures in word retrieval;
(b) circumlocutions;
(c) semantic errors;
(d) phonological errors and/or word fragments.

• Frequency effects (Caramazza & Hillis, 1989).

General notes on assessment

Assess and analyse responses to phonemic cueing.

Key assessment areas and available methods

Area of assessment	Examples of available assessment tools	Response type
Error analysis of naming	CAT 17: Naming objects	Picture naming
	PALPA 53: Picture naming	Picture naming
Frequency analysis of naming	CAT 17: Naming objects	Picture naming
	PALPA 54: Picture naming × word frequency	Picture naming

Additional assessment options

Area of assessment	Examples of available assessment tools	Response type
Repetition and reading aloud of words	PALPA 53: Picture naming × oral reading, repetition & written spelling	Repetition and reading aloud
Response to phonemic cueing	Informal or in CAT 17	Spoken naming

Interpretation

✓   Retained picture naming, oral reading and repetition of words implies an intact phonological output lexicon.

✗   Impaired access to the phonological output lexicon or an impaired phonological output lexicon is suggested by delays and failures in word retrieval (possibly characterised by a frequency effect), circumlocutions, semantic and phonological errors, and word fragments.

✗   Impaired picture naming with better preserved repetition and reading aloud may suggest impaired access to the phonological output lexicon, rather than impairment to the word forms within the lexicon. Note, however, that repetition and reading (at least for regular words) can be done sub-lexically. Where nonword repetition or reading are good, better performance in repetition or reading than naming is probably attributable to the use of sub-lexical processes, rather than better access to lexical representations.

✗   Correct word retrieval following phonemic cueing suggests that the phonological output lexicon is intact and that access is impaired.

Box 5.1 A case of impairment to the phonological output lexicon (lexical anomia): Client EE (Howard, 1995)

EE was a 46-year-old postman who suffered a head injury falling from a ladder while painting his house. He was 4–5 years post-onset at the time of testing. His speech was fluent and grammatical, although there was evidence of word-finding difficulties. In reading aloud and writing he made errors with irregular words (surface dyslexia and dysgraphia). He scored within the normal range on the three picture and three spoken word versions of Pyramids and Palm Trees (Howard & Patterson, 1992) indicating intact recognition of pictures and intact access to semantic information. On standard assessments of naming, he presented with a severe anomia. His ability to name the pictures of the Hundred Picture Naming Test (Howard & Franklin, 1988) was tested on three occasions to examine the consistency of retrieval, the variables affecting naming performance and the effect of different cues. EE showed a high degree of consistency in the items named correctly. (Not all clients with impairment to the phonological output lexicon show the same high degree of consistency.) His errors were mainly no responses or circumlocutions containing appropriate semantic information. He did not improve in naming with phonemic cues or extra time and semantic errors could not be elicited by phonemic miscues. His naming performance was affected by word familiarity but there was no effect of the semantic or phonological properties of words (e.g. imageability or number of phonemes). For the same one hundred items, EE showed accurate auditory lexical decision and auditory comprehension. Howard argues that EE has intact semantic information but has lost specific lexical items within the phonological output lexicon.

```
Phonological
assembly
```

Indicators during assessment

- Impaired naming, oral reading and repetition characterised by:

    (a) phonological errors/neologisms in all output tasks;
    (b) *conduite d'approche* resulting in sequences of phonological errors.

- Possible production of circumlocutions in naming.
- Length effects in all tasks requiring spoken output.

Key assessment areas and available methods

Area of assessment	Examples of available assessment tools	Response type
Error analysis of naming	CAT 17: Naming objects	Picture naming
	PALPA 53: Picture naming	Picture naming
Effects of syllable length on naming	CAT 17: Naming objects	Picture naming
	Nickels Naming Test	Picture naming
Effect of syllable length on repetition	PALPA 7: Repetition: syllable length	Repetition
Sub-lexical phonological input-to-output conversion	PALPA 8: Repetition: nonwords	Repetition

Interpretation

✓   Retained picture naming or oral reading, or repetition of words and nonwords, implies intact phonological assembly.

✗   Impaired phonological assembly is suggested by target-oriented phonological errors in all output tasks.

✗   Reduced performance with repetition of longer words (and nonwords) relative to shorter words (and nonwords) (length effect) implies impairment of phonological assembly or subsequent processes.

✗   If repetition of nonwords is more difficult than repetition of words, this implies that the phonological assembly is more impaired than the lexicons, as the person cannot rely on lexical information to perform the task. This could also be accounted for by an impairment to sub-lexical phonological input-to-output conversion.

Box 5.2 A case of impairment to phonological assembly: Client MB (Franklin *et al.*, 2002)

MB was a retired 83-year-old lady. She had a left middle cerebral artery infarction. She was about 4 months post-onset at the time of testing. Her spontaneous speech consisted of the production of some automatic words and phrases. She produced many phonological errors and neologisms. Her auditory comprehension was functional in conversation and she had good single-word comprehension. Despite good auditory comprehension, she had difficulty on an auditory rhyme judgement, possibly indicating a specific segmentation problem. Her writing was limited and she produced many spelling errors. On formal testing of her spoken output, naming, reading aloud and repetition were all impaired, with naming being most difficult. In all tasks, she produced phonological errors consisting of both the omission and substitution of phonemes. These errors resulted in both real word and nonword errors. Some errors were repeated attempts at the target, resulting in responses that were either closer to the correct response or the correct response itself (conduite d'approche). There was an effect of length in all three tasks that was directly related to the number of phonemes in the word. There was no effect of frequency or imageability. MB had greater difficulty in nonword repetition and reading aloud than in the same tasks with real words. Her errors were again phonological, with a length effect for reading aloud. There was no effect of length on the repetition of nonwords, due to a floor effect. Franklin *et al.* suggest that MB has a post-lexical deficit affecting phonological assembly, specifically in phoneme encoding.

Notes

1   Some versions of this model also include a phonological output buffer that holds phoneme strings during the process of phonological assembly. It is also suggested that a phonological output buffer plays an important role in some short-term memory tasks. There is substantial evidence that the process of phonological assembly is distinct from an output buffer (see, for example, Howard & Nickels, 2005; Vallar & Shallice, 1992). Impairments in short-term memory have no necessary impact on single-word phonological production (Shallice & Warrington, 1977a). Because the process of phonological assembly is clearly necessary for word production (Levelt *et al.*, 1999), and there is no clearly established need for a buffer, we have called this process 'phonological assembly'.

2   Frequency effects have been attributed to semantic deficits (Hodges, Patterson, Oxbury & Funnell, 1992), mapping of semantics to the phonological output lexicon (Barry, Morrison & Ellis, 1997; McCann *et al.*, 1988) and the phonological output lexicon (Howard, 1995).

6 Written comprehension and reading

Model of reading

Figure 6.1 shows the processes involved in the comprehension and reading aloud (oral reading) of written words. Three stages are involved in reading words for meaning (reading comprehension): visual orthographic analysis, the orthographic input lexicon and the semantic system.

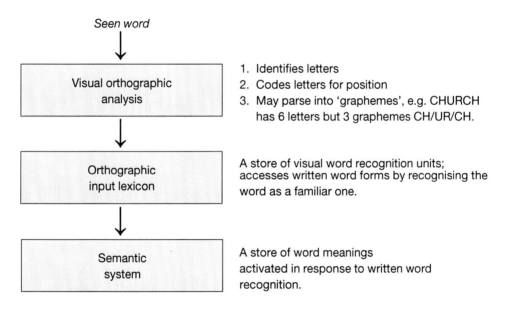

Seen word

| Visual orthographic analysis |
| 1. Identifies letters |
| 2. Codes letters for position |
| 3. May parse into 'graphemes', e.g. CHURCH has 6 letters but 3 graphemes CH/UR/CH. |

Orthographic input lexicon — A store of visual word recognition units; accesses written word forms by recognising the word as a familiar one.

Semantic system — A store of word meanings activated in response to written word recognition.

There are three routes that can be used to read words aloud. These are illustrated in Figure 6.1. The three routes for reading aloud share a varying number of components with the processes used in reading comprehension.

Semantic lexical route

This route involves reading words aloud via access to their meaning. It involves:

(a) recognition of a word in the orthographic input lexicon;
(b) access to the word's semantic representation; and
(c) retrieval of the spoken form from the phonological output lexicon.

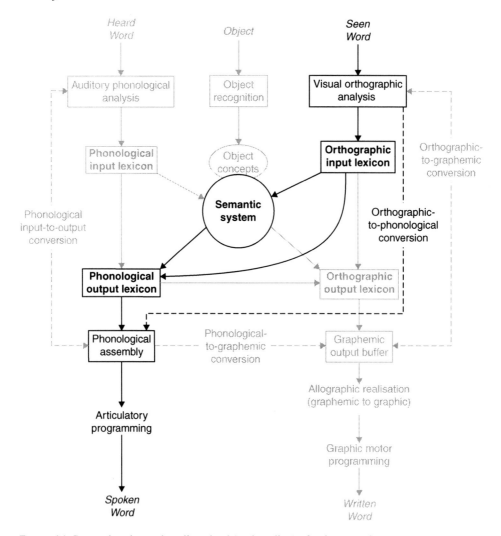

Figure 6.1 Comprehension and reading aloud (oral reading) of written words

This route can only process real, familiar words, and is not affected by spelling-to-sound regularity. It is required in the disambiguation of heterophonic homographs (words with the same spellings but different pronunciations) where the semantic context determines how the word sounds. For example:

There was a tear in her eye.
There was a tear in her dress.

Sub-lexical route (orthographic-to-phonological conversion)

Reading aloud via the sub-word level, orthographic-to-phonological correspondence is the 'sounding out route' or translation of visual analysis into an acoustic code that can be identified by the word recognition system. It involves:

(a) *Graphemic parsing* (within visual orthographic analysis). Dividing the letter string into units that correspond to phonemes, e.g. CH, TH, EE, A_E etc.
(b) *Grapheme-to-phoneme correspondences*. Some of these are simple correspondences between letters or graphemes (groups of letters) and sounds (e.g. B → /b/ or CH → /tʃ/), and some are context dependent (e.g. C → /s/ when followed by E or I, otherwise C → /k/).
(c) *Phonological assembly*. Blending a string of phonemes into a word.

This route allows the reading of nonwords that cannot be accessed within the lexicon. It also allows accurate reading of regular words. For irregular words, it will yield an incorrect pronunciation that will be a 'regularisation' (e.g. pronouncing PINT to rhyme with 'mint' or BEAR as 'beer').

Direct lexical route

This route involves reading aloud via a lexical but not semantic route. It involves:

(a) recognising the word in the orthographic input lexicon; and
(b) retrieving the phonology from the phonological output lexicon.

As only real, known words are represented in the lexicons, this routine can only process real words irrespective of their spelling-to-sound regularity. Words can be recognised and read aloud without semantic knowledge. For example:

Given the written word HYENA → 'hyena . . . hyena . . . what in the heck is that?' (Schwartz, Saffran & Marin, 1980, p. 261; see also Funnell, 1983).

The routine probably works better with more familiar words, so a frequency effect may be found. As reading is not semantically mediated, variables such as word imageability or concreteness should not affect performance. There is evidence for this route from patients with dementia (Schwartz *et al.*, 1980).

Note that regular real words (e.g. MINT) will be read correctly by any of these three 'routes'. Irregular words (e.g. PINT) will be read correctly by either lexical route, but will be 'regularised' (to /pɪnt/) when read by the sub-lexical route. Nonwords that have no lexical representation can only be read using the sub-lexical route.

Deficits of reading

Deficits in reading comprehension and reading aloud depend on the location of the impairment and whether alternative routes can be utilised. Typically, routes are not wholly abolished but some routines may work less effectively than others. Reading impairments have traditionally been characterised in terms of peripheral or central dyslexias. A description of the characteristic features of the main types can be found in Table 6.1. Table 6.2 contrasts the features of the central dyslexias.

> Visual orthographic
> analysis

A deficit in visual orthographic analysis results in visual reading errors (as seen in neglect, attentional or visual dyslexia). Impairment to visual orthographic analysis may also result in letter-by-letter reading.

Table 6.1 Characteristic features of different types of dyslexia

PERIPHERAL DYSLEXIAS

1 Neglect dyslexia (Ellis, Flude & Young, 1987)

This peripheral dyslexia occurs as a consequence of difficulty with the visual specification of the word at the level of visual orthographic analysis. It is not necessarily a consequence of a general visual neglect.

Characteristic features:

- Spatially determined visual errors that occur consistently at either the right-hand or left-hand end of words. A neglect point can typically be discerned in reading errors. In a large proportion of the errors, all the letters will be correct on the preserved side of the neglect point, and incorrect on the impaired side of the neglect point. For example:

Left neglect dyslexia   Right neglect dyslexia

    LOG → 'dog'   LOG → 'lot'
    RIVER → 'liver'   BOOK → 'boot'
    YELLOW → 'pillow'   BUCKET → 'buckle'

- Errors are typically very similar in length to the stimulus word.

2 Attentional dyslexia (Shallice & Warrington, 1977b)

This peripheral dyslexia occurs as a consequence of difficulty with the visual specification of the word at the level of visual orthographic analysis.

Characteristic feature:

- Errors involving interference/migration of letters from other words. For example:
  WIN FED → 'fin fed'

3 Visual dyslexia (Marshall & Newcombe, 1973)

This dyslexia occurs as a consequence of a difficulty identifying and recognising the visual form of the word either at the level of visual orthographic analysis or in subsequent access to the orthographic input lexicon.

Characteristic feature:

- Visual errors involving the misidentification of one word for a visually similar one (but without any strong tendency for errors to occur at one end of the word). For example:

    LEND → 'land'
    EASEL → 'aerial'
    CALM → 'claim'

4 Letter-by-letter reading (Warrington & Shallice, 1980; Patterson & Kay, 1982)

In letter-by-letter reading, letters of a word cannot be identified simultaneously and in parallel, so some or all of the letters of the word will be named (and sometimes misnamed) before a response is produced. This is a consequence of impaired visual orthographic analysis. Written words are identified by a reverse operation of the intact spelling system for oral spelling (Warrington & Shallice, 1980) or by serial rather than parallel access to the input lexicon (Patterson & Kay, 1982). For example:

    CHAIR → C H A I R . . . chair
    TABLE → T A B . . . table
    LAMP → L A N P . . . no . . . L A M . . . lamp
    TOOL → F O O L . . . fool

Characteristic features:

- Very slow reading, with reading latencies increasing linearly with the word letter length.
- Occasional, more rapid responses without overt letter naming for shorter words.

Note that about 50% of people who read letter by letter also show the features of surface dyslexia.

CENTRAL DYSLEXIAS

1 Surface dyslexia (Marshall & Newcombe, 1973)

Surface dyslexia results from impairment to lexically mediated reading with orthographic-to-phonological conversion relatively well preserved. The lexically mediated route may be impaired at different levels: the orthographic input lexicon, access to or within the semantic system, or access to or retrieval from the phonological output lexicon.

Characteristic features:

- Regular words (e.g. MINT, FEAR) are read better than irregular words (e.g. PINT, BEAR).
- Relatively well-preserved nonword reading (although many patients are somewhat worse at reading nonwords than matched real words).

Errors in reading consist of:

- Phonologically plausible errors (mostly regularisations, e.g. YACHT → '/jætʃt/', SEW → 'sue').
- Visual errors, e.g. SUBTLE → 'sublet'.
- Errors resulting from misapplication of letter-to-sound rules, e.g. failure to apply the 'rule of E' correctly: RAGE → 'rag'.

2 Deep dyslexia (Marshall & Newcombe, 1973)

Deep dyslexia is a result of reading via an impaired semantically mediated lexical route. Orthographic-to-phonological conversion is also impaired.

Characteristic features:

- The defining symptom of deep dyslexia is the occurrence of semantic errors in single-word reading, e.g. APE → 'monkey'.
- Unable to read nonwords.
- High-imageability words are read better than low-imageability words (more impaired on abstract words).
- Content words are read better than function words (although this difference may not be found with lists matched for imageability).

Other errors that are nearly always present include:

- Visual and/or semantic errors, e.g. CLING → 'clasp'.
- Visual errors, e.g. DOOR → 'doom'.
- Morphological errors, e.g. LOVELY → 'loving'.
- Occasional visual-then-semantic errors, e.g. SYMPATHY → 'orchestra'.
- Function word substitutions, e.g. HIM → 'was'.

3 Phonological dyslexia

Phonological dyslexia results from impaired orthographic-to-phonological conversion (the sub-lexical reading route) relative to lexical reading.

Characteristic features:

- Poor or non-existent nonword reading (and reading of unfamiliar words). Nonwords are often read as visually similar real words. For example:

  SOOF → 'soot'
  KLACK → 'slack'

- Preserved or relatively good real word reading unaffected by spelling-to-sound regularity.

If reading of words is impaired:

- High-imageability words are read better than low-imageability words (more impaired on abstract words).

- Content words may be read better than function words (although this difference may not be found with lists matched for imageability).
- Morphologically simple words are read better than morphologically complex words.

Errors in reading consist of:

- Visual errors.
- Visual and/or semantic errors.
- Morphological errors.

Note: Pure semantic errors do not occur in phonological dyslexia.

Table 6.2 Contrasting patterns of performance in different types of central dyslexia

Performance	Type of dyslexia		
	Surface dyslexia	Deep dyslexia	Phonological dyslexia
Nonword reading	✓	✗	✗
Regularity effects in reading aloud	✓	✗	✗
Imageability effects in reading aloud	✗	✓	✓ (possibly)
Grammatical class effects in reading aloud	✗	✓	✓ (possibly)
Semantic errors in reading aloud	✗	✓	✗

As visual orthographic analysis is shared in all aspects of reading, errors occur in reading comprehension and in the oral reading of words and nonwords. Real word reading is often but not necessarily better than nonword reading.

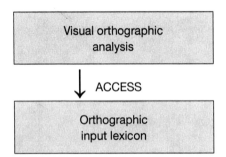

An impairment in accessing the orthographic input lexicon will affect the recognition and comprehension of words. Impairment results in the visual error characteristics of the visual dyslexias or in letter-by-letter reading. If orthographic-to-phonological conversion is retained, a pattern of reading characteristic of surface dyslexia is seen. Words and nonwords are read via the sub-lexical route, resulting in accurate reading of nonwords and regular words and regularisation errors for irregular words.

```
┌─────────────────┐
│  Orthographic   │
│  input lexicon  │
└─────────────────┘
```

A deficit in the orthographic input lexicon results in an impairment to reading comprehension and to lexically mediated reading aloud. If orthographic-to-phonological conversion is retained, a pattern of reading characteristic of surface dyslexia is seen. Words and nonwords are read via the sub-lexical route, resulting in accurate reading of nonwords and regular words and regularisation errors for irregular words.

A deficit within the lexicon results in difficulty determining whether a string of graphemes is a real word or not. Lexical decision and comprehension may occur via phonology, so irregular words are rejected (e.g. YACHT → 'that's not a word') but pseudo-homophones (e.g. BOAL, JALE, PHOCKS) are accepted and understood (as their corresponding real words). The meanings of real word homophones (e.g. MALE/MAIL or TWO/TO/TOO) are confused when meaning is accessed on the basis of phonology.

```
Semantic
system
```

A semantic deficit results in impaired comprehension of both auditory and written words and difficulty producing both spoken and written words (see semantic impairments in Chapter 4).

Impairment to the semantic system will affect reading aloud via the semantically mediated route. Imageability effects are typically present. If orthographic-to-phonological conversion is also impaired, then reading aloud will be characteristic of either deep or phonological dyslexia.

```
Orthographic-to-
phonological conversion
```

An impairment to orthographic-to-phonological conversion results in non-existent or poor reading of nonwords and novel words. Nonwords are often read as visually similar real words. Orthographic-to-phonological conversion is impaired in both deep and phonological dyslexia.

Assessments of reading

Exclude deficits of visual acuity and visual neglect through:

- Tests of vision (usually carried out by optician).
- Ensuring eye glasses are worn if prescribed.
- Checking influence of size of print.
- Line bisection/letter cancellation/star cancellation (Behavioural Inattention Test – Wilson, Cockburn & Halligan, 1987).

Exclude pre-morbid difficulties in literacy.

General notes on assessment

When testing reading, it is important to consider both reading comprehension and reading aloud. To assess reading comprehension, a test that considers the whole process (e.g. written word to picture matching) is a useful starting point. Clients should be encouraged to read the words silently. If written word comprehension is impaired, consider the pattern of errors made. Comparing the reading aloud of regular and irregular words of varying imageability and nonwords allows the clinician to hypothesise to what extent the three reading routes are impaired and preserved. One complication is that typically these routes are not wholly abolished but some routes may be working less effectively than others. More detailed assessments will then need to be carried out to determine what specific processes are impaired.

Word types

As a first step in assessing reading aloud, three types of word lists are useful:

1   Nonwords – that is, reading aloud single-syllable nonwords. Ideally, these would be matched in terms of length and orthographic complexity to real words.
2   Regular and irregular words. These matched sets should include low-frequency irregular words, as these are the items most likely to elicit regularity effects.
3   High- and low-imageability words.

The use of these three item sets allows conclusions to be drawn about three effects:

(a) A lexicality effect. Where nonwords are read less accurately than real words of equivalent difficulty, this implies impairment to orthographic-to-phonological conversion.
(b) A regularity effect. Where regular words are read more accurately than irregular words, this implies that lexical reading is impaired.
(c) An imageability effect. Where high-imageability words are read more accurately than matched low-imageability words, this implies impairment at the level of the semantic system, with some contribution of the semantically mediated route.

Error types

The second source of evidence available is the nature of the errors made in reading. These can be classified into the following categories:

1   Semantic errors: responses that are semantically related to the target, but the words are not visually related, e.g. APE → 'monkey'.
2   Visual/phonological errors: errors which are similar to the target in orthographic and/or phonological form. A common criterion for visual similarity is that at least 50% of the phonemes in the stimulus occur in the error response in approximately the same order (cf. Morton and Patterson, 1980), e.g. DOOR → 'doom'.
3   Mixed visual/semantic errors: errors that are both visually and semantically related to the stimulus, e.g. RAT → 'cat'.
4   Morphological errors: responses that share at least the root morpheme with the stimulus, but have errors in addition, deletion or substitution of morphemes. These errors will typically be found most often with stimuli that are morphologically complex, e.g. LOVELY → 'loving'.
5   Visual-then-semantic errors: errors in which a semantic error appears to follow a visual error, e.g. SYMPATHY → 'orchestra'.
6   Phonologically plausible errors: mostly 'regularisations' but also including relatively rare 'irregularisations', e.g. SPEAR → /spɛə/.

> Visual orthographic
> analysis

Indicators of impairment

- Reduced ability to recognise letters.
- Impaired reading comprehension and reading aloud with visual errors.
- Length effects (shorter words easier to read than longer words).

General notes on assessment

Impaired visual orthographic analysis will affect all reading tasks.

Key assessment areas and available methods

Area of assessment	Examples of available assessment tools	Response type
Written letter recognition	PALPA 18: Mirror reversal	Letter selection
	PALPA 19: Upper-case/lower-case letter matching	Letter selection
	PALPA 20: Lower-case/upper-case letter matching	Letter selection
	PALPA 21: Letter discrimination: Letters in words and nonwords	Tick/correct
Auditory and written letter recognition	PALPA 23: Spoken letter/written letter matching	Letter selection

Interpretation

✓ Good performance on letter recognition, discrimination and matching tasks implies that visual orthographic analysis is intact.

✗ Impaired visual orthographic analysis is suggested by difficulty with letter recognition and the presence of visual errors in reading of words and nonwords.

Additional specific assessment options

(a) Neglect dyslexia

Area of assessment	Examples of available assessment tools	Response type
Detection of neglect errors	One, few, many bodies test (as described in Patterson & Wilson, 1990) Tests for word-centred neglect	Reading aloud
Note distribution of incorrectly read words	Informal – ask client to read passage and note the spatial distribution of the errors made Tests for page-centred neglect	Reading aloud

(b) Letter-by-letter reading

Area of assessment	Examples of available assessments tools	Response type
Letter naming and sounding	PALPA 22: Letter naming/sounding	Naming/sounding letters
Length effect	PALPA 29: Letter length reading	Reading aloud

Box 6.1 A case of a letter-by-letter reader: Client CH (Patterson & Kay, 1982)

CH was an 81-year-old when he had a left CVA. He was right-handed and had worked as a chauffeur until his retirement. A CT scan showed damage in the left occipital and temporal lobes. He had a right homonymous haemianopia. He was 4 years post-onset at the time of testing. CH had normal comprehension and speech production. His spelling to dictation, both oral and written, was good although not perfect. His spelling errors were predominantly either phonologically acceptable alternatives (e.g. for 'definite' he wrote 'definate') or nearly phonologically acceptable (e.g. 'yaught' for 'yacht'). It was unclear to what extent these difficulties reflected his pre-morbid abilities. He was always able to identify words from their oral spelling. His reading was almost entirely letter by letter – that is, he named each letter before saying the word. His reading was very slow and reading latency increased linearly with word length. He had a severe deficit in naming individual letters, with a slight advantage for upper-case letters. This led to letter misidentifications resulting in reading errors (e.g. 'men' was read as 'h e n, hen'). Misidentifications between visually similar letters were most common. Other errors included the production of a word containing the same initial letter string as the target. If the letters were correctly identified and named, CH almost always produced the correct word, for words with regular and irregular spellings. Patterson and Kay propose that once CH had identified the correct letters, he used intact lexical knowledge of spelling to assign the correct pronunciation to the word.

> Orthographic
> input lexicon

Indicators of impairment

- Reduced ability to recognise a string of graphemes as a real word and to reject non-words. Rejection of irregular words as nonwords and acceptance of pseudo-homophones implies reliance on orthographic-to-phonological conversion.
- Visual errors in reading.

- Frequency effects (with high-frequency words being recognised more easily than low-frequency words).

And, if nonword reading is (relatively) intact:

- Regularity effects (exception words are more difficult to read aloud and regularisation errors occur, e.g. 'blewed' for BLOOD).
- Homophone errors occur in written comprehension (e.g. BERRY → 'to put in the ground', LISTEN → 'the boxer'[1]).

General notes on assessment

Impaired visual orthographic analysis will lower performance on tests of visual lexical decision and written comprehension. Reduced access to the orthographic input lexicon may result in visual dyslexia or letter-by-letter reading. Impairment to the lexicon will impair reading aloud via the semantic or direct lexical route. If impairment to the orthographic input lexicon is accompanied by intact orthographic-to-phonological conversion, reading will be characteristic of surface dyslexia.

Key assessment areas and available methods

Area of assessment	Examples of available assessment tools	Response type
Written lexical decision – illegal strings	PALPA 24: Visual lexical decision with 'illegal' nonwords	Written word selection
Written lexical decision – semantic involvement	PALPA 25: Visual lexical decision: imageability × frequency	Written word selection
Written lexical decision – regularity	PALPA 27: Visual lexical decision: spelling–sound regularity	Written word selection

Interpretation

✓ Good performance on written lexical decision tasks implies that the orthographic input lexicon is intact.
✗ Reduced performance on written lexical decision tasks implies impairment to the orthographic input lexicon.
✗ Different patterns of error may be seen depending on whether the client is able to access phonological information via orthographic-to-phonological conversion. The additional options will help to confirm whether this route is intact. If intact, the client will show characteristics of surface dyslexia.

Additional specific assessment options

Area of assessment	Examples of available assessment tools	Response type
Reading nonwords	CAT 23: Reading nonwords	Reading aloud
	PALPA 36: Nonword reading	Reading aloud
Spelling–sound regularity effect	CAT 20: Reading words	Reading aloud
	PALPA 35: Spelling–sound regularity and reading	Reading aloud
Access to semantics from written word form	PALPA 38: Homophone definitions and regularity	Spoken definition/ reading aloud
Access to pronunciation from written word form	PALPA 28: Homophone decision	Tick

Interpretation

✓   A regularity effect in reading and preserved reading of nonwords implies relatively intact orthographic-to-phonological conversion.

✗   If comprehension is based primarily on a phonological form, homophones will frequently be misunderstood. Where this occurs only with regular homophones (e.g. BERRY → to put in the ground) but not irregular homophones (e.g. BURY → that's not a word, /bjʊərɪ/), this suggests that the phonology on which comprehension is based is primarily sub-lexical orthographic-to-phonological conversion. Where, however, homophone errors also occur frequently with irregular homophones (e.g. BURY → grows on bushes, berry), phonology must sometimes depend on lexical and non-semantic ('direct route') recoding of orthography to phonology.

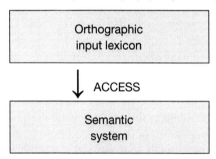

Indicators of impairment

•   Written words are recognised as real words but are difficult to understand.
•   Good access to semantics via the auditory modality but impaired access via the written modality.

General notes on assessment

Impairment to visual orthographic analysis or the orthographic input lexicon will also affect access to semantics. Impaired access to semantics from the orthographic input lexicon will affect reading aloud via the semantically mediated route, but both regular and irregular words may still be read via the direct lexical route.

Key assessment areas and available methods

Area of assessment	Examples of available assessment tools	Response type
Access to semantics from written word form	PALPA 38. Homophone definitions and regularity	Spoken definition/ reading aloud
Compare written and auditory comprehension of words	CAT 7/8: Comprehension of spoken/ written words	Picture selection
	PALPA 47/48: Spoken and written word to picture matching	Picture selection

Interpretation

✓ Comparable auditory and written comprehension with retained understanding of homophones implies input from the orthographic input lexicon to semantics is intact.

✗ Reduced written performance compared to auditory performance implies input to semantics from the orthographic input lexicon is impaired.

✗ Homophone errors in defining homophones may imply impaired access from the orthographic input lexicon to semantics, with access to semantics depending on a phonological code. If homophone errors occur only with regular homophones, this phonological code is generated using orthographic-to-phonological conversion. Where homophone errors occur with irregular homophones, this suggests that the phonology is sometimes derived lexically.

Box 6.2 A case of impairment to the phonological output lexicon (surface dyslexia): Client MP (Bub, Cancelliere & Kertesz, 1985)

MP was a 62-year-old woman who was struck by a car. She sustained trauma to the skull, particularly in the region of the left temporal lobe. She was tested approximately 3 years after the accident. She presented with a severe comprehension deficit, having difficulty understanding single auditory and written words and identifying semantic associates. Her speech was characterised by anomia and jargon. Compared with her speech, her oral reading was rapid and fluent. On formal testing of her reading, her oral reading of regular words was more accurate than her reading of exception words. She showed a strong frequency effect. MP was able to read nonwords accurately. She was able to read some exception words, particularly those of high frequency; lower frequency exception words were read using general spelling-to-sound rules resulting in regularisation errors. MP was unable to identify irregular words in a lexical decision task, but on a lexical discrimination task her performance was sensitive to the regularity of letter–sound correspondence. She had particular difficulty identifying exception words as words when paired with orthographically plausible nonwords. Bub *et al.* suggest that MP was able to use some lexical knowledge to pronounce words using a route not mediated via semantics but by direct lexical connections between orthographic and phonological representations. When this route could not be accessed, she used her knowledge of spelling–sound correspondence. Due to her lexical discrimination skills, they suggest her functional impairment was located at the level of phonological retrieval rather than at the level of the orthographic representation.

```
┌─────────────────────────────────┐
│            Semantic             │
│             system              │
└─────────────────────────────────┘
```

Indicators of impairment

*   If a semantic impairment, the person will have:

    (a) impaired comprehension for both auditory and written input modalities and
    (b) semantic errors in both spoken and written output (but semantic errors may also indicate impairment at other levels).

*   Imageability effects in all tasks requiring semantic processing.

General notes on assessment

In reading, a semantic deficit affects reading comprehension and the use of the semantically mediated route for reading aloud. If orthographic-to-phonological conversion is also impaired, the client will present with the characteristics of either deep or phonological dyslexia. The difference between the two types is the presence of pure semantic errors in deep dyslexia.

Key assessment areas and available methods

See also the assessment of semantic deficits in Chapter 4.

Area of assessment	Examples of available assessment tools	Response type
Compare written and auditory compensation of words	CAT 7/8: Comprehension of spoken/ written words	Picture selection
	PALPA 47/48: Spoken and written word to picture matching	Picture selection
Imageability effect (and interaction with frequency effect)	CAT 20: Reading words	Reading aloud
	PALPA 31: Imageability × frequency reading	Reading aloud

Interpretation

✓ Retained performance on spoken and written comprehension and production implies intact semantics.
✗ Comparable performance on spoken and written comprehension with the choice of semantic distractors implies a semantic deficit.
✗ Errors on low-imageability items versus high-imageability items may imply a central semantic problem.

Additional specific assessment options

Area of assessment	Examples of available assessment tools	Response type
Reading nonwords	CAT 23: Reading nonwords	Reading aloud
	PALPA 36: Nonword reading	Reading aloud
Grammatical class effect	CAT 22: Reading function words	Reading aloud
	PALPA 33: Grammatical class reading (controlled for imageability)	Reading aloud
Morphological complexity effect	CAT 21: Reading complex words	Reading aloud
	PALPA 34: Lexical morphology and reading	Reading aloud

Interpretation

✓ Retained ability to read nonwords implies intact orthographic-to-phonological conversion.

✗ Reduced ability to read nonwords implies an impairment to orthographic-to-phonological conversion.

✗ Reduced performance in reading aloud verbs and function words relative to nouns (grammatical class effects) may imply syntactic–semantic difficulties. As both verbs and function words are lower in imageability than nouns, increased difficulty reading may also be due to an imageability effect.

✗ Morphological complexity effects have been found in deep dyslexia; these may be semantic in nature (Funnell, 1987).

Box 6.3 A case of impairment to semantic lexical reading and impaired orthographic-to-phonological conversion (deep dyslexia): Client GR (Marshall & Newcombe, 1966; Newcombe, Oldfield, Ratcliff & Wingfield, 1971; Newcombe & Marshall, 1980)

GR was a 19-year-old soldier who was injured in Normandy in 1944 when a bullet penetrated his brain in the region of the left sylvian fissure and emerged in the superior parietal lobe of the left hemisphere. His speech was non-fluent and agrammatic with word finding difficulties in constrained tests and in spontaneous speech. GR's performance in reading aloud was characterised by relatively good reading of common, concrete nouns but errors on other words. He was completely unable to read nonwords. His errors in reading aloud were a combination of semantic circumlocutions (e.g. for TOMATO → 'Can't pronounce it . . . don't like them myself . . . they're red') and semantic errors (e.g. ARSENIC → 'poison'). There was also evidence of semantic difficulties in other formal tests. He made a high proportion of semantic and semantic/visual errors in spoken and written word–picture matching. He had difficulty sorting written words into semantic categories and made errors when matching spoken words to written words within semantic categories. GR presented with marked difficulties in spoken naming with increased naming latencies for low-frequency words. He produced predominantly circumlocutions (described as misnaming errors). For example, for SYRINGE he produced 'a thing for pushing medicine . . . injection'.

Orthographic-to-
phonological conversion

Indicators of impairment

- Reading nonwords (i.e. pronouncing unfamiliar strings of letters) will be difficult.

General notes on assessment

Orthographic-to-phonological conversion is impaired in both deep and phonological dyslexia.

Key assessment areas and available methods

Area of assessment	Examples of available assessment tools	Response type
Reading nonwords	CAT23: Reading nonwords	Reading aloud
	PALPA 36: Nonword reading	Reading aloud

Interpretation

✓ Retained ability to read nonwords implies intact orthographic-to-phonological conversion.

✗ Impaired orthographic-to-phonological conversion is suggested by a reduced ability to produce nonwords and novel words.

Box 6.4 A case of impairment to orthographic-to-phonological conversion (phonological dyslexia): Client WB (Funnell, 1983)

WB was a man who had a left hemisphere CVA at the age of 58. He was previously employed as a transport manager. His speech was non-fluent but not agrammatic and was slightly dysarthric. He presented with relatively good functional comprehension but impaired comprehension of syntactic structures. His reading aloud was characterised by an inability to read nonwords, to produce the sounds for isolated letters and to read isolated suffixes. His reading aloud of words was around 90% accurate with no effect of imageability, word class, regularity or morphological complexity. He was able to read function words and suffixes when attached to appropriate or phonologically legal words. He produced very few semantic errors in real word reading. Funnell argues that WB's reading of real words was a consequence of direct word links between orthography and phonology and not semantic mediation, as he made semantic errors in the written comprehension of single words. His reading aloud of words was significantly superior to his ability to make semantic judgements about those words; although he was at chance in matching written MITTEN to GLOVE or SOCK, he could read almost all of the words correctly.

Note

1 Sonny Liston was world heavyweight boxing champion 1962–4.

7 Written word production

Model of written production (spelling)

Figure 7.1 shows the processes involved in written word naming of objects/pictures. The processes involved in copying written words are shown in Figure 7.2. Four stages are involved in writing words to convey meaning: the semantic system, the orthographic output lexicon, the graphemic output buffer and allographic realisation.

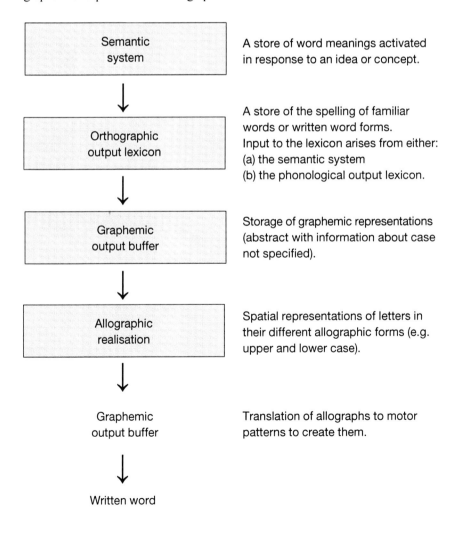

Semantic system	A store of word meanings activated in response to an idea or concept.
Orthographic output lexicon	A store of the spelling of familiar words or written word forms. Input to the lexicon arises from either: (a) the semantic system (b) the phonological output lexicon.
Graphemic output buffer	Storage of graphemic representations (abstract with information about case not specified).
Allographic realisation	Spatial representations of letters in their different allographic forms (e.g. upper and lower case).
Graphemic output buffer	Translation of allographs to motor patterns to create them.
Written word	

When writing words to dictation, there are three routes that can be used. These are illustrated in Figure 7.3.

Semantic lexical route

This route involves writing with access to meaning and is the usual spelling mechanism. It involves: (a) activation from the semantic system and (b) access to the word within the orthographic output lexicon. This route is necessary to correctly spell homophones.

Sub-lexical route (phonological-to-graphemic conversion)

Writing via phonological-to-graphemic conversion is the 'sounding out route'. It involves the segmentation of a word into phonemes and then translation of the phonemes into graphemes. This route is used for the writing to dictation of unfamiliar words and nonwords.

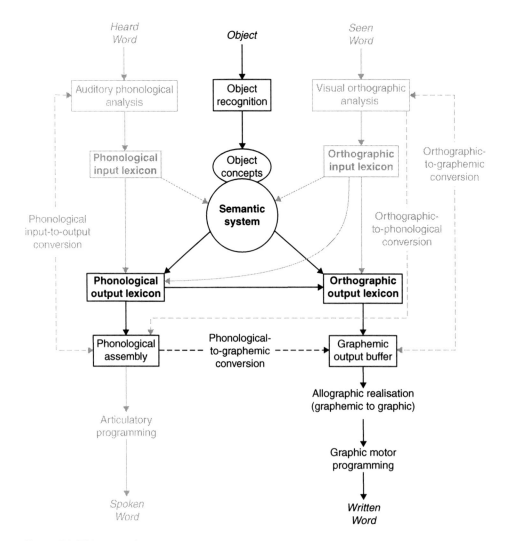

Figure 7.1 Written naming

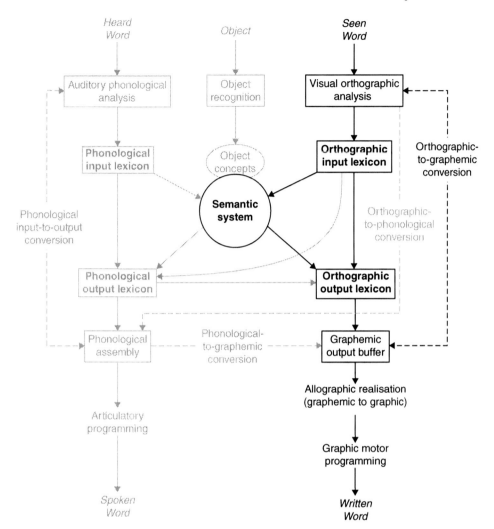

Figure 7.2 Copying written words

Direct lexical route

This route involves writing to dictation via a lexical but not semantic route. It involves: (a) retrieving the word's phonology from the phonological output lexicon and (b) activation of the word within the orthographic output lexicon. As only real, known words are represented in these lexicons, this routine can only process real words, irrespective of their sound-to-spelling regularity. This results in being able to write irregular words without semantic knowledge.

Deficits of written production (spelling)

Deficits in writing depend on the location of the impairment and whether alternative routes can be utilised. Writing impairments have traditionally been characterised in terms of deep dysgraphia, surface dysgraphia and phonological dysgraphia. Table 7.1 describes the main features of each.

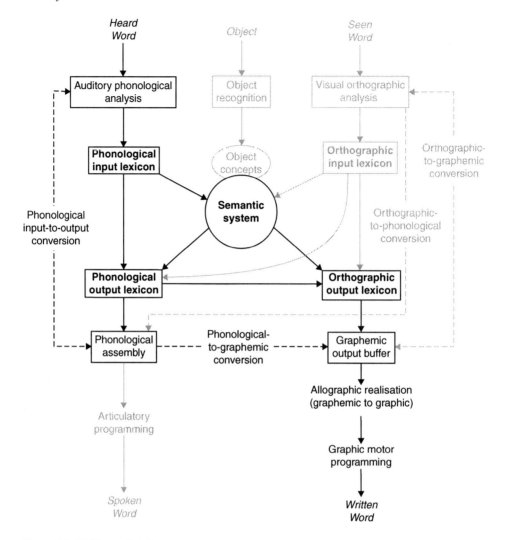

Figure 7.3 Writing to dictation

Table 7.1 Characteristic features of different types of dysgraphia

DYSGRAPHIAS

1 Deep dysgraphia (Bub & Kertesz, 1982)

Deep dysgraphia results from writing via an impaired semantic route. Access to the orthographic output lexicon is impaired with an additional deficit in phonological-to-graphemic conversion.

Characteristic features:

- The defining feature of deep dysgraphia is the presence of semantic errors in writing, e.g. TIME → 'clock'.
- Nonword spelling is impaired – typically impossible or close to impossible.

- High-imageability words are written more accurately than low-imageability words.
- Content words are written more accurately than function words.

2 Phonological dysgraphia (Shallice, 1981)

Phonological dysgraphia results from a difficulty in sub-lexical writing to dictation with relatively good lexical writing. The writing impairment can result from an impairment to sub-lexical phonological-to-graphemic conversion (when nonword repetition is unaffected) or in sub-lexical auditory-to-phonological conversion (when both nonword repetition and writing nonwords to dictation are impaired).

Characteristic features:

- Very poor writing of nonwords to dictation.

Real word writing to dictation may be close to perfect, but if real word writing is impaired:

- Structurally similar and morphological errors in writing to dictation.
- Better writing of high- than low-imageability words.

3 Surface dysgraphia (Beauvois & Derouesne, 1981)

Surface dysgraphia results from impairment to lexically mediated writing with phonological-to-graphemic conversion well preserved.

Characteristic features:

- Regular words and nonwords are written more accurate

- Correct production of some high-frequency, irregular w

- Confusion between the spelling of homophones, e.g. S/

Errors:

(a) Regularisation errors in the spelling of irregular word:
(b) Errors involving partial knowledge of irregular wor 'sward'.

```
┌─────────────────────────────┐
│                             │
│         Semantic            │
│         system              │
│                             │
└─────────────────────────────┘
```

A semantic deficit results in impaired comprehension of both auditory and written words and difficulty producing both spoken and written words (see semantic impairments in Chapter 4).

Impairment to the semantic system will affect writing to convey meaning and writing to dictation via the semantically mediated route. Imageability effects are typically present. If phonological-to-graphemic conversion is impaired, then writing will be characteristic of deep dysgraphia.

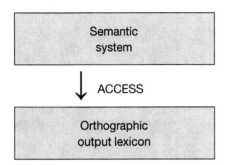

A deficit in accessing the orthographic output lexicon results in impaired writing via the semantic lexical route. Words may still be written via phonological-to-graphemic conversion or the direct lexical route. The comprehension of spoken and written words and spoken word production will be preserved. If phonological-to-graphemic conversion is also impaired, writing will be characteristic of deep dysgraphia.

Orthographic output lexicon

An impairment in the orthographic output lexicon results in impaired writing via the semantic lexical and the direct lexical route. If writing via phonological-to-graphemic conversion is preserved, writing will be characteristic of surface dysgraphia. A frequency effect in writing may be evident. A deficit within the orthographic output lexicon results in confusion when writing homophones.

Graphemic output buffer

Impairment to the graphemic output buffer results in difficulty writing words and nonwords, although nonwords are often significantly worse than words (Sage & Ellis, 2004). Written naming, writing to dictation, delayed copying, typing and oral spelling are affected.[1] Although the graphemic output buffer is post-lexical, there is increasing evidence that performance is still influenced by lexical or semantic variables e.g. word frequency, imageability, age of acquisition (Sage & Ellis, 2004).

   Spelling errors include: (a) additions, (b) deletions, (c) substitutions and (d) transpositions of letters. An effect of word length on spelling will be present. Letter formation is intact.

Allographic realisation

Impairment to allographic realisation results in letter substitutions in both words and nonwords. All writing is impaired but oral spelling is retained.

Graphic-to-motor realisation

Impairment results in impaired selection of movements (Baxter & Warrington, 1986). Words can be spelled orally. Error types present in writing single letters include: (a) substitutions, (b) incomplete letters and (c) the fusion of two letters.

The ability to describe the shape of the letters is retained. Copying is unaffected (i.e. it is not an apraxic disorder). It is possible to have a selective difficulty in writing either upper-case letters (Destreri *et al.*, 2000) or lower-case letters (Patterson & Wing, 1989).

> Phonological-to-graphemic
> conversion

An impairment to phonological-to-graphemic conversion results in non-existent or poor writing of nonwords. Nonwords are often written as similar real words. Phonological-to-graphemic conversion is impaired in both deep and phonological dysgraphia.

Assessments of written word production

Exclude deficits of visual acuity, visual neglect and motor dyspraxia through:

- Tests of vision (usually carried out by optician)
- Ensuring eye glasses are worn if prescribed
- Line bisection
- Tests for motor dyspraxia
- General positioning and posture (liaise with physiotherapist)

Exclude pre-morbid difficulties in literacy.

General notes on assessment

When assessing writing, written picture naming of a variety of stimuli is a useful starting point. It is important to note to what extent the client produces the word verbally before written naming. Consider the error types produced to form a hypothesis about the level of impairment. Writing to dictation of regular and irregular words of varying imageability and nonwords can help to confirm the diagnosis. If an impairment to peripheral processes (graphemic output buffer, allographic realisation or graphic-to-motor realisation) is suspected, contrast written performance with copying, oral spelling and the use of a letter board/letter tiles or typing. When assessing spelling, it is important to recognise that some clients will be using their non-dominant hand and to consider pre-morbid spelling ability.

Word types

In assessing written production of words, four types of word stimuli are useful:

1   High- and low-imageability words.
2   High- and low-frequency words.

3   Regular and irregular words. These sets should include low-frequency irregular words, as these are the items most likely to elicit regularity effects.
4   Words varying in syllable length, e.g. one-, two-, three-syllable words.

In each case, it is important to ensure that the words used are within the client's pre-morbid vocabulary. Analysis of performance on these variables allows conclusions to be drawn about four effects:

(a)   An imageability effect. Where high-imageability words are spelled more accurately than matched low-imageability words, this may imply impairment to the semantic system.
(b)   A regularity effect. Where regular words are spelled more accurately than irregular words, this may imply impairment at the level of the orthographic output lexicon or in access to it.
(c)   A frequency effect. Where high-frequency words are spelled more easily than low-frequency words, this may imply impairment at the level of the orthographic output lexicon.
(d)   A length effect. Where shorter words are accessed more easily than longer words, this may imply impairment at the level of the graphemic output buffer or at another post-lexical level.

Error types

The second source of evidence available is the nature of the errors made in written production. These can be classified, for example, into the following categories:

1   Additions, e.g. TABLE → TARBLE.
2   Deletions, e.g. TABLE → TALE.
3   Substitutions, e.g. TABLE → TAPLE.
4   Transpositions of letters, e.g. TABLE → TALBE.
5   Incomplete letters.
6   The fusion of two letters.
7   Morphological errors (addition, deletion or substitution of an affix), e.g. TABLE → TABLES.
8   Semantic errors, e.g. TABLE → CHAIR.
9   Regularisation/phonologically plausible errors, e.g. TABLE → TAYBULL.

Key assessments of written naming

Naming assessment	Control factors
CAT 25: Writing picture names	Not controlled, mix of high/low frequency, high/low imageability and regular/irregular words
PALPA 53: Picture naming × oral reading, repetition and written spelling	Regular and irregular words matched for word frequency, familiarity, concreteness, age of acquisition, letter length, and number of syllables

In addition, any of the assessments of noun and verb retrieval described in Chapter 5 could be used to investigate written naming.

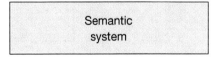

Semantic
system

See assessment in Chapter 4.

Indicators of impairment

- If a semantic impairment, the person will have:

  (a) impaired comprehension for both auditory and written input modalities and
  (b) semantic errors in both spoken and written output (but semantic errors may also indicate impairment at other levels).

- Imageability effects in all tasks requiring semantic processing.

General notes on assessment

In writing, a semantic impairment affects writing to convey meaning and the use of the semantic lexical route in writing to dictation. If phonological-to-graphemic conversion is also impaired, the client will present with the characteristics of deep dysgraphia. Additional assessment options are available to determine whether other characteristics are present.

Key assessment areas and available methods

Area of assessment	Examples of available assessment tools	Response type
Error analysis of naming	PALPA 53: Picture naming × oral reading, repetition & written spelling	Written naming
Imageability effect	PALPA 40: Spelling to dictation: imageability & frequency	Writing to dictation

Interpretation

✓ Retained performance on spoken and written comprehension and production implies intact semantics.
✗ Semantic errors in written naming alongside semantic errors in comprehension and spoken naming imply impairment of the semantic system.
✗ Reduced performance when spelling low-imageability words relative to high-imageability words (imageability effect) implies impairment of the semantic system.

Additional assessment options

Area of assessment	Examples of available assessment tools	Response type
Imageability effect	PALPA 40: Spelling to dictation: imageability & frequency	Writing to dictation
Grammatical class effect	PALPA 42: Spelling to dictation: grammatical class × imageability	Writing to dictation
Morphological complexity effect	PALPA 43: Spelling to dictation: morphological endings	Writing to dictation

Interpretation

✓   Reduced performance when spelling low-imageability words relative to high-imageability words (imageability effect) implies impairment of the semantic system or impaired access to the orthographic output lexicon.

✗   Reduced performance spelling verbs and function words relative to nouns (grammatical class effects) may imply syntactic–semantic difficulties. As words such as function words are lower in imageability, greater difficulty in spelling may also be due to an imageability effect.

✗   Morphological complexity effects have been found in deep dysgraphia (Badecker, Hillis & Caramazza, 1990).

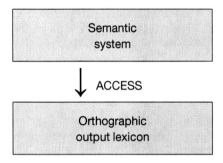

Indicators of impairment

•   Semantic errors in writing without semantic errors in reading, auditory comprehension or naming.

•   Imageability effects.

General notes on assessment

If access to the orthographic output lexicon is impaired alongside impaired phonological-to-graphemic conversion, writing will be characteristic of deep dysgraphia. Regular and irregular words may still be written via the direct lexical route.

Box 7.1 A case of impairment to the semantic system and phonological-to-graphemic conversion (deep dysgraphia): Client JC (Bub & Kertesz, 1982)

JC was a 21-year-old lady who suffered a left hemisphere CVA in the middle cerebral artery territory. She was 4 months post-onset at the time of testing. Her speech was non-fluent and agrammatic, with some word-finding difficulties in confrontation naming. Her comprehension of single words and short sentences was generally intact but she experienced difficulties with the comprehension of sequential commands. On formal testing of her writing, she was unable to write nonwords to dictation, producing confabulatory responses or real words that sounded similar to the target (e.g. CLIMPANY → 'balcony'). In real word writing, she produced semantic errors (e.g. TIME → 'clock'). Her writing of words was also characterised by an imageability effect (concrete nouns written more accurately than abstract nouns) and a word class effect (nouns written more accurately than verbs). She was unable to write function words. In contrast, reading and repetition of both words and nonwords was accurate.

Orthographic output lexicon

Indicators of impairment

*   Frequency effects on irregular words.
*   Reduced ability to spell homophones.

General notes on assessment

If the orthographic output lexicon is impaired and phonological-to-graphemic conversion is preserved, writing will be characteristic of surface dysgraphia. Additional assessments can be used to determine the presence of a regularity effect with regularisation errors in the production of irregular words.

Key assessment areas and available methods

Area of assessment	Examples of available assessment tools	Response type
Error analysis of naming	PALPA 53: Picture naming × oral reading, repetition & written spelling	Written naming
Frequency effect	PALPA 54: Picture naming × word frequency	Written naming
	PALPA 40: Spelling to dictation: imageability & frequency	Writing to dictation
Regularity effect	PALPA 44: Spelling to dictation: regularity	Writing to dictation
Writing of homophones	PALPA 46: Spelling to dictation: disambiguated homophones	Writing to dictation

Interpretation

✓   Good performance in the writing of low-frequency, irregular words implies an intact orthographic output lexicon.
✗   Reduced performance when spelling irregular words relative to regular words (regularity effect) implies impairment at the level of the orthographic output lexicon with spared phonological-to-graphemic conversion.
✗   A tendency to regularise exception words may also be seen with spelling of homophones, suggesting difficulties with the orthographic output lexicon.
✗   Reduced performance when spelling low-frequency words relative to high-frequency words (frequency effect) implies impairment of the orthographic output lexicon.

Box 7.2 A case of impairment to the orthographic output lexicon (surface dysgraphia): Client TP (Hatfield & Patterson, 1983)

TP was a lady who had a left posterior cerebral haemorrhage at the age of 50. She was 4 months post-onset at the time of testing. Her auditory comprehension of single words and sentences was generally accurate. She had a severe naming difficulty. She was able to repeat both single words and sentences. TP's writing was characterised by many spelling errors. For example, in a picture description task she wrote 'she is stil lafing about the to men being cros' instead of 'she is still laughing about the two men being cross'. In writing to dictation, her writing of regular words was significantly better than her writing of exception words, although occasional irregular words were spelled correctly. Her spelling errors were mainly the production of phonologically plausible responses (e.g. ANSWER   'anser'). She also sometimes confused visually similar letters (e.g. 'p' and 'b'). She was unable to disambiguate homophones in writing. Hatfield and Patterson suggest that TP's spelling reflects a reliance on a phonological spelling routine, with a minimal contribution of word-specific spelling.

```
Graphemic
output buffer
```

Indicators of impairment

- Generalised spelling errors (additions, deletions, subtractions and transpositions of letters for both words and nonwords).
- Length effects.

General notes on assessment

Impairment to the graphemic output buffer will affect all writing tasks.

Key assessment areas and available methods

Area of assessment	Examples of available assessment tools	Response type
Length effect	PALPA 39: Spelling to dictation: letter length	Writing to dictation
Real and nonword comparison	PALPA 45: Spelling to dictation: nonwords	Writing to dictation
Copying	CAT 24: Copying	Copying
	Informal immediate and delayed copying of words and nonwords	Copying

Interpretation

✓ Preserved written naming, writing to dictation and the copying of long and short words and nonwords imply an intact graphemic output buffer.

✗ Reduced performance when spelling longer words relative to shorter words (length effect) implies impairment of the graphemic output buffer.

✗ Generalised spelling errors in the writing and copying of words and nonwords imply impairment to the graphemic output buffer.

Box 7.3 A case of impairment to the graphemic output buffer: Client FV (Miceli, Silveri & Caramazza, 1985, 1987)

FV was 60 years old when he had a CVA. He was a lawyer. A CT scan showed a very small lesion in the uppermost portion of the angular gyrus and the lowermost portion of the superior parietal lobe with very minor involvement of the sub-cortical white matter. Initially, he presented with a mild aphasia but this resolved and he returned to work. When tested as an outpatient, he showed no aphasia but a severe writing disorder. His speech was fluent, with a varied vocabulary and a normal range of syntactic structures. He performed within the normal range on tests of spoken production and comprehension and was able to read words and nonwords correctly. His spontaneous writing was grammatical with a good vocabulary but contained frequent spelling errors. On formal testing, he was able to write single letters to dictation but made errors on sequences of letters. In written naming and writing to dictation, he made frequent spelling errors. His errors involved the substitution, omission, addition or transposition of letters, resulting in the production of nonwords. His writing accuracy was not affected by grammatical class, frequency or abstractness but was affected by length; short words were spelled more accurately than long words. He made more errors when writing nonwords than words but his errors were the same. FV often seemed to be aware of his errors and could correct about 80% of them when they were presented to him as errors. He could also identify his errors as nonwords when they were presented in a lexical decision task. FV was able to copy words and nonwords accurately even following a delay of up to 10 seconds. Miceli *et al.* propose that an impairment in the graphemic output buffer could account for FV's performance in writing but cannot explain his accurate delayed copying. An impairment in phonological-to-graphemic conversion cannot explain his increased accuracy in writing words compared to nonwords. They propose a model in which the information within the graphemic output buffer is refreshed not only via phonological-to-graphemic conversion but also via the orthographic output lexicon (possibly via the phonological output lexicon).

```
Allographic
realisation
```

Indicators of impairment

• Substitutions of letters for both words and nonwords.

Key assessment areas and available methods

Area of assessment	Examples of available assessment tools	Response type
Comparison of oral versus written spelling	Informal – any test of spelling	Oral and written spelling
Real and nonword writing	PALPA 39: Spelling to dictation: letter length	Writing to dictation
	PALPA 45: Spelling to dictation: nonwords	Writing to dictation

Interpretation

✓ Comparable written and oral spelling implies intact allographic realisation.
✗ Reduced performance in written spelling relative to oral spelling implies impaired allographic realisation.
✗ Letter substitutions in both real words and nonwords imply impaired allographic realisation.

> Graphic-to-motor
> realisation

Indicators of impairment

• Impaired movements and writing of single letters.

Key assessment areas and available methods

Area of assessment	Examples of available assessment tools	Response type
Spontaneous writing	Analysis of error types	Written spelling/letters
Copying ability	Ability to copy letters	Written copying

Interpretation

✓ Correct letter formation in copying and writing tasks implies intact graphic-to-motor realisation.
✗ Impaired movements during writing and impaired copying of letters, resulting in incorrect letter formation, would suggest involvement of graphic-to-motor realisation.

> Phonological-to-graphemic
> conversion

Indicators of impairment

• Writing of nonwords will be difficult.

General notes on assessment

Phonological-to-graphemic conversion is impaired in both deep and phonological dysgraphia.

Key assessment areas and available methods

Area of assessment	Examples of available assessment tools	Response type
Writing of nonwords	PALPA 45: Spelling to dictation: nonwords	Writing to dictation

Interpretation

✓ Retained ability to write nonwords implies intact phonological-to-graphemic conversion.

✗ Impaired phonological-to-graphemic conversion is suggested by a reduced ability to write nonwords and novel words to dictation.

Box 7.4 A case of impairment to phonological-to-graphemic conversion: Client PR (Shallice, 1981)

PR was a right-handed computer salesman who had an infarction in the territory of the left middle cerebral artery in his mid-fifties. At the time of testing, his speech was fluent with varied word choice but limited grammatical constructions. He scored within the normal range on tests of auditory comprehension and naming. His reading aloud was characteristic of a mild phonological dyslexia, with slightly impaired reading of nonwords (e.g. ITE → 'it'). His spontaneous writing was slow and laboured due to slight motor and formulation difficulties and was characterised by function word and verb errors. On testing, he showed a marked difference between his ability to write matched sets of words (94% correct) and nonwords (18% correct). His errors writing nonwords were mainly no responses. When he was able to attempt nonwords, he commented that he was using a real word mediator to facilitate his spelling. He was unable to write letters to single phonemes or clusters but could write letters in response to their letter names. His errors writing real words were a combination of no responses, structurally similar errors (e.g. ABSORPTION → 'absolve') and derivational errors (e.g. ASCEND → 'ascent'). He had particular difficulty writing function words. PR was able to repeat the function words and nonwords he was unable to write. He did, however, show some impairment on tasks of phonological segmentation.

Note

1 To accommodate the presence of people with better oral spelling than written spelling, it has been suggested that there are separate output buffers for written and oral spelling (Lesser, 1990; Pound, 1996). It is unclear whether this modification to the model is necessary.

8 Object and picture recognition

Model of object and picture recognition

Several stages are involved in recognising objects from visual input (either from pictures or from the actual object). The scheme given below elaborates on our basic model in Figure 1.1 (see page 5).

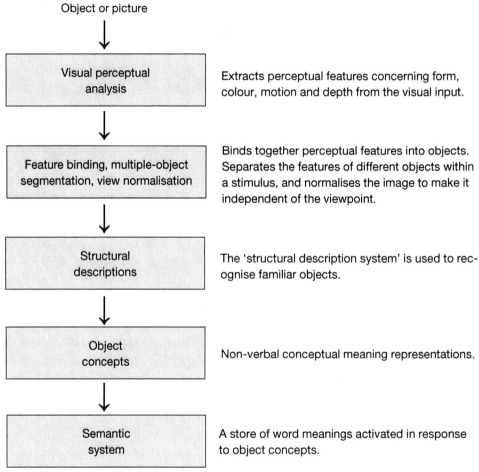

Object or picture

Visual perceptual analysis	Extracts perceptual features concerning form, colour, motion and depth from the visual input.
Feature binding, multiple-object segmentation, view normalisation	Binds together perceptual features into objects. Separates the features of different objects within a stimulus, and normalises the image to make it independent of the viewpoint.
Structural descriptions	The 'structural description system' is used to recognise familiar objects.
Object concepts	Non-verbal conceptual meaning representations.
Semantic system	A store of word meanings activated in response to object concepts.

Note that objects can be recognised in other ways – that is, from touch (tactile input) or from audition – at least for objects with characteristic noises. Note also that deficits in object recognition are typically due to lesions in regions such as the occipital and inferior temporal lobes (normally supplied by the posterior cerebral artery) that are typically intact in people with aphasia due to stroke (which usually follows lesions in the territory of the middle cerebral artery) (Farah, 1990; Riddoch & Humphreys, 2001). Striking deficits in object perception are therefore unusual in this population.

The inferior temporal lobes, and particularly the fusiform gyrus and surrounding regions, are important for face recognition (De Haan, 2001). As a result, disordered face recognition (prosopagnosia) frequently occurs in conjunction with object recognition difficulties. The medial temporal lobe, particularly the hippocampus and adjacent cortex, is important for episodic memory (Parkin, 2001). These structures are usually supplied by the posterior cerebral artery and, as a result, a degree of amnesia (both retrograde and anterograde) is frequently associated with object recognition difficulties.

Deficits of object recognition

```
Visual perceptual
analysis
```

Deficits may occur in:

(a) Shape perception.
(b) Motion perception – akinetopsia.
(c) Colour perception – achromotopsia.
(d) Depth perception.

```
Feature binding, multiple-object
segmentation, view normalisation
```

'Apperceptive' visual agnosias are deficits in object perception where elementary visual features are correctly extracted from the stimulus. The difficulties may lie in segmentation of the visual array and/or in binding together the features of objects. Recognition of pictures of objects from unusual (non-prototypical) views is typically poor. Line-by-line copying of a drawing is typically possible even where it is not recognised. Recognition of objects in other sensory modalities (e.g. by touch, sound or smell) is better than visual object recognition.

```
Structural
descriptions
```

'Associative' agnosias can result from an impairment of structural descriptions. People with a deficit at this level have good performance in tasks testing more peripheral visual properties, including unusual view matching, but perform poorly in object decision (discriminating objects from non-objects). They also, typically, have difficulty in other tasks tapping stored perceptual knowledge, including object drawing to command, and answering questions about the shape of objects (e.g. does a leopard have a long tail?).

> Object
> concepts

'Associative' agnosias may also result from an impairment of object concepts. Object decision tasks can be performed well, but people with a deficit at this level have difficulty in retrieving conceptual information about objects with all modalities of input. Semantic difficulties at this level can be category-specific. The most frequent category-specific disorders are impairment of 'animate' items (animals, plants and foods) relative to artefacts, or vice versa. Other more specific conceptual semantic disorders (e.g. of animals alone) are more rarely found (Capitani, Laiacona, Mahon & Caramazza, 2003; Caramazza & Mahon, 2003).

Box 8.1 A case of apperceptive visual agnosia: Client HJA (Humphreys & Riddoch, 1987; Riddoch & Humphreys, 1986)

HJA was in his sixties when he suffered a stroke following an emergency operation for a perforated appendix. A CT scan showed bilateral lesions near the occipital pole, but sparing the primary visual cortex. He had a bilateral loss of the superior half of the visual fields. He had severe difficulty in recognising visually presented objects and pictures, although he was able to copy them line-by-line – showing that he could perceive them. He had lost all colour vision (achromotopsia) – a natural consequence of the lesion that affected V4, the area responsible for colour vision, bilaterally. Aside from these visual difficulties, his language was intact; he had no difficulty in naming to definition, or in naming objects from their characteristic sounds. He could read laboriously letter-by-letter, but found this exhausting and unsatisfying. Recognition of pictures was much worse when they overlapped, but improved when they were presented as silhouettes, reducing the overall complexity of the drawing. Humphreys and Riddoch describe him as having an 'integrative visual agnosia' – 'intact registration of form elements, along with an impaired ability to integrate the elements into perceptual wholes' (p.105).

Assessments of object recognition

Exclude:

Exclude deficits of visual acuity and visual neglect through:

- Test of visual acuity (usually carried out by optician)
- Line bisection (e.g. from the Behavioural Inattention Test; (Wilson *et al.*, 1987).

As major visual perceptual impairments are rare in post-stroke aphasia, the optimal strategy is to first test for good access to object concepts (see final section below). Only if significant impairment is found would it be worthwhile to examine earlier stages of processing.

> Visual perceptual
> analysis

Indicators of impairment

- Difficulty in recognising visually presented stimuli (objects, pictures) with relatively intact recognition of objects presented through other modalities.
- Difficulty in discrimination or matching of stimuli on the basis of shape, size, colour, spatial location and/or motion.

Key assessment areas and available methods

Area of assessment	Examples of available assessment tools	Response type
Shape perception	VOSP[1]: Shape detection screening test	Yes/no
	BORB[2] 1: Copying of elementary shapes	Drawing
Length discrimination	BORB 2: Length match task	Same/different
Size discrimination	BORB 3: Size match task	Same/different
Orientation discrimination	BORB 4: Orientation match task	Same/different
Spatial location	BORB 5: Position of gap match task	Same/different
	VOSP 5: Dot counting	Number
	VOSP 6: Position discrimination	Pointing
	VOSP 7: Number location	Number

1 The Visual Object and Space Perception Battery (Warrington & James, 1991)
2 Birmingham Object Recognition Battery (Riddoch & Humphreys, 1993)

Interpretation

✓ Retained object recognition implies intact shape perception.
✓ Retained ability to name or match colours implies that colour recognition is intact.
✗ Impaired recognition of visually presented objects relative to tactile presentation is necessary for an impairment at this level.

Note that poor performance on shape copying may also be due to a constructional dyspraxia (drawing impairment) or visual neglect.

> Feature binding, multiple-object
> segmentation, view normalisation

Indicators of impairment

- Difficulty in recognising visually presented stimuli (objects, pictures) with relatively intact recognition of objects presented through other modalities.
- Difficulty in segmentation of superimposed object drawings and/or in recognition of objects from unusual views.

Key assessment areas and available methods

Area of assessment	Examples of available assessment tools	Response type
View normalisation	VOSP 2: Silhouettes	Name or describe object
	VOSP 4: Progressive silhouettes	Name or describe object
	BORB 7: Minimal feature view task	Pointing
	BORB 8: Foreshortened view task	Pointing
Object segmentation and feature binding	BORB 6: Overlapping figures task	Naming or matching

Interpretation

✓   Retained object recognition implies intact feature binding, object segmentation and view normalisation.

✗   Impaired recognition of visually presented objects relative to tactile presentation is necessary for an impairment at this level.

✗   Impaired recognition of unusual views and overlapping figures.

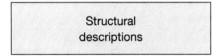

Structural descriptions

Indicators of impairment

•   Difficulty in recognising visually presented stimuli (objects, pictures) with relatively intact recognition of objects presented through other modalities.

•   Difficulty in object decision and drawing from memory.

Key assessment areas and available methods

Area of assessment	Examples of available assessment tools	Response type
Object decision	BORB 10: Object decision	Yes/no
Drawing from memory	BORB 9: Drawing from memory	Drawing

Interpretation

✓   Retained object recognition implies intact structural descriptions.

✗   Impaired recognition of visually presented objects relative to tactile presentation is necessary for an impairment at this level.

✗   Impaired object decision and drawing from memory implies impaired structural descriptions.

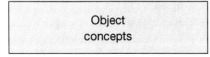

Object concepts

Indicators of impairment

- Poor retrieval of conceptual knowledge from any stimulus modality, even when tested in tasks not requiring any (overt) language. The impairment may be category-specific.

Key assessment areas and available methods

Area of assessment	Examples of available assessment tools	Response type
Object concepts	CAT 2: Semantic memory	Picture selection
	Pyramids and Palm Trees: Pictures only version (Howard & Patterson, 1992)	Picture selection
	BORB 12: Associative match task	Picture selection
	BORB 11: Item match task	Picture selection
Category-specific disorders	The Category-Specific Naming Test (McKenna, 1998)	Naming or word-to-picture matching

Interpretation

- ✓ Retained ability to match and name related concepts implies intact object concepts.
- ✗ Impaired matching of concepts (across modalities) implies difficulties with object concepts (although may be category-specific).

Part 3

Therapy

9   Introduction to therapy

Aphasia therapy continues to be characterised by many, very different approaches that reflect the variety of viewpoints both about the nature of the impairment in aphasia and about the aims of the therapy process (Howard & Hatfield, 1987; Basso, 2003; Whitworth, Webster & Morris, 2014). This diversity not only reflects the great variety of symptoms seen in individual clients, the varying severity of the aphasia and the impact that language impairments have both for the client and for their communication partners, but also the different approaches to treatment from therapists. More recently, the World Health Organisation's International Classification of Functioning, Disability and Health (ICF) (World Health Organisation, 2001) has sharpened the focus on the psychosocial and environmental aspects of aphasia therapy (e.g. Pound, Parr, Lindsay & Woolf, 2000). While these aspects of aphasia therapy have formed part of our clinical practice for some time now (e.g. Holland, 1982; Green, 1982), a real benefit of this discussion has been a realisation that therapies motivated by cognitive neuropsychology and those focused on other domains can come together in an integrated and congruent manner (Martin, Thompson & Worrall, 2007).

Notwithstanding the importance of considering the person with aphasia in context, approaches focusing on the impairment nevertheless have their roots in the underlying view held as to what aphasia is and what therapy can consequently aim to achieve. These have often been classified into two main groups (Albert, Goodglass, Helm, Rubens & Alexander, 1981; Seron, 1984). First is the belief that aphasia reflects an impairment of access to language, or damage to language processes or representations. With therapy, language functions can be restored, relearned or retrained. The second approach is based on the assumption that the impaired processes are themselves irremediable. Therapy must draw on compensatory strategies (other language and communication skills) to take over those impaired functions.

As in the preceding chapters of this volume, our discussion of therapy is presented from the theoretical viewpoint of cognitive neuropsychology. This view holds that language functions can be retrained or re-accessed through targeted intervention and will often directly target impaired processes. Based, as we have emphasised, on an analysis of both impaired and retained language-processing abilities, this approach also provides a basis for the development of therapy approaches centred on the development of compensatory strategies that draw on retained functions. Other reviews of aphasia therapy are available that have different aims but nonetheless cross-over with some of this literature (e.g. Robey, 1998; Bhogal *et al.* 2003; Moss and Nicholas, 2006; Cherney *et al.*, 2008), with the Cochrane library (Greener *et al.*, 1999; Kelly *et al.*, 2010; Brady *et al.*, 2012) providing a further source of scrutiny of therapy impact within certain research paradigms, e.g. randomised controlled trials (RCTs).

Building on the discussion of therapy set out in the first edition of this volume, this chapter has a number of aims. First, it will introduce some of the contextual factors that provide the current backdrop to aphasia therapy, placing therapies motivated by cognitive neuropsychology in a holistic context, and leading into a discussion of a cognitive neuropsychological perspective on aphasia therapy and possible mechanisms of change. Second, the main methodologies used by clinicians or researchers when applying cognitive neuropsychological therapies in practice are discussed, setting out the key principles recommended for clinicians to adhere to when setting up and evaluating therapy. Finally, the chapter introduces the template used for evaluating aphasia therapies that underpins Chapters 10 through 14, where a large, but not exhaustive, number of studies reported in the literature are detailed.

A holistic context

The holistic nature of aphasia therapy is non-contentious and therapy motivated by a cognitive neuropsychological approach forms an important component of such a view. The ICF model (World Health Organisation, 2001) provides a context whereby the impairment is a fundamental aspect of a person's condition, alongside the environmental and personal domains that contribute to the psychosocial impact of the condition (see Simmons-Mackie & Kagan, 2007, for an overview of the ICF in aphasia). Kagan and colleagues' development of the A-FROM model (Aphasia Framework for Outcome Measurement) (Kagan *et al.* 2008) has provided an aphasia-specific interpretation of the ICF framework model that has 'provided an opportunity to structure our thinking around the diversity within aphasia management' (Whitworth, Webster and Morris, 2014, in press). Placing quality of life at the centre of its schematic representation of the different parameters of aphasia (see also Cruice, Worrall & Hickson, 2000, for a discussion on quality of life in aphasia), the A-FROM promotes transparency both between and within different approaches.

   Cognitive neuropsychological therapy can take place both alongside other therapy approaches and be integrated with other approaches. Indeed, therapy targeted directly at the impairment will often need to be accompanied by therapy aimed at promoting overall communication and support to deal with the psychological and psychosocial effects of aphasia on clients and their carers (Brumfitt, 1993, Cunningham, 1998; Code & Herrmann, 2003; Holland, 2007; Worrall, Brown, Cruice, Davidson *et al.*, 2010). Pound *et al.* (2000), for example, describe therapy focusing on helping clients to cope with language loss and the effects of that disability on their everyday life. Holland (1982) describes methods of facilitating functional communication, the Life-Participation Approach to Aphasia (LPAA) is set out by Chapey and colleagues (Chapey *et al.*, 2008) to address re-engaging in life, while many studies provide robust evidence of working with communication partners of people with aphasia (Booth & Perkins, 1999; Booth & Swabey, 1999; Lesser & Perkins, 1999; Turner & Whitworth, 2006a, 2006b). These approaches are well documented elsewhere and will not be discussed here. Integration of approaches might be reflected in the use of highly personal vocabulary in improving word retrieval, or structuring reading strategies around return to specific employment. We would agree with Pound and colleagues that 'the multi-faceted nature of aphasia demands a flexible, integrated approach to therapy and support' (Pound, Parr, Lindsay & Woolf, 2000).

   We believe that all treatment for aphasia should reflect an individual client's communication needs and wishes for communication and their priorities for treatment. These priorities often include therapy targeted towards impairments in the language-processing system and cognitive neuropsychology provides a unique opportunity to identify and treat these impairments. Direct treatment for the impairment does not, however, mean that therapy is not relevant to the real-life needs of the person with aphasia or that it is focused on communication *per se*. The ultimate goal of all therapy motivated by a cognitive neuropsychological approach is the use of communication skills within everyday settings and treatment should, like any other approach, employ materials and themes that are relevant and appropriate for the client. Similarly, evaluating efficacy of intervention must look beyond improvement within the language-processing system to the impact on real-life communication and the true and/or perceived benefits of improvement for the person with aphasia.

A cognitive neuropsychological perspective

Since the introduction of cognitive neuropsychology to the study of language breakdown in aphasia, there has been extensive debate about its contribution in determining therapy. Interested readers are directed to discussions in Howard and Hatfield (1987), Howard and Patterson (1989), Caramazza (1989), Basso (1989), Wilson and Patterson (1990), Hillis (1993), Lesser and Milroy (1993) and Nickels, Kohnen and Biedermann (2010). From a cognitive neuropsychological perspective, the aim of assessment is to understand the client's speech and language pattern in terms of the normal processing system, enabling targeted intervention to be developed for the individual. The assessment needs to be detailed enough to allow the identification of the impaired process or processes as well as those processing abilities that remain intact. Analysis of the surface symptoms is not sufficient to plan therapy, as the same surface symptoms may arise in various ways (Howard & Patterson, 1989). Sometimes, as Lesser and Milroy (1993) highlight, the actual therapy offered may not be radically different to traditional methods and techniques. The difference is that particular techniques targeting an aspect of the client's disorder are selected on the basis of a theoretical understanding of the underlying impairment.

Howard and Hatfield (1987) pointed out that identification of levels of breakdown and intact and impaired processes does not, in itself, *determine* the most appropriate and effective approach for therapy. It does, however, limit the range of possible treatments. As Basso and Marangolo (2000, p. 228) clearly and succinctly state:

> 'The most important contribution of cognitive neuropsychology to aphasia therapy lies in the massive reduction of the theoretically-motivated choices left open to the therapist. Clearly articulated and detailed hypotheses about representations and processing of cognitive functions allow rejection of all those strategies for treatment that are not theoretically justified. The more detailed the cognitive model, the narrower the spectrum of rationally motivated treatments; whereas the less fine-grained the cognitive model, the greater the number of theoretically justifiable therapeutic interventions.'

The cognitive domain and mechanisms of change

It should also be acknowledged that a normal language-processing model by itself is less useful than if it were accompanied by a fully developed theory of cognitive rehabilitation (Hillis, 1993). Several researchers have identified the need for the development of a theory of therapy, and have suggested the areas it should cover (e.g. Howard & Hatfield, 1987; Byng & Black, 1995; Wertz, 1999; Basso, 2003). The reciprocal nature of theory and therapy has also been explored by Nickels *et al.* (2010). Minimally, Hillis (1993) suggested that we need:

(a) a thorough analysis of the client's cognitive system pre- and post-therapy and a close examination of what changes have occurred;

(b) a proposed mechanism as to how change occurred; and
(c) a greater understanding as to which characteristics, both of the client and of their neuro-logical damage, relate to the outcome of therapy.

The use of assessment procedures to analyse a client's cognitive system is covered in the preceding chapters of this volume. Mechanisms of change have received little systematic attention, at the level of determining exactly why doing some therapy task results in a specific change in a person's language system. At a broad level, one can classify a number of different therapy approaches. Table 9.1 summarises one possible set of groupings, loosely based on systems developed by Howard and Hatfield (1987) and Lesser and Milroy (1993). These include six categories of therapy approaches: (1) reactivation, (2) relearning, (3) brain reorganisation, (4) cognitive-relay, (5) substitution and (6) compensatory strategies. Further analysis of the mechanisms of change occurring in aphasia therapy was made by Whitworth (1994). The studies in the following chapters predominantly use techniques that fall under the first four categories; substitution and compensatory strategies generally assume a loss of language function, although, as stated earlier, these are not incompatible. Some of the therapy studies use a combination of therapy tasks that incorporate the use of different strategies.

Table 9.1 Summary of different therapy approaches

Approach	Aim of therapy
Reactivation	To reactivate access to impaired language and processing abilities
Relearning	Impaired language procedures or knowledge are re-acquired through learning
Brain reorganisation	To encourage alternative parts of the brain to take over the impaired language function
Cognitive-relay	To seek an alternative route or means of performing the language function, i.e. use intact components of the language system to achieve the impaired function through indirect means (Luria, 1970)
Substitution	To encourage the adoption of an external prosthesis to promote communication
Compensation	To maximise the use of retained language and communication behaviours, without focusing on the impaired functions

While this system classifies the beliefs that therapists have had about how their therapies work, we would emphasise that there is, in most cases, little or no evidence that these are the *real* mechanisms of change. One example is Melodic Intonation Therapy developed by Albert, Sparks and Helm (1973). This therapy approach is based on a rationale of using music-like speech production intended to recruit processes in the intact right hemisphere. The approach can be broadly classified as 'brain reorganisation'. Functional brain-imaging work, however, has found no evidence that it does recruit right-hemisphere language (Belin *et al.*, 1996). The findings suggest that intact regions within the left hemisphere are responsible for the improvements.

Hillis's third domain is that of relating the effects of therapy to the characteristics of the patient, which leads us to a discussion of therapy design and measuring outcome in relation to the individual client. It has been documented extensively in the literature that significant improvement in performance does not by itself show that a specific therapy technique is effective. Improvement that is a direct and specific result of therapy must be distinguished from spontaneous recovery and non-specific effects of treatment due to such influences as support, social participation and encouragement. Single case study, or single-subject, methodology has predominantly been used to distinguish these causes of improvement, allowing inferences to be made about the effectiveness of treatment. Comprehensive reviews of the use and types of single case designs can be found in Howard (1986), Willmes (1990) and Franklin (1997). Tate, McDonald, Perdices, Togher, and Schultz (2008) further provide a protocol for rating the methodological rigour and quality of single-subject designs.

The basic experimental designs are described in Table 9.2, although experimental designs are often used in combination with one another. Where the experimental design has been stated or is transparent, this is reported in the reviews in the following chapters.

Table 9.2 Summary of single case study designs

Design	Format
Multiple baseline	Treatment is preceded and followed by testing of the process targeted in treatment and a series of other processes. The other processes may be unrelated and are expected to remain unaffected by treatment (control tasks), as well as be related and show generalised effects of treatment.
	Multiple baseline designs may be across behaviours (different processes) or across tasks (same process but in different contexts).
	If treatment is effective, performance on the treated process will improve, with no or minimal improvement on the control task(s) and, where there is generalisation, improvement to some degree on those related to the targeted process.
Control task	A simplified version of the multiple baseline design. Treatment is preceded and followed by testing of the process targeted in treatment and an unrelated, control process.
	If treatment is effective, performance on the treated process will improve, with no or minimal improvement on the unrelated process.
Repeated baseline	Treatment is preceded by repeated testing of the process to be targeted in treatment.
	If treatment is effective, significant gains will be found in performance post-treatment and improvement will be significantly greater during the treatment phase than during the baseline period.
Item-specific design	Treatment is preceded by testing of performance on items to be treated and untreated items.
	If treatment is effective and the effects are item-specific, there will be significant gains seen on treated items, with no or minimal improvement on untreated items (unless generalisation occurs across items).
Cross-over design	Two phases of treatment preceded and followed by the testing of two processes. Process 1 treated initially followed by treatment for Process 2 (this may also involve the cross-over of items as well as different processes).
	If treatment is effective, significant gains will be found in Process 1 only (or the first set of items) following the first phase of treatment, with significant gains in Process 2 (or the second set of items) following the second phase of treatment.

While single case methodology provides a valid way to design and measure change for the individual, our basis for distinguishing between the people with aphasia who will benefit from a treatment approach and those who will not actually rests with an extension of this design, ultimately enabling therapists to choose the most effective treatment approach. Receiving little systematic attention early on (although see Nettleton and Lesser, 1991, for an early attempt in this direction), Howard (2003) and others (Schwartz & Dell, 2012) argue that this question can be most productively addressed by using a case series approach that allows a closer examination of the nature of improvement in relation to the characteristics of the people with aphasia (see Best, Herbert, Hickin, Osborne & Howard, 2002; Conroy, Sage & Lambon Ralph, 2009a, 2009b; Fillingham, Sage & Lambon Ralph, 2006; for examples of this approach). Through formalising replication of the same assessment and therapy procedures across a group of clients, a case series directly enables us to confirm or refute findings from single case designs and closely study individual differences. We have, for example, obtained stronger evidence of the effectiveness of therapy for word retrieval (e.g. Hickin, Best, Herbert, Howard & Osbourne, 2002), been able to explore the presence of memory and executive problem solving difficulties on therapy outcome (e.g. Lambon Ralph, Snell, Fillingham, Conroy & Sage, 2010), client preferences (e.g. Fillingham *et al.* 2006; Conroy *et al.*, 2009b) as well as examine how nouns and verbs respond differently to the same types of therapies (Conroy *et al.*, 2009a, 2009b). Beeson, Rising & Volk (2003) have also used this type of design to address the relationship between therapy outcome, motivation and communicative need following writing therapy.

Designing therapy studies in clinical practice

The increase in aphasia therapy studies motivated by a cognitive neuropsychological approach has been commensurate with a refinement of the single case design – a symbiotic relationship, perhaps. The need to apply a systematic approach to planning, implementing and evaluation therapy outcomes is clear. All clinicians want and need to know that the treatment that they have given to a client is effective. If the client improves, there are basically three possibilities:

1. *'Spontaneous recovery': the client would have improved without the intervention.*
   If that is the case, we should see more-or-less equal improvement in periods with treatment and without treatment, and more-or-less equal improvement in treated and untreated tasks.
2. *'Charm'/placebo effects: the client improves simply as a result of interaction with the clinician.*
   If only all our clients would improve just because a clinician is there! Unfortunately that is not what happens in reality, but we need to be able to show that 'charm effects' are not responsible for improvement. 'Charm improvements' should be found equally for treated and untreated items, and equally for treated and untreated tasks, but these improvements should occur only during the periods when treatment is provided.
3. *Treatment effects: the client improves as a result of the treatment.*
   For the clinician, this is clearly the best outcome; it shows that what (s)he did benefited the client's language performance. Evidence for this will be found when (a) there is improvement only during the period of treatment (although, in some circumstances, there may be carryover into post-therapy periods), (b) there is greater improvement on treated items than a matched untreated items or, if there is generalisation of treatment effects within a task, greater improvement is seen in the treated task than in untreated and (preferably) unrelated task.

To be confident of teasing apart these possibilities, and to then interpret treatment effects against a theoretical position, clinicians need to apply key principles of single case design within the clinical setting. While there is no doubt that adhering to the principles of good treatment study design enables robust conclusions to be drawn, it is recognised, that in clinical practice and, indeed, in research that takes places in a regular clinical environment, all elements may not be practically realisable. Understanding the impact of this, on interpretation of the findings is important. These principles are set out below and attention drawn to the implications for when these principles are not met. A fuller discussion of many of these recommendations is set out in Howard, Best & Nickels (submitted).

In the hypothesis setting phase:

- A clear hypothesis as to the client's level of breakdown should be supported by assessment data. While this may be comprehensive, economical use of assessments is encouraged.

In the pre-therapy phase:

- The primary outcome measures should be established at the outset, i.e. what is the main measure that will enable the clinician to measure that change has occurred, and where is change expected? Identification of other measures to capture generalisation to, for example, other items or other contexts, will also be necessary at this stage.
- Assessments should be selected that contain sufficient number of items such that statistical procedures can be applied to them to detect change. Larger item sets will increase confidence in the results after therapy. In certain studies, larger item sets are also required to enable a proportion of the items to be used as control items, i.e. placed into an untreated set for comparison with treated items. Where small numbers of items of used, this introduces error when statistical procedures are applied, and also may limit the overall impact of therapy.
- Ideally there should be a selection phase and a baseline phase in selecting items for use in therapy. Therapists often want to select items for treatment that the client finds hard. The selection phase might consist of one, two or three trials on a large set of items and choosing the items that were consistently wrong. One might think that if an item was wrong three times, it would always be wrong without intervention/help. That would, however, be incorrect. Howard *et al.* (1985b) chose the hardest-to-name items over three assessments and, on average, the 12 participants named around 30% of items correctly on the first testing occasion *before* any treatment had happened (this is an example of a phenomenon called 'regression to the mean'). Howard *et al.* (submitted) argue that the selection phase and baseline phase must be distinguished where the therapist wants to concentrate treatment on difficult items. The alternative is to abandon a selection phase and take all of the items into the study, irrespective of their pre-therapy performance.
- Baseline assessments should preferably be repeated over at least two or three occasions to gain insight into variability and stability of behaviour. If not adhered to, the conclusions do not permit comparison of the slope (i.e. rate of change) within the pre-therapy period to the therapy period. Howard *et al.* (submitted) argue that obtaining stability of performance during the baseline phase is not required or indeed possible (as it requires affirming a null hypothesis); the best that one can do is put limits on the rate of change.
- Where the design involves comparison of treated and untreated items, items should be *randomly* allocated into two sets – those to be treated and those untreated, i.e. control items. This is often known as matching of item sets. These should also be matched on performance where the two groups contain the same proportion of correct and incorrect items; they can also be matched on other variables known to affect performance (for

example, in the case of word retrieval, word length, frequency or imageability). The lack of a control set will not permit generalisation to be explored.

- Identification of suitable control measures, i.e. those behaviours that are not expected to change following the intervention. This may be achieved by using the same behaviour as its own control (i.e. baseline period vs. treatment period), using untreated items as a control, or using an untreated language modality or behaviour as a control. An example of using an untreated modality may be electing to monitor syntactic comprehension when treating word retrieval, while an example of using an untreated behaviour may be in electing to monitor tense markers while treating plurals. While identifying suitable control measures is not always an easy task, the absence of such a feature does reduce confidence around spontaneous change and clinician charm.
- Ideally, the length of time in contact with the clinician pre-therapy should be equivalent to the length of time of the therapy period. This controls for the charm effect. In many therapy studies where therapy is delivered over a long period of time or where clinical constraints apply, this condition is prohibitive. In such cases, other design elements can be included (e.g. use of untreated items, or involvement in a non-experimental period of contact, such as conversation groups, pre-therapy) and the influences of charm considered in interpretation.

In the therapy phase:

- Therapy should be replicable from the description of the protocol. The therapy should be set out in sufficient detail to enable another clinician or researcher to repeat the study, including the aims, resources used, the instructions and feedback given, hierarchies used, methods of recording, and criteria used to progress within the protocol. Where therapy is not clear, the results of the single case design cannot be truly tested.
- The therapy phase should specify a set number of sessions, motivated by previous evidence, theoretical position or feasibility. This contrasts to the design which continues therapy until success has been reached, often meeting a pre-set criterion, or when untreated items show no/minimal improvement by comparison (e.g. Thompson, 2006). The implications of not specifying the number of intervention sessions leads directly to invalidating statistical analysis of the data (see Howard *et al.*, submitted).
- Probing of untreated items during the therapy phase should be considered against two prevailing view points. One view argues that probing untreated items during the therapy phase should be minimised, as this may provide inadvertent therapy to those items (repeated presentation, even without treatment, results in improvement (see Howard *et al.*, submitted for detailed arguments)). Thompson (2006) argues the opposite, maintaining that probing both treated and untreated items during therapy provides essential information, particularly in being able to show that the improvement coincides precisely with the onset of treatment. Both views are considered in detail in Howard *et al.* (submitted). One consideration may be important: the time taken to probe performance at the beginning of each session for treated and untreated items will necessarily reduce the time available for treatment.

In the data analysis phase:

- Statistical procedures should be used where possible to ensure that the findings have not occurred by chance. Advice on statistical procedures should be sought where appropriate. Howard *et al.* (submitted) offer advice on appropriate statistical procedures.

- Generalisation of therapy to untreated items/tasks should also be analysed. This may involve, for example, the improvement during therapy of matched untreated items, relative to the baseline; these can be evaluated statistically in exactly the same way as treated items.
- Analysis of impact on real-life tasks and activities should be considered where appropriate; this may involve client and family perceptions of change.

Framework for therapy evaluations: recognising the right therapy

The challenge for speech-language pathologists, therapists and other professionals involved in the treatment of aphasia is to determine techniques that will be effective for the remediation of particular deficits in particular individuals. Byng and Black (1995) outline a number of critical factors that are involved in therapy and which emphasise that therapy is not just about the task and the materials used but a combination of the task, the psycholinguistic concepts conveyed and the interaction between the therapist and client. The parameters used by Byng and Black (1995) to compare and contrast a range of therapies used with clients with sentence-processing difficulties form the basis of the subsequent review format. These have applicability across the spectrum of therapeutic interventions and include:

(a) the focus of therapy, i.e. the language impairment that is being worked on;
(b) the design of the task, i.e. how the task is introduced, the nature of the stimuli, the interaction between the therapist and client, and the type of feedback/facilitation given; and
(c) the hypothesised mechanism of change.

These parameters should provide sufficient detail about the therapy to allow the replication of the technique and to characterise the similarities and differences between techniques.

The purpose of the reviews in the following chapters is to provide an overview of therapy techniques available for the treatment of aphasia and to allow therapists to consider and select therapy techniques that may be effective for their clients. We include studies that meet three main criteria:

1   Clients have been described in sufficient detail to determine the impaired and retained processes, allowing the extent of similarity with other clients to be determined.
2   Therapy is described in sufficient detail to be replicated.
3   An adequate experimental design was used so that treatment efficacy can be determined.

The number of studies that unquestionably met these criteria is limited. Consequently, studies have been included that meet the majority of the criteria and caveats made where information has been unavailable or extrapolated. Each study has been reviewed in the same format, the template of which is shown in Table 9.3. The purpose of this is to facilitate comparison of studies. The reviews are by no means an exhaustive account; this would indeed be an ambitious aim given the growing number of studies being reported in the literature. Instead, only a representative example has often been included to exemplify a particular type of therapy, or to highlight a certain variation; this is particularly true in the section looking at naming therapy, where there is a considerable number of studies. Attempts have also been made to restrict the reviews to studies that have been published and are therefore widely available. While dissertations and symposium proceedings, such as those collated for the British Aphasiology Society, provide a rich source of material, their more restricted availability has prevented them from being discussed at length here.

Table 9.3 Template for therapy reviews

Title, author, date and place of publication of paper

Focus of therapy

- Targeted deficit – impaired process being treated

Therapy approach

- Approach used (see Table 9.1)

Subject details

General information

- Personal information given about client, e.g. age, sex, educational background
- Details of medical history and information given about incident resulting in the aphasia

Overall pattern of language impairments and preservations

- Performance on pre-therapy assessments and author's interpretation of retained and impaired aspects of language

Length of time post-onset

Therapy

Aims of therapy

- Aims of therapy
- Duration of therapy (including frequency and length of sessions and time period)
- Therapy design to evaluate efficacy

Task

- General format and presentation of task

Materials

- Stimuli used (including psycholinguistic nature of stimuli in terms of length, frequency, regularity, etc.)

Hierarchy

- Details on the stages and progression of therapy

Feedback on error

- Therapist response or type of facilitation if the client did not produce a correct response

Feedback if correct

- Therapist response or type of facilitation if the client produced a correct response

Outcome

- Results of measures taken pre- and post-therapy
- Overall pattern of improvement seen and the extent to which the improvement is a consequence of the direct treatment received
- Improvements on task stimuli
- Across task/across stimuli
- Functional improvements
- Hypothesised mechanism of change

Other comments

- Any other relevant information
- Replications of study
- Any improvements suggested by the authors of the study
- General comments on the design of the study and the adequacy of the descriptions of the client and therapy

---

The studies reviewed in Chapters 10–14 are summarised at the beginning of each chapter in a table. Detailed reviews follow in order of mention in the table (page numbers of full reviews are also reported in the summary table).

10 Therapy for auditory comprehension

Summary of auditory comprehension studies

Only a limited number of studies have used a cognitive neuropsychological framework to assess and understand auditory comprehension impairments in people with aphasia. Equally, few studies have rigorously evaluated any subsequent therapy with these clients. Those studies reviewed here are listed in Table 10.1.

There have been a group of studies which have investigated the impact of therapy at the level of auditory phonological analysis. These studies focus on improving clients' ability to discriminate between similar sounds and words, supporting auditory discrimination with visual cues. Gieleweski (1989) described spoken word-to-picture matching tasks, systematically varying the similarity of phonemes and availability of articulograms and lip reading. This study is not described in detail here as it is not a robust study of efficacy; an illustrative case study is provided but the client was still in the period of spontaneous recovery and the widespread gains seen cannot be attributed directly to the therapy. Gieleweski's work was, however, the precursor to the other studies detailed here. Morris, Franklin, Ellis, Turner and Bailey (1996) stringently test the efficacy of a range of therapeutic activities designed to improve phoneme discrimination. This study, like Gieleweski (1989), systematically controls the phonological similarity of stimuli and initially uses cued articulation and lip reading to support discrimination. A wide range of therapy tasks is used and the authors suggest such a range may be necessary to maintain client motivation. An extensive set of therapy materials based on the tasks described in Morris *et al.* (1996) is available in the Newcastle University Aphasia Therapy Resources: Auditory Processing (Morris, Webster, Whitworth & Howard, 2009). Similar tasks are used in the first phase of therapy in the Maneta, Marshall and Lindsay (2001) and the Tessier, Weill-Chounlamountry, Michelot and Pradat-Diehl (2007) studies although in the latter study the tasks are presented on computer.

The studies provide some evidence that auditory discrimination can improve as a consequence of therapy. Gains in phoneme discrimination were seen in both the Morris *et al.* and Tessier *et al.* studies. JS (Morris *et al.* 1996) also showed improved repetition although significant gains were not seen in spoken word comprehension and the functional impact of therapy was not considered. The client in the Tessier *et al.* (2007) study showed more widespread gains, with generalisation to both comprehension and functional activities (conversation and use of the telephone). Phoneme discrimination therapy was not effective for PK (Maneta *et al.* 2001); his lack of improvement was attributed to the severity of his difficulties. Functional gains in interaction were achieved in the second phase of indirect therapy which involved training his wife to use particular compensatory strategies. These strategies

Table 10.1 Summary of auditory comprehension therapy studies reviewed here

Level of impairment	Therapy studies	Therapy tasks
Auditory phonological analysis	Study 1: Morris *et al.* (1996, p. 103)	• Phoneme-to-grapheme matching • Phoneme discrimination • Spoken word–picture matching • Spoken word–written word matching • Word judgement (correct/incorrect) • CV/VC judgement (correct/incorrect) Initially lip reading allowed, progression to free voice and then tape. Decreasing number of distinctive features different in the pairs
	Study 2: Maneta *et al.* (2001, p. 105)	• Minimal pair judgement • Indirect therapy focusing on changing the communicative behaviours of client's wife
	Study 3: Tessier *et al.* (2007, p. 107)	Computer-presented therapy • Phoneme discrimination • Phoneme recognition
Auditory phonological analysis, phonological input lexicon and semantic system	Study 4: Grayson *et al.* (1997, p. 109)	• Spoken word-to-picture matching (rhyming distractors) with lip reading
Access to the semantic system (via auditory input)	Study 5: Francis *et al.* (2001a, p. 112)	Implicit Auditory Therapy • Silent reading of definitions of words followed by writing of word • Silent reading and matching of written word triads (synonym judgement) Explicit Auditory Therapy • Reading and listening to word definitions followed by repetition of word • Reading, listening to and matching of written word triads (synonym judgement)
Semantic system	Study 6: Behrmann and Lieberthal (1989, p. 114)	• Spoken word and written word–picture matching tasks used alongside discussion of distinctive features and identification from semantic cues with increasing semantic relatedness
	Study 7: Bastiaanse *et al.* (1993, p. 116)	• Spoken word-to-picture matching (semantic distractors) • Other semantic tasks e.g. semantic categorisation
	Study 8: Morris and Franklin (2012, p. 118)	• Picture name verification task

could be used alongside direct approaches within a holistic framework. Maneta *et al.* (2001) do, however, reinforce that the introduction of these strategies required a structured programme of modelling, repeated practice and feedback.

Grayson and colleagues (Grayson, Hilton & Franklin, 1997) describe a multi-faceted therapy approach for LR who presented with multiple difficulties in auditory comprehension. The range of therapy tasks described in Bastiaanse, Nijober and Taconis' (1993) study could target access to words in the auditory input lexicon or the semantic system, although the case reported focuses only on the semantic system. Francis, Riddoch and Humphreys (2001a) describe and contrast two therapies used with a client KW who had problems accessing the semantic system from the phonological input lexicon (word meaning deafness). The authors conclude that the client benefited most from the therapy that had a combined focus on both spoken and written comprehension (i.e. focusing on both impaired and unimpaired processes). Crucially, both therapies resulted in item-specific gains, emphasising the need to select words relevant to the client. Both Bastiaanse *et al.* (1993) and Behrmann and Lieberthal (1989) address the semantic system using auditory input only, using a diverse range of semantic tasks. In contrast, Morris and Franklin (2012) consider the effectiveness of a specific semantic therapy (picture name verification) with two clients. For one client, therapy resulted in significant gains for both treated and untreated items due to improved access to the semantic system. The other client showed no gains, leading the authors to explore the possible factors contributing to the differential success of this task.

There are several reasons why there may be a paucity of studies of therapy for spoken word comprehension. First, most people with aphasia show substantial recovery in understanding single words during the first few months post-onset. As a result, there are few good candidates for therapy aimed at this level in the chronic stages. Therapy for people with substantial impairments in word comprehension is most likely to be suitable in the early stages and it is difficult to design studies that can convincingly demonstrate the specific effects of treatment during the early period when most spontaneous recovery occurs; the study by Grayson *et al.* (1997) is a notably successful exception. Secondly, therapy typically draws upon intact systems to support treatment of impaired processes. For example, treatment of word production often uses (relatively) intact processes, such as word comprehension and word repetition, to facilitate output. While input processes can aid word production, word production cannot aid auditory comprehension. Moreover, most people with severe difficulties in word comprehension have even more severe difficulties in output modalities because they are, typically, globally aphasic. The result is that there are normally few people with other intact abilities that could support spoken word comprehension. The most promising possibility is written word comprehension. It is not at all uncommon for people with difficulties in understanding spoken words to have better understanding of written words, perhaps partly because written words are much less fleeting. Francis *et al.* (2001a) describe such an approach with KW, a client with word meaning deafness. He developed a strategy of visualising the written form of words, enabling him to access meaning and define words that were spoken to him. The written form is also used as one of the compensatory strategies introduced to PK's wife in the indirect therapy phase in the Maneta *et al.* (2001) study. Spoken comprehension may also be aided by lip reading and there is some evidence from initial assessment data and gains in therapy (although non-significant) that this may be beneficial for some clients (Maneta *et al.*, 2001).

EVALUATIONS OF THERAPY STUDIES

Study 1

Morris, J., Franklin, S., Ellis, A. W., Turner J. E. and Bailey, P. J. (1996). Remediating a speech perception deficit in an aphasic patient. *Aphasiology, 10*, 137–158.

Focus of therapy: Auditory phonological analysis (word sound deafness).

Therapy approach: Reactivation.

Client details

General information

JS was a 73-year-old man who was a retired factory worker. He had a single left CVA resulting in a global aphasia. A CT scan showed areas of low attenuation in both hemispheres, particularly in the left basal ganglia. Assessment of hearing showed a threshold of 20dB (in ambient noise) with some high frequency loss (8000Hz).

Overall pattern of language impairments and preservations

JS's verbal output was restricted to the occasional single-word, stereotypical phrases and neologisms. He relied predominantly on 'yes' and 'no' and non-verbal methods to communicate. Auditory comprehension was characterised by impaired pre-phonetic auditory processing as shown by impaired performance on assessments of gap detection, formant frequency discrimination, frequency modulation detection and pitch discrimination. At a phonemic level, he had impaired auditory discrimination of minimal pairs and single words. Written comprehension was also impaired, although to a lesser extent, supporting a diagnosis of central semantic impairment. The authors suggest that JS had difficulties in auditory phonological analysis (word sound deafness) with additional central semantic and output difficulties.

Time post-onset

JS was 1 year post-onset when this therapy commenced.

Therapy

Therapy aimed to improve phonological discrimination. Therapy consisted of twelve sessions over a 6-week period. A multiple-baseline with control task therapy study design was used to measure efficacy.

See Table 11.1 on p. 123 for outline of therapy procedure.

Outcome

JS improved significantly on tasks involving minimal and maximal pair discrimination and pre-phonetic auditory discrimination tasks. There was a trend for improvement in the tests of

	1. Phoneme–grapheme matching	2. Phoneme discrimination	3. Spoken word/picture matching	4. Spoken word/written word matching	5. Word judgement	6. Same or different
Task	Matching spoken phonemes to written letters.	Same/different judgements of phonemes.	Matching spoken words to pictures.	Matching spoken words to written words.	Judge whether word matches picture.	Same/different judgements of words.
Materials	C + /ə/stimuli matched to choice of 3 letters.	Pairs of C + /ə/.	CVC words. Distractors phonologically related. Differed in either initial or final consonant.	CVC words. Distractors phonologically related. Differed in either initial or final consonant.		CV or VC nonwords. Judged whether same or different.
Hierarchy	*Phonological similarity* a. Three distinctive features different, b. Two distinctive features different, c. One distinctive feature different.	*Presentation* a. With lip reading, b. Free voice, c. Tape recorder.	None	None	None	None
Feedback on error	Information regarding accuracy. Repeated with reduced level of difficulty					
Feedback if correct	Information regarding accuracy					

auditory lexical decision and auditory synonym judgement. There was a significant improvement in repetition but no improvement in naming performance. No improvement was seen in the control task of written synonym judgement.

JS showed a significant improvement in his ability to discriminate speech sounds that generalised across auditory comprehension tasks. This improved discrimination also aided his repetition. Improvement was attributed to the therapy programme. No improvement was noted in unrelated tasks. No information was provided as to whether this improvement was maintained once therapy was discontinued or about improvements in functional comprehension.

Other comments

With rigorous initial assessment and reassessment data presented, this study permits a thorough evaluation of the therapy with the reported client. It is discussed in sufficient detail to replicate the therapy. The authors suggest the range of therapy tasks may be necessary to maintain client motivation. JS is also described (with more details of therapy) in Morris and Franklin (1995).

Study 2

Maneta, A., Marshall, J. & Lindsay, J. (2001) Direct and indirect therapy for word sound deafness. *International Journal of Language and Communication Disorders, 36(1)*, 91–106.

Focus of therapy: Auditory phonological analysis.

Therapy approach: Phase 1, Reactivation; Phase 2, Compensation.

Client details

General information

PK was a monolingual English speaker who had a CVA at the age of 79 years. Before retiring, he had been a university lab technician. A CT scan showed a left temporo-parietal infarct with enlargement of the left lateral ventricle. The CVA resulted in a right hemiparesis which resolved and a persistent severe aphasia. He had no hearing difficulties.

Overall pattern of language impairments and preservations

PK produced neologistic jargon with occasional recognisable words and some stereotyped phrases. He could use yes/no reliably. PK was able to understand single written words but written sentence comprehension was impaired. Auditory comprehension was poor. Performance across all single-word auditory tasks was severely impaired, with performance on only one task (word-to-picture matching) above chance. Performance on the auditory tasks did not improve with lip reading. Repetition was also severely impaired but significantly improved with lip reading. Picture naming was significantly better than repetition. The authors suggest PK had word sound deafness (difficulties in auditory phonological analysis). In interaction with his wife, the impairment resulted in frequent and prolonged communication breakdown as his wife did not have appropriate strategies to aid communication.

Time post-onset

PK was 5 years post-onset when the therapy described in this study commenced.

Therapy

Therapy consisted of two phases. Phase 1 of therapy aimed to improve PK's auditory discrimination using lip reading and cued speech. Phase 2 aimed to change the communicative behaviours of PK's wife (FK).

A multiple-baseline, single case study design was used. Both phases consisted of twelve, 30 minute sessions across 6 weeks.

Phase 1: Auditory discrimination

Task	1. Phoneme-to-grapheme matching Matching spoken phoneme to written letter	2. Spoken word/written word matching Matching spoken word to written word	3. Spoken word-to-picture matching Matching spoken word-to-picture
Materials	C + /ə/stimuli matched to choice of three letters	CVC word matched to one of three to phonologically related written words	CVC word matched one of three pictures of phonologically related words
Hierarchy	Colour coding to emphasise phonetic grouping and articulatory positioning. *Phonological similarity* Level 1: At least two distinctive features Level 2: one distinctive feature *Visual Cues* a. With cued speech b. With lip reading only		
Feedback on error	Verbal and visual feedback. Repetition of stimulus with additional cues		
Feedback if correct	Verbal and visual feedback		

Phase 2: Communicative strategies

Phase 2 of therapy aimed to change the communicative behaviours of PK's wife, FK. FK was given an advice booklet summarising PK's strengths and weaknesses and outlining a variety of strategies. Strategies were modelled by the therapist and then practised by FK, with the therapist giving feedback. The strategies included writing down key words or phrases, restructuring messages to convey one piece of information and checking PK's understanding.

Outcome

Following phase 1, no significant gains were seen on the auditory tasks or in repetition. There was a small but consistent trend of improvement when lip reading information was available but gains did not reach significance. Following phase 2, there was no change in PK's auditory comprehension but he was able to understand his wife much better due to her use of writing and simplified/chunked information. PK did not benefit from direct discrimination therapy. The authors propose that PK's impairment was more chronic and severe than that of the client reported by Morris *et al.* (1996) and therefore less amenable to therapy. The indirect therapy resulted in fewer communication breakdowns.

Other comments

The changes in communication were assessed using a series of biographical questions and the authors acknowledge this may not be representative of natural interaction. Phase 1 of therapy is similar to the tasks described by Morris *et al.* (1996). The authors suggest that it is possible that gains in auditory discrimination might have been achieved with a more extensive therapy. In phase 2, the authors acknowledge the strategies were simplistic but suggest that FK needed the structured programme of repeated modelling, practice and feedback in order to learn and apply them.

Study 3

Tessier, C., Weill-Chounlamountry, A., Michelot, N. and Pradat-Diehl, P. (2007) Rehabilitation of word deafness due to auditory analysis disorder. *Brain Injury, 21(11)*, 1165–1174.

Focus of therapy: Auditory phonological analysis (referred to as auditory analysis system in paper).

Therapy approach: Reactivation (errorless learning).

Client details

General information

The client was a 65-year-old, right-handed, French speaking woman, She had a cerebral infarction resulting in auditory agnosia and word deafness. An MRI scan showed multiple lesions in the brainstem, attributed to bilateral sub-cortical vascular disease. She presented with mild cerebellar disease. She had a mild hearing loss due to presbycusis.

Overall pattern of language impairments and preservations

The client presented with intact verbal naming, verbal and written expression and written comprehension. Verbal comprehension and repetition were impaired (when tested without lip reading) at single-word and sentence level. The authors suggest an impairment in phoneme discrimination and recognition corresponding to an auditory analysis disorder.

Time post-onset

The client was 10 months post-onset when therapy commenced.

Therapy

The study aimed to determine whether specific auditory processing rehabilitation would improve communicative abilities. Therapy consisted of twelve, 1-hour sessions carried out twice a week (ten sessions of phoneme discrimination and two sessions of phoneme recognition). A repeated, multiple-baseline single case study design was used (described as ABCA design). The client was assessed twice prior to therapy (4 months and 1 week pre-therapy), between the two therapies and twice post-therapy (immediately and 1 month after). Therapy was presented via computer.

Task	1. Phoneme discrimination Presentation of same or different phoneme pairs.	2. Phoneme recognition Matching heard phoneme to visual representation from choice of all 25 phonemes.
Materials	25 phoneme pairs (13 vowel pairs and 12 CV pairs).	25 phonemes
Hierarchy	*Phoneme complexity* Vowels before consonants, open back vowels before close back vowels. *Visual support* (a) Presentation of visual representation of both heard phonemes with flickering. (b) Presentation of visual representation of both heard phonemes with flickering after delay. (c) Presentation of visual representation of first phoneme. (d) No visual presentation of either phoneme.	*Visual support* (a) Visual representation of target phoneme flickering during auditory presentation. (b) Visual representation of target phoneme flickering after delay. (c) No flickering.
Feedback on error	Not stated	Not stated
Feedback if correct	Not stated	Not stated

Outcome

Prior to therapy, performance on phoneme discrimination and recognition was stable. After ten therapy sessions, the client made no errors on trained phoneme discrimination and untrained phoneme recognition improved from 64% to 84%. After two additional therapy sessions, phoneme recognition reached 100% accuracy. Performance on both tasks remained stable 1 month post-therapy. Therefore, therapy resulted in significant improvement in phoneme discrimination and recognition. Following therapy, there was also a significant improvement in the repetition of syllables, single words and sentences and in spoken comprehension (with and without visual cues). A test of communication handicap showed significant improvement in communication in daily life for conversation and on the telephone. There was no change in environmental sound recognition. The generalisation to non-trained tasks, particularly verbal comprehension, and transfer to daily life demonstrates the efficacy of therapy. The gains are likely to be due to therapy as the client was beyond the period of spontaneous recovery, had a stable performance prior to therapy and there was no change on an unrelated task. The authors propose gains in comprehension are seen as the client had no co-occurring aphasia. The discrimination and recognition therapies are reported as complementary, targeting the same process.

Other comments

The study provides a comprehensive evaluation of the therapy. Although the therapy described is computer based, some aspects could be replicated without a computer. The authors discuss the similarities and differences between the clients and therapy tasks discussed in this and the Morris *et al.* (1996) study. They also discuss the role of top-down support from the lexicon and short-term verbal memory in phoneme discrimination.

Study 4

Grayson, E., Hilton, R. & Franklin, S. E. (1997). Early intervention in a case of jargon aphasia: efficacy of language comprehension therapy. *European Journal of Disorders of Communication, 32*, 257–276.

Focus of therapy: Auditory phonological analysis, the phonological input lexicon and the semantic system.

Therapy approach: Reactivation.

Client details

General information

LR was a 50-year-old man who worked as a sales director. He had a CVA resulting in a dense right hemiplegia and visual agnosia. A CT scan showed an infarct in the left temporoparietal region.

Overall pattern of language impairments and preservations

LR presented with a severe auditory and written comprehension impairment at the single-word and sentence levels. His speech was characterised by English jargon and neologisms. He was unable to repeat, read aloud or write. Word retrieval did not improve with presentation of semantic or phonemic cues. On testing before the therapy, LR was significantly impaired in minimal pair discrimination, auditory lexical decision, picture matching of both spoken and written words, and general word semantics. He was also impaired in sentence comprehension. The authors hypothesised that LR had an impairment of pre-lexical processing (auditory phonological analysis), difficulty accessing the lexical form within the phonological input lexicon and a central semantic impairment. He also had an additional syntactic comprehension deficit.

Time post-onset

Therapy began 4 weeks post-onset.

Therapy

Therapy consisted of three phases, each corresponding to a separate aim:

1   To improve LR's semantic ability.

2   To continue to improve LR's semantic ability and improve auditory comprehension.
3   To increase LR's ability to process up to three key words in sentence-level therapy.

The first therapy phase consisted of 1-hour sessions, 5 days per week, for 4 weeks. The second phase consisted of three 15-minute sessions each week for 3 weeks. The duration and frequency of the third phase of therapy was not specified. A cross-over design was used to evaluate treatment efficacy, where LR was reassessed following each phase of therapy.

Phase 1: Semantic therapy

Task	**1. Spoken/written word to object/ picture matching** Sentence with key word at end. Task was to select appropriate object or picture.	**2. Categorisation task** Sorting pictures into categories.	**3. Matching of written word associates** Choosing associates from word lists.
Materials	Common objects, pictures of objects and corresponding written words.	Pictures within categories. Categories used not stated.	Sheet of ten words divided into two columns.
Hierarchy	a. Two choices-target/ unrelated b. If 80% correct – Gradual increase in number of choices (up to six) – Increased relatedness to target	a. Two distant categories b. Increasing semantic relatedness c. Increased number of groups d. Written words as well/instead of pictures e. Verbal presentation with no written/ picture stimulus	Number of items reduced if difficulty.
Feedback on error	a. Repetition b. Gesture c. Semantic information d. Combination of above	a. Attention drawn to choice b. Given name c. Further information d. Gesture e. Written information f. Combination of above	a. Reading words b. Additional semantic information c. Gesture
Feedback if correct	a. Verbal reinforcement b. Repetition of name c. Visual feedback – ticks	Visual feedback – ticks	Visual feedback – ticks

Phase 2: Auditory training and semantic therapy

The semantic component of the therapy was the same as for the first phase but the n of words and pictures were increased.

Task	1. Spoken word-to-picture matching with rhyming foils Spoken word matched to choice of three pictures. Lip reading encouraged.	2. Spoken word-to-picture matching with minimal pairs Spoken word matched to choice of two pictures. Lip reading encouraged.
Materials	Hand drawn pictures of three rhyming words. 5 sets of pictures	Black-and-white minimal pair photographs
Hierarchy	None	None
Feedback on error	a. Feedback regarding incorrect b. Item repeated c. Repetition of task until correct picture given	a. Feedback regarding incorrect b. Item repeated c. Repetition of task until correct picture given
Feedback if correct	a. Verbal reinforcement b. Visual feedback (ticks)	a. Verbal reinforcement b. Visual feedback (ticks)

Phase 3: Sentence therapy

Task	1. Selection of three named objects in a sequence Sequence of words. Client must select corresponding objects from a choice of five. Lip reading encouraged.	2. Spoken sentence to action picture matching Spoken sentence. Match to action pictures.
Materials	Unrelated objects	Action pictures
Hierarchy	a. Increased number of distractor items (5 to 9) b. Initial gestural support	Number of key words a. 2 key words b. 3 key words Number of distractors a. 4 pictures b. 8 pictures
Feedback	Not stated	Not stated

Outcome

Following the first phase of therapy, LR showed significant improvement in written word–picture matching. Following phase 2 of therapy, significant improvement was seen in minimal pair selection and in spoken word–picture matching, but no further improvement was seen in written word comprehension. Auditory sentence comprehension did not change significantly following phase 1 or 2 of therapy but improved significantly following phase 3.

Overall, therapy resulted in significant improvements in auditory discrimination, auditory and written single-word comprehension, and auditory sentence comprehension. The patterns of improvement suggest specific effects of treatment. Some evidence of generalisation was noted, as effects were not item-specific. Functional comprehension was also shown to have improved. LR's speech also improved post-therapy with a reduction in neologisms and inappropriate responses. While improvement in verbal output cannot conclusively be attributed to therapy (as opposed to spontaneous recovery), the authors believe that LR's improvement in auditory to semantic processing could underlie improved expressive communication and suggest how this may be so.

Other comments

The authors suggest that the pattern of impairment, timing of therapy and therapy approach were similar to those reported by Jones (1989). The current case study was conducted by a clinician working in a busy rehabilitation setting who acknowledged that collating pre-therapy baseline assessment data would have been useful, but difficult, given the importance of early intervention for the client. The specific effects of treatment following the three phases of the therapy programme would, however, suggest that the improvement is partly a consequence of therapy rather than spontaneous recovery alone. The study is an excellent example of how treatment effects can be demonstrated in the early stages of recovery.

Study 5

Francis, D. R., Riddoch, M. J. and Humphreys, G. W. (2001a). Cognitive rehabilitation of word meaning deafness. *Aphasiology, 15*, 749–766.

Focus of therapy: Access from the phonological input lexicon to semantics (word meaning deafness).

Therapy approach: Explicit auditory therapy, Reactivation. Implicit auditory therapy, Compensation.

Client details

General information

KW was a 63-year-old Jamaican-born man who emigrated to England as a young adult. He was a retired bus driver who enjoyed attending further education classes. He had a CVA that resulted in a left parietal infarct.

Overall pattern of language impairments and preservations

KW was unable to understand words unless they were written down. His speech was characterised by a slight anomia and some phonemic jargon aphasia. On formal testing, he was able to match environmental sounds to pictures and to match spoken and written words. His judgement of word and nonword minimal pairs was intact. He had minor problems with lexical decision in both the spoken and written modalities, performing just outside the normal range. He scored within the normal range on the three-picture version of the Pyramids and Palm Trees Test (Howard & Patterson, 1992). He had difficulty accessing the meaning of spoken words, finding it difficult to match spoken words to pictures, to define spoken words and perform auditory synonym judgements. His auditory comprehension performance was characterised by imageability and frequency effects. His performance on tasks assessing access to semantic information from written words was significantly better than his auditory comprehension. The authors proposed that KW had word meaning deafness, with preserved early auditory processing and lexical access but impaired auditory access to meaning despite preserved orthographic access to the same information. In spelling, KW showed some of the characteristics of surface dysgraphia, with a high proportion of phonologically based errors and some confusion of homophones. He showed no regularity effect, as he was able to write some irregular words. His writing thus reflected a heavy reliance on the sub-lexical route alongside some use of a lexical writing route.

Time post-onset

KW was 4 years post-onset at the time of the current study.

Therapy

Therapy aimed to improve the comprehension of spoken words, contrasting the effectiveness of two types of therapy: implicit auditory therapy and explicit auditory therapy. Implicit auditory therapy targeted auditory comprehension only indirectly via the silent reading of written words. Explicit therapy directly targeted KW's difficulty in accessing semantic information from spoken words. The therapy was carried out by KW at home using worksheets completed 3–4 times a week. Each phase of therapy lasted for 2 weeks. A cross-over item-specific design was used to demonstrate efficacy.

	1. Implicit auditory therapy		**2. Explicit auditory therapy**	
Task	*1. Reading of definitions*	*2. Written synonym judgement*	*3. Reading and listening to definitions*	*4. Written and auditory synonym judgement*
	Silently read the definition, try to 'fix the meaning' of the word and then write the word down four times whilst thinking of the word's meaning.	Silently read written word triads and match the treated word to another word in the triad.	Read the definitions whilst listening to a taped version, try to 'fix the meaning' of the word and then repeat the word four times whilst thinking of the meaning.	Listen to and read each triad of words and then match the treated word to another in the triad.
Materials	Seventy-eight words that KW was able to define from the written word but not from the spoken word. Words divided into three matched sets of 26 words. One set for each therapy and a control set.			
Hierarchy	None	None	None	None
Feedback on error	Not stated		Not stated	
Feedback if correct	Not stated		Not stated	

Outcome

Before therapy, baseline performance in defining the spoken words was stable with comparable accuracy across the three word sets. At the end of therapy one (implicit therapy), improvement was seen in the definitions of the treated words but there was a significant decline in performance 2 weeks later. Following therapy two (explicit therapy), improvement was seen in the definitions of the treated words. No improvement was seen in performance on the control set following either therapy. During therapy, definitions were learned quicker with therapy one than therapy two. When the treatment sets were compared, there was no significant difference in the degree of improvement immediately post-therapy. A significant difference was, however, seen 2 weeks post-therapy with the effects of the explicit therapy being more durable. Both therapies resulted in item-specific improvement with no generalisation to untreated words.

In contrast to the authors' predictions, explicit auditory therapy was not more effective than implicit therapy immediately post-therapy. KW improved following the implicit therapy as he adopted a compensatory strategy. The therapy involved repeated writing of the words and thus his spelling improved. During the post-therapy baseline, he was able to visualise the correct spelling enabling access to the word's meaning via the written form. The explicit therapy may have had a more durable effect, since it directly improved the link between the auditory representation of the word and its meaning. Alternatively, hearing the word alongside the written form may have enabled KW to visualise the written form when he heard the word in isolation. The improvements seen are likely to be due to therapy, as KW was a long time post-onset and performance was stable before therapy.

Other comments

Information about KW's assessment can be found in Hall and Riddoch (1997). The study shows the successful development of a strategy that compensated for KW's difficulties in accessing the meaning of words from spoken words, although this meant that the efficacy of the implicit therapy could not be assessed. It also shows that direct treatment of the impairment resulted in improvement in the auditory comprehension of a small set of words, over a very short period of therapy.

Study 6

Behrmann, M. and Lieberthal, T. (1989). Category-specific treatment of a lexical–semantic deficit: a single case study of global aphasia. *British Journal of Disorders of Communication*, *24*, 281–299.

Focus of therapy: Semantic system (via auditory and written comprehension).

Therapy approach: Reactivation.

Client details

General information

CH was a 57-year-old male engineer who suffered a cerebral infarct resulting in dense hemiplegia and global aphasia. A CT scan showed a left middle cerebral infarct, involving the frontal, temporal and parietal lobes as well as the internal capsule.

Overall pattern of language impairments and preservations

On initial testing, CH's speech was restricted to jargon. He was unable to repeat or read words aloud. Both auditory and written lexical decision were impaired but performance was above chance. Written and spoken single-word comprehension were impaired with selection of semantic distractors. Some ability to compute broad semantic representations was retained, but CH was impaired in tasks requiring access to more detailed semantic representations (e.g. synonym judgement). In a category sorting task, the ability to sort animals was significantly higher than chance, but performance on other categories was not significantly different from chance. CH was considered to present with a semantic deficit.

Time post-onset

CH was at least 3 months post-onset when therapy commenced.

Therapy

Therapy was designed to improve written and spoken comprehension of single words via category-specific rehabilitation. Therapy consisted of fifteen 1-hour sessions (five sessions per category) over a 6-week period, plus additional home exercises. A control task therapy study design was used to demonstrate the efficacy of therapy.

Task	1. Explain distinctive features	2. Presentation of picture alongside written/ verbal label	3. Selection of picture from semantic cues	4. Spoken/ written word matching
Materials	Pictures within three categories of transport, furniture and body parts. Corresponding words.			
Hierarchy	a. Generic (superordinate features) b. Distinctive features		a. Distant semantic distractors b. Close semantic distractors	a. Distant semantic distractors b. Close semantic distractors
Feedback on error	Not stated	Not stated	Not stated	Not stated
Feedback if correct	Not stated	Not stated	Not stated	Not stated

Home exercises included written word–picture matching and using a dictionary to identify the semantic features of the categories and individual items within those categories.

Outcome

CH showed improved sorting of treated items into categories with some generalisation to untreated items within the treated categories of transport and body parts. Some generalisation was noted to untreated categories, but in two of the three categories it was non-significant. Performance improved on other semantic tasks involving wide semantic discrimination, but no improvement was recorded on narrow semantic judgements. CH's performance on the control task (syntactic comprehension) remained unchanged. CH's semantics, therefore, improved for the treated categories and change can be attributed to therapy. The authors proposed that CH was able to use newly learned semantic information to sort items into categories and that he could carry over this newly acquired knowledge to items sharing class membership and semantic features. Changes were also seen in his broad semantic knowledge and his ability to access superordinate information. No information is given regarding the functional impact of therapy.

Other comments

The authors suggest that hierarchical, category-specific semantic therapy is useful in the remediation of semantic deficits as this reflects the normal organisation of information.

Study 7

Bastiaanse, R., Nijober, S. and Taconis, M. (1993). The Auditory Language Comprehension Programme: a description and case study. *European Journal of Disorders of Communication, 28*, 415–433.

Focus of therapy: Semantic system (via auditory comprehension). The programme targets access to the auditory input lexicon and semantics, but the case reported here was trained on the semantic level only.

Therapy approach: Reactivation.

Client details

General information

Mr S was a 37-year-old former teacher and a native speaker of Dutch. Involvement in a traffic accident resulted in a brain contusion and a frontoparietal skull fracture. A craniectomy was performed to decompress a haematoma in the parietotemporal part of the left hemisphere, leaving Mr S with a right hemiparesis, homonymous hemianopia and aphasia.

Overall pattern of language impairments and preservations

Mr S presented with severely impaired auditory and written comprehension of single words and sentences. Errors on auditory and written comprehension tasks were predominantly semantic in nature. Expressively, Mr S was unable to retrieve single words in a naming test; responses were characterised by semantic jargon and perseverations. Spontaneous output was fluent and paragrammatic, with no communicative value. Mr S was diagnosed with a Wernicke's type aphasia with a prominent semantic deficit. In addition, the authors considered Mr S had difficulties with symbolic functions and so therapy on the ALCP was preceded by Visual Action Therapy (Helm-Estabrooks, Fitzpatrick & Barresi, 1982).

Time post-onset

Mr S was 3 months post-onset when therapy commenced.

Therapy

Therapy aimed to improve auditory comprehension of single words using the Auditory Language Comprehension Programme (ALCP). The ALCP is a hierarchical programme with a Base-10 format. Stages are repeated until the client performs without error. The programme has three levels:

1 Phonological level – items linked phonologically (similar vowels).
2 Semantic level – items linked semantically.
3 Complement level – items linked phonologically, via lexical–morphological correspondence or via a combination of phonological and semantic correspondence.

Mr S was treated using the semantic level and hence only the efficacy of this section is considered here. The ALCP was used between two and five times per week for 12 weeks. In addition to the ALCP tasks, association and categorisation tasks, and training of written word comprehension, were also carried out. The frequency with which these tasks were used and their precise nature were not reported. A multiple-baseline therapy design was used to monitor efficacy.

Task	**Spoken word–picture matching task** Spoken word presented with a choice of four pictures.
Materials	High frequency, highly imageable nouns. Unrelated distractors bore no relationship with either target or other distractors. Semantically related distractors linked to target via coordination or collocation.
Hierarchy	**Semantic relatedness across four blocks** a. Three unrelated distractors b. Two unrelated distractors, one related distractor c. One unrelated distractors, two related distractor d. Three related distractors **Length within each block** a. Polysyllabic words b. Monosyllabic words
Feedback on error	Distractor concept discussed and contrasted with target.
Feedback if correct	Concept discussed via additional tasks listed as: pointing to object in room/on himself, producing/imitating corresponding gesture, giving a description, drawing/copying the object, producing the corresponding sound, visual presentation of word or presenting characteristics of object.

Outcome

Mr S completed the ALCP semantic stage, achieving 100% successful performance. Significant improvement was reported in auditory comprehension of single words, with some generalisation to untreated stimuli on a spoken word–picture matching test. Significant improvement on tests of written single-word comprehension and auditory sentence comprehension were also recorded. Spontaneous output had also significantly improved despite still being characterised by word-finding problems. Paragrammatism, while still present, had diminished. While Mr S improved on trained stimuli, the authors suggest that he still may not have access to the full meaning of the target.

Improvement was reported in all aspects of comprehension and production. The authors do not state how therapy can account for such improvement. The authors argue, however, that the increased improvement in single-word auditory comprehension, compared to sentence comprehension, is indicative of effective therapy.

Other comments

Any improvements that were due to therapy were probably a consequence of the tasks as a whole rather than just the spoken word–picture matching task; however, these are not described in sufficient detail to evaluate how therapy may have worked. Improvement may also have been a consequence of spontaneous recovery, rather than specific effects due to therapy. The therapy is, however, described in sufficient detail to replicate and evaluate the effects in a more rigorous way.

Study 8

Morris, J. and Franklin, S. (2012) Investigating the effect of a semantic therapy on comprehension in aphasia. *Aphasiology, 26(12)*, 1461–1480.

Focus of therapy: Semantic system.

Therapy approach: Reactivation.

Client details

Two clients are discussed in the study.

General information

AD was 68 years old when he had a stroke. A CT scan showed slightly reduced attenuation in left temporal and occipital regions. He had a right-sided hemi-spatial neglect but compensated well for this. He was within normal limits on tests of object recognition. AD had left education at 16 and was a company director prior to retirement. JAC was 58 years old when he had his stroke. A CT scan showed an area of low density in the left anterior parietal region. He wore glasses but had no additional stroke-related visual difficulties. JAC was a retired teacher. Neither client had mobility difficulties. No information is provided about their hearing.

Overall pattern of language impairments and preservations

AD's comprehension of everyday language was impaired when conversation was not in context or contained rapid topic shift. He was dependent on his wife to facilitate communication. His spontaneous output was characterised by word-finding difficulties. JAC also had spoken language comprehension difficulties resulting in problems understanding tasks and transfer between tasks. His spoken output was predominantly English jargon with some neologisms. He showed limited awareness of communication breakdown. If prompted, he was sometimes able to write single words but did not do this spontaneously.

Participants were assessed on tests accessing semantic information from spoken, written and pictorial input. On picture matching tests, both AD and JAC made errors in both spoken and written versions, with semantic and semantic and phonologically related errors. AD's performance was outside the normal range on both versions. JAC's performance was just within the elderly control range on the auditory version. In synonym judgement, AD showed impairment on both versions but written synonym judgement was superior to spoken performance. JAC also had difficulties with performance on both versions outside the normal range. For picture verification, both AD's and JAC's performance was again impaired in both spoken and written modalities, with an advantage for written presentation. Their main difficulty was in rejecting semantic foils. Both participants also showed impaired performance on the three-picture version of Pyramids and Palm Trees (Howard & Patterson, 1992). AD and JAC showed normal performance on a range of tasks examining auditory/phonological processing but showed some difficulty with longer minimal pairs and auditory lexical decision. They also showed difficulties with picture naming, with no effect of frequency. JAC produced mainly perseverative errors. AD produced primarily no responses with a small number of semantic errors.

The authors conclude both AD and JAC had difficulties accessing semantic information, including lexical and conceptual semantic knowledge. Superior performance on written tasks compared to spoken tasks was explained by additional mild auditory processing deficits.

Time post-onset

AD was 14 months and JAC was 16 months post-onset at the time of the study.

Therapy

The study examined the effectiveness of a specific semantic therapy, picture name verification, in improving comprehension. Prior to the study, repeated baselines for auditory synonym judgement and lexical decision were carried out over a 3 month (JAC) and 7 month period (AD). Performance did not significantly vary across assessment times, with the exception of AD's performance on synonym judgement during the initial two assessments (5 months apart). A single case study design comparing performance on treated and untreated items was used to monitor therapy outcome. AD and JAC were seen twice weekly. AD was seen for nine, 60–90 minute sessions. JAC was seen for twelve, 30–40 minute sessions. They both had the same number of exposures to the treated items.

Task	**Picture name verification** Picture shown followed by a word (either target or semantically related foil) which had to be accepted or rejected.
Materials	200 black & white line drawings divided into 100 treated items and 100 untreated items. Equal number of natural & artefact items. Sets balanced for number of items correct at baseline, frequency and overall category. Semantic foils were category coordinates.
Hierarchy	None
Feedback on error	Two words (correct & foil) written down and participant asked to choose word which matched picture. Salient similarities and differences between two items discussed.
Feedback if correct	State correct

Outcome

Within therapy, AD demonstrated a lack of consistent improvement across sessions. Post-therapy, there was no improvement on picture verification or on other comprehension tasks. There was a slight improvement in naming, with more self corrections and semantic errors. Within therapy, JAC showed a steady general improvement with an increased ability to reject semantic foils. Post-therapy, there was a significant improvement on picture verification across both treated and untreated items; gains were maintained 4 months post-therapy. JAC's performance on other semantic tasks was assessed to determine generalisation. There were no gains on another picture verification task involving semantic and phonological foils. On the auditory version of Pyramids and Palm Trees, there was no significant improvement. No change was seen on written picture verification, auditory synonym judgement or picture naming. The authors do not report whether there was any impact on everyday comprehension.

Despite similar performance on pre-therapy assessments, AD and JAC responded differently to therapy. JAC showed improved performance on the therapy task with generalisation to untreated items and some generalisation to another auditory comprehension task. The authors suggest JAC's improved performance reflects improved access to semantic information from the auditory modality rather than in the semantic system itself. AD showed no significant improvement. The authors explore differences between JAC and AD in terms of the extent of differences between spoken and written comprehension, the severity of the conceptual semantic deficit and differences in spoken output. JAC's performance in picture verification was influenced by the degree of semantic relatedness between the target and semantic foil. AD's performance was not affected by semantic relatedness. AD's lack of improvement is attributed to his conceptual difficulties with the presence of semantic distracters making the therapy confusing.

Other comments

Other studies of semantic therapy have used a range of semantic tasks. This study looked at a specific task, picture name verification; this was chosen as the participants' semantic difficulties were particularly prominent in this task.

11 Therapy for noun retrieval and production

Summary of noun-naming studies

Studies targeting word retrieval form the bulk of the therapeutic literature and address a range of issues at the centre of the cognitive neuropsychological approach. Due to the large number of studies, this review of the literature is by necessity selective; there is a focus on studies that reflect the diversity of therapy tasks available and which highlight particular issues related to the therapeutic process and factors influencing treatment outcome. Historically studies initially focused on the retrieval of nouns, with nouns dominating both the diagnostic and therapy literature. More recently, there have been an increasing number of studies investigating whether similar therapy approaches can be applied to verb retrieval. These studies are reviewed in Chapter 12. Similarly, a number of studies have compared therapy with nouns and verbs; these are also discussed in the following chapter.

Many cognitive neuropsychological therapies for word retrieval have their antecedents in the experimental studies of facilitation in the mid-1980s (Patterson, Purell & Morton, 1983; Howard, Patterson, Franklin, Orchard-lisle & Morton, 1985a). Howard *et al.* (1985a) drew a distinction between three kinds of effects: (i) cueing: the immediate effects of a treatment; (ii) facilitation: the effects of a single treatment, measured some time later (5 minutes, 40 minutes, 1 day, etc); (iii) therapy: the effects of multiple treatment encounters delivered over many sessions over an extended period of time. So, for example, with a first phoneme cue, the cueing effect would be accuracy in word retrieval, the facilitation effect would be accuracy in naming, for example, 1 hour later, and the therapy effect would be the long-term improvement in word retrieval after multiple encounters with the target cued with the first phoneme. Howard *et al.* (1985a) argued that it is likely that effective cues would be effective facilitators, and that effective facilitators would be effective therapy methods. The only systematic test of this hypothesis is from Best, Herbert, Hickin, Osborne and Howard (2002) who provided evidence that, with phonemic/orthographic cues, participants with larger facilitation effects benefited more from treatment. Facilitation studies are not reported in detail in the subsequent chapters with the focus on multiple or repeated naming of items within a therapy context.

Therapy for word retrieval has focused on improving access to the word's meaning within the semantic system, improving access to the lexical representation of the word within the phonological output lexicon or strengthening the connection between meaning and word form. Only relatively few studies have investigated therapy for post-lexical deficits affecting phonological assembly. Table 11.1 summarises the studies focused on noun retrieval. In contrast to the other therapy chapters, the table summarises the level of impairment (described as the focus of therapy within the reviews) and the target of therapy, i.e. the type or level of processing targeted in the therapy tasks. These are broadly characterised under semantic, phonological, semantic/phonological and orthographic and will be discussed in depth below.

A number of studies reported also compare different therapy techniques with a single participant or across participants with the same or different therapies.

There is a complex relationship between the *nature of the underlying deficit* and the *tasks* used in therapy, hence the distinction between the focus and target of therapy. Nickels (2002b) provides a comprehensive discussion about the difference between semantic and phonological impairments and semantic and phonological therapy tasks. Semantic impairments affect spoken and written comprehension, as well as spoken and written word retrieval. Semantic errors may be present across modalities and performance is influenced by imageability. Firstly, a consideration of the tasks used to assess comprehension and production is important to the interpretation of the therapy literature on word retrieval. The multiple choice/forced choice formats of comprehension tasks may require less detailed semantic information than that required to retrieve the appropriate word. Good comprehension of high-imageability single words, for example, is often seen as demonstrating that the semantic system is intact and that the nature of the deficit is phonological. While this may indeed be the case for certain people, further in-depth assessment of semantics using more demanding tasks or materials (e.g. synonym judgements or comprehension of low-imageability words) may reveal impairment of semantics undetected on other tasks (for further discussion, see Cole-Virtue & Nickels, 2004). The implication of this is that the clinician needs to be alert to the possibility of a different underlying deficit from that reported, i.e. involving a compromised semantic system. One solution to this would be a recommendation that semantics is reported in more depth than simply single-word comprehension using word-to-picture matching. Secondly, mild semantic impairments commonly occur with more severe deficits in later stages of word retrieval (e.g. Nickels, 2002a, DeDe, Parris & Waters, 2003).

Semantic tasks have been used with people with both semantic and phonological impairments with the aim of facilitating word retrieval. Semantic tasks focus on the meaning of words and their referents. Examples of semantic tasks include word-to-picture matching, word–picture verification, feature matching/verification, generation of semantic features, categorisation, relatedness judgements and the provision of semantic information in cues. Tasks often involve pictures, with the provision of verbal and/or written labels differing between tasks. *Phonological tasks* promote access to the word, with examples including repetition, reading aloud and the provision of phonological and orthographic cues by the therapist. Other phonological tasks ask participants to reflect more explicitly on the phonology of the word, for example, counting syllables, identifying the initial phoneme or performing rhyme judgements. There is, however, a blurring between tasks as there may be inherent activation of semantics when working on phonology and vice versa. For example, when performing word-to-picture matching, the person may retrieve the spoken word and the meaning of the word may be activated during a repetition task, particularly if the word is repeated in the presence of a picture. Howard (2000) suggested that semantic and phonological therapies are effectively indistinguishable with both providing meaning–phonology pairings. Some tasks, labelled semantic/phonological, explicitly pair the two; examples include naming with both semantic and phonological cues and combining a semantic task, e.g. word-to-picture matching with repetition or reading aloud.

There are a number of studies, labelled orthographic, where the participant is taught or encouraged to draw on their orthographic knowledge to facilitate their retrieval of spoken words. These approaches are appropriate for participants who have more preserved written production or at least partial access to initial letters or word forms. A number of different studies are described: the provision of an alphabet board (Howard & Harding, 1998), the identification of initial letters with a computer then producing a phoneme cue (Bruce & Howard, 1987, Best *et al.* 1997), the teaching of orthographic-to-phonological conversion

Table 11.1 Summary of studies targeting noun retrieval

Level of impairment	Therapy studies	Area targeted in therapy	Therapy tasks
Semantic system	Study 1: Rose and Douglas (2008, p128)	Semantic comparison of verbal, gesture and combined treatment.	• Verbal treatment: Generation of semantic features if unable to name • Gesture treatment: Generation of iconic gesture if unable to name • Gesture and verbal treatment: Combination of generation of features and iconic gesture if unable to name
Semantic system and/or phonological output lexicon (either within or across clients)	Study 2: Nettleton and Lesser (1991, p130)	Semantic	• Word-to-picture matching (name, function and written form) • Semantic judgements (category and attributes) • Categorisation
		Phonological	• Repetition of picture name • Naming with progressive phonological cues
	Study 3: Howard *et al.* (1985b, p133)	Semantic	• Spoken word-to-picture matching with semantic distracters • Written word-to-picture matching with semantic distracters • Yes/no question about item meaning
		Phonological	• Repetition of picture name • Phonemic cueing • Rhyme judgement
	Study 4: Nickels and Best (1996, p135)	Semantic	• Yes/no questions about function • Relatedness judgements • Spoken and written word-to-picture matching
	Study 5: Kiran and Thompson (2003, p139)	Semantic	• Picture naming • Category sorting • Identifying semantic attributes • Yes/no questions about semantic features
	Study 6: Marshall *et al.* (1990, p142)	Semantic/ Phonological	• Written word-to-picture matching with reading aloud
	Study 7: Pring *et al.* (1993, p144)	Semantic/ Phonological	• Word-to-picture matching with reading aloud • Picture-to-word matching with reading aloud
	Study 8: Hillis (1989, p146)	Semantic/ Orthographic	• Spoken and written naming with orthographic and semantic cues
	Study 9: Hillis and Caramazza (1994, p148)	Semantic/ Phonological Orthographic	• Naming followed by a hierarchy of cues, including sentence completion, initial phoneme, and modelling the word • Teaching of orthographic-to-phonological conversion • Teaching of phonological-to-orthographic conversion

Table 11.1 Continued

Level of impairment	Therapy studies	Area targeted in therapy	Therapy tasks
	Study 10: Best *et al.* (1997, p152)	Semantic Orthographic	• Written naming • Written word-to-picture matching with copying • Initial letter identification on computer with repetition of computer generated phoneme
	Study 11: Hickin *et al.* (2002, p155)	Phonological Comparison of phonological and orthographic cues	• Spoken naming with progressive phonological cues • Spoken naming with progressive orthographic cues
	Study 12: Herbert *et al.* (2003, p157)	Phonological Semantic/ Phonological	• File of pictures with progressive orthographic cues • Elicitation of items within conversational tasks
	Study 13: Best *et al.* (2008, p159)	Phonological	• Spoken naming with progressive orthographic and phonological cues • Elicitation of items within conversational tasks
	Study 14: Fillingham *et al.* (2006, p161)	Phonological Comparison of errorful and errorless learning	• Errorful: Picture naming with progressive grapheme and phonological cues • Errorless: Picture naming with written word and spoken word for repetition
	Study 15: Leonard *et al.* (2008, p164)	Phonological	• Phonological component analysis (PCA): Naming of picture followed by generation of phonological features and repeated naming
	Study 16: DeDe *et al.* (2003, p166)	Orthographic	• Written naming • Tactile cues • Self-generated phonological cues
Phonological output lexicon (or access to it)	Study 17: Le Dorze *et al.* (1994, p168)	Semantic	• Formal-semantic therapy – tasks involving semantic comprehension with spoken or written word • Spoken word-to-picture matching • Written word-to-picture matching • Semantic judgement – yes/no questions • Semantic therapy – tasks involving semantic comprehension where word form not present • Spoken definition to picture matching • Written definition to picture matching • Semantic judgement – yes/no questions
	Study 18: Boyle and Coelho (1995, p170)	Semantic	• Guided verbalisation of semantic features (supported by visual–semantic feature chart) during picture naming
	Study 19: Lowell *et al.* (1995, p172)	Semantic	• Self-generated semantic cue words read aloud by therapist • Client attempts to name picture

	Study 20: Francis *et al.* (2002, p174)	Semantic	• Circumlocution-induced naming (CIN): Talking around topic until word named

	Study 21:
	Spencer *et al.*
	(2000, p175)
		Semantic/
		Phonological
			• Semantic and phonological cueing hierarchy
			  using superordinate category, rhyme,
			  phoneme and grapheme cues

	Study 22: Miceli *et al.* (1996, p177)	Phonological	• Reading of target items (with and without picture) • Repetition of target items • Picture naming
	Study 23: Robson *et al.* (1998, p180)	Phonological	• Syllable judgement • Initial phoneme judgement • Dual judgement of syllable and phoneme • Judgement tasks with naming using first sound as self-cue
	Study 24: Nickels (2002a, p182)	Phonological Comparison of approaches	• Attempted picture naming • Reading aloud • Delayed written copying of word following silent reading

	Study 13 in
	Chapter 13: De
	Partz (1986,
	p273)
		Orthographic	• Generation of code word for each letter
			• Segmentation of initial phoneme from code
			  word
			• Production of phoneme on presentation of
			  grapheme
			• Phoneme blending

	Study 14 in
	Chapter 13:
	Nickels (1992,
	p275)
		Orthographic	• Generation of code word for each letter
			• Segmentation of initial phoneme from code
			  word
			• Production of phoneme on presentation of
			  grapheme
			• Phoneme blending

	Study 25: Bruce and Howard (1987, p184)	Orthographic	• Initial letter identification on computer with repetition of computer generated phoneme
	Study 26: Howard and Harding (1998, p186)	Orthographic	• Use of alphabet board
Phonological ***output lexicon*** ***and phonological*** ***assembly***	Study 27: Waldron *et al.* (2011a, p188)	Phonological	• Phoneme discrimination • Self-monitoring
Phonological ***assembly***	Study 28: Franklin *et al.* (2002, p190)	Phonological	• Phoneme discrimination • Self-monitoring

	Study 29:
	Waldron *et al.*
	(2011b, p192)
		Phonological	• Phoneme discrimination
			• Naming with minimal contrast pairs,
			  articulatory–kinematic and orthographic
			  cues
			• Self-monitoring

to facilitate the production of self-generated phonemic cues or the reading aloud of written responses (De Partz, 1986, Nickels, 1992, Hillis & Caramazza, 1994) and using written naming to support verbal production (Hillis, 1989, DeDe *et al.*, 2003). The studies are very varied, reflecting the diversity between individual patterns of strengths and weakness in spoken and written production, and highlight the importance of detailed assessment prior to the introduction of a cognitive-relay or compensatory strategy.

Semantic therapy tasks generally result in improvement in the production of treated words, although not every semantic task produces the same effect within or across participants. The study by Nickels and Best (1996) highlights the complex interaction between the client's underlying impairment, the nature of the tasks, the person's accuracy in performing the semantic task and the relationship between feedback and performance. Boyle (2010) in her discussion of 'semantic feature analysis' therapy similarly emphasises that subtle differences between therapy tasks may influence treatment outcome. In a small proportion of studies, where either semantic tasks have been employed or the deficit has been of semantic origin, generalisation to untreated items has been reported (e.g. Hillis, 1989, Boyle & Coelho, 1995, Nickels & Best, 1996). A number of factors should be noted when considering this apparent generalisation. Firstly, some studies test a very limited number of control items. Secondly, untreated items are sometimes repeatedly probed during the therapy period and generalisation may reflect these repeated attempts at naming (Howard, 2000; Nickels, 2002a, Boyle, 2010). Finally, when gains are seen in the retrieval of untreated words post-therapy, these gains are often transient and are often not maintained at follow-up (Nickels & Best, 1996). Kiran and Thompson (2003) found generalisation to untreated words was greatest when therapy focused on atypical items within a semantic category. Despite the centrality of the semantic system, many studies do not consider the impact of therapy on comprehension and other semantic tasks. When assessed, some gains have been reported (e.g. Rose & Douglas, 2008) when tasks have explicitly contrasted semantic features.

Phonological therapy tasks have similarly been reported to result in improved production of treated words when used with people with either semantic and/or phonological output lexicon impairments. Therapy is thought to either strengthen the connection between meaning and the lexical representation or increase the activation of the target word. In both cases, the likelihood of the word being successfully retrieved is increased. A small proportion of individuals show generalisation to untreated items (e.g. Leonard, Rochon & Laird, 2008; Hickin, Best, Herbert, Howard & Osborne, 2002; Best, Greenwood, Grassly & Hickin, 2008; Best, Greenwood, Grassly & Hickin *et al.*, 2013). Leonard *et al.* (2008) suggest this generalisation may be a consequence of spreading activation within the phonological system or the development of a strategy. Alternatively, generalisation may reflect improvement in post-lexical phonological assembly or strengthening of bidirectional connections between phonemes and lexical items (see discussion in Greenwood *et al.*, 2012). Overall, the strong likelihood of item-specific gains following therapy emphasises the need to work on words that are functionally relevant and useful to the client (see discussion in Renvall, Nickels & Davidson, 2013a, 2013b on functionally relevant items). In addition, although many of the studies show statistically significant improvements in naming, improvement is often rather limited (in terms of the number of items learned). In aphasia, therefore, it appears that it is not just the ability to retrieve known words that is impaired, but the ability to re-learn words may also be affected.

The orthographic therapies are strategy based, with the written letter or word acting as a cue for spoken word retrieval. Some therapies rely on re-teaching orthographic-to-phonological conversion to produce a phoneme cue or to read the word aloud. Generalised gains are predicted and are seen but gains are restricted by impairment in related skills, e.g. extent of difficulties in written naming, the success of initial phoneme cues and the ability to blend phonemes (Nickels, 1992; Hillis & Caramazza, 1994). In studies using a computer to generate the cues (Bruce & Howard, 1987; Best, Howard, Bruce & Gatehouse, 1997), generalised gains have been reported for clients when using the aid but also improvements in unaided performance. Participant JOW (Best *et al.*, 1997) showed highly significant gains in his ability to find the words without the aid. The authors, therefore, conclude that the aid was not a prosthesis but helped him to find the words independently, possibly via the use of sub-lexical cues.

Therapy targeting phonological assembly has received much less attention. Franklin *et al.* (2002) targeted phoneme discrimination and self-monitoring ability, with a view to improving the detection and correction of phonological errors. The therapy has been replicated in two studies by Waldron, Whitworth and Howard (2011a, 2011b). MB, the client in the original study, showed generalisation to untreated words and gains across reading aloud, repetition and naming. Clients in the subsequent studies failed to show these generalised gains. Waldron and colleagues explore possible reasons for this, considering the implications of co-occurring lexical and motor speech deficits and the potential value of incorporating a production task.

Few studies have investigated the relative effectiveness of tasks targeting semantic and phonological processing; this may reflect the overlap and similarity between the tasks. Nettleton and Lesser (1991) investigated the effects of model-appropriate and model-inappropriate therapy for clients with semantic, phonological output lexicon and phonological assembly impairments. Semantic therapy for semantic impairments and phonological therapy for lexical deficits resulted in significant improvement. Inappropriate semantic therapy for clients with phonological assembly deficits resulted in no improvement. The authors conclude that therapy should be motivated by an understanding of the impairment. On the other hand, Howard *et al.* (1985b) used phonological and semantic treatment techniques for word retrieval in a cross-over trial with 12 people with aphasia. The participants varied in the degree to which they improved, but both treatment techniques resulted in approximately equal improvement. A later re-analysis by Howard (2000) showed that there was a strong correlation between the amount of improvement with each therapy method. There was no evidence that any subject improved with just one treatment approach.

A number of studies have investigated the effects of different therapy tasks focused on the same level of processing. As previously stated, Nickels and Best (1996) showed that different semantic tasks resulted in differential gains but there has been no systematic evaluation of the impact of different tasks across participants. Other studies have shown minimal differences between therapy tasks. Rose and Douglas (2008) found that verbal, gesture and combined verbal and gesture treatment resulted in similar gains. Hickin *et al.* (2002) found there was no significant difference between the effects of phonological and orthographic cues. Fillingham, Sage and Lambon Ralph (2006) found limited difference between the effects of errorless and errorful learning, although a number of participants showed a significant difference in favour of errorful therapy either immediately post-therapy or at follow-up. Fillingham and colleagues, however, highlight that although the therapies were equally effective for most of the participants, all preferred the errorless learning as it was less frustrating. This emphasises the importance of considering client preference alongside the likely impact of therapy.

Within the studies of word retrieval, the move away from single case studies to case series studies is evident. These case series studies have formalised replications of therapy with standard assessment and therapy procedures across a group of clients. These studies have provided strong evidence that therapy can be effective and have facilitated systematic comparison of therapy across participants, enabling a greater understanding of the factors that underpin individual variability. These factors have included the origin of the naming deficit, with the presence of a semantic impairment limiting gains (Hickin *et al.*, 2002; Leonard *et al.*, 2008), the severity of the naming impairment (Leonard *et al.*, 2008), the presence of co-occurring language deficits (Waldron *et al.*, 2011a) and co-occurring cognitive deficits (Fillingham *et al.*, 2006). They have also contributed to a wider understanding of factors influencing the therapy process, for example, the number of naming attempts (Fillingham, Sage & Lambon Ralph, 2005) and active engagement in therapy either by the generation of features (Leonard *et al.*, 2008) or the selection of cues (Best *et al.*, 2008).

Reactivation therapy for word retrieval has typically involved repetitive constrained activities with a resultant increase in the naming of treated items. The aim of therapy is, however, to improve word retrieval in everyday activities and in conversation. Herbert, Best, Hickin, Howard & Osborne (2003) describe an interactional therapy which aimed to bridge the gap between constrained therapy and conversation. Participants generated lists of words related to a particular topic, e.g. shopping, holidays, and then had conversations around these topics. While participants had access to a file of target words with orthographic cues, there was no pressure to produce the target words and participants did not produce every item during each session. Following therapy, gains were seen in the retrieval of treated items. The positive gains of interactional therapy were not, however, replicated in a later study (Best *et al.*, 2008). There is some evidence that gains in anomia therapy can extend beyond picture naming. Herbert *et al.* (2008) demonstrated that performance on naming tasks was related to lexical retrieval in conversation, suggesting that gains in naming performance should result in gains in connected speech. Therapy for word retrieval has been shown to result in gains on lexical measures in conversation for some participants (Spencer, Doyle, McNeil, Wambaugh, *et al.*, 2000, Greenwood *et al.*, 2012) but connected speech measures are often not included in the studies. Best *et al.* (2008) showed that anomia therapy also resulted in improved participation in everyday activities and positive gains in how individuals perceived their difficulties. Further exploration of these wider gains is needed.

EVALUATIONS OF NOUN STUDIES

Study 1

Rose, M. and Douglas, J. (2008) Treating a semantic word production deficit in aphasia with verbal and gesture methods. *Aphasiology, 22(1)*, 20–41.

Focus of therapy: Semantic system.

Target of therapy: Semantic (Gesture).

Therapy approach: Reactivation.

Client details

General information

JB was a 51-year-old, right-handed woman. She had a cerebral infarction resulting in a focal abnormality in the left posterior frontal lobe adjacent to the sylvian fissure in Broca's area, with slight involvement of the insular cortex. She left school at 15, undertook vocational training and eventually established her own company. She had normal visuo-spatial and visuo-constructional skills and verbal memory span.

Overall pattern of language impairments and preservations

JB presented with a mild category specific anomic aphasia. Functional comprehension was intact. Oral expression was fluent and grammatically correct until a word-finding difficulty occurred, resulting in a semantic error or pausing. Semantic errors were present across modality, with impaired spoken and written word matching and spoken and written naming. There was a strong imageability effect present in spoken and written synonym judgement. There was also some impairment in picture semantics. JB's naming showed no frequency or word length effects, with naming errors specifically related to the categories of tools, musical instruments and animals. The authors suggest JB had poor semantic processing with normal phonological processing.

Time post-onset

JB was 40 months post-onset at the time of the study.

Therapy

The study investigated the relative effectiveness of gesture, verbal and combined gesture and verbal treatments. A multiple-baseline across conditions design was used to monitor the effects of the three different treatments, with therapies applied simultaneously to different word sets. The order of treatment was varied across sessions. Ten baseline sessions were carried out, followed by fourteen treatment sessions. Sessions were 45 minutes in duration and took place 3 times per week in her home.

Task	Verbal treatment	Gesture treatment	Combined verbal and gesture treatment
	Present picture and ask participant to name. If not named correctly in 20 seconds, provide cues dependent on treatment. No further cues when correct response produced.		
Materials	Four sets of stimuli. Group A – control words, mixed category. Group B – musical instruments, verbal treatment. Group C – tools, gesture treatment. Group D – animals, verbal and gesture treatment. Sets balanced for word frequency, imageability and baseline error rate.		
Hierarchy	None	None	None
Feedback on error	1. Describe function and attempt to name 2. Describe shape and attempt to name 3. Contrast erroneous productions with target in terms of use and shape and then attempt to name 4. Verbal model for repetition	1. Produce iconic gesture and attempt to name 2. Contrast gesture associated with erroneous production with target gesture and attempt to name 3. Verbal model for repetition	1. Steps 1 and 2 of verbal 2. Steps 1 and 2 of gesture 3. Copy verbal and gesture model
Feedback if correct	Not stated	Not stated	Not stated

Outcome

Baseline performance was stable. Treatment led to marked and rapid improvements in all three treatment conditions. Group D words treated via combined verbal and gesture treatment took six sessions to reach criterion. Group C treated via gesture took eight sessions and Group B treated via verbal treatment took fourteen sessions. There was no change in the control words until they subsequently received the combined treatment. Statistical analysis showed significant treatment effects and large effect sizes for all three conditions. Naming accuracy was maintained at 1 month and 3 months post-treatment.

The relative effectiveness of the three treatment conditions was examined in terms of the rate of item acquisition (slope parameters) and stability of acquisition (variance in power curve residuals). There were no significant differences between combined verbal and gesture and verbal alone or combined and gesture alone. The difference between relative variance of verbal and gesture was significant but there was no difference in slope (rate of acquisition). Generalised improvement was seen in the Western Aphasia Battery aphasia quotient, use of nouns in procedural discourse around treated topics, the three-picture version of Pyramids and Palm Trees (PPT) and spoken and written naming. There was no improvement in reading comprehension, Raven's matrices or letter cancellation.

The three treatments resulted in improved naming of treated items and generalised gains in a number of tasks requiring lexical and conceptual semantic processing. Generalisation was not, however, seen in the naming of control items. The authors discuss the similarity of the approach to semantic feature analysis therapy, with a focus on shape and function. The lack of generalisation to the control set was attributed to a dosage effect, with a sufficient amount of therapy being required before the effects were seen. Change on the test of conceptual semantics (PPT) was partially attributed to improved knowledge of the treated categories and partially to a more generic strategy of analysing details of pictures more carefully.

Other comments

The authors acknowledge that JB showed a specific and mild semantic level impairment, emphasising the need to replicate therapy in participants with more extensive semantic impairments. They also acknowledge the limitation of the simultaneous design, recognising that the three treatment conditions could interact with one another. The different treatments were applied to different word categories which may have influenced the results.

Study 2

Nettleton, J. and Lesser, R. (1991). Therapy for naming difficulties in aphasia: application of a cognitive neuropsychological model. *Journal of Neurolinguistics*, 6, 139–157.

Focus of therapy: Semantic system and phonological output lexicon.

Target of therapy: Semantic and phonological.

Therapy approach: Reactivation.

Client details

Six participants were included in the study.

General information

PD was a 55-year-old man who had worked as a car park attendant. FF was a 68-year-old former labourer. DF was a 63-year-old housewife. MC was a 57-year-old housewife. MH was a 72-year-old woman who had previously owned a bakery. NC was a 74-year-old woman who had worked as a nursing sister. All participants had had a left CVA. Only PD and NC had had a CT scan and they presented with left parietal damage.

Overall pattern of language impairments and preservations

PD had a fluent aphasia. FF had a fluent aphasia with 'empty speech' and poor auditory comprehension. DF had severe word-finding difficulties. MC was non-fluent and agrammatic. MH presented with higher level comprehension problems, fluent speech and word-retrieval difficulties. NC had moderate comprehension difficulties, fluent speech and word-finding difficulties.

The clients were allocated to one of three groups based on an analysis of errors on the Boston Naming Test (Goodglass, Kaplan & Weintraub, 2001), their performance on spoken word-to-picture matching, and a comparison of their performance on comprehension and repetition tasks. PD and FF were considered to have a semantic impairment. They scored below the normal range on picture matching, selecting close semantic distractors. They produced mainly semantic errors on the Boston Naming Test and could be phonemically cued to produce a semantic associate of the target word which they then accepted as correct. DF and MC were considered to have an impairment of the phonological output lexicon. They scored within the normal range on picture matching and produced circumlocution errors in naming. Their repetition performance was equivalent to their performance on auditory comprehension tasks. MH and NC also scored within the normal range on picture matching. They produced phonological errors on the Boston Naming Test and presented with difficulties in repetition. They were considered to have an impairment at the level of phonological assembly (referred to by Nettleton & Lesser as the phonological output buffer).

Time post-onset

The clients varied considerably in their time post-onset. FF was 3 months, PD was 6 months, MH was 8 months, DF was 1 year, NC was 3 years and MC was 8 years post-stroke.

Therapy

The study aimed to compare performance on 'model-motivated' therapy versus 'model-inappropriate' therapy. PD and FF received appropriate semantic therapy, DF and MC received appropriate phonological therapy, and MH and NC received inappropriate semantic therapy. Therapy consisted of 1-hour sessions, twice a week for 8 weeks. A repeated multiple-baseline therapy design was used to compare performance on treated and untreated items.

(a) Semantic therapy

Task	Word-to-picture match a. by spoken name b. by function c. by written name	Yes/no judgements about pictures a. category information. b. attributes	Categorisation Sorting pictures into categories
Materials	Selection of object line drawings from a set of 50 treated items		
Hierarchy	Increasing semantic relatedness	None	None
Feedback on error	Not stated	Not stated	Not stated
Feedback if correct	Not stated	Not stated	Not stated

(b) Phonological therapy

Task	Repetition of picture name	Rhyme judgement Judging whether the spoken name of the picture rhymes with another word	Naming with progressive phonemic cues
Materials	Names of objects from a set of 50 treated items	Selection of object line drawings from a set of 50 treated items	Selection of object line drawings from a set of 50 treated items
Hierarchy	None	None	None
Feedback on error	Not stated	Not stated	Not stated
Feedback if correct	Not stated	Not stated	Not stated

Outcome

Following appropriate semantic therapy, PD showed significant improvement in his naming of the treated items. This improvement was maintained 2 months post-therapy. There was no significant change on untreated items. FF showed a non-significant trend of improvement with a qualitative change in his errors (more closely related semantic associates following therapy). Following appropriate phonological therapy, both DF and MC showed significant improvement on the treated items. MC also showed significant gains in his naming of untreated items. Following model-inappropriate semantic therapy, MH and NC showed no significant improvement on either treated or untreated items.

Appropriate semantic and phonological therapy for the four clients resulted in improvement, although this improvement was not significant for FF. The improvement seen is likely to be a consequence of therapy, as the clients were beyond the phase of spontaneous recovery and showed a relatively stable pre-therapy baseline. Inappropriate semantic therapy for the clients thought to have a difficulty at the level of phonological assembly resulted in no improvement.

Other comments

The authors propose that the results of this study suggest that clients with naming difficulties should not be treated as a homogeneous group but that therapy should be motivated by an analysis of their impairment. The study suggests that semantic therapy is not appropriate for clients with phonological assembly difficulties but does not address whether semantic therapy has value for clients with phonological output difficulties.

Study 3

Howard, D., Patterson, K. E., Franklin, S., Orchard-Lisle, V. and Morton, J. (1985b). Treatment of word-retrieval deficits in aphasia: a comparison of two therapy methods. *Brain*, *108*, 817–829.

Focus of therapy: Semantic system and/or phonological output lexicon (locus not specified).

Target of therapy: Semantic/phonological.

Therapy approach: Reactivation.

Client details

General information

Twelve clients were involved in the study. All clients had specific word-finding problems as a consequence of acquired aphasia, no severe visual problems or visual agnosia, and were able to repeat single words.

Overall pattern of language impairments and preservations

On the Boston Diagnostic Aphasia Examination (Goodglass, Kaplan & Barresi, 2001), six clients were identified as having a Broca's aphasia, four as having a mild conduction aphasia and two as having anomic aphasia.

Time post-onset

All clients were at least 6 months post-onset and usually several years post-onset.

Therapy

This study aimed to compare the relative improvement in naming ability following phonological and semantic therapy. Each client received phonological and semantic therapy with 4 weeks intervening between therapy methods. Six clients had 2 consecutive weeks of treatment with each method and six had 1 week of treatment with each method. Therapy was carried out over 4 consecutive days in either the 2 weeks or the 1 week, depending on which group they were assigned to (i.e. the first group received therapy on 8 days). The length of the therapy session was 1 hour. An item-specific treatment design was used to monitor the effects of therapy.

Task	Semantic therapy	Phonological therapy
	1. Spoken word-to-picture matching with semantic distractors	1. Repeating the picture name
	2. Written word-to-picture matching with semantic distractors	2. Attempting to produce the name with the aid of a phonemic cue
	3. Answering a yes/no question requiring the patient to access the meaning of the name e.g. 'Is a cat an animal?'	3. Judging whether the word rhymed with another word
Materials	300 line drawing pictures of objects (Set A) For each picture the following were prepared: 1. a sheet containing the picture and three semantically related distractors 2. a card with targets written name on 3. a semantic judgement for each picture e.g. 'Is a cat an animal?' 4. a second set of different pictures of the same 300 objects (Set B)	
Hierarchy	None	
Feedback	Not specified	

Outcome

Clients were assessed on naming of their 80 test pictures by daily pre-tests, and naming of all 300 pictures, 1 week and 6 weeks after completion of therapy. All 12 clients showed a significant improvement in naming the treated items over naming controls in daily pre-tests. This advantage increased as treatment progressed. There was no significant difference between semantic and phonological therapy. Post-therapy, naming of the treated words improved significantly compared with the naming of the control words. There was a small but statistically reliable improvement for the clients as a group on both picture sets A and B. Eight of the 12 clients showed significant improvement, one client being able to name 40% of the pictures she could not previously name after only 4 hours of therapy, while four of the clients showed no change. Semantic therapy and phonological therapy resulted in equal improvement in the naming of treated items. Improvement was not maintained 6 weeks post-therapy.

Other comments

This study shows, however, that even with small amounts of therapy (4–8 hours), significant improvements in naming can be made. Improvement was unrelated to the duration of therapy, age of client, time post-onset or type of aphasia. The authors propose that the semantic representation is accessed during the course of semantic therapy. This representation is 'primed' and is more easily accessible for later naming. Phonological therapy, however, was hypothesised to act at the level of the phonological output lexicon with the effects being shorter lasting. The difference is considered to reflect the properties of these two levels of lexical representation. The authors propose that the use of good facilitating tasks such as those used here in the semantic therapy can act as a 'first stage' therapy to activate words before those words are used in a second stage therapy that maximises their communicative value. The data in this study are re-analysed in Howard (2000), showing that for each participant the amount of improvement was approximately equal in the two treatment periods.

Study 4

Nickels, L. and Best, W. (1996). Therapy for naming disorders (Part II): specifics, surprises and suggestions. *Aphasiology, 10(2)*, 109–136.

Focus of therapy: Semantic system and phonological output lexicon.

Target of therapy: Semantic.

Therapy approach: Reactivation.

Client details

Three participants were included in the study.

General information

AER was a 69-year-old man who was a retried engineer. PA was a 54-year-old woman who worked as a secretary. TRC was a 47-year-old male fishmonger. All participants had had a left hemisphere CVA.

Overall pattern of language impairments and preservations

All three participants were reported to have 'fair' comprehension in a conversational setting. AER had non-fluent, agrammatic speech. TRC and PA had fluent speech, described as being empty with marked word-finding difficulties. TRC could sometimes write a word he was unable to say. PA was often able to indicate the initial letter. Both TRC and PA's naming improved when given phonological cues and this sometimes aided word retrieval. Participants were assessed on the Pyramids and Palm Trees, auditory and written word-to-picture matching and synonym judgement and spoken and written naming.

   AER showed impaired comprehension of pictures and spoken and written words, especially low-imageability items. Written comprehension was more impaired than spoken. Spoken naming was characterised by semantic errors. AER was unable to write. The authors described AER has having a semantic impairment, with an additional impairment processing written stimuli. TRC also showed impaired comprehension of both spoken and written words, with spoken comprehension worse than written. He produced semantic errors in spoken and written naming, with slightly better performance in written. The authors proposed TRC had a semantic impairment with an additional deficit in accessing representations in the phonological output lexicon. PA showed a similar pattern to TRC with impaired spoken and written comprehension and naming. As well as semantic errors, she produced phonological errors particularly with longer words. The authors suggest she had difficulty at multiple levels, semantic system, access to semantics from spoken words and deficit subsequent to phonological output lexicon.

Time post-onset

AER and TRC were both 4 years post-onset. PA was 6 years post-stroke at the time of the study.

Therapy

The three participants all received multiple phases of different types of semantic therapy. Each participant and their therapy is, therefore, presented separately with discussion of general issues raised by the authors at the end.

Therapy for AER

The first type of therapy involved yes/no questions. Therapy was carried out by the therapist for 20 minutes, twice a week for 3 months, resulting in a total of 8 hours of therapy. The second therapy was relatedness judgements. AER did this therapy independently at home, spending 1½ hours a week spaced over 2 to 3 days for 12 weeks. An additional phase of this therapy followed, with his wife giving feedback on performance; this phase took place over 6 weeks. The third type of therapy, word-to-picture matching, was carried out independently at home. AER carried out this task for approximately 15 minutes per day, 4 days a week for 8 weeks. In each case, an item-specific design was used to compare performance on treated and untreated items, before and after therapy.

Task	*Yes/No questions* Questions about function of object presented auditorily.	*Relatedness judgements* Given picture or written words and asked to decide whether it is related to other items.	*Written word-to-picture matching* Matching a written word to four semantically related pictures or a picture to four words.
Materials	Fifty-nine target pictures for naming. Sixty untreated. Matched for baseline accuracy.	Sixty items that were untreated in Task 1.	One hundred pictures for naming. Fifty treated and 50 untreated matched for baseline accuracy.
Hierarchy	None	1. Picture material only 2. Written word target with picture choices 3. Written words only	None
Feedback on error	Not stated	None initially. In second phase, feedback following judgement and discussion of reasons.	No feedback
Feedback if correct	Not stated		No feedback

Outcome for AER

The first phase of therapy (yes/no questions) resulted in no improvement in naming of treated or untreated items. There was, however, significant improvement on another unrelated naming assessment; these gains were maintained 6 months later. Therapy encouraged AER to focus on the functional attributes of the object. The authors suggest that performance improved on the unrelated naming test as the function of these objects was useful in distinguishing them from a close semantic associate, e.g. 'rake' from 'hoe'. The therapy involving relatedness judgements was very difficult for AER. The initial phase without feedback resulted in significant improvement for the treated items. Following the same therapy with feedback, there was additional significant improvement for treated items and significant improvement for untreated items. Gains were maintained 1 month later. The authors discuss that the differences may result from additional therapy or the feedback given. AER found the word-to-picture matching therapy easy and made minimal errors. He always attempted to read the words aloud. Therapy resulted in a significant improvement for both treated and untreated items, but treated items were significantly better than untreated. One month later, only treated items were significantly better than before therapy. Gains for treated items were also significant 1 year later. Word-to-picture matching with semantically related distracters was effective in improving long-term naming of treated items. The authors conclude that not every semantic task produces the same therapy effects. They discuss the influence of the task, the person's accuracy in performing the task independently and the relationship between feedback and performance.

Therapy for PA

Therapy aimed to improve PA's word finding, comparing the effects of a semantic and non-semantic task. Tasks were carried out by PA at home with treatment lasting a week and practice carried out on four to five occasions. A repeated baseline, item-specific design was used to monitor the impact of therapy on treated and untreated items.

Task	*Letter cues* Presentation of picture for naming with letter cues if unable to name.	*Written word-to-picture matching* Presentation of picture with either correct word or semantic associate with person making yes/no judgement or matching picture to one of 4 written words.	*Lexical therapy* Presentation of picture for naming
Materials	Sixty-six pictures divided into 33 treated and 33 untreated. Treated set began with /s f d b/. Sets matched for baseline accuracy.	Untreated set from task	Two sets of 27 items matched for baseline accuracy. One treated and one untreated.
Hierarchy	1. Initial naming 2. If unsuccessful, find initial letter on cue card 3. If unable to name, read aloud name on reverse of picture	None	If unable to name, read aloud name on reverse of picture.
Feedback on error	No feedback	Name of picture on reverse to allow checking of decision.	No feedback
Feedback if correct	No feedback		No feedback

Outcome for PA

During the initial baseline, non-significant improvement was seen with repeated testing. Following letter cue therapy, significant improvement was seen in the naming of treated items with no change on untreated items. No change was seen after word-to-picture matching; these tasks did not facilitate PA's naming. Lexical therapy resulted in significant improvement in the naming of the treated set with no change on untreated items. When the same treatment was repeated with previously untreated items, those words also showed significant gains. The authors conclude that PA had to say the target words for therapy to be successful, possibly strengthening the links between the semantic system and the phonological output lexicon.

Therapy for TRC

Therapy aimed to improve written and spoken naming using semantic judgement tasks. Following an initial baseline assessment over a 2 month period, written word-to-picture matching tasks were introduced. Therapy was carried out independently, with two variations of the task (one word to four pictures and one picture to four words) carried out on alternative days. TRC was due to do the task which took around 10 minutes, 5 days a week for 4 weeks. Given Tec's time constraints, the equivalent of 3 days work was uncompleted. Following reassessment, a second phase of therapy consisted of spoken word-to-picture matching. TRC again was intented to be carrying out therapy independently 5 days a week for 4 weeks with tasks lasting 5 to 10 minutes and during this phase, therapy was completed. An item-specific design comparing treated and untreated items in both spoken and written naming was used.

Task	**Written word-to-picture matching** Either matching a written word to four semantically related pictures of matching a picture to four written words.	**Spoken word-to-picture matching** Either matching one spoken word to four semantically related pictures or one picture to choice of two spoken words.
Materials	One hundred pictures for naming divided in treated and untreated sets. Sets balanced for baseline naming accuracy in spoken and written naming.	
Hierarchy	None. Variations alternated.	None. Variations alternated.
Feedback on error	No feedback	No feedback
Feedback if correct	No feedback	No feedback

Outcome for TRC

During written word-to-picture matching, TRC often attempted to say the word but would move on if unsuccessful. Following written word-to-picture matching therapy, spoken and written naming showed significant improvement. One week post-therapy, significant improvement was seen on both treated and untreated items. One month later, performance had declined but significant gains were still evident for both treated items in both spoken and written modalities. At 1 month, there was no longer significant improvement for untreated items. The second period of therapy comprising spoken word-to-picture matching resulted in no significant change. Written word-to-picture matching produced gains in both output modalities, suggesting that therapy effects were not dependent on overt production. Spoken word-to-picture matching resulted in no gains. The authors suggest that this may be a consequence of TRC having a more severe impairment of spoken word comprehension, resulting in less facilitation from the spoken version of the task.

Other comments

The authors provide a general discussion about the outcomes for the three participants. All of the participants had a semantic impairment and were given 'semantic therapy' but gains differed across participants and tasks. All participants had written word-to-picture matching therapy. AER and TRC showed the same pattern of gains, with long lasting improvement on treated items and transient gains for untreated items. PA showed no improvement. The authors discuss these findings in relation to the need for word production, task difficulty or accuracy and the nature of the semantic deficit. Suggestions of further investigations to determine how semantic treatments work are discussed. A considerable proportion of the therapy described in the study was carried out independently by the participants at home. A previous period of therapy with TRC is described in Nickels (1992).

Study 5

Kiran, S. and Thompson, C.K. (2003). The role of semantic complexity in treatment of naming deficits: Training semantic categories in fluent aphasia by controlling exemplar typicality. *Journal of Speech, Language and Hearing Research, 46*, 608–622.

Focus of therapy: Semantics and the phonological output lexicon.

Target of therapy: Semantic.

Therapy approach: Reactivation.

Client details

Four participants were included in the study.

General information

Participants included three women and one man, aged between 63 and 75 years. All participants were right-handed and had had a single left hemisphere stroke in the territory of the middle cerebral artery. They were all at least high school educated. They had adequate hearing and no visual impairment.

Overall pattern of language impairments and preservations

Participants presented with fluent aphasia, with impaired comprehension and naming difficulties. On assessment of spoken and written, single-word comprehension, there was some variation between participants but all showed some impairment. Difficulties were also present in single-word repetition and oral reading. The authors suggest participants had impairments in the semantic system and the phonological output lexicon.

Time post-onset

Participants were between 9 months and 99 months post-onset.

Therapy

Therapy aimed to improve naming, examining the impact of semantic complexity on generalisation. The authors predicted that training atypical (more complex) items would facilitate greater generalisation to untrained items. A multiple, repeated baseline design across participants and behaviours was used to examine the acquisition of trained items and generalisation to untrained items within and across categories. Treatment was preceded by three or five baseline probes. During treatment, eight examples were trained at a time. Naming probes for the treated category were administered every second treatment sessions. Treatment was discontinued on that sub-set when naming accuracy of 7/8 was achieved for two consecutive sessions or a total of twenty sessions. Naming probes for untreated categories were completed at the end of each sub-set. A follow-up probe was completed 6 to 10 weeks after treatment. Treatment took place in a 2 hour session twice a week.

Two categories were treated, with the order of categories trained and the typicality of sub-sets counterbalanced across participants. Bird names were trained first in participants 1 and 2, with vegetable names trained first in participants 3 and 4. Typical exemplars were trained first in participants 1 and 3 with atypical exemplars treated first in participants 2 and 4.

Task	*Picture naming*	*Category sorting* Sorting of pictures under written category headings.	*Feature selection* Given target picture and features for category. Participant selects six features pertinent to target and then reads aloud.	*Yes/no questions* Participants asked semantic feature questions about target item.
Materials	Twenty-four items within each category (birds, vegetables) – eight typical, eight intermediate typicality and eight atypical. All low-frequency words. Sub-sets matched for frequency and syllable length. Three untreated categories (fruits, animals, musical instruments) with 12 items in each. Thirty features for each treated category, 15 general features applicable to all items within category, 15 specific features applicable to at least two items. Twenty distracter features related to other categories. Features either physically, functionally, characteristically or contextually related to items.			
Hierarchy	All four tasks done for each item. When consistent accuracy achieved in category sorting, that task carried out at start of session rather than for each item.			
Feedback on error	Not stated	Examiner places picture under correct category label.	Not stated	Not stated

Feedback if correct	Explanation that subsequent tasks focus on understanding more about item.	Not stated	Not stated	Not stated

Outcome

All participants demonstrated stable baseline performance except participant 3 who showed some fluctuation on one sub-set. Treatment for participant 1 started with typical examples of birds. Participant 1 showed gains on trained items, meeting criterion after 7 weeks. No generalisation was seen to untrained intermediate or atypical items. Gains were seen on these items when specifically trained, with training for all 24 items taking 25 weeks. No gains were seen on the untreated vegetable naming category. As participant 1 found therapy frustrating, vegetables were trained using atypical exemplars first. Training resulted in improved naming of trained atypical items in 8 weeks, with generalised gains in the naming of untrained intermediate and typical items.

Participant 2 initially received treatment on atypical exemplars of birds. Criterion was reached for trained items in 11 weeks, with generalisation to both intermediate and typical items. No change was seen on the untreated category. With training on atypical vegetables, the treatment effect was replicated within 6 weeks.

Participant 3 received treatment for typical vegetables first. Training resulted in gains on treated exemplars with no generalisation to untrained items. Intermediate and atypical items improved when treatment was applied. The treatment of the first category took a total of 28 weeks so the second category was not treated.

Participant 4 received treatment on atypical items first and showed a similar treatment effect to participant 2. Naming of trained items reached criterion in 6 weeks for vegetables and 9 weeks for birds, with generalised improvement in naming of more typical items.

All participants showed maintenance of gains 6 to 10 weeks post-therapy. As well as the reduction in errors and increasing number of correct responses, all participants showed significant changes in error type. All participants showed a decrease in the proportion of general responses and an increase in specific errors following treatment. The order of treatment had no effect on the nature of the errors produced. All participants showed some improvement in auditory comprehension on a general aphasia battery (WAB) and across semantic tests. Minimal change was seen on naming tests.

In summary, semantic therapy resulted in gains in the naming of trained items. Training of atypical examples resulted in gains for untrained typical items. No generalisation to atypical items was seen following training of typical items. The authors propose that the generalisation is present as the more complex items share features of the category prototype as well as disparate features, resulting in activation of both typical and atypical features. Training typical items resulted in repetitive activation of general features whereas training atypical items highlighted featural variation. Starting treatment with atypical items was also more time efficient as less treatment sessions were needed. The authors attribute the wider gains in semantic processing to the explicit judgement about semantic features that were both imageable and non-imageable. Gains are likely to be a consequence of therapy and there was no influence of time post-onset or severity of aphasia.

Other comments

This study does not consider whether gains are statistically significant. Wider gains on the semantic tests are considered as overall mean gain across tests. The study relates its finding to therapy studies in other domains, e.g. sentence processing (Thompson, 2003) where complexity has been shown to influence generalisation. The authors suggest that the findings challenge the long-standing clinical assumption that treatment should begin with simpler tasks and progress to more complex ones.

Study 6

Marshall, J., Pound, C., White-Thomson, M. and Pring, T. (1990). The use of picture/word matching tasks to assist word retrieval in aphasic patients. *Aphasiology, 4*, 167–184.

Focus of therapy: Semantics and access to the phonological output lexicon.

Target of therapy: Semantic/phonological.

Therapy approach: Reactivation.

Client details

Three clients are reported in this study. A further group study involving seven clients is also reported but not discussed here.

General information

RS was a 45-year-old company director who had a single left CVA. IS was a 76-year-old retired civil servant who also had a single left CVA. FW was a 76-year-old woman (no previous occupation reported) who had a left CVA and additional emotional distress which was treated unsuccessfully with anti-depressants.

Overall pattern of language impairments and preservations

RS presented with good functional comprehension. His comprehension of concrete words was retained but he had some difficulty understanding low-imageability words. He was within normal limits on the three-picture version of Pyramids and Palm Trees (Howard & Patterson, 1992). His speech was characterised by a marked anomia, particularly for verbs. In naming, he produced a lot of no responses. He was helped by phonemic cues but could not be induced to produce semantic errors by inappropriate cues. He was able to read aloud both high- and low-imageability words accurately. It is suggested that he was unable to access the phonological output lexicon from semantics.

   IS presented with functional comprehension in conversation and hesitant, non-fluent output with word-retrieval difficulties. She made errors in single-word, auditory and written comprehension tasks (selecting semantic distractors) and was outside normal limits on Pyramids and Palm Trees. In naming, she produced a combination of semantic and phonological errors. Her reading aloud of words was quite good but she was unable to read nonwords. It is suggested that her naming difficulties resulted from a combination of impaired semantics and impaired access to the phonological output lexicon.

FW had a similar pattern of performance to IS. She had impaired spoken and written comprehension alongside her naming difficulties. She produced both semantic and phonological errors in naming and was helped by phonemic and graphemic cues. Her reading aloud was not assessed. It is suggested FW had a primary semantic impairment and difficulty accessing the phonological output lexicon.

Time post-onset

RS was 10 months post-onset, IS was 3 months post-onset and FW was 5 months post-onset.

Therapy

Therapy aimed to improve picture-naming ability via access to semantic information. RS received 3 hours of therapy over 2 weeks, IS received 5 hours over 4 weeks (2½ hours each stage), while FW received 3½ hours over 3 weeks, which was then extended for a further three weeks. An item-specific therapy design was used to investigate the effects of therapy on treated and control items.

Task	**Semantic matching** Client presented with a drawing and five written words (target + four semantically related foils). Client required to read aloud all words and then select correct name.
Materials	Drawings of low-frequency words; written form of target and four semantically related distractors for each target. RS: 50 drawings; 25 treated items and 25 controls (matched for equal correctness). IS: 100 drawings; 50 treated in two consecutive stages of 25 words; 50 controls. FW: 50 drawings; 25 treated items and 25 controls (matched for equal correctness). Frequency higher than for other clients.
Hierarchy	None
Feedback on error	Not stated
Feedback if correct	Not stated

Outcome

RS showed significantly better naming of treated items than of untreated items immediately post-therapy. This was maintained 4 weeks later. IS also demonstrated a significant difference between improvements on both treated sets compared to performance on untreated items. Smaller gains, however, were seen with untreated items. No differences were seen between untreated and treated items for FW, although significant improvement was seen for both sets at the end of the second therapy period.

Both RS and IS made significant gains in treated items following semantic therapy despite having different underlying naming deficits, leading the authors to suggest that clients with both intact and impaired semantic systems respond to semantic therapy. Some uncertainty is highlighted by the authors, however, over the initial extent of semantic involvement in the case of IS based on the improvement seen on later testing. While RS showed no generalisation to untreated control items, small benefits were present for IS. FW made smaller gains than RS and IS; these were not treatment-specific but reflected significant overall improvement. FW's emotional state was considered to influence her performance.

Other comments

This study shows that a simple semantic task can benefit clients with different underlying impairments. Some generalisation of therapy effects is seen in IS's performance. The relationship is discussed between significant measurable gains following therapy and clinical worth, or impact to the client in a more generalised communicative sense.

Study 7

Pring, T., Hamilton, A., Harwood, A. and Macbride, L. (1993). Generalisation of naming after picture/word matching tasks: only items appearing in therapy benefit. *Aphasiology, 7*, 383–394.

Focus of therapy: Semantic system and access to the phonological output lexicon.

Target of therapy: Semantic/phonological.

Therapy approach: Reactivation.

Client details

Five clients were involved in the study.

General information

The participants had all had a CVA. No information is provided on the age, gender, employment history or specific neurological deficits of the clients.

Overall pattern of language impairments and preservations

All clients had predominantly expressive problems with prominent word-retrieval difficulties and only mild deficits in single-word comprehension, with performance on low-imageability words more impaired than on high-imageability words. Their sentence comprehension was functional in conversation. They all showed only mild impairments in the reading aloud of high-imageability words. Four of the clients, MM, DL, BR and PB, had a Broca's type aphasia. MM and PB had deficits in verb retrieval and sentence construction. DL and BR had less severe lexical and grammatical deficits. RH presented with severe naming difficulties and is described as having a 'recovered Wernicke's dysphasia'. In naming tasks, the clients produced omissions and circumlocutions, alongside some semantic errors.

Time post-onset

The clients were all more than 2 years post-onset. MM was more than 12 years, PB was more than 4 years, and DL, BR and RH were all between 2 and 3 years post-stroke.

Therapy

Therapy aimed to improve naming using semantic tasks. Therapy took place daily for 2 weeks. The initial session was supervised as were sessions when a new set of items was introduced. The client carried out all other sessions unsupervised and recorded responses on a stimulus sheet. Task 1 was used in the therapist-led sessions. Task 2 was carried out independently. An item-specific design was used to measure efficacy.

Task	*1. Word-to-picture matching* Read aloud four words (target + three distractors) and select one to match the picture.	*2. Picture-to-word matching* Read aloud three words and match each word to correct picture.
Materials	Seventy-two black-and-white line drawings in each of three semantic categories; corresponding written (typed) words.	As for Task 1. Six pictures presented each time (three targets and three distractors)
Hierarchy	None	None
Feedback on error	Not stated	Not stated
Feedback if correct	Not stated	Not stated

Outcome

For all clients, significant improvements were seen in treated items and related distractors following therapy; treated items, however, improved significantly more than related distractors. Related distractors improved significantly more than related unseen items, and unseen related items and controls did not differ. This study demonstrates that naming of items used in therapy tasks improved, with significant improvement seen both immediately following therapy and at follow-up 1 month later. Naming of treated items improved significantly more than all other items. No generalisation to unseen items occurred, regardless of whether these were in the same semantic domain or unrelated.

The tasks in this study combine phonological and semantic processing. The authors propose that the improved naming of the items used as related distractors is a consequence of the greater degree of semantic relatedness between items than in previous studies. The authors suggest semantic task that explicitly draw attention to the relatedness of items may be more effective.

Other comments

This study involved a small number of clients only and the clients were described as atypical therapy candidates with relatively mild problems. There was no clear level of deficit for each client.

Study 8

Hillis, A. (1989). Efficacy and generalisation of treatment for aphasic naming errors. *Archives of Physical Medicine and Rehabilitation, 70*, 632–636.

Focus of therapy: Semantic and phonological output lexicon.

Target of therapy: Semantic/orthographic.

Therapy approach: Reactivation.

Client details

Two participants are included in this study, referred to as Patient 1 and Patient 2.

General information

Patient 1 was a 51-year-old right-handed man who had a thromboembolic stroke. A CT scan revealed a large area infarct in the left frontoparietal area. Patient 2 was a 63-year-old right-handed woman who was seen following her second CVA. A mild CVA in the left occipital area 3 years previously had left no residual speech or language difficulties. Her second CVA occurred in her left parietal area.

Overall pattern of language impairments and preservations

Patient 1 had severely impaired comprehension; yes/no responses were at chance levels. Verbal output was characterised by a low volume and perseverative syllables. While his reading comprehension was also severely impaired, written word-to-picture matching was relatively good (27/32 items), with errors being predominantly semantic. Patient 2 had intact auditory and written comprehension in the presence of severely impaired output. Spoken output was fluent with a low use of content words. Naming and repetition were profoundly impaired; errors in repetition showed semantic involvement. She was unable to name items to definition, either verbally or in writing.

Baseline assessment of naming showed that both clients made similar semantic errors in spoken naming; Patient 1 made errors in comprehension and writing as well. The homogenous pattern of semantic errors seen in Patient 1 led the authors to propose a unitary impairment in word meaning (the semantic system). Patient 2's output-specific deficits were considered to suggest two separate sources of errors for spoken and written naming – that is, a breakdown in (a) the ability to retrieve the correct phonological representation for spoken naming and (b) the ability to hold the written representation of the word while it was being written.

Time post-onset

Patient 1 was 3 months post-onset at the beginning of the study, although language assessment occurred at 7 weeks post-onset. Patient 2 was 15 months post-onset from her second CVA.

Therapy

Therapy aimed to improve written and spoken naming of nouns and verbs. Patient 1 had 1 to 2 hours of therapy, 5 days per week. The total number of weeks was not reported.

The amount and length of therapy for Patient 2 was not reported. A multiple-baseline design across items was used to evaluate efficacy of therapy and generalisation across items and modalities.

Task	*Written naming* Client asked to write the name of the picture, provided with cues if unable.	*Spoken naming* Client asked to name the picture, provided with cues if unable.
Materials	Fifty black-and-white line drawings of familiar nouns and verbs. Ten nouns (stimulus Set 1) and ten verbs (stimulus Set 2) used which client could not name (spoken or written). Other items used as controls. Baseline measures of all items were obtained over five sessions. Both tasks were carried out on Set 1 (nouns) before progressing to Set 2 (verbs) when 90% accuracy in naming nouns in both modalities was achieved.	
Hierarchy	1. Picture stimulus (independent written name) 2. Scrambled anagram and two distractors 3. Scrambled anagram without distractors 4. Initial letter cue 5. Verbal name (correct writing to dictation) 6. Written name presented briefly (correct delayed reproduction)	1. Picture stimulus + What's this called? 2. Can you write the word? Now read it 3. What do you do with it? or What does he do? 4. Function provided 5. Written word provided 6. Verbal sentence completion 7. Initial phoneme cue
Feedback on error	Proceed through hierarchy until response is successful.	
Feedback if correct	When correct, present earlier cues in reverse order. Client encouraged to then say word but no feedback provided on spoken production.	

Outcome

For Patient 1, both spoken and written naming improved following treatment of written naming, with generalisation in both modalities to untrained nouns in the same semantic categories. There was no generalisation from nouns to verbs. Verbs subsequently treated also showed improvement. Gains were maintained nine sessions after therapy had discontinued (length of time unreported). For Patient 2, improvement was seen following both written and spoken naming therapy, although this improvement was specific to the trained modality – that is, the simultaneous gains seen in Patient 1 following written naming therapy were not evident with the second client. There was some minor evidence to suggest a trend towards generalisation to untrained stimuli in spoken naming only. No comment was made on maintenance.

While the therapy programme had positive results for both clients, the author highlights the finding that identical treatment can improve performance of different clients for different reasons. She proposed that the contrasting results are likely to be attributed to differences in the clients' underlying deficits. The generalisation of Patient 1's improvement was considered to relate to the impairment of word meaning, while the lack of generalisation in the case of Patient 2 reflected the impairment of two distinct processes.

Other comments

The cueing hierarchies within the study were devised by observing the sorts of stimuli that sometimes elicited a correct response.

Study 9

Hillis, A. E. and Caramazza, A. (1994). Theories of lexical processing and rehabilitation of lexical deficits. In M. J. Riddoch and G. W. Humphreys (Eds.), *Cognitive neuropsychology and cognitive rehabilitation*. London: Lawrence Erlbaum Associates Ltd.

Focus of therapy: Semantic system and phonological output lexicon. Some of the therapies targeted orthographic-to-phonological conversion and phonological-to-orthographic conversion (POC) (referred to in this book as phonological-to-graphemic conversion).

Target of therapy: Semantic/phonological and orthographic.

Therapy approach: Reactivation with KE, JJ and HW. Cognitive-relay strategies with HW, SJD and PM.

Client details

General information

HW was a 64-year-old woman who had experienced left parietal and occipital strokes. SJD was a 44-year-old woman with a left frontoparietal infarct. PM was a 50-year-old left-handed woman with a PhD. She had a left fronto-temporal-parietal and basal ganglia stroke. KE was a 51-year-old college-educated man with a left frontoparietal infarct. JJ was a 67-year-old retired corporate executive with a left temporal and basal ganglia stroke. HW, SJD, KE and JJ were all right-handed.

Overall pattern of language impairments and preservations

HW and SJD produced fluent, grammatical speech with some morphological errors. PM's speech was grammatical but hesitant and slightly slurred. HW, SJD and PM had normal comprehension of single words but difficulty in the auditory comprehension of syntactically complex, semantically reversible sentences. HW produced semantic errors in naming and oral reading. Naming of verbs was impaired compared with nouns. In naming tasks, she responded well to phonemic cues. SJD produced semantic errors in written naming and writing to dictation. Performance was worse for verbs than nouns, with semantic and/or morphological errors. She also omitted or substituted function words in writing. PM made semantic errors in both spoken and written tasks, although performance was more accurate in spoken tasks. She was unable to read or spell nonwords or any items she could not name. KE and JJ presented with impaired single-word comprehension and produced semantic errors in all tasks. KE's naming responded well to phonemic cueing. For JJ, oral reading and writing to dictation were more accurate than naming, suggesting intact orthographic and phonological conversion mechanisms. We would interpret JJ and KE as having semantic difficulties and HW, SJD and PM as having difficulties accessing phonology.

Time post-onset

All of the clients were at least 6 months post-onset. KE was 6 months and JJ was 9 months post-stroke. HW was two and a half, SJD was four and PM was 2 years post-stroke.

Therapy

Therapy had different aims for the different clients.

(1) For HW, therapy aimed to teach orthographic-to-phonological conversion (OPC) rules and to increase activation of items for naming. She received twelve sessions on oral reading to aid verb retrieval, five sessions each on action and object naming via naming therapy A (see below) and twenty sessions of naming therapy B.
(2) For SJD, the aim of therapy was to teach phonological-to-orthographic conversion (POC) rules as a self-monitoring strategy to block semantic errors. She received twelve sessions on POC cueing and forty-three sessions on self-monitoring.
(3) For PM, therapy aimed to teach both OPC and POC rules. She received five sessions on POC therapy before it was abandoned. She then received twelve sessions of OPC therapy.
(4) For KE and JJ, therapy aimed to increase activation of items for naming. KE had five sessions each on object and action naming via naming therapy A. JJ had twenty sessions of naming therapy B.

A multiple-baseline across-behaviours design was used to measure the effects of intervention on treated and untreated naming tasks.

Therapy 1: Teaching of conversion rules

Task	Teaching of POC rules (SJD, PM)	Teaching of OPC rules (HW, PM)
Materials	Thirty phonemes divided into three sets of ten. Each set worked on until 100% performance.	Three sets of phonemes.
Hierarchy	1. Point to the letter that makes the sound /phoneme/. 2. Think of a word that starts with /phoneme/. 3. A word that starts with /phoneme/ is (key word). Point to the letter that makes the first sound of (key word). 4. Write (key word). Point to the letter that makes the sound of (key word). 5. (Target letter) makes the first sound of (key word). /Phoneme/ is the first sound of (key word). (Target letter) makes the sound /phoneme/. Point to (target letter). e.g. B makes the first sound of 'baby'. /b/ is the first sound of 'baby'. B makes the sound /b/. Point to B).	Not specified – assumed to be similar to that of POC therapy.
Feedback	Feedback not stated.	

Therapy 2: Naming therapy

Task	Oral reading of verbs to facilitate oral naming (HW)	Naming therapy A Picture naming using a cueing hierarchy (HW, KE)	Naming therapy B Oral reading and word-to-picture matching (HW, JJ) Word-to-picture matching involved identifying correct picture from set of 40.
Materials	Forty pictures depicting transitive verbs, randomly divided into two sets A and B. When 100% performance was obtained on Set A, Set B was targeted.	Pictures of 50 objects and ten actions (items not given). When 100% performance was obtained on Set A, Set B was targeted.	Set of 40 printed words and pictures of those 40 items (items not given), divided randomly into two sets for ach session, one to the oral reading treatment and one to the word/picture matching treatment.
Hierarchy	None	Cueing hierarchy: a. sentence completion b. initial phoneme c. word itself as a spoken model When 90% performance obtained on nouns, the verb set was targeted in the same way.	None
Feedback	If unable to read word, phonemic cueing or modelling used until correct response elicited.		If unable to read word, phonemic cueing was used. In word-to-picture matching, items that were initially incorrect were corrected and repeated after intervening items, until a correct response was obtained.

Outcome

The results are set out here sequentially according to client, including information on improvements across tasks and stimuli, functional generalisation and proposed mechanisms of change.

Client HW

HW was unable to learn OPC procedures sufficiently to aid oral production. Naming performance improved on the treated verbs (from 30% to 90% correct). In response to naming therapy A, oral naming of treated items improved (nouns from 50% to 80%, verbs from 10% to 70%). Following naming therapy B, oral reading improved naming of some items. Word-to-picture matching did not show improvement. With respect to generalised improvement across tasks and stimuli, HW was unable to blend those phonemes she could translate (see Nickels, 1992, for similar results). Verb naming improved but did not generalise to untreated items. Following therapy A, there was no generalisation to untreated items. Following therapy B, this was not tested. When considering generalised impact on daily living, those OPC rules learned by HW did not cue retrieval of phonological form (cf. Nickels, 1992). This was not stated for other treatments. The proposed mechanism of change for HW was the lowering of threshold activation for treated verb items by increasing the frequency of production. With therapy A and B, this was probably as for verb therapy above, again lowering the threshold of activation of phonological representations, because errors were hypothesised to arise at the phonological output level. The word-to-picture matching treatment was considered unsuccessful because errors were not due to a semantic level deficit.

Client SJD

SJD learned POC rules for targeted phonemes. She improved to 100% phoneme-to-grapheme translation. SJD showed a generalised effect whereby performance increased on all words. Functionally, the quantity and accuracy of written verb production in narrative improved (this was monitored each session during a paragraph-writing task). With respect to a proposed mechanism of therapy, SJD's ability to convert phonology to orthography was considered to 'block' semantic paragraphias. The ability to convert phonology to appropriate graphemes might cue access to the orthographic representation for output.

Client PM

PM was unable to learn POC rules but OPC therapy was successful. PM improved to 60% phoneme-to-grapheme translation before ceasing therapy. Grapheme-to-phoneme translation improved from about 20–30% to around 90%. PM's spelling improved only on specifically trained verbs (using a cueing hierarchy unstated). Grapheme-to-phoneme conversion skills allowed PM to produce phonemes to written words and hence cue accurate oral reading. Oral reading of 144 untrained items improved from 76% to 89%; however, oral naming did not improve. No functional improvement was seen with PM. Her OPC skills did not facilitate naming, because she could not retrieve the spellings of words she could not name. PM's lack of success on POC procedures might be due to differences in type or severity of deficit, even though this was postulated to be at the same locus as SJD. Success in improved reading through OPC procedures could be due to any of the many processes involved in the conversion, and it is suggested that the contrast with the lack of success in HW might be due to a difference in the precise component that is affected in the deficit or in the level of severity.

Client KE

KE improved his oral naming of all treated items from 10 to 100%. Improvement on object naming generalised to untreated items within the same semantic category. Improvement in oral naming also generalised to written naming of the same items and those of the same semantic category. Functional improvements were not stated. With KE, cueing might have provided additional activation of the target, making it available for further processing (this does not explain generalisation to other items).

Client JJ

JJ's oral reading therapy did not improve naming performance. Word-to-picture matching did, however, improve naming. As with HW, JJ's word-to-picture matching resulted in cumulative facilitation in naming; on average, one to two previously misnamed pictures were named correctly in the session following treatment. Generalisation was not tested with JJ. As with KE, functional improvements were also not stated. For JJ, teaching distinctions (or activating features that distinguish) between related items was the proposed mechanism of therapy because errors arise at the semantic level. Oral reading treatment was unsuccessful because errors arise before the phonological output level.

Other comments

This is a complex study that examined the efficacy of a variety of therapy techniques. The authors suggest that if the deficit is semantic, word-to-picture matching therapy can help, but not if the deficit is only at the phonological output level (note that semantic errors are not necessarily due to a semantic deficit). This is in contrast to many studies that have shown improvements in naming performance for clients with phonological output difficulties, following word-to-picture matching tasks and other semantic tasks (e.g. Marshall *et al.*, 1990; Le Dorze *et al.*, 1994; see discussion in Nickels, 2002b). A suggested improvement to the study would be to check for generalisation to untreated items after word-to-picture matching therapy.

Study 10

Best, W., Howard, D., Bruce, C. and Gatehouse, C. (1997). Cueing the words: A single case study of treatments for anomia. *Neuropsychological Rehabilitation, 7(2)*, 105–141.

Focus of therapy: Semantics and access to phonological output lexicon.

Target of therapy: Semantic and orthographic.

Therapy approach: Reactivation.

Client details

General information

JOW was a 72-year-old man. He had previously run his own business. He had a left hemisphere stroke. No CT scan information was available.

Overall pattern of language impairments and preservations

JOW presented with good comprehension in conversation. He had anomic aphasia with fluent speech interrupted by frequent word-finding difficulties. On testing, he was within normal limits on a variety of auditory input tasks. He had good semantic processing in all tasks involving pictures and concrete words. His comprehension of abstract words in tasks not involving pictures showed some impairment. Picture naming was severely impaired. Naming accuracy was influenced by operativity and imageability. He produced a lot of non-specific lead in comments, no response errors and perseverative errors. His perseverative errors often shared some meaning with the target word. JOW showed some benefit from initial phoneme cues, more benefit from additional phonology and the most benefit from written letter cues. His repetition was good. His reading aloud was impaired but significantly better than his naming; reading of high-imageability words was better than reading of low-imageability words. His written naming was poor with a high proportion of no response errors and did not differ significantly from his spoken naming. JOW was described as having a mild impairment at the lexical semantic level in production. Good performance in picture semantics suggested his problem was specific to lexical meaning. There is extensive discussion of the evidence supporting this diagnosis.

Time post-onset

JOW was more than 2 years post-stroke at the time of the study.

Therapy

Therapy took place over a period of 10 months. Treatment aimed to improve word retrieval. Initially a pilot study looked at the impact of eight tasks, each carried out independently by JOW for a week. Tasks consisted of a semantic task, a written lexical task (written picture naming and copying), reading aloud, a spoken lexical task (spoken naming and reading aloud), a semantic and output task, delayed copying and written naming. The pilot study showed no benefit from the majority of tasks but JOW did show some item-specific improvement following the written lexical treatment. Following the pilot study, two treatment studies were carried out. The first study contrasted semantic and lexical treatments. The second used a cueing aid (as described by Bruce & Howard, 1987). Naming was assessed pre-therapy, after each phase of therapy and at follow-up. Word retrieval in composite picture description and during the description of a room was also assessed as well as performance on control tasks. In study 1, each phase of treatment was carried out for 3 weeks with six attempts at each target item. In study 2, treatment took place once a week for 5 weeks for about an hour.

	Study 1		Study 2
Task	**Lexical therapy** Presented with picture and asked to write name.	**Semantic therapy** Picture presented with four semantically related written words. Underline target word and copy.	**Cueing aid therapy** Picture naming with cueing aid.
Materials	Seventy-two pictures. Two sets of 36, one for lexical therapy and one for semantic therapy.		Fifty hard to name items for therapy. Fifty control items. Fifty easy to name items as fillers.

Hierarchy	None	None	1. Press initial letter. If failed, go to four. 2. Encourage repetition of cue. 3. Name picture. If failed, go to seven. 4. Therapist points to three letters for JOW to select correct one. 5. Encourage repetition of cue. 6. Name picture. If failed, go to seven. 7. Present name for repetition.
Feedback on error	Not stated	Not stated	As above
Feedback if correct	Not stated	Not stated	Not stated

Outcome

Study 1

In contrast to the pilot study, JOW's spoken naming did not benefit from the lexical treatment. The semantic tasks resulted in significant improvement in spoken naming of both treated and untreated items. Gains were not, however, maintained 1 month later. The authors explore differences between JOW's written responses in the pilot and main studies. They conclude that in the pilot phase JOW was writing the words via the semantic system, whereas in the main study, he was just copying the words. In the pilot study, the effects of treatment may have disappeared by the time of reassessment.

Study 2

During treatment, the number of items JOW named after cueing increased dramatically. Following therapy, JOW's naming of treated items, filler items and control items improved significantly. There was no difference between naming with the aid and naming without the aid. Gains were maintained at 5 weeks and 15 months post-treatment. Following therapy, there was an increase in the number of content words used during picture description and naïve listeners rated his ability to find the words and transmit the message higher post-therapy. There was no change on the control tasks and on written naming. JOW did improve in his ability to do letter sound conversion. The authors suggest the aid was not a prosthesis to help word retrieval but improved his own ability to find the words. Treatment did not improve JOW's access to initial letters but rather the initial letter knowledge he had was being used in spoken word production. The authors discuss how treatment with the aid could have improved spoken naming. JOW did not use letter to sound conversion as a conscious strategy to aid word finding. The aid could have facilitated the use of sub-lexical cues or facilitated the lexical retrieval of a set of items beginning with the letters used in therapy. The authors suggest either hypothesis relies on the cascading of activation within the processing model, with the summation of information facilitating naming.

Other comments

The authors highlight the importance of looking at how tasks are carried out, the information available during tasks and the responses during treatment when considering therapy gains.

The study is an excellent example of using the response to therapy to contribute to theoretical discussion about models of language processing.

Study 11

Hickin, J., Best, W., Herbert, R., Howard, D. and Osborne, F. (2002). Phonological therapy for word-finding difficulties: a re-evaluation. *Aphasiology, 16*, 981–999.

Focus of therapy: Participants with semantic and/or phonological difficulties (access to phonological output lexicon or phonological output lexicon).

Target of therapy: Phonological.

Therapy approach: Reactivation.

Client details

Eight participants were included in the study.

General information

Participants were between 38 and 77 years old and had had a single left hemisphere CVA. Limited background information was provided.

Overall pattern of language impairments and preservations

Of the eight participants, four presented with anomic, three with Broca's and one with mixed/Wernicke's type of aphasia. All presented with word-finding difficulties as a significant aspect of their aphasia. None had severe comprehension difficulties or verbal dyspraxia. Participants were tested on a wide range of single-word assessments investigating spoken and written comprehension, spoken and written naming, reading and repetition and tests of auditory discrimination and short-term memory. Participants varied in the severity of their naming difficulties and the extent to which semantic and phonological impairments contributed to their naming difficulties.

Time post-onset

Participants were between 2 and 8 years post-onset.

Therapy

Therapy aimed to improve picture naming via phonological and orthographic cueing. The effect of giving a choice of cues on naming success was evaluated. This study forms part of a larger study; only the first treatment phase is reported in this paper. Treatment sessions were once per week over the 8 weeks and lasted between 1 and 1½ hours. A repeated, multiple-baseline therapy design was used; clients were assessed on two occasions before therapy and once after therapy.

Task	Picture naming with phonological cueing	Picture naming with orthographic cueing
Materials	One hundred words (drawn from assessment of 200) divided into two sets of 50 words matched for baseline naming accuracy. Fifty words were used for phonological cueing and 50 words used for orthographic cueing. Twenty additional client-selected (high functional impact) words were orthographically cued. All 120 items were presented once per session, either phonological cued words followed by orthographic cued words, or vice versa.	
Hierarchy	Cueing hierarchy: a) initial phoneme of the target word (with schwa) and an unrelated distractor b) the first syllable of target and distractor c) the whole word of target and distractor d) repetition of the target word Number of distractors increased from one (first two sessions) to two (second two sessions) to three (final four sessions).	Cueing hierarchy: a) initial grapheme of the target word and an unrelated distractor b) the first syllable written of target and distractor c) the whole word written of target and distractor d) repetition of the target word Number of distractors increased from one (first two sessions) to two (second two sessions) to three (final four sessions).
Feedback on error	Proceed through hierarchy until response is successful.	Proceed through hierarchy until response is successful.
Feedback if correct	Not stated	Not stated

Outcome

Significant improvement in spoken naming of the original 200 items was found in seven of the eight clients. Five of the clients who showed overall improvement improved significantly more on treated items than untreated items. Of these five clients, one client improved significantly on untreated items, suggesting some generalisation, while the other four clients showed item-specific improvement. The two other clients who improved showed no significant difference between treated and untreated items. There were no significant differences between the effects of phonological and orthographic treatment for any participant, although one participant showed a non-significant trend towards benefiting more from phonological cues. Seven clients showed some improvement in naming self-selected words with the change for three reaching statistical significance. Individual responses to therapy are discussed in the light of pre-therapy assessment findings.

The authors suggest that the effectiveness of the different cueing approaches may be due to the client being required to make a choice at each stage. Against this is their finding that in the facilitation study there was no effect of making a choice of cue. The study design does not, however, exclude whether this may simply be due to repeated practice. The item-specific benefits of phonological therapy seen in previous studies are reinforced by this study and are considered to result from activation of 'individual mappings from semantics to phonological representations'.

Other comments

The authors discuss the relationship between facilitation and treatment in relation to the eight clients and show that short-term benefits may predict response to therapy. The facilitation part of the study is reported in Best *et al.* (2002). The second treatment phase is reported in Herbert *et al.* (2003).

Study 12

Herbert, R., Best, W., Hickin, J., Howard, D. and Osbourne, F. (2003). Combining lexical and interactional approaches to therapy for word-finding deficits in aphasia. *Aphasiology, 17(12)*, 1163–1186.

Focus of therapy: Participants with semantic and/or phonological difficulties (access to phonological output lexicon or phonological output lexicon).

Target of therapy: Semantic/phonological.

Therapy approach: Reactivation.

Client details

Six participants were included in this study. Participants were involved in a larger study reported in Best *et al.* (2002) and Hickin *et al.* (2002).

General information

Six clients aged 38–77 years old were involved in this study. All had had a single left hemisphere CVA.

Overall pattern of language impairments and preservations

The people with aphasia all had prominent word-finding difficulties. Participants were assessed on a range of tests investigating semantic and phonological processing. Three participants had non-fluent Broca's aphasia, one with a phonological naming impairment, one with a semantic impairment and one with mixed semantic–phonological difficulties. Two participants presented with fluent anomic aphasia, with an impairment in the mapping between semantics and phonology (access to the phonological output lexicon). The final participant had Wernicke's aphasia and had a semantic impairment. Participants varied in the severity of the anomia and overall aphasia.

Time post-onset

Participants were between 3 and 8 years post-onset at the time of the study.

Therapy

Participants had already completed an initial phase of therapy involving phonological and orthographic cues reported in Hickin *et al.* (2002). The second phase of therapy aimed to enable participants to use treated words in tasks approximating to conversation. Therapy took place once a week for a total of 8 weeks, with each session lasting 1 to 2 hours. A repeated multiple design with control task design was used to evaluate efficacy. Performance was assessed twice pre-therapy, after Phase 1, after Phase 2 and 8 weeks post-therapy.

Task	Interactional therapy
Materials	One hundred words, 50 which had received therapy in Phase 1 and 50 untreated in Phase 1. Words selected for functional relevance. Twenty additional client-selected words. Control set of 100 words of similar composition. Treated words sorted into conversational categories. Each treated item presented in file with picture and progressive orthographic cues.
Hierarchy	Sessions 1 and 2: Naming to definition or request game with picture and orthographic cues to elicit target. Sessions 3 and 4: Production of lists related to topics e.g. shopping, family, holiday. Sessions 5 to 8: Conversations around self-selected topics.
Feedback on error	Facilitation of conversation
Feedback if correct	Therapist response within conversation

Within sessions, participants had access to picture and orthographic cues and relevant items were reviewed prior to conversation but there was no pressure to produce the word. In sessions, participants were not exposed to all 120 items.

Outcome

To allow comparison with the current therapy, the results of Phase 1 therapy were summarised. One participant showed no gains during Phase 1. Five participants made significant gains in picture naming; the gains of four participants were item specific. One participant showed generalisation with significant improvement in both treated and untreated items.

Following Phase 2, the impact of therapy was assessed for Treated Treated (TT) items (items that were treated in both Phase 1 and 2) and Untreated Treated (UT) items (items treated only in Phase 2). Five participants showed significant improvements in the UT set. One participant also showed significant gains in the TT set. There was no change in the items not treated in Phase 2.

Participants were also assessed in a task assessing noun production in everyday communication with performance scored in terms of target achieved and the production of a communicatively appropriate response. There was no change in the production of target words for any participant. One participant showed an improvement in the number of communicatively appropriate responses. Participants were also asked their views about communication via a questionnaire. The questionnaire showed considerable variability, indicating possible poor test–re-test reliability. There was no change on the control tasks.

Improvement is likely to be due to therapy as participants were not in spontaneous recovery and there was no change on the control tasks. For the majority of participants, therapy effects were specific to treated items.

The interactional therapy encouraged the communicative use of the target words and participants were not exposed to all words in each session. Nevertheless, therapy resulted in specific gains in picture naming for five of the six participants. One participant who did not respond to Phase 1 therapy benefited from Phase 2, enjoying the interaction and benefiting from the reduced constraint within the conversation. Another participant showed the opposite pattern, improving during the structured phase but finding the lexical search required in Phase 2 more problematic. Interactional therapy resulted in no additional gains for TT items for four of the participants benefiting from the treatment probably as they had previously reached ceiling performance for each participant. The authors discuss the notion of ceiling effects in treatment sets, suggesting the ceiling relates to the nature of their word-finding deficit and variables affecting naming and that improvement in some items may result in deterioration in other items.

Other comments

The authors question the use of the communicative views questionnaire as an outcome measure, considering the variability in response. The authors also provide some cautionary notes regarding the use of personal words.

Study 13

Best, W., Greenwood, A., Grassly, J. and Hickin, J. (2008). Bridging the gap: can impairment-based therapy for anomia have an impact at the psycho-social level? *International Journal of Language and Communication Disorders, 43(4)*, 390–407.

Focus of therapy: Participants with semantic and/or phonological difficulties (access to phonological output lexicon or phonological output lexicon).

Target of therapy: Phonological.

Therapy approach: Reactivation.

Client details

The study involved eight participants.

General information

Participants included three men and five women, aged between 42 and 75 years. Some of the participants were working at the time of their CVA, with a variety of occupations. Brief information was provided about their conversational partners and major life events that occurred during the period of the study.

Overall pattern of language impairments and preservations

Five of the participants presented with non-fluent aphasia and three presented with fluent aphasia. They all had word-finding difficulties that formed a significant part of their aphasia. They varied in the severity of their naming difficulty and overall aphasia. Participants were assessed on a range of language measures; results of key tests of semantic and phonological processing were provided but were not discussed.

Time post-onset

Participants were between 1 and 7 years post-onset at the time of the study.

Therapy

Therapy aimed to improve word finding and evaluate the impact of therapy on the individual's perception of their everyday communication. The Communication Disability Profile (CDP) (Swinburn & Byng, 2006) was used to evaluate each individual's activity, social participation, external influences on communication and emotional consequences. A multiple repeated baseline with control task design was used to monitor efficacy, with a particular focus in this study on the relationship between picture naming and the activity section of the CDP. Performance was assessed twice prior to therapy, after each phase of therapy and at 8 weeks follow-up. There were two phases of therapy which each consisted of 8 weekly sessions. Phase 1 of therapy was cueing therapy and was similar to that reported in Hickin *et al.* (2002, p155) although combined orthographic and phonological cues were used. Phase 2 of therapy centred around structured exchanges and elicitation of items in conversation and was similar to that reported in Herbert *et al.* (2003, p157). Detailed descriptions of the format and outcome of these therapies can be found in the relevant reviews.

Outcome

One participant died after the second phase of therapy so follow-up data was not available. Most participants (six) showed some change during the pre-therapy baselines suggesting that focused assessment may improve word retrieval; change was, however, smaller than that seen during therapy. There was significant change in the naming of treated items following cueing therapy for all eight participants. There was very little change in naming following the second (interactional) phase of therapy. Gains in naming performance were maintained at the follow-up assessment.

The quantitative scores from the CDP and the relationship between participants' scores on the activity section and naming performance were considered. There was a strong correlation between participant's scores on the activity section of the CDP and naming during the two baseline assessments and there was a significant change in the activity ratings over the course of the study. With regard to the relationship between naming and a participant's activity, there was a significant correlation at baseline. The relationship between change in word finding and the change in CDP activity rating approached significance across the group but varied patterns of performance were seen across participants. At the final assessment, all seven participants tested viewed ease of participation as greater and four showed a change in a positive direction with respect to emotional consequences.

The study replicated findings that cueing therapy resulted in significant gains in the naming of treated items that were maintained at follow-up. Contrary to findings by Herbert *et al.* (2003), interactional therapy resulted in minimal gains. The strong relationship between changes in naming and activity ratings suggest that word-retrieval therapy can impact on activity. The authors, however, discuss the complex relationship between language impairment and CDP ratings, with consideration of different communication strategies, support available and other life events.

Other comments

This study has a more limited focus on individual language performance and the impact of therapy. The authors discuss that the CDP provides a rich source of information about individual's views about their aphasia and its impact. The study used only the quantitative information but the qualitative information may be important in planning therapy and formulating goals and for interpreting the changes reported.

One of the participants, TE, is described in more depth in Greenwood *et al.* (2012). As the therapy protocol is set out above, the later study is not reviewed in detail in this volume but the reader is referred to Greenwood *et al.* (2012) for a focused discussion of TE. TE presented with fluent anomic aphasia, with good semantic processing and a possible deficit in mapping semantics to phonology and in phonological assembly. TE was presented as a single case study as he demonstrated generalisation in naming untreated items and positive changes on broader measures of word retrieval in connected speech. The authors describe his performance at baseline, after each phase of therapy and at follow-up, followed by detailed consideration of how therapy might have worked, exploring his overall profile of performance and the nature of the therapy task. Accounts related to semantic processing and accessing phonological forms from semantic representations were rejected. The authors favour an account that intervention strengthened the connections between phonemes and lexical items via bidirectional connections. They recognise however, that there was no evidence to rule out some strengthening of orthographic-to-phonological connections, improvement in post-lexical phonological assembly or changes at more than one level of processing.

Study 14

Fillingham, J.K., Sage, K. and Lambon Ralph, M.A. (2006). The treatment of anomia using errorless learning. *Neuropsyhological Rehabilitation, 16(2)*, 129–154.

Focus of therapy: Participants with semantic, phonological and mixed semantic–phonological deficits.

Target of therapy: Phonological.

Therapy approach: Reactivation.

Client details

The study included eleven participants.

General information

The participants included two women and nine men, aged between 40 and 80 years. They had an acquired neurological deficit after left hemisphere damage, with lesion site varying across participants. They had a variety of employment histories.

Overall pattern of language impairments and preservations

Participants all presented with anomia and were able to repeat and/or read aloud with a high degree of accuracy. Three participants were described as having mild aphasia with the other participants presenting with more severe aphasia of a variety of types. Participants were assessed on a range of language tests including picture naming, reading and repetition of words and nonwords and spoken and written word comprehension. In addition, neuropsychological assessments were carried out investigating episodic memory for verbal and non-verbal stimuli, non-verbal problem-solving and executive function, auditory working memory and attention. Participants varied in the severity of their anomia, the extent to which semantic and/or phonological impairments contributed to their naming difficulties and the co-occurrence of cognitive deficits.

Time post-onset

All participants were at least 6 months post-onset at the time of the study.

Therapy

Therapy aimed to improve the anomia, contrasting the effects of errorless and errorful learning. A multiple-baseline design was used across time periods with performance on items treated with errorless therapy, items treated with errorful therapy and control items compared. The initial baseline was repeated three times and then naming was assessed after the initial phase of errorless therapy, after the second phase of errorful therapy and at 5 weeks after each therapy phase. Each therapy phase consisted of ten sessions, given twice weekly for 5 weeks. The treated items were cycled through three times in each session.

Task	*1. Errorless therapy*	*2. Errorful therapy*
Materials	Three sets of 30 nouns, one for errorless, one for errorful and control set. Sets matched for accuracy, word frequency, number of phonemes and number of syllables.	
Hierarchy	Picture plus written and spoken name given with a request to repeat twice initially, listen again, then three more times.	1. Picture plus first grapheme and phoneme 2. Two graphemes and phonemes (first syllable if multisyllabic) 3. Whole word in spoken and written form and person asked to repeat
Feedback on error	Given additional repetition	Move to next cue
Feedback if correct	Not stated	Not stated

As participants were able to repeat with a high degree of accuracy, it was assumed that there would be minimal errors in the errorless therapy.

Outcome

Therapy outcome was reported for each phase of therapy, at follow-up and the overall effect of therapy (comparison of results at follow-up with baseline accuracy), with a comparison of the effects of errorless and errorful learning. Two of the participants showed no significant therapy effect, with no gains following either therapy. Eight participants showed a significant and equal effect of both therapies on trained words. One participant showed a significant difference in favour of errorful over errorless treatment immediately post-therapy. Minimal generalisation was seen to untreated items but gains did reach significance at a particular time period following different therapies for some participants. At follow-up, there was a significant long-term improvement for nine participants, five who showed benefit from both therapy types and four who demonstrated long-term gains only for items treated with errorful therapy. There was a significant difference favouring errorful over errorless items for two participants.

The study investigated the relationship between gains immediately post-therapy and at follow-up and baseline language and cognitive performance. None of the language measures correlated with therapy outcome. Overall the therapy effect immediately post-therapy and at follow-up was significantly correlated to performance on topographical and word sub-tests of the Camden Memory Test, Wisconsin Card Sorting Test, the three word version of Pyramids and Palm Trees and participants' self rating of performance. People who responded better to therapy had better recognition memory, executive function and self-monitoring skills. The two participants who showed a significant benefit for errorful learning had the strongest working and recall memory and attention.

Significant improvements in naming were seen for nine participants. Two participants showed a greater benefit from errorful therapy. No participants showed an advantage for errorless over errorful. Gains are likely to be due to therapy due to stable baseline performance. Therapy outcome was not related to initial language performance. The authors discuss the potential role of cognitive skills in therapy.

Other comments

Although errorless and errorful therapies were equally effective for most of the participants, the authors report that all participants preferred errorless learning as they found it more rewarding and less frustrating. Following the original study (although later publication), two additional studies were carried out involving some of the same participants. Fillingham *et al.* (2005a) investigated the effect of removing feedback from training, with slight modifications to the format of the errorful therapy and reduced naming attempts for each item. The study replicated the finding that errorful and errorless therapy were equally effective. There was no effect of removing feedback. Some of the participants learned fewer items in this study, possibly due to a reduced naming of naming attempts. A third study (Fillingham *et al.*, 2005b) was, therefore, carried out to investigate the influence of number of naming attempts. This study used therapy without feedback but increased the naming attempts in line with the original study. Percentage improvement in the third study was in line with the original study, suggesting the increased number of naming attempts resulted in greater success in learning the item. Across both replications, the status of participants' language skills did not predict therapy outcome; executive problem-solving skills and recognition memory predicted naming improvement. The data from the series of studies was used in a study examining the relationship between gain after anomia therapy and performance on language and cognitive tasks (Lambon Ralph *et al.*, 2010). Two overarching factors were found to predict therapy gains:

(1) a cognitive factor combining attention, executive function and visuo–spatial memory and (2) a phonological factor resulting from reading aloud and repetition. Factors were independent predictors of both immediate and longer term therapy gains. Pre-treatment naming ability also predicted gain following anomia therapy.

Study 15

Leonard, C., Rochon, E. and Laird, L. (2008) Treating naming impairments in aphasia: Findings from a phonological components analysis treatment. *Aphasiology, 22(9)*, 923–947.

Focus of therapy: Participants with semantic, phonological and mixed semantic–phonological deficits.

Target of therapy: Phonological.

Therapy approach: Reactivation.

Client details

The study included ten participants.

General information

The participants included six men and four women, aged between 52 and 73 years, with a mean education level of 13.9 years. They were right-handed, English speakers who had had a single left hemisphere CVA. The participants had normal visual perceptual abilities and eight of the ten participants were within normal limits for hearing.

Overall pattern of language impairments and preservations

Of the ten participants, six had Broca's aphasia, two had anomic aphasia, one had mixed non-fluent aphasia and one had Wernicke's aphasia. At screening, they had to be less than 75% accurate in naming. Participants were assessed on a range of tests investigating semantic and phonological processing. Participants varied in the severity of the naming impairment and the extent to which semantic and/or phonological impairments contributed to their anomia.

Time post-onset

Participants ranged from 1½ to 17 years post-onset.

Therapy

The study investigated the use of phonological component analysis (PCA) to improve naming. A single subject multiple-baseline across-behaviours design was used. Probes of naming performance were carried out three times before therapy. Treated items were probed every second session during therapy; untreated items were proved every third session. Therapy took place 3 times per week for approximately an hour. Three lists of items were treated, with criterion for moving to the next list set at 80% correct over two consecutive sessions or a total of fifteen sessions. Maintenance of previously treated items was probed every three sessions.

Task	**Phonological component analysis**
	Picture placed in centre of feature analysis chart and client attempts to name the picture. Guided verbalisation of five phonological features: rhyme, first sound, first sound associate, final sound and number of syllables. Features written down. After generation of features, client asked to name target again. Clinician reviews features and client asked to name target again.
Materials	Thirty coloured photographs of items the client had been unable to name on at least 2/3 occasions. Divided into three lists of ten. Lists equated for category, frequency and number of syllables.
Hierarchy	None
Feedback on error	If unable to generate features, participant asked to choose from a list of three. If unable to name after feature generation or review, given correct response and asked to repeat.
Feedback if correct	Positive feedback

Outcome

Initial baseline performance was stable for eight of the ten participants. Two participants showed some variability. Visual analysis of the data suggested that six of the ten participants demonstrated robust treatment effects on all three lists. One participant showed clear treatment effects for two lists. There was some level of maintenance at 1 month follow-up. The treatment effect for these participants was confirmed by looking at effect size and the standard deviation method, with performance exceeding two standard deviations above the mean on two consecutive occasions reflecting improvement. Three participants did not make any gains. Three of the seven participants with a treatment effect showed generalisation to untreated items shown by significant gains on an unrelated naming test. Significant correlations were found between response to treatment and scores on the initial naming test and oral reading test. Gains in treatment were greatest for participants with better oral reading and less severe initial naming impairments. There were trends indicating a positive relationship between treatment response and repetition and a negative relationship between treatment response and the presence of a semantic deficit.

The authors suggest the treatment approach was effective with seven of the ten participants showing notable improvements in the naming of treated items. The long lasting effects of phonological treatment were attributed to the active engagement of participants in therapy, with people who benefited more from therapy generating more features independently. Generalisation to untreated items was seen for three participants. The authors suggest this generalisation may be due to spreading activation within the phonological system (similar to spreading activation within the semantic system following semantic feature analysis) or the development of a strategy. The authors explore potential factors influencing the response to treatment including initial severity of impairment, underlying phonological abilities, presence of a semantic impairment and aphasia type.

Other comments

PCA was modelled on semantic feature analysis (SFA) therapy designed for remediation of semantic naming deficits. The participant whose deficits were more phonologically based compared to other participants did not benefit from PCA therapy. The authors attribute this lack of improvement to the severity of her naming impairment and the presence of other deficits.

Study 16

DeDe, G., Parris, D. and Waters, G. (2003). Teaching self-cues: A treatment approach for verbal naming. *Aphasiology, 17(5)*, 465–480.

Focus of therapy: Semantic system and phonological output lexicon (and AOS).

Target of therapy: Orthographic and phonological.

Therapy approach: Cognitive relay.

Client details

General information

LN was a 49-year-old man who had a stroke in the territory of the left middle cerebral artery with a subsequent haemorrhage in the left basal ganglia. He was a college graduate who worked as vice president of a large restaurant chain.

Overall pattern of language impairments and preservations

LN's comprehension was functional in conversation. On testing, his spoken comprehension of concrete words was intact. Abstract word comprehension and complex sentence comprehension was impaired. Written comprehension was more impaired than spoken, with mildly impaired lexical decision and difficulties accessing meaning, particularly for morphologically complex words. Spoken production was non-fluent and was characterised by severe anomia, articulatory groping, inconsistent phonemic substitutions and prolongation errors. Word length and frequency did not impact on naming performance. He was unable to produce the first sound of words but could often identify the first letter from a choice of three. Word and nonword repetition was a relative strength. LN was unable to write words to dictation or in written naming but was often able to write the first letter. The authors suggest that LN had a mild semantic impairment with additional deficits in the visual input lexicon. His oral and written production was severely impaired but his ability to access partial information about written words was stronger than accessing phonological information. His aphasia was accompanied by a moderate apraxia of speech.

Time post-onset

LN was 4 years post-onset at the time of the study.

Therapy

Therapy aimed to train LN to cue himself to produce verbal names by using a combination of written naming and tactile cues. It was hypothesised that the stronger access to lexical information in the written modality would support spoken production and that the tactile cues would support the apraxia of speech. Tactile cues associated specific phonemes with hand shapes and positions. The authors predicted gains in treated words with generalisation to words beginning with targeted phonemes. A multiple, repeated baseline design was used, with repeated probes of trained and control items, generalisation probes starting with the same phonemes and reassessment of verbal and written naming post-therapy. Treatment took place once per week for 13 weeks. The 24 treatment items were targeted each once per session in sessions lasting approximately an hour. A video version of the treatment programme was made to facilitate more intensive input. LN used the home video four to five times per week. At the end of the study, LN used the video at home for half of the trained items, with maintenance evaluated 6 weeks post-therapy. During the period of therapy, LN also participated in 1 hour of group treatment focused on counselling and multi-modality communication.

Each of the stages of the modified cueing hierarchy was used for each item.

Task	Stage 1: Written Naming	Stage 2: Tactile Cues	Stage 3: Phonological Cues
Materials	Forty-eight words divided into 24 trained words beginning with /d f t k/ and 24 control words beginning with /b p s g/. Three one syllable and three two syllable words beginning with each phoneme. Target and control sets matched for word frequency. Words were chosen to be functionally useful and were depicted in colour photographs.		
Hierarchy	1. Presentation of picture and asked to write name 2. Choice of first letters 3. Mix of letters/ blanks and asked to complete 4. Clinician writes word for copying	Initial teaching of tactile cues. 1. Produce cue independently 2. Choice of pictures depicting four cues 3. Clinician models cue	1. Presentation of picture and asked to verbally name 2. Phonological cue (first sound or syllable) 3. Clinician produces word for repetition
Feedback on error	Next stage of hierarchy	Next stage of hierarchy	Next stage of hierarchy
Feedback if correct	Not stated	Not stated	Not stated

Outcome

Following therapy, LN was able to write all of the trained words. Treatment gains were seen in the verbal production of trained words compared to control words. At 6 weeks, there was a loss of treatment gains, with no difference between words practised on the video and those not practised. It was difficult to monitor generalisation to untrained words beginning with target and control phonemes but the authors suggest there was not strong evidence of generalisation. Post-therapy, however, LN's performance improved on both verbal and written naming tasks. Throughout therapy, LN required prompts to use the cueing strategies. The authors suggest that a programme focusing on the self generation of phonemic cues can be effective. They suggest the writing component of the treatment programme was more critical to the observed gains in verbal naming than the tactile cues. LN showed little spontaneous use of tactile cues and the authors suggest this may be due to resistance to alternative modes of communication.

Other comments

The home video programme was used to provide more intensive practice. However, home practice alone was not effective in maintaining treatment effects. The authors highlight a number of limitations of the study, e.g. not teaching tactile cues for control phonemes and carrying out treatment probes at the end of the session. The reported gains in the study were small and no statistical comparisons were carried out.

Study 17

Le Dorze, G., Boulay, N., Gaudreau, J. and Brassard, C. (1994). The contrasting effects of a semantic versus a formal–semantic technique for the facilitation of naming in a case of anomia. *Aphasiology, 8*, 127–141.

Focus of therapy: Access to the phonological output lexicon from the semantic system.

Target of therapy: Semantic.

Therapy approach: Reactivation.

Client details

General information

RB was a 56-year-old right-handed man who had a non-haemorrhagic single CVA, confirmed by CT scan, in the vicinity of his left carotid artery. He was a policeman before the incident. He was a bilingual speaker in French and English.

Overall pattern of language impairments and preservations

At the time of the study, RB was described as having a moderately severe, mixed aphasia. Spoken output was characterised by syntactically well-formed sentences with severe word-finding difficulties. A slight articulatory difficulty was present. On testing, he had moderately impaired picture naming. Errors consisted predominantly of no responses and some semantic errors; no phonological errors were present. Repetition was good. Good auditory and written comprehension of single words was present, although this decreased with sentences. Oral reading was mildly impaired. Writing was limited to copying.

Time post-onset

Therapy was commenced when RB was 10 months post-onset.

Therapy

Therapy aimed to compare the relative effects of a semantic technique and a formal-semantic technique in the treatment of anomia. These techniques are discussed in the paper; the key difference between the techniques was the use of the word form in the formal-semantic technique and the use of a definition (with no usage of the word form) in the semantic technique. Therapy consisted of three 1-hour therapy sessions per week for a total of eleven sessions. Therapy sessions included formal-semantic and semantic techniques rotated on each stimulus. Within each session, the naming of items treated in previous therapy sessions was tested using a maintenance test. Items to be treated within the session were tested before and after therapy. An item-specific therapy design contrasting the effects of the two treatments was used.

Task	*Formal-semantic therapy*	*Semantic therapy*
	Tasks involved semantic comprehension with the presentation of the word form a. Spoken word-to-picture matching b. Written word-to-picture matching c. Semantic judgement – yes/no questions	Tasks involved semantic comprehension. Word form not presented a. Matching spoken definition to picture b. Matching written definition to picture c. Semantic judgement task as in formal-semantic therapy
Materials	225 pictures which were named incorrectly in naming assessment. Twenty stimuli were drawn from these pictures in each session. Ten pictures treated via semantic technique, ten via semantic formal technique. Fourteen stimulus cards for use in word and definition matching tasks. Each card contained six pictures. a. Target b. Three semantic distractors c. Two unrelated distractors	
Hierarchy	No hierarchy	No hierarchy
Feedback on error	Not stated	Not stated
Feedback if correct	Not stated	Not stated

Outcome

Naming improved significantly for the items treated with the formal-semantic technique immediately post-therapy but the improvement was not maintained 2–3 days later. There was no change in naming for the items treated with the purely semantic technique. No change was evident on formal aphasia testing. There was, however, a reported improvement in RB's ability to convey information in a picture description task.

The authors propose that formal-semantic therapy resulted in improved naming performance immediately post-therapy but these gains were not maintained 2–3 days post-therapy. Semantic therapy resulted in no significant improvement. The authors suggest that the presentation of the word form is, therefore, critical for the facilitation of naming. No theoretical explanation is offered for the apparent generalisation to a picture description task but they suggest that the semantic technique involving use of definitions may have provided a useful model of circumlocution.

Other comments

The formal-semantic therapy is a replication of Howard and colleagues' (1985b) semantic therapy.

Study 18

Boyle, M. and Coelho, C. A. (1995). Application of semantic feature analysis as a treatment for aphasic dysnomia. *American Journal of Speech and Language Pathology, 4*, 94–98.

Focus of therapy: Phonological output lexicon (or access to it).

Target of therapy: Semantic.

Therapy approach: Reactivation.

Client details

General information

HW was a 57-year-old right-handed male. He was a retired postal worker with a high school education. A CT scan showed a left frontoparietal ischaemic infarct.

Overall pattern of language impairments and preservations

HW presented with a Broca's type aphasia with a mild apraxic component. Spontaneous speech was characterised by frequent pauses, nonword fillers and incomplete word attempts. Picture naming was impaired. He showed retained auditory comprehension of single words. While no reference was made to HW's exact level of breakdown, he was not reported to have a primary deficit involving the semantic system.

Time post-onset

HW was 65 months post-onset when therapy started.

Therapy

Therapy aimed to improve naming performance. Therapy consisted of three, 1-hour sessions per week, with a total of sixteen sessions over 7 weeks (seven sessions Stage 1, nine sessions Stage 2). There was a 1-week break between Stages 1 and 2 of therapy. A repeated-measures multiple-baseline design across tasks was used to evaluate the efficacy of therapy.

Task	**Naming and semantic feature analysis** Picture placed in centre of feature analysis chart and client attempts to name the picture. Guided verbalisation of the semantic features (group, use, action, properties, location and association)

Materials	Forty-eight Snodgrass and Vanderwart (1980) black-and-white line drawings divided into three groups:
	 a) Treatment Group (34 pictures). HW was unable to name these on two/ three occasions. Treatment group further divided into:
	  i) Few exemplar condition (seven pictures)
	  ii) Many exemplar condition (remaining 27 pictures)
	 b) Control Group – seven pictures not named correctly on three/three occasions
	 c) Easy Group – seven pictures named correctly on three/three occasions easy group pictures used to provide success in therapy.

Hierarchy	Stage 1. Few exemplars condition: training of the same seven pictures each session with the seven easy pictures interspersed for periodic success. Stage 2. Many exemplars condition: 27 pictures randomised into three sets of nine and with seven easy pictures interspersed into each set.
Feedback on error	1. Clinician provided semantic feature orally and in writing 2. If unable to name picture after all features written on chart request for repetition of picture name and review of all features
Feedback if correct	1. Client guided through features chart even when target is named.

The criterion for the transition between Stages 1 and 2 and for the conclusion of treatment was 100% success over three consecutive sessions.

Outcome

HW demonstrated significant improvement in the naming of task stimuli (reaching 100% accuracy). This was maintained 2 months post-treatment. Naming performance also significantly improved for the untreated control items. There was no generalisation to connected speech (as measured by Nicholas and Brookshire's, 1993, protocol that looks at words as information-carrying units), although a clinically important functional improvement in communication was found on the Communicative Effectiveness Index (Lomas *et al.*, 1989).

Naming performance therefore improved significantly for both treated and untreated pictures. The authors propose that this improvement is a consequence of internalising the prompts in the semantic feature chart facilitating self-cueing and thus a consequence of therapy. A stable baseline had been established before therapy, although no control tasks were reported. HW was a long time post-onset and improvement was therefore unlikely to be a consequence of spontaneous recovery. No carryover into spontaneous speech was noted.

Other comments

This study reports limited assessment data on the client, making interpretation difficult. HC's word-retrieval deficit is likely to be post-semantic, so input to the semantic system may well be activating access to the phonological output lexicon. The authors suggest that direct treatment of word retrieval in connected speech may be necessary to achieve improvement at that level. They further noted that functional improvement evident on the Communicative Effectiveness Index (Lomas *et al.*, 1989) may be due to either the reporter's (client's daughter) desire for improvement and for therapy to continue, or may indicate a mismatch between connected speech measures and functional measures.

Boyle (2010) reviews a range of studies which reported the use of 'semantic feature analysis' treatment. The review highlights that whilst therapies share a similar focus on semantic features, the paradigms have a number of differences that may influence treatment outcome. The main difference is whether semantic features are generated (labelled semantic feature generation) or selected/verified (labelled semantic feature review). An example of a study involving feature review is Kiran and Thompson (2003) on p139. Lowell *et al.* (1995), described on p172, involves initial feature generation and then review of self-generated features in subsequent sessions. Boyle (2010) also considers the potential influence of the number of features, whether the participant is monolingual or bilingual, the frequency of generalisation probes and the quantity of treatment. Boyle concludes that treatments involving semantic feature generation or review result in improved naming of treated items in participants with mild or moderate aphasia. Studies reporting generalisation (with the exception on Lowell *et al.*, 1995) involved repeated probing (as in this original study), and therefore, gains on untreated items may be the result of repeated attempts to name during the treatment phase.

Study 19

Lowell, S., Beeson, P. M. and Holland, A. L. (1995). The efficacy of a semantic cueing procedure on naming performance of adults with aphasia. *American Journal of Speech – Language Pathology, 4*, 109–114.

Focus of therapy: Phonological output lexicon (or access to it).

Target of therapy: Semantic.

Therapy approach: Reactivation.

Client details

General information

This study examines three patients who each presented with aphasia following a single left CVA. BB was 74 years old, BG was 76 years old and SB was 66 years old.

Overall pattern of language impairments and preservations

BB and SB presented with a conduction-type aphasia. BG presented with an anomic aphasia. All presented with naming difficulties, despite retained single-word auditory and written comprehension and relatively unimpaired semantics.

Time post-onset

The clients were all at least 9 months post-onset when therapy was commenced. BB was 16 months post-onset, BG was 9 months post-onset and SB was 30 months post-onset.

Therapy

Therapy aimed to improve naming of items consistently not named correctly over three pre-therapy baseline assessments. Therapy consisted of three sessions per week for 2 weeks for list 1 and then the equivalent for list 2. A multiple-baseline and cross-over design was used. Therapy consisted of two tasks, one task for the 'trained' group of items and one task for the 'untrained' items. If multiple responses were given, the best response was scored. Recognisable phonological errors with one to two phonological substitutions were counted as correct. A criterion of 5/6 items named correctly in two consecutive sessions with a combined accuracy of > 50% in each of three training sessions was set for the trained items.

Task	1. Trained items	2. Untrained items
	Four self-generated cue words read aloud by client and therapist. Client then asked to name the picture.	Client asked to name the picture.
Materials	Thirty-six black-and-white line drawings named incorrectly on 3 occasions Three groups: • Twelve 'trained'. Trained items had written cue cards • Twelve 'untrained' semantically related • Twelve 'untrained' unrelated Groups were divided into two lists for therapy (six of each group) 18 items within each list seen two–three times in each session	
Hierarchy	None	None
Feedback on error	Written feedback of 3 written choices given and client asked to read target aloud.	Written feedback of 3 written choices given and client asked to read target aloud.
Feedback if correct	Not stated	Not stated

Outcome

Criterion was reached by BB and BG for both sets of trained items. Naming for the untrained items also improved, but only for those items which were probed on every cycle. Performance was maintained 1 week post-therapy. Naming performance also improved for test items not selected for treatment. SB did not reach criterion for trained items. No improvement in naming performance was evident. Performance on a control task involving the production of morphology remained unchanged for all three clients.

Therapy resulted in improved naming performance in BB and BG. The improvement seemed to be a consequence of therapy, as the clients were stable before therapy and no improvements were noted on the control task. Similar gains in naming performance seen in the untrained items suggest that improvement may be a consequence of repeated exposure to the items and the use of the written feedback. The authors propose that the improved naming of items not selected for the 'trained' or 'untrained groups' reflects an internalisation of a semantic self-cueing strategy. No improvement was seen in SB's naming performance. The authors suggest that this lack of improvement may be a consequence of a greater impairment of semantic/phonological access and the semantic activation provided by the cues was not sufficient to overcome the deficit. SB also performed poorly on non-verbal cognitive tasks compared with BB and BG.

Other comments

The limited initial assessment data reported in this study means that the precise impairment of the three clients cannot be identified. The authors suggest that SB's poor performance on non-verbal cognitive tasks may be influential in the lack of improvement seen with this client and that these cognitive limitations may preclude the use of this strategy.

Study 20

Francis, D. R., Clark, N. and Humphreys, G. W. (2002). Circumlocution-induced naming (CIN): a treatment for effecting generalization in anomia? *Aphasiology, 16*, 243–259.

Focus of therapy: Access to the phonological output lexicon.

Target of therapy: Semantic.

Therapy approach: Reactivation.

Client details

General information

MB was a 78-year-old woman who had retired from her job as a cleaner prior to her left middle cerebral artery CVA. A CT scan also showed bilateral aneurysms of the internal carotid arteries. She had a right-sided hemiplegia.

Overall pattern of language impairments and preservations

In the initial months following her CVA, MB's initial comprehension difficulties spontaneously resolved, leaving her with specific problems in name retrieval. She produced visual, semantic and unrelated errors in naming. Francis *et al.* conclude a possible mild visual recognition deficit in the presence of more severe difficulties accessing the phonological output lexicon. She showed little evidence of spontaneous circumlocution. Both frequency and category effects were present.

Time post-onset

MB was 2–3 months post-onset at the time of the study.

Therapy

Therapy aimed to use circumlocution as a treatment (instead of as a strategy) to improve access to words. Therapy consisted of thirteen therapy sessions over a 4 week period (three to four sessions per week). The sessions were approximately 15–30 minutes long and conducted when MB was an inpatient. A multiple-baseline across-behaviours therapy design was used.

Task	**_Circumlocution-induced naming (CIN)_**
	Client attempts to name each picture. Circumlocution ('talk around the topic') is encouraged until correct name is spoken.
Materials	Twenty black-and-white drawings (half animate, half inanimate, low-frequency nouns). All pictures used in each session.
Hierarchy	None
Feedback on error	Clinician verbally reinforces information provided by client by restating what has been said. Phonological cue may be provided sparingly. Correct name not to be provided by clinician.
Feedback if correct	Not stated

Outcome

A small but significant improvement in spoken naming was found on untreated items (only pictures not included in therapy were reassessed). A qualitative change was seen in the type of errors produced by MB. A non-significant increase was seen in visual–semantic errors, while unrelated errors showed a significant reduction post-therapy. Circumlocutory errors did not change. Performance did not change on control measures, suggesting that improvement was a result of therapy. Treatment effects were maintained on testing 2½ weeks later.

Francis *et al.* suggest that MB's success following therapy was directly related to the client having to 'look up' items in her phonological output lexicon rather than being provided with the correct item through such methods as repetition or reading aloud. This had the effect of strengthening access to phonology from semantics, a fact reinforced by the greatest change being seen with low-frequency words rather than high-frequency words. The authors suggest that this may occur through (a) 'exercising' the impaired link between intact semantics and intact phonology, or (b) directly improving semantics through the detailed descriptions generated in circumlocution, allowing the lexical representation to be accessed more easily. They argue that, if circumlocution had only been developed as a compensatory strategy, more circumlocution would have been seen post-therapy; this did not happen.

Other comments

Francis *et al.* stress the use of a technique that is usually reserved for the generalisation phase of therapy and suggest that therapy using this method may avoid the item specificity that is usually associated with improving deficits at the level of the phonological output lexicon. Issues related to clinical research within an inpatient setting are also discussed.

Study 21

Spencer, K. A., Doyle, P. J., McNeil, M. R., Wambaugh, J. L., Park, G. and Carroll, B. (2000). Examining the facilitative effects of rhyme in a patient with output lexicon damage. *Aphasiology*, *14*, 567–584.

Focus of therapy: Phonological and orthographic output lexicons.

Target of therapy: Semantic/phonological.

Therapy approach: Reactivation.

Client details

General information

NR was a 47-year-old right-handed native English-speaking woman with aphasia following a left parietal haemorrhage. She had completed a 2-year art degree.

Overall pattern of language impairments and preservations

NR presented with conduction aphasia. She had relatively intact single-word comprehension but impaired sentence comprehension. Naming, repetition and oral reading were impaired with phonological errors and neologisms, particularly as word length increased. She was unable to repeat or read nonwords. NR was unable to do rhyme judgement tasks involving pictures but performed better on tasks involving written words, relying on the orthographic similarity of the words. NR's difficulties were interpreted as insufficient access to phonological information and faulty encoding of the phonological representations retrieved from the lexicon. Similarly in writing, written naming and writing to dictation of words and nonwords were impaired, with errors of letter substitution, insertion and deletion. This was interpreted as an inability to access and manipulate orthographic representations.

Time post-onset

NR was 12 months post-onset when therapy began.

Therapy

Therapy aimed to provide partial phonological information and thereby enhance access to the phonological output lexicon and the orthographic output lexicon. NR received daily therapy totalling one hundred and ten sessions over 7 months. A multiple-baseline and item-specific design was used.

Task	*Semantic category rhyme therapy (SCRT)* Naming using a systematic cueing hierarchy. 1. Client provided with superordinate semantic category and rhyming word and asked to name the target (e.g. *'Name a four-legged animal that rhymes with course'*). 2. Rhyme pair repeated by client. 3. Written word presented and client asked to copy word. 4. Word produced verbally again by client.
Materials	Four lists of 17 pairs of rhymed words (each list from four different semantic categories – four-legged animals, household items, carpenters tools, articles of clothing). The first member of each pair provided the phonological cue, and the second was the target for oral and written naming. Twelve of each set were targeted for treatment and five were not treated (control items) (with the exception of tools where no control items were present).

Hierarchy	None
Feedback on error	1. Phonemic cue provided with a 5 second response time permitted. 2. Graphemic cue, with a 5 second response time. 3. Therapist says the rhyme-target pair and provides written target word. Client asked to say the word pair, copy the target word, and say the word pair once more.
Feedback if correct	1. After correct verbal response, response confirmed by the therapist and the rhyme pair repeated by the client ('horse/course'). 2. After correct written response, client asked to repeat the word pair again.

The hierarchy for presentation and feedback is clearly documented diagrammatically in the article.

Outcome

Results were analysed using both visual inspection and statistical evaluation. NR demonstrated significantly improved oral and written naming for treated items, with continued improvement following the cessation of therapy and generalisation to untreated items. Improvement was better than would be expected if only maintenance of skills had occurred. Improvement was also seen in naming, nonword repetition and in the percentage of correct information units in connected speech (an index of accurate, relevant and informative words in connected speech, as described in Nicholas and Brookshire, 1993). No change was recorded on the control task that measured auditory sentence comprehension.

In normal processing, activation of the semantic system following input to the phonological input lexicon would activate the corresponding phonological representation in the output lexicon. Damage to the phonological output lexicon would diminish or prevent this activation. The authors proposed that improvement in accessing the target words was facilitated by providing a rhyme, where activation of the phonological representation of the rhyme word spread to other entries in the output lexicon with similar sounds. Furthermore, by providing semantic information at the start of each therapy task in addition to the rhyme, stronger activation of the target word's phonological and orthographic representation was also facilitated. The pattern of delayed generalisation was explained by the authors as possibly resulting from 'retrieval inhibition' or 'lateral inhibition'.

Other comments

The number of control items in this study (*n* = 5) was small, making any interpretation of treatment effects on untreated items difficult.

Study 22

Miceli, G., Amitrano, A., Capasso, R. and Caramazza, A. (1996). The treatment of anomia resulting from output lexical damage: analysis of two cases. *Brain and Language, 52,* 150–174.

Focus of therapy: Phonological output lexicon.

Target of therapy: Phonological.

Therapy approach: Reactivation.

Client details

Two case studies are reported.

General information

RBO was a 38-year-old right-handed female who suffered a ruptured A–V malformation of the left posterior communicating artery. Following surgery, RBO presented with a global aphasia, right hemiplegia, hypoesthesia and hemianopia. A CT scan showed a large lesion involving deep and superficial structures of the left parietal and temporal lobes. RBO worked as a flight attendant. GMA was a 60-year-old right-handed male who suffered a left hemisphere stroke, leaving him with aphasia and no motor deficits. A CT scan showed involvement of the left temporal lobe. GMA had degrees in mathematics and engineering.

Overall pattern of language impairments and preservations

RMO's comprehension of isolated words remained intact with reasonable ability to convert words and nonwords (auditory and visual presentation) into verbal or written responses. Errors were phonologically or visually related to the target. Naming was severely impaired and was characterised primarily by failure to respond. Slow, mildly dysarthric output with evidence of complex grammatical structures was present; grammaticality judgements were reliable but comprehension of reversible sentences was poor. Mild buccofacial dyspraxia and reduced verbal memory were also reported. GMA presented with a similar, but milder, pattern to RBO. Comprehension was spared at the single-word level in the presence of fluent grammatically complex output. Picture naming, however, showed a mild impairment (100/120 items; nouns > verbs) and was characterised by omissions and circumlocutions, with infrequent phonological and semantic errors. Nonword transcoding tasks showed relative preservation. Both RBO and GMA present with selective damage to the phonological output lexicon.

Time post-onset

RBO was 18 months post-onset when the programme began. GMA was seen approximately 12 months post-onset.

Therapy

Therapy aimed to strengthen the phonological representation and subsequent access to it through repeated reading and repetition of the word. An item-specific therapy design was used.

(a) Client RBO

Two stages of therapy were involved based on two sets of stimuli. Each stage involved five, 1-hour sessions over 5 consecutive days with 3 days in between the two stages (total period approximately 13 days).

Task	Reading (Stage 1) and Repetition (Stage 2) of target items
Materials	Ninety pictures RBO consistently failed to name but could comprehend (range of familiarity and semantic categories). Randomly assigned to three sets of 30 items (Set 1 – 30 reading items for Stage 1, Set 2 – 30 repetition items for Stage 2, Set 3 – 30 untreated items).
Hierarchy	Stage 1 (using Set 1): Written word presented and RBO asked to read aloud. All 30 items repeated ten times. Stage 2 (using Set 2): Target word spoken by examiner and RBO asked to repeat it.
Feedback on error	Corrected as many times as necessary until correct response produced.
Feedback if correct	Not stated

(b) Client GMO

The treatment procedure was similar to that given to RMO. Key differences were in (a) the reduced number of items (80 items), (b) the inclusion of three stages of therapy, and (c) the length of therapy in each stage being extended to 7 consecutive days with 7 days of non-treatment between each stage (total period of approximately 5 weeks).

Task	Reading with picture (Stage 1), reading without picture (Stage 2) and picture naming (Stage 3) of target items
Materials	Eighty pictures GMA could not name consistently (failed minimum 2/3 presentations) but could comprehend (range of familiarity and semantic categories). Randomly assigned to 4 sets of 20 items (Set 1 – Stage 1, Set 2 – 20 items for Stage 2, Set 3 – Stage 3, Set 4 – 20 untreated items).
Hierarchy	Stage 1 (using Set 1): Stimulus picture and corresponding written word presented at same time. GMA required to look at picture and read word aloud. Stage 2 (using Set 2): Only written word presented and GMA required to read word aloud. Stage 3 (using Set 3): Only picture presented and GMA required to name it.
Feedback on error	During Stage 3, when GMA could not name an item, a phonemic cue (initial sound, initial syllable, second syllable, etc.) was given until correct name produced. Correct response was necessary before next item introduced.
Feedback if correct	Not stated

Outcome

For RBO, naming improved significantly for the items in both sets of treatment stimuli, regardless of modality of stimulus presentation (reading and repetition). Only treated items were named more accurately. There was no generalisation to untreated items. Improvement was maintained when tested 3 weeks after the end of treatment. As with RBO, GMA's naming improved significantly for the items in all three sets of treatment stimuli. Only treated items were named more accurately. There was no generalisation to untreated items, not even to semantically related items. Significant improvement was maintained during a 17 month follow-up period, although a decrease in response accuracy was noted over time.

The authors propose that picture-naming performance in both clients could be accounted for by selective damage to the phonological output lexicon. Improvement can be expected where exercises rely on the spoken production of words. The lexicon is therefore remediable but only on an item-specific basis. No generalisation can be expected to occur. The authors suggest that the mechanism of change may be due to one of the following: improving lexical access mechanisms, increasing activation levels of lexical representations or repairing damage to lexical representations.

Other comments

The authors highlight the unknown but critical influence of other parameters (e.g. neuropsychological, psychological and neurological factors) and stress the need for further investigation of these.

Study 23

Robson, J., Marshall, J., Pring, T. and Chiat, S. (1998). Phonological naming therapy in jargon aphasia: Positive but paradoxical effects. *Journal of the International Neuropsychological Society, 4*, 675–686.

Focus of therapy: Access to the phonological output lexicon.

Target of therapy: Phonological.

Therapy approach: Aimed to develop a strategy but worked via reactivation.

Client details

General information

GF had a left CVA aged 55 years. A CT scan revealed a large cerebral infarct in the territory of the left posterior cerebral artery and posterior branches of the middle cerebral artery. She was a right-handed monolingual English speaker who left school at 18 years and worked as an orthopaedic masseuse.

Overall pattern of language impairments and preservations

GF's comprehension was described as adequate in conversation. She had fluent speech characterised by empty English jargon, verbal paraphasias and paragrammatisms. On testing, she showed retained spoken comprehension of concrete words, with a significant decline with abstract words. Her non-verbal (picture) semantic skills were intact. Written comprehension was impaired for both concrete and abstract words. Her naming was at floor with predominantly no response errors, often accompanied by comments on her failure to name the item. Semantic cues were ineffective. Phonological cues were mildly facilitative (around 30%). Reading aloud and word repetition were significantly better than naming. She was unable to repeat nonwords. The authors attribute her word retrieval difficulties primarily to a problem accessing the phonology from semantics. The phonological representations were considered to be available based on her greater success with word repetition. The authors suggest the jargon output was underpinned by her severe anomia.

Time post-onset

GF was 2 years post-onset at the time of the study.

Therapy

The study considered whether phonological therapy would improve naming, monitoring the effects of therapy on the naming of treated and untreated items that were either phonologically related or unrelated. Performance on tasks investigating phonological awareness was also assessed. A multiple-baseline with control task design was used to monitor efficacy, with performance assessed pre-therapy, immediately post-therapy and 8 weeks after treatment. Therapy aimed to introduce a self-cueing strategy with the authors predicting gains in naming, possible use of overt self-cueing and improved performance on the phonological judgement tasks. Therapy took place over a 6 month period with forty therapy sessions of approximately 20 minutes (a total of 14 hours of therapy).

Task	Syllable judgement	Initial phoneme judgement	Dual judgement	Judgement tasks with naming
	Point to 1 or 2 to indicate number of syllables in word.	Point to grapheme on card that corresponds to the first sound.	Identify number of syllables and grapheme.	As dual judgement and then encouraged to produce sound as self-cue.
Materials	Twenty-four treated words beginning with /k b s f m n/. 48 untreated, 24 phonologically related and 24 phonologically unrelated. Sets balanced for frequency and syllabic structure: Twelve one syllable and twelve two syllable words. Fifty additional words beginning with same initial consonants. Therapy tasks used core set of 24 items and random selection of additional items.			
Hierarchy	1. Exaggerated intonation 2. Normal spoken production 3. Picture stimuli 4. Non-picture stimuli – objects or verbal description	*Phoneme choice* 1. Choice of two – no shared features 2. Increased choices and more shared features 3. Choice of all 6 consonants *Presentation* 1. Spoken word and picture 2. Picture only 3. Non-picture stimuli		If unable to produce phoneme, phoneme given and asked to repeat phoneme and attempt name.

Feedback on error	Spoken word given with syllabic information highlighted.	Correct phoneme identified and produced.	Asked to revise. Correct phoneme identified and produced.	Not stated
Feedback if correct	Not stated	Not stated	Not stated	Not stated

GF moved through all tasks. Although the steps were planned, GF often spontaneously named the item after the initial judgement task. The conscious cueing process in the final task was often unsuccessful.

Outcome

Therapy resulted in significant improvement in the naming of treated and both sets of untreated items. Gains were maintained at 8 weeks follow-up. 'No' response errors remained the most frequent and the response to phonemic cues was unchanged. Significant improvement was also seen on a naming task and test of word repetition, with non-significant gains in reading aloud. Gains were maintained 8 weeks post-therapy. Performance on assessments of phonological judgement and phoneme discrimination remained poor. There was no improvement in unrelated control assessments investigating semantic processing. There was also no change in written naming. GF's spontaneous speech was not formally evaluated. The authors report a new ability to access specific vocabulary in conversation. GF's family reported that conversation with GF was easier, that she was more confident speaking to others and was attempting to use the telephone.

Therapy resulted in significant and long-term gains in picture naming which generalised to untreated items. Gains are likely to be a consequence of therapy as GF was 2 years post-onset, had stable baseline performance and showed no gains on control tasks. The authors explore whether the generalised gains in naming were a consequence of GF learning a self-cueing strategy. They conclude that the lack of overt self cueing and unchanged performance on phonological judgement tasks suggest that gains do not reflect a strategy but that improvement was due to improved access to the lexicon.

Other comments

The authors suggest the study provides some evidence that the naming disorder in jargon aphasia can respond to phonological therapy. They suggest, however, that GF may be different to other people with jargon output as she had good self-monitoring and relatively well-preserved auditory comprehension. The authors acknowledge the long duration of treatment but emphasise that GF could only tolerate short sessions and there were only 14 hours of therapy in total.

Study 24

Nickels, L. A. (2002a). Improving word finding: practice makes (closer to) perfect? *Aphasiology, 16*, 1047–1060.

Focus of therapy: Phonological output lexicon.

Target of therapy: Phonology.

Therapy approach: Reactivation.

Client details

General information

JAW was a 60-year-man who worked, until his CVA, as a carpenter. A CT scan showed a left middle cerebral artery infarct.

Overall pattern of language impairments and preservations

JAW had a fluent aphasia, characterised by impaired naming. Auditory comprehension was poor, with an impairment considered to be present at a pre-lexical level of processing. Semantic processing was within normal limits for high-imageability words but was impaired for abstract and low-imageability words. A severe naming deficit showed significant frequency effects and consistent but non-significant length effects. These difficulties were considered to arise from a phonological processing deficit. Written naming was also poor but considered to arise from problems with the graphemic output buffer. Given his auditory processing and phonological output difficulties, repetition was poor. Reading was also impaired, in particular his ability to read using the orthographic-to-phonological conversion route.

Time post-onset

JAW was over 12 months post-onset.

Therapy

Therapy aimed to improve picture naming through repeated presentation of the same stimulus items, investigating any differences between the three tasks of (a) attempted naming, (b) reading aloud and (c) delayed copying in improving naming performance. Three treatment phases were completed with JAW, each corresponding to 6 consecutive days of therapy and 1 day of assessment. Between each week of therapy, JAW had a 1-week non-therapy period.

Task	*Attempted naming* Naming pictures	*Reading aloud* Reading words	*Delayed copying* Read word, turn over page and silently write picture name.
Materials	102 pictures divided into three sets of 34 (a Naming set, a Reading set and a Copying (control) set) – matched for baseline spoken naming accuracy and approximately for length and frequency. The Reading and Copying set were presented as written words.		
Hierarchy	None	None	None
Feedback	No feedback or correction.	No feedback or correction.	No feedback or correction.

Outcome

Significant improvement in spoken naming was found following each of the three treatment phases. Improvement was item-specific and was maintained 2 weeks after the end of the final therapy period. Written naming did not improve following attempted naming but did show significant improvement following reading aloud and delayed copying.

Nickels argues that improvement was due, first, to the variability in JAW's naming abilities; his inconsistency in naming reduced as the lexical item was activated over and over again. Second, successful naming of the word led to 'long-term priming of subsequent retrieval' of that word. Priming of mapping from semantics to phonology is common to each of these tasks, although the two tasks of reading aloud and delayed copying have the added advantage of also accessing phonology via spelling. This study reports the benefits involved in word finding even when a word is attempted but not named. It further reports success in the absence of any feedback or correction being given. Finally, it proposes that practice is a powerful component of subsequent word-finding success.

Other comments

This study shows that repeated opportunities to say the name of items may improve word retrieval; this repeated practice may explain the generalisation seen in some studies.

Study 25

Bruce, C. and Howard, D. (1987). Computer generated phonemic cueing: an effective aid for naming in aphasia. *British Journal of Disorders of Communication, 22*, 191–201.

Focus of therapy: Phonological output lexicon.

Target of therapy: Orthographic.

Therapy approach: Compensation.

Client details

General information

Five people who had suffered cortical lesions were involved in the study.

Overall pattern of language impairments and preservations

All clients were non-fluent and classified as having Broca's aphasia and word-retrieval difficulties. They had no visual agnosia or severe articulatory difficulties, and were able to repeat single concrete content words. All had failed to name more than 50 pictures in a previous study but had been able to indicate the initial letter of a significant proportion of picture names. Three clients benefited significantly from phonemic cues. The remaining two clients either named items when they were shown the initial letter or named to some extent following a cue. No information is given on comprehension abilities or the proposed location of the clients' impairments.

Time post-onset

All clients were more than 6 months post-onset.

Therapy

The study aimed to evaluate the effects of a microcomputer as an aid for a cueing strategy in naming. Following pre-testing, each client had five sessions using the microcomputer with a set of 50 items that had not been named correctly (Set A). A further set of items (Set B) was compiled, not assessed and used as control items. At the conclusion of therapy, all items from both sets (A and B) were presented for naming in two sessions, 1 week apart. An item-specific design across tasks (with and without aid) was used with each client.

Task	**Picture naming with a computer aid for cues** Picture presented for naming, client identifies first letter and computer provides phoneme.
Materials	150 drawings from Cambridge pictures, beginning with letters P C F S T B D M L. Set A had 50 treated pictures (combined with a further 50 fillers), Set B had 50 untreated (and unseen) pictures. Apple II microcomputer with recorded digitised speech of the nine phonemes. Computer produced phoneme + schwa.
Hierarchy	a. Clients located and then pressed the initial letter on the keyboard. The aid converted this into a phoneme. b. Clients encouraged to repeat phoneme and use this to cue word production. • For first three sessions, clients had to use aid even if they could name spontaneously. • In the final two sessions patient used aid only when failed to name correctly in 5 seconds. In these sessions the numbers named with and without cue were recorded.
Feedback on error	If client failed to name, therapist provided phonemic cue.
Feedback if correct	Not stated

Outcome

There were significant differences between the clients in their response to therapy, with different levels of benefit from the aid and between treated and untreated words seen. As a group, there was a significant effect of using the aid compared with not using the aid. A significant effect of treatment was also found, whereby better performance was recorded for naming treated Set A than untreated Set B. The effects of using the aid generalised across Sets A and B. No significant change in performance was noted 1 week after testing.

When looked at individually, client-specific effects of treatment were found. All clients learned to use the aid; four clients showed significantly better naming with the aid compared with the control condition. In some cases, clients improved naming performance without the use of the aid, although they were still assisted by use of the aid (in one case, the client's improvement in unaided naming was comparable to aided performance). Clients also increased their ability to identify initial letters of words that they could not name. Therapy with the aid, therefore, had variable effects, both in increasing unaided performance of naming as well as increasing naming performance when used as a prosthetic device.

The machine-generated cue was proposed to act in the same way as a therapist-generated cue, providing extra activation to the phonological word forms within the lexicon.

Other comments

While the information available on the clients in this study is less comprehensive than for other studies, the target of therapy was clear and it showed clear benefits for some clients. A closer examination of each client's pre-therapy abilities may inform the discussion as to why clients responded differently to such an approach.

Study 26

Howard, D. and Harding, D. (1998). Self-cueing of word retrieval by a woman with aphasia: why a letter board works. *Aphasiology, 12,* 399–420.

Focus of therapy: Access to the phonological output lexicon.

Target of therapy: Orthographic (via input orthography).

Therapy approach: Cognitive relay.

Client details

General information

SD was a 46-year-old woman. She had a CVA secondary to a myocardial infarction which resulted in aphasia and right hemiplegia. She had worked and studied in management but was not working at the time of her CVA.

Overall pattern of language impairments and preservations

SD presented with a severe naming impairment that was characterised by a marked improvement in her ability to retrieve the name when shown an alphabet board. Naming errors were characteristically omissions or semantic errors. Some impairment was seen in spoken comprehension, related to auditory analysis and complex sentence comprehension, but no difficulties were seen with written word comprehension (comprehension of written grammar not assessed). SD had a reading impairment consistent with deep dyslexia. She was unable to write letters independently but could copy letters and used a typewriter adeptly. When asked to write the name of objects or write words to dictation, she typed none of them accurately but was always able to write the correct initial letter. She was able to type the appropriate letter when given the phoneme but was unable to give sounds for letters. The authors suggest that SD has an impairment in mapping from semantics to the phonological output lexicon. SD was able to identify the first letter of words but was unable to form letters herself and thus the authors suggest that the alphabet board acts as a cueing strategy.

Time post-onset

SD was 20 weeks post-onset at the time of the study.

Therapy

The study aimed to improve naming performance by providing a written cue and to consider the effect of different types of cues on word retrieval. Intervention with SD consisted of one session where an alphabet board was introduced. Subsequent sessions attempted to determine the relative benefits of a range of different cues and to systematically evaluate how the alphabet board was aiding naming.

Task	*(a) Provision of an alphabet board* *(b) Evaluating range of cues* • extra time • use of alphabet board • provision of initial letter of target • provision of spoken name of initial letter of target • provision of phonemic cue
Materials	Alphabet board
Hierarchy	Not applicable
Feedback on error	Not stated in initial therapy. Progressed to next item in evaluation study.
Feedback if correct	Not stated

Outcome

SD was able to name items that she had previously not named when provided with (a) a phonemic cue, (b) the written initial letter or (c) an alphabet board (reaching 78–96% accuracy). These cues were significantly more effective than when given extra time or the spoken letter name (achieving 14–23% correct). SD's ability to self-cue was attributed by the authors to a lexically mediated cascade of activation from input orthography to output phonology. Her increased naming performance was possible due to her intact knowledge of the word's initial letter. A lack of benefit from the spoken name of the initial letter suggested that the written form was essential. The success of phonemic cues was explained by the likelihood that the target word was close to activation and could be, as when provided with partial orthographic information, activated with partial phonological information.

Other comments

In this study, the cognitive neuropsychological approach provides an explanation as to why a particular technique was useful to the client. It also stresses the importance of detailed assessment of a client's performance on a wide range of tasks. The authors explain the implications of this study for the logogen model of information processing, postulating different routes from the visual input lexicon to either the phonological output lexicon or a semantic lexicon as possible ways of accounting for the pattern seen in SD.

Study 27

Waldron, H., Whitworth, A. and Howard, D. (2011a) Therapy for phonological assembly difficulties: a case series. *Aphasiology, 25*, 434–455.

Focus of therapy: Phonological assembly and phonological output lexicon.

Target of therapy: Phonological assembly.

Therapy approach: Reactivation.

Client details

Four participants were included in the study.

General information

All participants were right-handed, monolingual English speakers who had aphasia following a stroke. No information was given about education or employment history. SD was a 75-year-old woman who had a left parietal infarct. BB was a 76-year-old woman with a left middle cerebral artery infarct. HS was a 63-year-old man who also had a left parietal infarct. PL was an 82-year-old man with a left middle cerebral infarct.

Overall pattern of language impairments and preservations

In auditory processing, HS was within normal limits. BB and PL showed a similar level of impairment on minimal pair discrimination and auditory lexical decision. SD's performance in minimal pair discrimination was at chance but she performed better in auditory lexical decision. Performance was not related to pure tone audiometry results. On tests of phonological processing, SD was impaired across tasks involving auditory and picture rhyme judgement and written homophone decision. BB, HS and PL showed a tendency to perform better on homophone decision and auditory rhyme judgement compared to picture rhyme judgement. Poor performance on picture rhyme judgement could be due to deficits in lexical retrieval or in the link between phonological assembly and auditory analysis. None of the participants had a severe impairment in accessing the semantic representations of concrete words from either spoken or written input. On the Pyramids and Palm Trees assessment and a recognition memory test, HS was within normal limits, BB and PL scored just below normal performance and SD showed a significant impairment. SD and BB were unable to perform the Wisconsin Card Sorting Test, a test of executive function. HS and PL had some success but still performed below average. On tests of spoken production, all participants were impaired across modalities with a large number of phonological errors, indicative of an impairment of phonological assembly. PL showed additional characteristics of apraxia of speech including vowel distortion, slowed speech rate and articulatory groping. SD, BB and HS had co-occurring lexical retrieval difficulties shown by lower scores and semantic errors in picture naming and an effect of word frequency for SD.

Time post-onset

SD and PL were both 5 months post-onset. BB was 32 months and HS was 45 months post-onset.

Therapy

Therapy replicated the procedure described by Franklin *et al.* (2002) and consisted of two phases. Phase 1 aimed to improve auditory discrimination and consisted of six sessions. Phase 2 aimed to improve the monitoring of speech errors and took place over fourteen sessions, six sessions of external monitoring, four sessions of indirect monitoring and four sessions of direct internal monitoring. Participants were seen twice a week, with sessions of around 45 minutes. Participants were given homework based on therapy tasks to carry out between sessions. A multiple-baseline therapy design across tasks, materials and time was used with assessment twice pre-therapy, after each phase of therapy and 2 months after therapy.

Task	*Phoneme discrimination* Hearing spoken sounds/words and matching them to written material	*Self-monitoring* Hearing spoken words and judging whether the productions are correct/incorrect. Then to identify the location of the error within the word
Materials	Sixty-five words from the Nickels Naming Test. Set of 65 untreated items matched for syllable length, frequency and baseline accuracy (first attempt).	
Hierarchy	a) Deciding whether spoken words are long/short b) Spoken to written phoneme matching c) Identification of initial phoneme d) Identification of final phoneme e) Identification of rhyming word	a) External monitoring (Examiner off-line) – therapist produces word for client to judge b) Indirect monitoring (off-line) – client names picture and recorded response is played back to her for monitoring c) Direct internal monitoring (on-line) – client names picture and is immediately asked to judge production
Feedback on error	Not stated	Once errors identified, production of correct target word
Feedback if correct	Not stated	Not stated

Outcome

Client SD

After Phase 1, SD showed a significant improvement in naming and repetition of treated items. There was no change in untreated items. There was no change in SD's naming or repetition after Phase 2. Two months post-therapy, there was a decrease in naming of treated items but performance remained significantly higher than pre-therapy. There was no change in reading aloud and repetition and reading of nonwords remained at floor. After therapy, SD showed a significant improvement in auditory discrimination of word minimal pairs but no change in auditory lexical decision.

Client BB

After Phase 1, BB showed significant improvement in naming of treated items, with no change in untreated items. There was no change in naming after Phase 2 and gains in treated items were not maintained 2 months post-therapy. There was no change in repetition or reading aloud after either phase of therapy. Post-therapy, there was no change in nonword repetition or reading, auditory minimal pair discrimination or lexical decision.

Client HS

HS showed a significant improvement in naming of treated items after Phase 1, with a further significant increase after Phase 2. There was no change in naming of untreated items. Gains in naming were maintained 2 months post-therapy and at that time, retrieval of untreated items was also significantly higher than pre-therapy. HS showed no improvement in repetition after Phase 1 but a significant improvement in repetition of both treated and untreated words after Phase 2. There was no change in reading of treated items after either therapy phase but reading of untreated items improved significantly after Phase 1. There was no significant change in nonword reading or repetition.

Client PL

PL showed no significant change after either therapy phase for the naming of treated or untreated items. There was, however, a significant improvement across the five naming trials for both treated and untreated items. There was no significant change in repetition. The reading aloud of treated words improved significantly after Phase 1 but reduced again after Phase 2. There was no change in reading of untreated words. Post-therapy, there was no change in reading or repetition of nonwords, auditory discrimination and auditory lexical decision.

  SD, BB and HS showed gains in the naming of treated items. All of the clients had a combination of impairments in both phonological assembly and lexical retrieval. The authors attribute gains to improvement in the mapping between semantics and lexical phonology. PL showed limited improvement after therapy. He showed a similar amount of change during untreated periods as treatment periods, suggesting that overall improvement cannot be attributed reliably to therapy effects. The authors suggest his limited improvement could be due to a range of factors, e.g. age, limited opportunities for social interaction, the severity of his spoken output difficulties, hearing loss and the presence of apraxia of speech.

Other comments

The case series replicates therapy described in Franklin *et al.* (2002). None of the four participants responded in the same way as the original client, MB (Franklin *et al.*, 2002). The authors explore possible reasons for this, describing the different profiles of the clients and considering the implications of co-occurring deficits.

Study 28

Franklin, S., Buerk, F. and Howard, D. (2002). Generalised improvement in speech production for a subject with reproduction conduction aphasia. *Aphasiology, 16*, 1087–1114.

Focus of therapy: Phonological assembly (phonological encoding).

Target of therapy: Phonological assembly.

Therapy approach: Reactivation via a strategy of self-monitoring.

Client details

General information

MB was an 83-year-old retired lady. She suffered a left middle cerebral artery infarction.

Overall pattern of language impairments and preservations

MB presented with a reproduction conduction aphasia. Spontaneous speech was character-ised by the production of automatic words, phonological errors and neologisms. She had retained single-word comprehension and auditory matching span. Naming, repetition and oral reading were all impaired with phonological errors, particularly with longer words. There was no effect of frequency or imageability. She made repeated attempts at the target word (*conduite d'approche*). Production of nonwords was less accurate than real word production. MB's impairment was located at the level of phonological assembly, specifi-cally a problem of phoneme retrieval during phonological encoding. She also presented with impaired auditory rhyme judgement and some sentence-level difficulties in written comprehension.

Time post-onset

MB was about 6 months post-onset when therapy began.

Therapy

Therapy aimed to improve MB's perceptual processing and monitoring skills as a strategy for improving the detection and correction of errors in speech production. It was hypothesised that spoken word production would improve for both treated and untreated words. Therapy consisted of a total of twenty-one sessions (seven sessions in Phase 1, fourteen sessions in Phase 2) of around 30–45 minutes. Sessions were twice weekly. A multiple-baseline therapy design across tasks, materials and time was used.

Task	**Phoneme discrimination** Hearing spoken sounds/words and matching them to written material.	**Self-monitoring** Hearing spoken words and judging whether the productions are correct/ incorrect. Then to identify the location of the error within the word.
Materials	Sixty-five words from the Nickels Naming Test (set matched to an untreated set of 65 items).	Twenty words each session taken from treated 65 item set.

Hierarchy	a) Deciding whether spoken words are long/short b) Spoken to written phoneme matching c) Identification of initial phoneme d) Identification of final phoneme e) Identification of rhyming word	a) External monitoring (Examiner off-line) – therapist produces word for MB to judge b) Indirect monitoring (off-line) – MB names picture and recorded response is played back to her for monitoring c) Direct internal monitoring (on-line) – MB names picture and is immediately asked to judge production
Feedback on error	Not stated	Once errors identified, production of correct target word
Feedback if correct	Not stated	Not stated

Outcome

Following Phase 1, there was a significant improvement in naming. A further significant improvement in naming was seen following Phase 2. The improvement was maintained 4 months post-therapy. There was no significant difference between treated and untreated items. Following therapy, there was an overall decrease in MB's *conduite d'approche*, and when multiple responses were produced they more often resulted in correct productions.

Therapy resulted in significant improvement in the naming of both treated and untreated words. Improvement was also seen in the repetition and reading aloud of both words and nonwords. Generalisation to spontaneous speech was seen with a significant increase in the production of phonologically accurate words. As MB had stable naming performance before therapy and there was no change on a control task of written sentence comprehension, naming improvement is unlikely to be due to spontaneous recovery. The authors suggest that therapy resulted in an improved ability to select phonemes during phonological encoding. It is proposed that improvement was not due to improved self-monitoring skills.

Other comments

With rigorous initial and reassessment data, this is a thorough evaluation of the therapy but it is not clear what aspect of therapy is responsible for the improvements seen. Waldron *et al.* (2011a, 2011b) replicate this therapy approach with a number of clients with more limited generalisation effects.

Study 29

Waldron, H., Whitworth, A. and Howard, D. (2011b) Comparing monitoring and production based approaches to the treatment of phonological assembly difficulties in aphasia. *Aphasiology, 25(10)*, 1153–1173.

Focus of therapy: Phonological assembly.

Target of therapy: Phonological assembly.

Therapy approach: Reactivation.

Client details

General information

RD was a 87-year-old, right-handed man. A CT scan at the time of the stroke showed a middle cerebral artery infarct. He was a native English speaker who had been in the armed forces prior to retirement. He had some hearing loss which was within the normal range for a man aged over 80 years. RD performed within the normal range on a recognition memory test and an assessment of executive function and problem-solving skills.

Overall pattern of language impairments and preservations

RE's spoken and written comprehension for single words was intact, with relatively well-preserved picture semantics. He showed a mild impairment in auditory minimal pair discrimination and lexical decision. He also showed some difficulty with written rhyme judgement and homophone decision for pairs involving nonwords. He had impaired nonword reading and repetition. His spoken production was impaired across all modalities, with repetition being the least affected and naming the most impaired. His errors were mainly phonologically related nonwords. He was aware of his errors and produced occasional self-corrections. There was a significant effect of word length on real word repetition and reading, with no effect of frequency on any task. He showed some hesitancy and groping but did not show any prosodic abnormalities or distorted articulation. The authors suggest that RE has impaired phonological encoding with some features of apraxia of speech.

Time post-onset

RE was 3 years post-onset at the time of the study.

Therapy

Therapy consisted of two, 45 minute sessions per week. The first phase consisted of six sessions focusing on auditory discrimination. The second phase comprised eight sessions; this phase focused on production, involving minimal contrast pairs, articulatory–kinematic and orthographic cues. The third phase lasted eight sessions, four focused on external monitoring and four on direct internal monitoring. In contrast to Franklin *et al.* (2002), indirect monitoring with the tape recording and monitoring of responses was omitted.

Task	*Phoneme discrimination* Hearing spoken sounds/words and matching them to written material	*Production* Name picture of target word	*Self-monitoring* Hearing spoken words and judging whether the productions are correct/ incorrect and then identify the location of the error within the word

Materials	One hundred words containing high- and low-frequency items of varying syllable length. Words divided into two sets of 50, matched for baseline accuracy, syllable length and frequency. First set – treatment items for first & second phase of therapy. Second set untreated in Phase 1 and 2. Third set consisting of 25 words from Set 1 and 25 from Set 2 treated in Phase 3. For Phase 2, set of minimal contrast words which differed by single phoneme. For longer words, contrast word shared as many target phonemes as possible.		
Hierarchy	a) Deciding whether spoken words are long/short b) Spoken to written phoneme matching c) Identification of initial phoneme d) Identification of final phoneme e) Identification of rhyming word	a) CV words b) Longer words	a) External monitoring (Examiner off-line) – therapist produces word for client to judge b) Direct internal monitoring (on-line) – client names picture and is immediately asked to judge production
Feedback on error	Not stated	Progressive cues until correct response elicited: a) Articulogram of initial phoneme, with grapheme, written instructions re: articulation and mirror to encourage copying. b) Initial phoneme with above c) Written word d) Word for repetition e) Segmentation of word into syllables	Once errors identified, production of correct target word.
Feedback if correct	Not stated	a) Repetition of word × five b) Presentation of contrast word c) Repetition of contrast word with explanation of difference d) Alternate production of target and contrast word	

Outcome

RE showed a stable baseline in naming performance. There was a significant gain in spoken naming and repetition from pre-therapy to post-therapy. There was no change in reading aloud. Following Phase 1 of therapy, no significant change was seen in naming, reading aloud or repetition. The second production phase resulted in a significant improvement in naming, with a significant increase in naming of treated items but no change in untreated words. Phase 2 resulted in no change in reading aloud or repetition. The monitoring therapy in Phase 3 resulted in no further significant improvement. Across the time, there was a significant increase in the proportion of successful self-corrections in naming of treated items. There was no change in the self correction in naming of untreated items. There was no change in performance on the control task, written sentence comprehension.

There were significant gains in the naming of treated items after both the production and monitoring phase of therapy. Effects are likely to be due to therapy as RE had a stable baseline and there was no change on the control task. The authors discuss the differences between therapy outcome for MB (Franklin *et al.* 2002) and RE, exploring possible differences in initial presentation and hypotheses relating to the presence of lexical retrieval difficulties or apraxia of speech.

Other comments

This study is a partial replication of the therapy described in Franklin *et al.* (2002) and Waldron *et al.* (2011a), with the addition of a production phase. The authors highlight potential limitations of the study and discuss the possible advantages of the more direct, production focused approach. Due to the failure to replicate the generalised improvements seen in Franklin *et al.* (2002) and the different responses to the same therapy across this and previous studies (Franklin *et al.*, 2002 & Waldron *et al.*, 2011), the authors emphasise that the same therapy can work in different ways for different clients.

12 Therapy for verb retrieval and production

Summary of verb-naming studies

Over the last decade, there has been an increasing interest in the differences between nouns and verbs and whether therapy approaches that have been successfully applied to nouns can be similarly applied to verb retrieval. Within these studies, the primary focus is on treating verbs as single words, with relatively limited consideration of the role of the verb in sentence production. Therapy studies focused on verb retrieval are discussed in section A of this chapter. These studies, using techniques initially designed for nouns, have provided evidence that the same tasks can be effective. There are also a number of studies that have directly compared the effectiveness of therapy for nouns and verbs; these are discussed later in the chapter and are set out in section B. Some of the studies included in section A have acknowledged the relationship between verb retrieval and sentence production, either in the therapy approach or the measures to evaluate therapy outcome. The impact of therapy on constrained sentence production is often considered, with some studies also looking at change in connected speech. Studies have included tasks with sentence cues, generation of a sentence or consideration of the nouns that occur alongside the verb in a sentence. These studies have been included in this chapter as they either use these tasks alongside single word tasks or contrast sentence level therapy with single word therapy. A more detailed review of verb retrieval studies that includes both single word and sentence level therapies is seen in Webster and Whitworth (2012). Other studies where verb retrieval is treated only at sentence level have not been included. The cognitive neuropsychological model that forms the basis of this volume is restricted to a consideration of single words. Appropriate consideration of sentence level therapies where verb retrieval is treated alongside other sentence processing deficits would require full elaboration of the different theoretical positions for sentence comprehension and production; the reader is referred to Faroqi-Shah and Thompson (2012), Marshall (2013), Mitchum and Berndt (2001) and Webster *et al.* (2009) for further discussions of intervention for sentence processing difficulties.

A. Verb studies

As for nouns, therapy for verb retrieval has focused on improving access to the word's meaning, improving access to the lexical representation or strengthening the connection between the semantic system and the phonological output lexicon. A summary of the therapy studies focused on verb retrieval can be found in Table 12.1. Therapy for verb retrieval has primarily drawn on tasks shown to be effective for nouns and has included a variety of semantic tasks (e.g. semantic judgement, written word-to-picture matching, naming with semantic cues) and phonological tasks (e.g. rhyme judgement, repetition, naming with phonological cues).

Table 12.1 Summary of studies targeting verb retrieval

Level of impairment	Therapy studies	Area targeted in therapy	Therapy tasks
Semantic system	Study 1: Raymer and Ellsworth (2002, p. 199)	Comparison of semantic therapy, phonological therapy and rehearsal	• Semantic therapy – produce verb, answer questions about verb meaning and then repeat word • Phonological therapy – produce verb, answer questions about initial phoneme and rhyming words and then repeat word • Rehearsal – repetition of word
	Study 2: Webster *et al.* (2005, p. 202)	Semantic	• Written semantic tasks followed by naming • Written verb and noun association • Sentence generation following generation of nouns
	Study 3: Webster and Gordon (2009, p. 204)	Semantic	• Verb and noun association – read verb aloud, find related word and produce sentence
Semantic system and phonological output lexicon (either within or across subjects)	Study 4: Wambaugh *et al.* (2002, p. 206)	Comparison of semantic cueing (SCT) and phonological cueing (PCT)	• SCT – picture naming with progressive semantic cues • PCT – picture naming with progressive phonological cues
	Study 5: Rodriguez *et al.* (2006, p. 209)	Comparison of gesture + verbal treatment (GVT) and semantic–phonologic treatment (SP)	• GVT – presentation of verbal and gestural model before multiple productions • SP – multiple repetition of word with yes/no questions about semantic and phonological features
	Study 6: Wambaugh and Ferguson (2007, p. 211)	Semantic	• Semantic feature analysis – guided verbalisation of semantic features
	Study 7: Rose and Sussmilch (2008, p. 213)	Comparison of treatment approaches	• Repetition • Semantic therapy – generation of semantic features • Semantic-gesture therapy – gesture and verbal model with generation of gestures for semantic features • Gesture therapy – gesture and verbal model

Table 12.1 Continued

	Study 8: Conroy *et al.* (2009a) (p215)	Comparison of word and sentence cues	• Word cues – decreasing phonemic and orthographic cues
			• Sentence cues – sentence frame with decreasing phonemic and orthographic cues
	Study 9: Boo and Rose (2011) (p217)	Comparison of treatment approaches	• Repetition
			• Semantic therapy – generation of semantic features
			• Semantic-gesture therapy – gesture and verbal model with generation of gestures for semantic features
			• Gesture therapy – gesture and verbal model
			• Repetition–orthographic therapy – written word and verbal model
Phonological output lexicon(or access to it)	Study 10: Fink *et al.* (1992, p. 220)	Comparison of direct verb training (DVT) and verb repetition priming (VRP)	• DVT – retrieve verb, agent and patient arguments and produce sentence
			• VRP – repeat sentence containing verb and then describe picture
	Study 11: Marshall *et al.* (1998, p. 222)	Semantic	• Written word-to-picture matching
			• Written odd one out
			• Generation of noun to written verb
			• Generation of verbs to link noun phrases
			• Generation of verbs to verbal scenarios
	Study 12: Schneider and Thompson (2003, p. 225)	Semantic	• Picture naming with definitions emphasising semantic or argument structure information
	Study 13: Edwards and Tucker (2006, p. 227)	Semantic	• Sentence completion
			• Naming to definition
			• Picture naming to graded semantic and phonemic cues

Therapy has resulted in improved retrieval of treated verbs, with minimal generalisation to untreated verbs. Many of the verb studies have compared different treatment approaches, with limited evidence that methods are differentially effective.

Verbs contain semantic and syntactic information integral to sentence production. Acknowledging this relationship, therapy has included sentence cues (e.g. Conroy, Sage & Lambon Ralph, 2009a) or sentence completion tasks (e.g. Edwards & Tucker, 2006); these tasks elicit verbs within a sentence frame, which is perhaps a more natural paradigm than single action naming. Other studies ask participants to select nouns that go with the verb (e.g. Webster & Gordon, 2009), generate nouns related to the verb (e.g. Marshall *et al.*, 1998, Wambaugh & Ferguson, 2007) or combine the two (e.g. Webster, Morris & Franklin, 2005). With consideration of nouns that are semantically related to verbs and how they might be used in sentences, these tasks target verb argument structure alongside verb retrieval (see Webster & Whitworth, 2012, for more complete discussion of the role of verb argument structure in verb therapy studies).

In evaluating the effectiveness of therapy, some of the studies have considered the impact of improving verb retrieval on sentence production and the production of connected speech in picture description, narrative or conversation. When assessed, improvements in sentence production have been seen across studies focusing on verb retrieval in a single word context, sentence context and those combining work on verb and argument structure. Gains in the retrieval of treated verbs are accompanied by gains in sentence production around treated verbs (e.g. Marshall *et al.*, 1998, Schneider & Thompson, 2003) when participants do not have co-occurring sentence processing difficulties. These gains often extend to untreated verbs, although there is often a significant difference between gains in treated and untreated verbs (Schneider &Thompson, 2003). Improvements in connected speech have also been reported in some studies and it is important to consider these gains when evaluating the functional outcome of the therapies. For example, GR (Fink *et al.*, 1992) showed an increase in the proportion of words produced in a sentence and the proportion of well-formed sentences in a picture description task. NS (Webster *et al.*, 2005) produced fewer single phrases and more two argument structures around lexical verbs in narrative speech. In Edwards and Tucker's (2006) study, two of the three clients showed gains in conversation. These gains are primarily structural and are most apparent in studies that focus on argument and syntactic structure as well as verb retrieval.

EVALUATIONS OF VERB STUDIES

Study 1

Raymer, A.M. and Ellsworth, T. A. (2002). Response to contrasting verb retrieval treatments: a case study. *Aphasiology, 16*, 1031–1045.

Focus of therapy: Verb retrieval – semantic impairment.

Target of therapy: Semantic and phonological approaches.

Therapy approach: Reactivation.

Client details

General information

WR was a 54-year-old woman. She left school at 13 and worked as a hairdresser prior to a left hemisphere CVA. A CT scan showed a left dorsolateral frontal lesion encompassing Broca's area, the anterior insular region and sub-cortical white matter.

Overall pattern of language impairments and preservations

WR presented with a transcortical motor aphasia, with better preserved repetition than spontaneous speech. She had non-fluent sentence production. She had a mild impairment for both noun and verb retrieval producing semantically related errors. She also had a mild impairment in comprehension, making errors on picture to written word matching and picture to picture associate matching involving semantically related nouns and verbs. There was no significant difference between her performance on nouns and verbs in either comprehension or production. The authors propose her difficulties reflect a mild semantic impairment. Her verb retrieval difficulties were thought to be responsible (at least in part) for her sentence production difficulties.

Time post-onset

She was 3 months post-onset at the time of the study.

Therapy

The study contrasts the effects of three different types of verb retrieval therapy: phonologic, semantic and rehearsal therapies. WR was seen for two or three, 1 hour sessions per week over the course of 4 months. There was a 6 week holiday break between the semantic and rehearsal therapies. A multiple baseline (across behaviours) cross-over design was used. Performance on a control task (oral reading of abstract) was also monitored. During the treatment phases, training was preceded by a daily probe test assessing acquisition of the trained verbs, generalised sentence production for trained verbs, generalised verb naming and sentence production for untrained verbs and oral reading. Each treatment phase stopped when a 90% correct criterion for the naming of treated verbs was reached.

Task	1. Phonologic therapy	2. Semantic therapy	3. Rehearsal
	Name the verb and then answer two phonological Yes/No questions before going to rehearsal phase. Yes/No questions were about initial phoneme and a rhyming word Rehearsal – three repetitions of word, silent rehearsal, reattempted naming and then three further repetitions.	Name the verb and then answer two semantic Yes/No questions before going to rehearsal phase. Yes/No questions were about a coordinate verb and a related noun. Rehearsal – three repetitions of word, silent rehearsal, reattempted naming and then three further repetitions.	Rehearsal – three repetitions of word, silent rehearsal, reattempted naming and then three further repetitions.

Materials	Seventy verbs that WR had consistent difficulty naming. Three sets of 20 treated via phonologic, semantic and rehearsal therapy respectively. Ten control words. Sets of verbs matched for baseline performance and comparable for argument structure of verbs. Words within phonologic and semantic set of higher frequency than rehearsal set.		
Hierarchy	No hierarchy	No hierarchy	No hierarchy
Feedback on error	Discuss response accuracy following naming	Discuss response accuracy following naming	Not stated
Feedback if correct	Discuss response accuracy following naming	Discuss response accuracy following naming	Not stated

Outcome

Prior to therapy, naming performance was low and stable across multiple baselines. Following phonologic therapy, naming performance on treated words reached 90% criterion after six sessions; this reflected a significant gain when compared to baseline performance. No improvement was seen on untreated items (semantic and rehearsal set). Following semantic therapy, naming performance on treated words reached 100% criterion after four sessions, again reflecting a significant improvement. No improvement was seen on untreated (rehearsal set). Following rehearsal therapy, performance on treated items improved significantly but never reached criterion. When compared for naming accuracy, there was no significant difference between the three treatment sets at the final training probe or at the 1 month follow up.

Following each phase of verb retrieval therapy, significant improvements were seen in the production of grammatically and semantically correct sentences incorporating the target verbs. Although performance for semantic and phonologic verbs was greater than for rehearsal training verbs, there was no significant difference across treatment sets for sentence accuracy at the final training probe or in the 1 month follow up. There was no change in oral reading performance during the study. No information is given about the functional outcome of the therapy and whether it had any impact on spontaneous speech. The authors suggest that gains across all therapies may be consequence of the presence of the picture and the resulting semantic activation of the treated words. Gains are likely to be a consequence of therapy as WR had stable baseline performance, gains were specific to treated items and there was no change on the control task.

Other comments

Following each treatment phase, WR produced more accurate sentences, although sentence production never reached criterion due to the presence of errors involving the mis-selection or omission of noun or pronoun arguments. This reveals the impact of other difficulties on sentence production.

Study 2

Webster, J., Morris, J. and Franklin, S. (2005). Effects of therapy targeted at verb retrieval and the realisation of the predicate argument structure: A case study. *Aphasiology, 19(8)*, 748–764.

Focus of therapy: Verb retrieval – semantic impairment.

Target of therapy: Semantic (with sentence production).

Therapy approach: Reactivation.

Client details

General information

NS was a 49-year-old man who had a left CVA. No information is available about the site of the lesion. He had left school at 15 and worked for the civil service as a fisheries inspector prior to the CVA.

Overall pattern of language impairments and preservations

NS is described as having adequate comprehension for everyday speech. His speech was hesitant and characterised by word-finding difficulties and sentence fragments. He had mild difficulties in the comprehension of nouns and verbs. He had impaired retrieval of nouns and verbs, with verbs more impaired than nouns. On assessment of sentence comprehension, he had problems understanding reversible sentences. In sentence production, he had difficulty producing complete sentences, with particular problems producing sentences with an increased number of arguments. His narrative speech was characterised by a heavy reliance on single phrases and two argument structures; his two argument structures were based around the copula verb.

   The authors propose that NS's difficulties in sentence production are likely to be a consequence of multiple difficulties: a mild semantic impairment affecting noun and verb comprehension and retrieval, difficulty specifying the predicate argument structure (PAS) and problems with thematic role assignment.

Time post-onset

He was 6 years post-onset at the time of the study.

Therapy

Therapy aimed to improve (1) verb retrieval, (2) awareness of the relationship between verbs and nouns within sentences and (3) the production of 1, 2 and 3 argument structures. Therapy was given within an intensive 10 week block. The study describes individual therapy given in five, 45 minute sessions over 3 days each week. NS was also receiving 10 hours of group therapy each week.

Task	1. Verb naming	2. Verb and noun association	3. Sentence generation
	Semantic tasks e.g. spoken-word–picture matching, written-word–picture matching, written-word–picture matching followed by picture naming	Written worksheets with verbs. NS asked to identify the nouns that fulfil particular thematic roles	NS given the written verb and asked to think of words that could fulfil particular thematic roles, then asked to use the words to produce a sentence.
Materials	48 verbs selected by NS. Functional categories related to his hobbies, interests and everyday life.		
Hierarchy	No hierarchy	Increasing semantic relatedness of distracters, Use of distracters that could fulfil another role in sentence.	NS encouraged to think of more words, and think about the diverse meanings of verbs.
Feedback on error	If unable to retrieve the word, word presented for repetition.	If incorrect word chosen, target and error response contrasted, focusing on meaning of verb.	Not stated
Feedback if correct	Not stated	Not stated	Once sentence produced, the optional/obligatory nature of sentence components was discussed.

A multiple baseline across behaviours design with tests of single word and sentence production was used alongside control tasks of written noun naming and sentence comprehension.

Outcome

During the verb retrieval therapy, a significant change in the retrieval of the treated verbs was seen. There was no related improvement on a general test of verb naming, suggesting no generalisation to untreated verbs. In sentence production, NS retrieved more verbs; these were not always the target verb but were close semantic alternatives which allowed the production of the PAS (and the retrieval of the appropriate nouns). Following therapy, there was also a reduction in the omission of obligatory arguments. In narrative production, he produced fewer single phrases (although still a high proportion compared to normal speakers) and his two argument structures were built around more lexical verbs. There was no change in written naming or in sentence comprehension.

NS was 6 years post-onset prior to the therapy and there was no change on the control tasks. The improvements seen in verb retrieval and sentence production are therefore likely to be due to therapy. Therapy improved access to a personally useful set of verbs. The more generalised gains in sentence production are attributed to NS having a better awareness about the role of verb and a general strategy that enabled him to specify the arguments around the verbs be could produce.

Other comments

The authors acknowledge the possible contribution of group therapy to treatment outcome. The therapy approach combines work on verb retrieval and sentence production.

Study 3

Webster, J. and Gordon, B. (2009). Contrasting therapy effects for verb and sentence processing difficulties: A discussion of what worked and why. *Aphasiology, 23(10)*, 1231–1251.

Focus of therapy: Verb retrieval – semantic impairment.

Target of therapy: Semantic (with sentence production).

Therapy approach: Reactivation.

Client details

General information

MV was a 63-year-old woman who left school at 15. She had a variety of jobs and was a barmaid at a local club before retirement. She had aphasia as a result of a sub-arachnoid haemorrhage. A CT scan showed an extensive left temperoparietal intracerebral haematoma and mild obstructive hydrocephalus.

Overall pattern of language impairments and preservations

MV is described as having adequate comprehension for everyday speech. Her speech was non-fluent and consisted of mainly single nouns with some short phrases. Her spoken comprehension of single nouns was within the normal range but she presented with verb comprehension difficulties. Her single word repetition was retained and she was just outside normal limits in reading aloud. Her retrieval of both nouns and verbs was significantly impaired, with no difference between the two word types. She produced mainly 'no' responses with occasional semantic errors. On assessment, she found it difficult to understand reversible sentences. Her difficulties in sentence production seemed primarily to reflect her verb retrieval difficulties as sentences were abandoned at the point of the verb.

The authors suggest she had a semantic impairment affecting verb comprehension and verb and noun retrieval. Her word-retrieval difficulties, particularly for verbs, impacted her sentence production.

Time post-onset

She was 9 months post-onset at the time of intervention period 1 and 14 months post-onset at the start of intervention period 2.

Therapy

The study describes two periods of intervention. Intervention period 1 is only briefly described with a focus on intervention period 2.

Intervention Period 1

Therapy aimed to improve the retrieval of everyday nouns and verbs and to improve sentence comprehension and production. Therapy took place within an intensive 11 week block. The study describes individual therapy given in five, 45-minute sessions over 3 days each week. She was also receiving 10 hours of group therapy each week. Therapy consisted of divergent verb and noun retrieval tasks and verb-centred mapping therapy. Therapy resulted in no change in sentence production or comprehension. Formal assessments of noun and verb retrieval were not repeated but limited progress was seen in therapy sessions.

Intervention Period 2

Therapy aimed to improve the comprehension and production of 80 everyday verbs, the association of these verbs with common nouns and the production of sentences containing those nouns and verbs.

Therapy was carried out twice weekly in individual sessions of 45 minutes. Therapy was divided into two phases, A and B, each concentrating on a set of 40 verbs. Each phase lasted eight sessions and was preceded and followed by assessment. A multiple baseline across behaviours design was used with monitoring of treated and untreated verbs at the end of phase A.

Task	**Verb and noun association** Action pictures presented with written verb and a choice of four written nouns (target, semantically related distracter and two unrelated distracters). MV was asked to read out the action word, point to the word that went with it and then produce a sentence containing the two words.
Materials	Two sets of 40 verbs, set A and set B. Each set had related nouns that consisted of ten agents, 20 patients/objects and ten instruments or locations.
Hierarchy	No hierarchy
Feedback on error	If incorrect noun chosen, target and distracter were contrasted. If incorrect sentence production, correct sentence presented verbally but MV not asked to repeat.
Feedback if correct	Not stated

Outcome (Intervention Period 2)

During therapy, MV was consistently able to read the verb aloud and select the appropriate noun. There was a variable but steady improvement in her ability to produce an appropriate sentence. Following phase A of therapy, there was a significant improvement in her ability to retrieve the treated verbs with no change in the untreated verbs. Following phase B, there was a significant improvement in set B verbs. Gains in verb retrieval were maintained 6 months post-therapy. Gains in verb retrieval were accompanied by significant gains in verb comprehension. In sentence production to picture, each phase of therapy resulted in an increase in the number of correct and appropriate sentences. In sentence generation when given the verb, there was no change following phase A of therapy. Following phase B, there was a significant increase in the number of correct and appropriate sentences. Changes in sentence production were also seen on a formal test of sentence production where she was able to produce more nouns in the context of a sentence.

The gains in verb retrieval, verb comprehension and sentence production are likely to be a consequence of therapy. The authors attribute the gains in sentence production partly to improved retrieval of a set of verbs and partly to an improved awareness of verb argument structure.

Other comments

The authors consider the reasons why intervention period 1 was not effective, comparing it with the gains seen following intervention period 2. The therapy approach combines work on verb retrieval and sentence production.

Study 4

Wambaugh, J.L., Doyle, P.J., Martinez, A.L. and Kalinyak-Fliszar, M. (2002). Effects of two lexical retrieval cueing treatments on action naming in aphasia. *Journal of Rehabilitation Research and Development, 39(4),* 455–466.

Focus of therapy: Verb retrieval – 1 participant with mixed semantic–phonological impairment, 1 participant with phonological impairment.

Target of therapy: Semantic and phonological approaches.

Therapy approach: Reactivation.

Client details

The study describes three speakers with chronic aphasia.

General information

Speaker 1 was a 67-year-old man. He had 14 years education and worked as a real estate broker. Speaker 2 was a 57-year-old man. He had 16 years education and worked as a manager. Speaker 3 was a 74-year-old man. He had 12 years education and worked as a post office courier. All of the speakers were right-handed. No information was given about the site of their lesions/nature of their CVAs.

Overall pattern of language impairments and preservations

Speakers 1 and 2 presented with a mixed non-fluent aphasia. Speaker 3's aphasia type was not specified. All three speakers presented with word-retrieval difficulties of varying severity.

Speaker 1 named nearly 50% of nouns correctly. Speaker 3 had the most severe difficulties (around 5% correct). When naming verbs, speakers 1 and 2 produced predominantly semantically related nouns with a few semantically related verbs. Speaker 3 produced a mixture of errors, semantically related verbs, non-specific verbs, gestural responses and semantically related nouns. Speakers 1 and 2 were considered to have mixed semantic and phonological difficulties. Speaker 3 was considered to have predominantly phonological difficulties.

Time post-onset

Speaker 1 was 43 months, speaker 2 was 122 months and speaker 3 was 54 months post-onset.

Therapy

Therapy aimed to improve verb retrieval. Semantic Cueing therapy (SCT) was thought to facilitate retrieval at the lexical semantic level with phonological cueing therapy (PCT) targeting the lexical phonological level. A multiple baseline across behaviours design across behaviours was used for speaker 1 and speaker 2. Speaker 1 received SCT. Speaker 2 received PCT. Speaker 3 had SCT and PCT in an alternating treatment design. Therapy was preceded by baseline naming sessions (four sessions for speakers 1 and 2, three sessions for speaker 3). Participants received two to three sessions per week. It was intended that speakers 1 and 2 would receive treatment until they reached 90% criterion for two to three sessions or a total of fifteen sessions. Speaker 3 had twenty sessions.

Task	Semantic cueing (Speaker 1)	Phonological cueing (Speaker 2)	Semantic and phonological cueing (Speaker 3)
Materials	Three sets of 12 verbs matched for verb arguments structure, existence of nouns root and pre-therapy difficulty	Three sets of 12 verbs matched for verb arguments structure, existence of nouns root and pre-therapy difficulty	Three sets of six verbs matched for verb arguments structure, existence of nouns root and pre-therapy difficulty. Set 1 PCT. Set 2 SCT
Hierarchy	1. Picture naming 2. Picture naming with verbal description of target 3. Picture with sentence completion (non-specific sentence) 4. Picture with sentence completion (semantically loaded sentence) 5. Picture with verbal model for repetition	1. Picture naming 2. Picture naming with nonword rhyme 3. Picture with first sound cue 4. Picture with sentence completion including rhyme and first sound cues 5. Picture with verbal model for repetition	As described in SCT and PCT

Feedback on error	State correct/ incorrect. Sequential application of cues until correct response	State correct/ incorrect. Sequential application of cues until correct response	State correct/ incorrect. Sequential application of cues until correct response
Feedback if correct	State correct/ incorrect. Reversal of steps to elicit correct response at each of previous steps	State correct/ incorrect. Reversal of steps to elicit correct response at each of previous steps	State correct/ incorrect. Reversal of steps to elicit correct response at each of previous steps

During a pre-stimulation phase, the target item was presented in picture form alongside three picture foils (two semantically related on one unrelated) and had to match the spoken form with the target picture.

Outcome

In a previous study of noun retrieval, PCT and SCT were applied sequentially and repeatedly to four sets of nouns. Speaker 1 showed no response preference to SCT or PCT, speaker 2 showed a slightly better response to PCT and speaker 3 showed a superior response to PCT than to SCT.

In this study speaker 1 showed stable naming performance across all three sets during baseline. Following SCT to set 1, naming responses increased rapidly and met criterion at session four. Eight sessions were given in total due to variation in session seven. Improvement was also seen on the untreated set 2 verbs following treatment for set 1. Set 2 verbs continued to improve when treated and there was some improvement in the untreated set 3. Speaker 2 showed stable or declining performance across all 3 sets during baseline. When PCT was applied to set 1, there was an increase in correct naming responses but the criterion of 90% correct was not met after fifteen sessions. There was no change in the naming of untreated items. When PCT was applied to set 2, there was limited improvement and the trained set 1 items returned to baseline performance. During the baseline sessions, speaker 3 named only one or two items correctly. Upon application of SCT and PCT, there was a steady increase in correct responses for both sets of items. one hundred per cent correct performance was achieved for the items treated by SCT in sixteen sessions and for the items treated by PCT in seventeen sessions. No improvement was seen on the untreated items.

Change in each case was likely to be a consequence of therapy as all clients had a stable profile prior to therapy. The authors propose that the response of some of the clients to the verb treatment was different to that for nouns. Speaker 1's response to SCT applied to verbs was similar to his previous response to SCT noun therapy. Speaker 2's response to PCT differed from his previous noun therapy as he failed to reach criterion for either verb set. His relative improvement may, however, be similar as his baseline level was much lower. In contrast to the noun therapy, speaker 3 showed positive improvements across both treatment types. The authors suggest that this may be due to a focus on a smaller number of items.

Other comments

The study does not look at the statistical significance of any improvement seen and the number of treated items in each set is quite small. The authors comment that this study was not designed to compare the effects of verb and noun therapy and that the different effects should therefore be considered with caution. SCT and PCT are also compared in Wambaugh, Cameron, Kalinyak-Fliszar, Nessler & Wright (2004). This study looks at five people with aphasia, receiving sequential SCT and PCT for different verb sets. The effects of SCT and PCT were comparable; two subjects showed significant gains in treated verbs, two subjects showed limited gains and one subject showed no gains.

Study 5

Rodriguez, A.D., Raymer, A.M. and Gonzalez-Rothi, L.J. (2006). Effects of gesture + verbal treatment and semantic–phonologic treatments for verb retrieval in aphasia. *Aphasiology, 20(2/3/4)*, 286–297.

Focus of therapy: Verb retrieval – 1 participant with semantic impairment, 1 participant with mixed semantic–phonological impairment, 1 participant with phonological impairment.

Target of therapy: Semantic–phonological.

Therapy approach: Semantic–phonologic therapy – reactivation, GVT -cognitive relay strategy.

Client details

The study describes four people with aphasia.

General information

P1 was a 73-year-old man who was right-handed and had 14 years education. He had a lesion in the left temporo-parietal region. P2 was a 63-year-old man who was left-handed and had 12 years education. He had a lesion in the left sub-cortical white matter. P3 was a 52-year-old woman who was right-handed and had 12 years education. She had a lesion in the left temporo-parietal region. P4 was a 72-year-old man who was right-handed and had 12 years education. He had a large lesion in the left fronto-temporo-parietal region. P3 and P4 presented with significant limb apraxia.

Overall pattern of language impairments and preservations

The participants all had a verb retrieval impairment. P4 had an additional apraxia of speech. P1 and P2 had conduction aphasia. P3 presented with Wernicke's aphasia and P4 had Broca's aphasia. When compared on tests of verb naming, sentence completion and spoken word-to-picture verification, it was proposed that P1 had a mild phonologically based verb impairment, P4 had severe semantic difficulties and P2 and P3 had mixed semantic–phonological difficulties.

Time post-onset

Participants varied in their time post-onset, 8–96 months (P1, 8 months, P2, 9 months, P3, 24 months and P4, 96 months).

Therapy

Therapy aimed to improve the retrieval of verbs, comparing the effects of gesture + verbal treatment (GVT) and semantic–phonologic (SP) treatment. Participants received two to three, 60 minute sessions per week. Each phase of therapy lasted ten sessions. P1, P3 and P4 received GVT followed by SP with P2 receiving the opposite. A multiple baseline across behaviours and participants design was used. Participants were tested at baseline, with daily naming probes during each treatment phase and then at maintenance, 1 month post-therapy.

Task	Gesture + verbal treatment (GVT)	Semantic–phonologic (SP) treatment
	1. Presentation of picture with model of target word and gesture 2. Presentation of gesture with participant imitating × 3 3. Presentation of target word with participant repeating × 3 4. After 5 second pause, presentation of picture with participant asked to say what is happening	1. Presentation of picture with model of target word, participant practised word × 3 2. Presentation of four yes/no questions about semantic and phonological characteristics about item 3. Participant produces target word × 3 4. After 5 second pause, participant is asked to say what is happening in the picture
Materials	Sixty black-and-white drawings of one and two place verbs. Twenty for GVT treatment, 20 for SP treatment and 20 untreated controls. Balanced for level of accuracy, with attempts to balance word frequency and syllable length	
Hierarchy	None	
Feedback on error	If problems with gesture, manipulation of limb to form gesture If problems with repetition, segmentation of word for participant to produce syllable by syllable	Modelling of correct response
Feedback if correct	Reinforcement of correct response	Reinforcement of correct response

Outcome

For all participants, baseline measures were low and stable. No participant reached ceiling levels of performance before the ten sessions were completed. P1 showed large increases in the spoken naming of trained items in both GVT and SP treatment phases. P2 and P3 showed some gains in spoken naming of trained verbs in SP treatment but no gains in the GVT treatment. P4 showed no gains during either treatment phase. None of the participants showed any gains in the retrieval of untrained verbs, Following SP, none of the participants showed improved gestures for the trained items. 3/4 (P1, P3 and P4) participants showed increased use of gestures for trained items following GVT but there was no gain for gestures of the untrained verbs.

The authors suggest the gains seen for P1 were a consequence of his mild phonological impairment. The improvements made by P2 and P3 during the SP treatment were attributed to the fact that therapy activated the impaired naming mechanism to produce target word on at least some occasions. The lack of improvement made by P4 was attributed to his severe semantic impairment. The authors propose that GVT is effective for promoting gesture use even in participant with severe limb apraxia and that this may be a potential means of communication.

Study 6

Wambaugh, J.L. and Ferguson, M. (2007). Application of semantic feature analysis to retrieval of action names in aphasia. *Journal of Rehabilitation Research and Development, 44(3)*, 381–394.

Focus of therapy: Verb retrieval – semantic and phonological impairment.

Target of therapy: Semantic.

Therapy approach: Reactivation and compensation.

Client details

General information

The participant was a 74-year-old woman who had had a single left parietal CVA. She was a right-handed, native English speaker who had worked as a secretary.

Overall pattern of language impairments and preservations

The participant presented with a moderate anomic aphasia, with significant word-retrieval difficulties. She presented with deficits in semantic association in verb and noun comprehension, suggestive of semantic difficulties. In the retrieval of nouns and verbs, she made a majority of no response errors; her other errors were semantic errors and descriptions containing some semantic information. Occasional phonemic errors and problems with rhyme judgement suggested some difficulties at the phonological level. The authors suggest that the participant had a combination of semantic and phonological difficulties.

Time post-onset

The participant was 4 years, 2 months post-onset at the time of the study.

Therapy

The study aimed to investigate whether action naming would benefit from semantic feature analysis (SFA) therapy. The authors chose the treatment method as they thought it may promote generalisation and may be useful as a compensatory strategy. A multiple baseline across behaviours design was used to monitor the effects of treatment of trained and untrained actions and on discourse production. There was repeated assessment of action naming prior to therapy, continued monitoring during two phases of therapy and then follow up assessment at 2 and 6 weeks post-therapy. The participant received 45–60 minute sessions, three times a week. Each treated word set was trained until they reached criterion (80% correct in three consecutive sessions) or for a total of twelve sessions. Each session involved a probe and one run through of the therapy for each item in the word set.

Task	**Semantic feature analysis** Picture placed on semantic feature diagram and person guided through features and then asked to name. Features consisted of subject, purpose of action, part of body or tool used to carry out action, description of physical properties, usual location and related objects or actions.
Materials	Forty action names divided into four lists of ten words. Lists matched for frequency, age of acquisition, imageability and visual complexity. Argument structure balanced across lists in terms of the number of one and two place verbs. List 1 treated during phase 1 of treatment. List 2 treated during phase 2 of treatment. List 3 was exposure list, probed across sessions but not treated. List 4 only assessed pre- and post-therapy.
Hierarchy	No hierarchy
Feedback on error	If unable to respond, clinician provided correct verbal response and requested repetition. All features then reviewed.
Feedback if correct	Clinician gave feedback. Nature of feedback not stated.

Outcome

Performance was relatively stable (less than 20% variability) prior to therapy. Application of SFA to set 1 verbs resulted in improved accuracy of naming; 80% accuracy was reached on one occasion with an average 60% correct across the final three probes. There was no change in the retrieval of set 2 verbs. Application of SFA to set 2 verbs resulted in an overall improvement in accuracy, but performance on these items was variable. During treatment for sets 1 and 2, there was an improving but unstable performance on set 3 verbs; these were the verbs that were 'exposed' during sessions but not treated. Post-therapy, there was no change in the retrieval of set 4 verbs. At follow up, gains in the retrieval of sets 1 and 2 were maintained but performance on set 3 returned to baseline levels. Post-therapy, gains were also seen on a test of noun and verb retrieval. There were also changes in discourse production with an increase in the number of words and an increase in the number and percentage of words that were correct information units. The relative distribution of nouns and verbs in discourse remained unchanged.

The study shows a modest increase in the retrieval of trained action words but the authors question whether the gains are clinically significant. The authors were disappointed with the extent of gains and explore possible reasons for the minimal gains e.g. the uncertainty about the nature of the participant's verb retrieval deficits. There was no generalisation to the retrieval of the verbs in the untreated sets, although gains in an unrelated test of noun and verb retrieval were seen. There was improvement in verbal productivity and informativeness in discourse. The authors acknowledge that improvements in noun retrieval could be a consequence of the focus on nouns within treatment and improved semantic processing and that this may have enhanced the production of argument structure in discourse. They also consider that the gains in discourse may be a consequence of the participant's increased willingness to attempt verbal communication.

Other comments

The number of treated items in each set was quite small. The authors suggest modifications to the study, including extended baselines for discourse, multiple-probe procedure to reduce exposure to items, and repeated pre-treatment measurement of the limited exposure list.

Study 7

Rose, M. Sussmilch, G. (2008). The effects of semantic and gesture treatments on verb retrieval and verb use in aphasia. *Aphasiology, 22(7–8)*, 691–706.

Focus of therapy: Verb retrieval, MT – semantic impairment, MW and KC – phonological output lexicon.

Target of therapy: Semantic, phonological and gestural approaches.

Therapy approach: Reactivation.

Client details

Three participants were included in the study.

General information

The three participants all spoke English as their first and only language and had no history of developmental language difficulties, neurological or psychological deficits. KC was a 45-year-old woman with 16 years education who worked as a microbiologist. She had a left fronto-parietal infarct. MW was a 55-year-old woman with 12 years education. She was an administrator prior to having a sub-arachnoid aneurysm. MT was a 53-year-old woman who had 15 years education and worked as a nurse. MT had a bilateral frontal haemorrhagic stroke. All three presented with right hemiplegia and a moderate limb apraxia.

Overall pattern of language impairments and preservations

All participants presented with speech output consistent with Broca's aphasia. They had a significant verb retrieval deficit and difficulties with noun retrieval. The authors suggest MT's verb production deficit arose from impairment at the semantic level, as evidenced by poor verb comprehension. MW and KC had difficulties accessing the word form at the level of the phonological output lexicon. At sentence level, all had some degree of impairment in sentence comprehension and poor grammaticality judgement.

Time post-onset

KC was 7 years, MW was 5 years and MT was 3 years post-onset at the time of the study.

Therapy

The aim of the study was to compare the relative efficacy of semantic, repetition and combined semantic plus gesture treatments. A multiple baseline across conditions, single subject design was used. An initial phase of background testing and ten baseline sessions was followed by a treatment phase where three treatments were simultaneously applied to different verb sets; the order of treatments was varied session by session. A final treatment phase involved the use of the most successful treatment on another set of verbs. There were three, 1 hour sessions per week up to a maximum of twenty therapy sessions. Control items were probed each session but no feedback was given.

NB: The therapy techniques are not described in detail in this paper but are described in a later paper by Boo and Rose (2011).

Task	Repetition (MT and MW)	Semantic	Combined semantic and gesture	Gesture only (KC)
	Present picture and ask participant to name in one word. If incorrect, see different cues for different treatments.			
Materials	Set of 100 verbs mainly from Druks & Masterson (2000) divided into five sets – one for each treatment and two control sets. Sets balanced for familiarity, syllable length, presence and number of consonant clusters, age of acquisition, presence of homophonous noun and argument structure complexity and individual error rate.			
Hierarchy	None			
Feedback on error	Provide verbal model and ask to repeat × 3. Then present picture again for naming.	Ask for: 1. Associated object 2. Associated movement 3. Associated location 4. Associated subject In each case, if correct, move to next feature. If incorrect, provide model. Then present picture again for naming.	Provide gesture and verbal model and ask to repeat × 3. Ask participant to show you with his/ her hands: 1. Associated object. 2. Associated movement 3. Associated location 4. Associated subject In each case, if correct, move to next feature. If incorrect, provide model. Then present picture again for naming and for gesture.	Provide gesture and verbal model and ask to repeat × 3. Then present picture again for naming and for gesture.
Feedback if correct	Reinforce correct response.	Reinforce correct responses.	Reinforce correct response.	Reinforce correct response.

KC received gesture only, semantic and combined semantic and gesture treatments. For MT and MW, gesture only therapy was replaced by repetition only.

Outcome

During the baseline phase, variation for all three participants was in a restricted range. For KC, treatment led to a marked and rapid improvement in verb accuracy, with all three treated groups reaching 90–100% correct in eighteen treatment sessions. There was some improvement in untreated items but this was below that obtained for treatment items. For MW, treatment led to consistent gains for all treatment sets but criterion was not reached. Verb naming performance was maintained at 1 month follow up but showed a 20% decrease by the 3 month follow up. MT showed minimal gains in verb accuracy during treatment. Following fifteen treatments, the therapy protocol was revised by reducing the number of treated and control items but no further gains were seen over a further five treatment sessions.

Large treatment effect sizes were found for both KC and MW. There was no statistically significant difference between treatment conditions with regard to stability and rate of acquisition. For MW, the effect size for combined semantic and gesture treatment and the semantic treatment was almost twice that of the repetition only treatment. For KC, the effect size for semantic and gesture treatment was almost twice that of the combined semantic and gesture treatment, but this may be due to increased variability during the baseline. KC and MW also showed a significant increase in verb naming on unrelated verb assessment and an increase in the number of verbs in picture description and conversation. On a measure of self report, KC's spouse, MW herself and her spouse, and MT each reported enhanced communicative ability.

Other comments

Participants underwent a large number of baseline sessions. Treatments were applied simultaneously; this was considered appropriate as no generalisation to untreated items was predicted.

Study 8

Conroy, P., Sage, K. and Lambon Ralph, M.A. (2009a). A comparison of word versus sentence cues as therapy for verb naming in aphasia. *Aphasiology, 23(4)*, 462–482.

Focus of therapy: Verb retrieval – participants have semantic and/or phonological difficulties.

Target of therapy: Semantic–phonological.

Therapy approach: Reactivation.

Client details

The study described seven participants.

General information

Participants included five women and two men, aged between 43 and 85 years. They were all right-handed, monolingual English speakers. They had between ten and 16 years of education and had worked in various occupations. Participants had had a CVA at least 6 months prior and had no other history of significant neurological illness. All participants had normal or corrected hearing and vision.

Overall pattern of language impairments and preservations

Of the seven participants, two presented with fluent anomic aphasia, one with fluent jargon, three with non-fluent aphasia and one with non-fluent, agrammatic aphasia. At screening, they were required to score at least 75% correct on a word repetition task and between 10 and 90% correct on a test of noun and verb naming to be included in the study. Participants were assessed on a range of tests investigating naming, phonological processing, semantic processing, self monitoring, memory, executive and attention skills. Participants varied in the severity of their naming impairment, the extent to which semantic and/or phonological impairments contributed to their naming difficulties and the co-occurrence of cognitive deficits.

Time post-onset

Participants ranged from 16 months to 65 months post-CVA.

Therapy

Therapy aimed to improve noun and verb retrieval, contrasting the effects of word and sentence cues. A multiple baseline design was used across three time periods (pre-therapy, 1 week and 5 weeks post-therapy) with performance on items treated with word cues, items treated with sentence cues and control items compared. Performance was analysed at both group and individual level. Participants received ten sessions of therapy (two sessions each week for 5 weeks). Word and sentence cue therapy was carried out in parallel with the order of presentation counterbalanced across sessions. During each session, there were ten naming attempts for each treated word.

Task	1. *Word cue therapy*	2. *Sentence cue therapy*	
Materials	Three sets of 20 verbs. Set A – word cue therapy, Set B – sentence cue therapy and Set C – control items. Sets matched for length, imageability, frequency and number of arguments. All words were ones that participants had failed to name at baseline.		
Hierarchy	1. Picture plus written and spoken name given with a request to repeat initially twice, listen again, then three more times.	*Intransitive verbs* 1. Sentence in spoken and written form (pronoun for agent).	*Transitive verbs* 1. Sentence in spoken and written form (pronoun for agent).

	2. Picture plus a substantial grapheme and phoneme cue (CV in CVC and CVC in bisyllabic words) 3. Picture plus a minimal grapheme and phoneme cue (C in CVC words and CV for bisyllabic words) 4. Picture plus semantic cue in the form of brief definition of action and object 5. Picture only	2. Sentence frame with phonemic/ graphemic CV/ CCV for verb 3. Sentence frame with phonemic/ graphemic C/CC for verb 4. Sentence frame with line for verb 5. Sentence frame with written prompt . . . is . . .	2. Sentence frame with phonemic/ graphemic C/ CC for patient argument 3. Sentence frame with phonemic / graphemic CV/CCV for verb 4. Sentence frame with phonemic/ graphemic C/CC for verb 5. Sentence frame with written prompt . . . is . . . the . . .
Feedback on error	Go to previous level	Not stated	
Feedback if correct	Not stated	Not stated	

Outcome

At a group level, there was a borderline effect of therapy type (word > sentence). There was no decrease in naming accuracy at 5 weeks post-therapy. At an individual level, therapy resulted in significant gains in the retrieval of treated verbs. There was a small reduction in numerical accuracy at 5 weeks, but this only reached significance for one participant. One participant showed significant gains in the retrieval of the control verbs. There was no significant difference between the therapies in any individual. The gains in verb retrieval following single word cues generalised to the same items presented in video format. The functional gains of therapy were not considered. In contrast to predictions, sentence cues were not more effective than word cues and the authors explore possible reasons for this.

Other comments

The participants were also involved in the study of the effects of increasing and decreasing cues on verb and noun retrieval (Conroy, Sage & Lambon Ralph, 2009b).

Study 9

Boo, M. and Rose, M.L. (2011). The efficacy of repetition, semantic, and gesture treatments for verb retrieval and use in Broca's aphasia. *Aphasiology, 25(2)*, 154–175.

Focus of therapy: Verb retrieval, GF – verb deficit involving semantic, phonological output lexicon and apraxia of speech, PF – phonological output lexicon.

Target of therapy: Semantic, phonological and gestural approaches.

Therapy approach: Reactivation.

Client details

The study described two participants.

General information

GF was a 63-year- old woman who was a housewife. PF was a 57-year-old man who was a consultant. Both participants had had a left hemisphere stroke, were right-handed, spoke English as their first and only language and had no history of neurological or psychological deficits.

Overall pattern of language impairments and preservations

Both participants presented with speech output consistent with Broca's aphasia. They had a significant verb retrieval deficit. The authors suggest GF's verb production deficits were a consequence of impairments at multiple levels: semantic, access to the phonological output lexicon and severe apraxia of speech (the paper refers to lemma, phonological access/encoding and/or phonetic encoding). GF also presented with sentence level difficulties thought to be a mapping deficit. The authors suggest PF presented with an impairment at the output phonological level.

Time post-onset

GF and PF were both 21 months post-onset at the time of the study.

Therapy

The aim of the study was to compare the relative efficacy of semantic, repetition and combined semantic plus gesture treatment, monitoring generalisation to sentence production, picture description, story retell and discourse tasks. A multiple baseline, cross-over across conditions, single subject design was used. Ten baseline sessions were followed by four sequential phases of therapy. Each phase lasted ten sessions. Each session was approximately 1 to 2 hours, two to three times per week. The probe task of naming 100 items took place in each session. Sentence and discourse level tasks took place pre- and post-therapy.

Task	Repetition	Semantic	Combined semantic and gesture	Gesture only (PF)	Repetition–orthographic treatment (GF)
	Present picture and ask participant to name in one word. If incorrect, see different cues for different treatments.				
Materials	Set of 100 verbs mainly from Druks and Masterson (2000) divided into five sets – one for each treatment phase and one control set. Sets balanced for familiarity, syllable length, presence and number of consonant clusters, age of acquisition, presence of homophonous noun and argument structure complexity and individual error rate.				

Hierarchy	None				
Feedback on error	Provide verbal model and ask to repeat × 3. Then present picture again for naming.	Ask for: 1. Associated object. 2. Associated movement 3. Associated location 4. Associated subject In each case, if correct, move to next feature. If incorrect, provide model. Then present picture again for naming.	Provide gesture and verbal model and ask to repeat × 3. Ask participant to show you with his/her hands: 1. Associated object 2. Associated movement 3. Associated location 4. Associated subject In each case, if correct, move to next feature. If incorrect, provide model. Then present picture again for naming and for gesture.	Provide gesture and verbal model and ask to repeat × 3. Then present picture again for naming and for gesture.	Provide verbal model and ask to repeat × 3. Then present picture again for naming. If incorrect, present orthographic form and verbal model. Then present picture again for naming. If incorrect, present each syllable orthographically and with verbal model. If word has consonant clusters, present phoneme by phoneme. Then present picture again for naming.
Feedback if correct	Reinforce correct response.	Reinforce correct responses.	Reinforce correct response.	Reinforce correct response.	Reinforce correct response.

In order of mention, GF received repetition–orthographic treatment, semantic treatment, combined semantic and gesture treatment and then repetition only treatment. PF received repetition treatment, semantic treatment, combined semantic and gesture treatment and gesture only treatment.

Outcome

GF showed a significant increase in naming accuracy following each treatment except repetition only. At 1 month follow up, gains were maintained for items treated via repetition–orthographic and combined semantic and gesture treatments. PF showed significant improvement in naming accuracy in all treatment conditions except gesture only. Gains were maintained significantly above baseline levels for repetition and semantic treatments. Neither participant showed significant gains in naming of control items. On another assessment of verb naming, both showed significant gains for treated verbs with no change in untreated verbs. Neither participant showed improved noun naming suggesting specific verb retrieval training effect.

In sentence production, PF showed qualitative changes on a constrained sentence task which did not reach significance. In the discourse tasks (picture description, story-retell and conversation), both participants produced an increased proportion of verbs post-treatment but there was little change in type token ratio, due to a heavy reliance on light verbs. Both participants produced an increased proportion of relevant information as seen by an increase in correct information units (Nicholas & Brookshire, 1993). GF's sentence production remained agrammatic. PF produced significantly more well-formed sentences and a longer mean length of utterance in picture description but there was no change in story retell and conversation. GF's scores on a self report, communication perception measure significantly decreased, indicating a more positive perception of his difficulties but his daughter reported no change. There was no change in self reported scores for PF. Both PF and GF showed increases in the WAB aphasia quotient but only PF's score increased by more than five points, which is considered to be clinically significant.

Overall verb naming accuracy improved with no gains in untreated verbs. For each client, there was one treatment phase which did not result in significant gains.

Other comments

Participants underwent a large number of baseline sessions and naming was probed within every session. Although there was an unstable increase in the naming accuracy of these items, the authors suggest that repeated attempts at naming without feedback or correction can leave stimulus items resistant to treatment. Order of treatments was not varied across clients and the authors consider the order of treatment may have affected outcome, e.g. increased motivation in the first phase of treatment, number of errorful naming attempts prior to therapy. The authors suggest the number of treatments contrasted should be limited.

Study 10

Fink, R.B., Martin, N., Schwartz, M.F., Saffran, E and Myers, J.L. (1992). Facilitation of verb retrieval skills in aphasia: a comparison of two approaches. *Clinical Aphasiology, 21,* 263–275.

Focus of therapy: Verb retrieval – access to phonological output lexicon.

Target of therapy: Semantic (with sentence production).

Therapy approach: Reactivation.

Client details

General information

GR was a 64-year-old former engineer. He had a left CVA. A CT scan showed a large infarction in the territory of the left middle cerebral artery.

Overall pattern of language impairments and preservations

GR presented with a Broca's aphasia characterised by agrammatic speech production with an apraxic component. His spontaneous speech consisted of mainly single word utterances, with some two word utterances in constrained tasks. He had good functional comprehension but showed agrammatic comprehension on testing. GR found it difficult to produce verbs within sentences. He produced the nouns in the correct order, marking the verb with a gesture or click. His verb retrieval was aided by phonemic cueing. The authors propose that GR's difficulty was a consequence of reduced accessibility to the phonology of verbs.

Time post-onset

He was 8 years post-onset at the time of the study.

Therapy

Therapy aimed to facilitate lexical phonological access to verbs. A multiple baseline, cross-over design was used. Both therapy procedures treated the verb within the context of a sentence. Set 1 verbs were treated via direct verb training. Set 2 verbs were treated via verb repetition priming and then via direct verb training. No details were given about the frequency or duration of therapy.

Task	1. *Direct verb training*	2. *Verb repetition priming*
	Name the verb, report the agent and theme and then compose a sentence to describe the picture.	Repeat a sentence containing the verb and then describe a picture depicting the same action. Each of the verbs was elicited under three conditions: without a prime, with a single prime sentence and following three priming sentences.
Materials	Ten verbs that GR was unable to name. Five in set 1 treated via direct verb training, five in set 2 treated via repetition priming and then direct verb training. Five picture tokens of each verb.	
Hierarchy	Step 1. Repeated training on one picture token of verb Step 2. Training on five picture tokens	Step 1. Repeated training on one picture token of verb Step 2. Training on five picture tokens
Feedback on error	If verb not named, elicited via modelling and phonemic cueing	Not stated
Feedback if correct	Not stated	Not stated

In direct verb training, GR was repeatedly made aware of the target verb and noun phrases. In verb repetition priming, the target verb was embedded in the sentences but the participant was not told directly about the verb.

Outcome

Direct verb training resulted in improved access to the set 1 treated verbs. Following step 1 involving training on one exemplar, there was significant improvement to the untrained picture tokens. There was no generalisation to untreated verbs. Gains were maintained 6 months post-therapy. Verb repetition priming produced significant gains but improvement was only seen on 3/5 verbs. Significant improvement continued when set 2 verbs received direct verb training. Therapy resulted in no change in untreated verbs, but the use of semantically appropriate verbs increased. A change in GR's spontaneous speech was also noted, with an increase in the percentage of words produced within a sentence, an increase in the number of sentences, an increase in the percentage of syntactically well-formed sentences and an increase in the number of acceptable verb. The gains seen seem to be a consequence of the therapy.

The authors suggest that the direct verb training procedure, with its emphasis on retrieving verb and its arguments, stimulated semantic as well as phonological processing resulting in the changes in spontaneous speech and the increased number of semantically related verb errors.

Other comments

The therapy is described in sufficient detail to allow replication but the frequency and duration of therapy is not given. The treatment sets contain a very small number of items. Direct verb training combined verb retrieval and sentence production.

Study 11

Marshall, J. Pring, T. and Chiat, S. (1998). Verb retrieval and sentence production in aphasia. *Brain and Language, 63*, 159–183.

Focus of therapy: Verb retrieval – access to phonological output lexicon.

Target of therapy: Semantic.

Therapy approach: Reactivation.

Client details

General information

EM was 52 years old when she had a left CVA. At the time of her CVA, she was working as a receptionist in a sports centre. She was right-handed and a monolingual English speaker.

Overall pattern of language impairments and preservations

EM's spontaneous speech was consistent with a Broca's type aphasia, characterised by reduced phrase length, few verbs and few function words and inflections. Functional comprehension was relatively spared. On detailed assessment, her spoken naming of verbs was significantly impaired compared to nouns in picture naming and in naming to definition. A combination of errors was produced for verbs, including omissions, inappropriate verbs and structures, semantically related verbs and abandoned utterances. When verbs were produced, it was often within the context of a complete sentence. There was no effect of frequency on verb production. No noun/verb difference was observed in written naming. She had almost perfect single word comprehension of both nouns and verbs. Her reading of words was more accurate than her naming, particularly for verbs, despite very impaired nonword reading. The authors suggest that her difficulties with verbs were a consequence of impaired access of verb phonology from semantics. Comprehensive assessment of sentence comprehension and sentence production was carried out. Comprehension of semantically reversible sentences was generally accurate. When given a verb, she was able to produce appropriate sentences, suggesting her sentence construction deficits were related to her verb deficit.

Time post-onset

She was 18 months post-onset when therapy started.

Therapy

Therapy aimed to facilitate verb retrieval via semantic tasks with a view to improving sentence production. Therapy initially consisted of a comprehension phase (ten, 1 hour sessions) and a production phase (ten, 1 hour sessions) over a 14 week period. An item specific design with additional control tasks (production of abstract words) was used. Details of the therapy tasks are taken from Marshall (1999).

Comprehension tasks

Task	1. Written word-to-picture matching Select written verb to match picture from choice of five: target, two semantic distracters and two phonological distracters. Then read the word aloud.	2. Odd one out Select the odd one out from three written verbs.	3. Noun production Given written verb and asked to produce as many associated nouns as possible. Encouraged to imagine an event using the verb to see the objects involved.
Materials	Seventy verbs from five semantic categories (35 to be treated, 35 frequency matched verbs as controls) Categories: (a) Non-action, e.g. 'pity' (b) Change in location/possession, e.g. 'buy' (c) Locative, e.g. 'pack' (d) Change of state, e.g. 'cook' (e) Manner of movement, e.g. 'drive' Verbs were treated in category with each category receiving two sessions of therapy. Task 1 was carried out before Task 2 and Task 3.		
Hierarchy	No hierarchy	1. Judgement based on manner information 2. Judgement based on thematic information	Once initial nouns produced, encouraged to think about a different event.

Feedback on error	Not stated	Not stated	Not stated
Feedback if correct	Following selection, EM had to explain why she had eliminated semantic distracters with aid of cues if needed.	Not stated	Not stated

Production tasks

Task	Verb generation 1 Given two written noun phrases and asked to think of verb to connect them.	Verb generation 2 Production of verb to spoken scenario
Materials	Seventy verbs from five semantic categories (35 to be treated, 35 frequency matched verbs as controls) Categories: a) Non-action e.g. 'pity' b) Change in location/possession e.g. 'buy' c) Locative e.g. 'pack' c) Change of state e.g. 'cook' v) Manner of movement e.g. 'drive' Verbs were initially treated in category with each category receiving one session of therapy. Then five sessions with all verbs.	
Hierarchy	Two levels of cue: (1). Therapist encourages EM to imagine an event. EM mimes part of event. (2). Five written options (as in WWPM)	Two levels of cue: (1). Encourage EM to produce gesture. (2). Five written options (as in WWPM)
Feedback on error	Not stated	Not stated
Feedback if correct	If written choices used, list removed and verb produced without cue.	If written choices used, list removed and verb produced without cue.

Outcome

Therapy resulted in significant gains in access to the treated verbs, with a small but non-significant change in the retrieval of untreated control verbs. Sentence production showed corresponding gains, Improvement in sentence production was highly significant around treated verbs and just significant around untreated verbs. There was no change in the control tasks, involving abstract word production, suggesting that change can be attributed to therapy.

Improvements in verb retrieval were accompanied by a corresponding gain in sentence production. The authors suggest that the gains in sentence production around untreated verbs may be due to low baseline performance on the untreated verbs or generalisation to verbs within the same semantic category. Within the paper, there is extensive discussion about the relationship between verb retrieval and sentence production, with the conclusion that both the semantics and phonology of a verb are required to construct sentences.

Other comments

Therapy for EM is also described in Marshall (1999). This chapter presents the therapy and the impact of therapy on story-retell and narrative production in more detail and also describes a second period of therapy looking at promoting the use of general verbs and improving connected speech.

Study 12

Schneider, S. and Thompson, C.K. (2003). Verb production in agrammatic aphasia: the influence of semantic class and argument structure properties on generalisation. *Aphasiology, 17(3)*, 213–241.

Focus of therapy: Verb retrieval – access to the phonological output lexicon.

Target of therapy: Semantic.

Therapy approach: Reactivation.

Client details

Seven participants were involved in the study.

General information

All of the participants presented with aphasia as a consequence of a single left hemisphere thromboembolic CVA. They were monolingual English speakers. Six of the participants had some college training and one had a degree. Other background information is limited.

Overall pattern of language impairments and preservations

The participants all had non-fluent speech characteristic of Broca's aphasia. Performance on key assessments of single word and sentence production and comprehension are presented. The participants had varying degrees of impairment in naming and repetition. Participants presented with lexical comprehension abilities that were superior to sentence comprehension, with particular difficulties with reversible sentences. Comprehension of verbs was superior to verb retrieval. On constrained sentence production, all participants except participant 6, had more difficulty as verbs increased in complexity (number of arguments). In narrative production, the participants (except participant 7) produced more simple sentences than complex sentences, produced less than 50% of grammatical utterances, produced more nouns than verbs and produced simple rather than complex verbs.

Time post-onset

The participants were between 39 and 132 months post-onset at the time of the study.

Therapy

Therapy aimed to improve verb naming, with monitoring of generalisation across verb classes based on semantic and argument structure information and to sentence production. Two types of therapy were contrasted: semantic verb retrieval therapy and argument structure therapy. A single subjects cross-over design in combination with multiple baselines across subjects and behaviours. Therapy consisted of baseline phase, application of first treatment, application of second treatment, application of third treatment if no generalisation seen and then assessment of maintenance at 3 weeks post-therapy. Trained items were probed at the start of each session, half of the untrained items were probed each session and then sentence production was probed at the end of each session. Different treatment approaches and different verb sets varied systematically across participants. Criterion for trained items was set at 90% correct across three consecutive sessions. Criterion for generalisation was set at 30% increase over baseline performance. Twelve treatments sessions were given in each treatment phase.

Task	*Semantic verb retrieval therapy*	*Argument structure retrieval therapy*
Materials	Black-and-white verb pictures. 102 verbs, 40 three place verbs (20 motion, 20 change of state) and 40 two place verbs (20 motion, 20 change of state). Divided into 2 sets – trained and untrained, matched for syllable length, picturability, phonological complexity and frequency. Twenty-two one place verbs (11 motion, 11 change of state) as additional monitor of generalisation.	
Hierarchy	1. Presentation of item. 2. Presentation of definition based on meaning e.g. 'The items you are going to see all describe a motion. This motion can be shown by movement in a particular direction, movement from one place to another or a particular way of moving. This picture shows jump. It shows a sudden movement from on to another.' 3. Naming of picture – tell me what is happening in the picture.	1. Presentation of item. 2. Presentation of definition based on meaning e.g. 'The items you are going to see all show someone doing something to someone (or something). That is someone doing the action and someone (something) receiving the action. This picture shows jump. It shows the girl is jumping the rope. The girl is person doing the jumping and the rope is the thing being jumped.' 3. Naming of picture – tell me what is happening in the picture.
Feedback on error	Modelled word for repetition	Modelled word for repetition
Feedback if correct	State correct and move onto next item	State correct and move onto next item

Outcome

Individual results were displayed graphically for each of the participants. Statistical significance of treatment effects only discussed at group level. All participants had a stable baseline performance. During treatment, there was rapid acquisition of the trained verbs, with no significant difference between therapy types. Gains were maintained at follow up. There was minimal generalisation to untrained verbs with performance for most participants remaining at baseline levels. Participant 4 showed some within verb category generalisation from trained to untrained three place verbs. Participants 3 and 4 showed some across verb category generalisation during the second treatment phase. The participants showed significant improvement in sentence production, with sentence production around trained verbs being significantly better than sentence production around untrained verbs. Gains in sentence production were not dependent on therapy type. Following therapy, statistical significant changes were seen in repetition and naming and in sentence production on formal assessments. Gains were also seen in narrative speech; there was an increase in the percentage of grammatical sentences and in the correct use of obligatory one and two place verbs and optional three place verbs. These changes did not reach statistical significance.

The semantic and argument structure therapies were both effective in facilitating verb retrieval. There was no significant difference between the therapies. In contrast to the authors' predictions, minimal generalisation was seen to untrained items. Improved verb retrieval resulted in improved sentence production around the trained verbs. The authors suggest that improved access to the verb facilitates improved access to the verb's argument structure which in turn promotes sentence production.

Other comments

Treatment effects were likely to be a consequence of therapy but generalised gains in repetition and naming were also seen across the group.

Study 13

Edwards, S. and Tucker, K. (2006). Verb retrieval in fluent aphasia: a clinical study. *Aphasiology, 20(7)*, 644–675.

Focus of therapy: Verb retrieval – accessing phonological output lexicon.

Target of therapy: Semantic.

Therapy approach: Reactivation.

Client details

The study described three male participants with fluent aphasia.

General information

JR was a 37-year-old man who had worked as a mechanical engineer, He had a large left cerebral haematoma. JD was a 63-year-old man who had worked as a risk and safety manager. He had a large left parietal infarct. CB was a 75-year-old man who had worked as an insurance/wine merchant. No information was available about the site of his lesion.

Overall pattern of language impairments and preservations

All three participants had impaired verb retrieval compared to noun retrieval and verb comprehension was significantly better than verb retrieval. Participants varied in terms of the severity of their word-retrieval difficulties and the extent of concurrent sentence level impairments. JR presented with an anomic aphasia and was the least impaired in both noun and verb retrieval. He presented with difficulties on tests of sentence comprehension and production, with no significant difference between the two. The authors propose that he had difficulty retrieving verbs with additional syntactic difficulties. On the control tasks, he had spared repetition of words but difficulty with nonword repetition and made some errors in writing to dictation.

JD presented with a mild Wernicke's aphasia. He had more severe naming difficulties than JR, particularly for verbs. He showed relatively strong sentence comprehension compared to sentence production. The authors propose his difficulties at sentence level were primarily due to his verb retrieval difficulties. On the control tasks, repetition of words was better than repetition of nonwords and he had significant difficulties in writing to dictation.

CB presented with a Wernicke's type aphasia. His noun retrieval was at a similar level to JR but his verb retrieval difficulties were less severe than JR's. His verb retrieval was very slow compared to both JR and JD. He had impaired sentence production and comprehension. Like JD, the authors propose that CB has verb and syntactic difficulties but his difficulties were more severe than JD's. On the control tasks, repetition of both words and nonwords was impaired, although he also had significantly more difficulty with nonwords. He made some errors in writing to dictation but his writing was more preserved than both JD and JR.

Time post-onset

JD was 7 months, JD was 6 months and CB was 18 months post-onset at the time of the study.

Therapy

Therapy aimed to improve verb retrieval with the expectation of generalised gains in sentence production. A multiple baseline, single subject design was used across five time periods (three pre-therapy, immediately post-therapy and 2 to 3 months post-therapy). Performance on tests of verb and noun retrieval, of sentence production and comprehension, on a range of connected speech tasks (picture description, narrative and conversation), and on control tasks of repetition and writing to dictation was compared across time periods. Participants received twice weekly session of 45 minutes in the clinic. JD had a total of twenty-five sessions over 4 months, CB had twenty-three sessions over 4 months and JR had sessions over a 2 month period. Therapy was accompanied by daily home practice (2 × 10 minute sessions on non-treatment days and 1 × 10 minute session on treatment days).

Task	Sentence completion	Naming verb to definition	Picture naming
Materials	Set of 100 verbs from Druks and Masterson (2000) divided into two sets – treated and control. Sets balanced for frequency, age of acquisition, familiarity, word length, imageability, visual complexity and argument structures.		
Hierarchy	Four levels of treatment focusing on different verb types (in assumed level of difficulty) 1. Transitive verbs e.g. kick 2. Intransitive/unergative verbs e.g. smile 3. Optional transitive/unergative e.g. eat 4. Optional transitive/unaccusative e.g. sink		

Feedback on error	When incorrect or unable to name, series of cues given until person able to produce verb. 1. Phonemic cue 2. Part word cue 3. Multiple choice from three orally presented words: target, semantic distracter and phonological distracter 4. Repetition	When incorrect or unable to name, series of cues given until person able to produce verb. 1. Phonemic cue 2. Part word cue 3. Multiple choice from three orally presented words: target, semantic distracter and phonological distracter 4. Repetition	When incorrect or unable to name, series of cues given until person able to produce verb. 1. Semantic cue 2. Phonemic cue 3. Part word cue 4. Multiple choice from three orally presented words: target, semantic distracter and phonological distracter 5. Repetition
Feedback if correct	Not stated	Not stated	Not stated

Tasks 1, 2 and 3 were carried out in order for each set of verbs. It was assumed that Tasks 1–3 became increasingly more difficult due to a reduction in the amount of cues. Sentence completion was considered to involve both semantic and syntactic cueing, definitions only semantic cues and naming no cues.

Outcome

There were no significant changes in performance for any of the three participants in the three pre-therapy baselines, although there was some variability in scores. For JR, scores on treated verbs were higher post-therapy but failed to reach significance (as close to ceiling pre-therapy). Verb retrieval was, however, quicker post-therapy. There was no change in the retrieval of the untreated verb set and no change on test of verb naming. There was a non-significant increase in scores for sentence production and comprehension. There was variability across the connected speech tasks with an increase in the percentage of grammatically correct sentences seen only in conversation immediately post-therapy and in picture description at follow up. There was no change in performance on the control tasks.

For JD, there was significant improvement in his ability to retrieve the treated verbs post-therapy and this was maintained at follow up. There was no significant change in his ability to retrieve the control set of verbs but his performance on another verb naming test did improve significantly. As with JR, verb retrieval was significantly quicker post-therapy. On the test of sentence production and in conversation, there was a significant improvement in the percentage of well-formed sentences immediately post-therapy but this was not maintained at follow up. No significant change was seen in sentence comprehension or on the control tasks.

For CB, there was significant improvement in the retrieval of the treated verbs post-therapy with a corresponding increase in the speed of retrieval. Significant change was seen in the retrieval of the control set of verbs at follow up and significant improvement was also seen on another test of verb naming. No significant improvement was seen in sentence production on the constrained test or in connected speech. A significant improvement was seen in sentence comprehension post-therapy. No change was seen on the control tasks.

Change in each case was likely to be a consequence of therapy as all clients had a stable profile prior to therapy and there was no change seen on the control tasks for any client. There was some overlap in the treated verbs and the verbs in the naming task which may account for the significant improvement seen for JD and CB. The connected speech data was quite difficult to interpret. The authors propose that the repetitive nature of treatment may have resulted in improved awareness about verbs, increasing the likelihood of producing verbs and sentence structures. The repetitive nature of treatment and the focus on verbs was also thought to account for the comprehension gains seen in CB's performance.

Other comments

A brief description of this study can also be found in Edwards, Tucker, and McCann (2004). The study took place in a clinical setting and the paper discusses service delivery issues and the possible role of home practice. McCann and Doleman (2011) replicated the therapy with three people with non-fluent aphasia. All participants showed gains in single verb retrieval but two of three showed no change in sentence production. The production of connected speech was not assessed.

B. Verb and noun studies

The studies of verb retrieval, using techniques initially designed for nouns, have provided some evidence that the same tasks can be effective. Table 12.2 lists studies treating nouns and verbs that have used the same therapy approach. There have also been a series of studies designed to compare the effects of therapy on noun and verb retrieval; these are summarised in Table 12.3 and are subsequently reviewed. These studies confirm that verbs and nouns can be treated using the same techniques, but there is some evidence that improving action naming may be more difficult to achieve than improving noun naming (Conroy, Sage & Lambon Ralph, 2009c). Conroy and colleagues suggest the increased complexity of verbs may result in reduced learning of verbs and/or increased vulnerability to loss post-therapy.

EVALUATIONS OF VERB AND NOUN STUDIES

Study 14

Raymer, A.M., Singletary, F., Rodriguez, A., Ciampitti, M., Heilman, K.M. & Gonzalez-Rothi, L.J. (2006). Effects of gesture + verbal treatment for noun and verb retrieval in aphasia. *Journal of the International Neuropsychological Society, 12*, 867–882.

Focus of therapy: Participants with semantic, phonological and mixed semantic–phonological deficits.

Target of therapy: Semantic–phonological (gesture).

Therapy approach: Reactivation.

Client details

Nine people with aphasia were included in the study.

Table 12.2 Studies using the same approach to treat nouns and to treat verbs

Overall target of therapy	Specific approach	Studies treating nouns in Chapter 11	Studies treating verbs in Chapter 12
Semantic	Semantic task e.g. picture matching followed by naming	• Study 2: Nettleton and Lesser (1991, p. 130) • Study 6: Marshall *et al.* (1990, p. 142) • Study 7: Pring *et al.* (1993, p. 144)	• Study 2: Webster *et al.* (2005, p. 202) • Study 3: Webster and Gordon (2009, p. 204) • Study 11: Marshall *et al.* (1998, p. 222)
Semantic	Semantic feature analysis Generation of semantic features	• Study 18: Boyle and Coelho (1995, p. 170)	• Study 6: Wambaugh and Ferguson (2007 p. 211) • Study 7: Rose and Sussmilch (2008, p. 213) • Study 9: Boo and Rose (2011, p. 217)
Semantic	Spoken naming with semantic cues Naming followed by answering semantic questions	• Study 5: Kiran & Thompson (2003 p. 139)	• Study 1: Raymer and Ellsworth (2002, p. 199) • Study 4: Wambaugh *et al.* (2002, p. 206) • Study 12: Schneider and Thompson (2003, p. 225)
Semantic–phonological	Spoken naming with cueing hierarchy with semantic and phonological cues	• Study 8: Hillis (1989, p. 146) • Study 21: Spencer *et al.* (2000, p. 175)	• Study 5: Rodriguez *et al.* (2006, p. 209) • Study 13: Edwards and Tucker (2006, p. 227)
Phonological	Spoken naming with phonological cues Naming followed by answering phonological questions	• Study 2: Nettleton and Lesser (1991, p. 130)	• Study 1: Raymer and Ellsworth (2002, p. 199) • Study 4: Wambaugh *et al.* (2002, p. 206)
Phonological–orthographic	Repetition and reading aloud	• Study 22: Miceli *et al.* (1996, p. 177) • Study 24: Nickels (2002, p. 182)	• Study 7: Rose and Sussmilch (2008, p. 213) • Study 9: Boo and Rose (2011, p. 217)
Phonological-orthographic	Spoken naming with phonological and orthographic cues	• Study 11: Hickin *et al.* (2002, p. 155)	• Study 8: Conroy *et al.* (2009a, p. 215)
Gestural	Gesture therapy Gestural verbal therapy Semantic-gesture therapy	• Study 1: Rose and Douglas (2008 p. 128)	• Study 5: Rodriguez *et al.* (2006, p. 209) • Study 7: Rose and Sussmilch (2008, p. 213) • Study 9: Boo and Rose (2011, p. 217)

Table 12.3 Studies directly comparing the effect of therapy for nouns and verbs

Level of impairment	Therapy studies	Area targeted in therapy	Therapy tasks
Semantic system and phonological output lexicon (either within or across subjects)	Study 14: Raymer *et al.* (2006, p. 230)	Gesture + verbal treatment	• GVT – presentation of verbal and gestural model before multiple productions
	Study 15: Raymer *et al.* (2007, p. 234)	Semantic– phonological therapy	• Multiple repetition of word with yes/no questions about semantic and phonological features
	Study 16: Conroy *et al.* (2009c, p. 236)	Comparison of errorless and errorful therapy	• Errorful – picture naming with progressive semantic, grapheme and phonological cues • Errorless – picture naming with written word and spoken word for repetition
	Study 17: Conroy *et al.* (2009b, p. 238)	Comparison of decreasing an increasing cue therapy	• Decreasing cue – picture naming with written word and spoken word for repetition, gradual decrease in cues • Increasing cue – picture naming with progressive semantic, grapheme and phonological cues

General information

Participants included three women and six men, aged between 49–70 years. All, except one, were right-handed. Participants had had a left CVA at least 4 months prior to the study, with lesion location varying across participants. All of the participants had mild to moderate limb apraxia with the exception of one participant who was severely impaired.

Overall pattern of language impairments and preservations

Of the nine participants, one presented with conduction aphasia, two with Wernicke's aphasia and six with Broca's aphasia. The participants all had word-retrieval impairments (<75% accuracy) for both nouns and verbs with an intact ability to repeat. Two participants had phonological impairments for both nouns and verbs. Three participants had a semantically based impairment for both nouns and verbs. Two participants had a mixed semantic–phonological impairment for both nouns and verbs and two presented with mixed patterns of semantic or phonological difficulties across nouns and verbs.

Time post-onset

Participants varied in their time post-onset. Two participants were less than a year post-onset. The other participants ranged from 16–62 months post-onset.

Therapy

Therapy aimed to improve the retrieval of nouns and verbs via gesture + verbal treatment and to monitor the impact on the production of gesture. Participants received three to four, 60 minute sessions per week, with the exception of one participant who received treatment 2 days per week. Each phase of therapy lasted ten sessions and treated either nouns or verbs. The order of treatment for nouns and verbs was randomly assigned. A multiple baseline across behaviours and participants design was used. Participants were tested at baseline, with daily probes during each treatment phase and then at maintenance, 1 month post-therapy. During each training trial, each target word and gesture was produced nine times.

Task	*Gesture + verbal treatment (GVT)*
	1. Presentation of picture with model of target word and gesture
	2. Presentation of gesture with participant imitating × 3
	3. Presentation of target word with participant repeating × 3
	4. Presentation of picture with participant asked to say what is happening
Materials	Forty nouns and 40 verbs. Twenty of each trained and 20 untrained. Balanced for level of accuracy, with attempts to balance word frequency and syllable length.
Hierarchy	None
Feedback on error	If problems with gesture, manipulation of limb to form gesture If problems with repetition, segmentation of word for participant to produce syllable by syllable
Feedback if correct	Reinforcement of correct response

Outcome

The authors consider the effects of therapy in terms of effect size (comparison of mean performance in treatment with mean performance in baseline, divided by the standard deviation during baseline) and gain scores (comparison of mean of final four treatments sessions to mean of prior phase). Gains were only considered significant if changes were present on both measures. No difference was seen between the treatment phases. One participant showed no improvement on any measure. Significant improvement was seen on trained items for six participants, four on trained nouns and four on trained verbs. Increases for both nouns and verbs were seen in two participants. There was no difference between nouns and verbs and no change on the untrained items. Large improvements in gesture production for the trained items were seen for eight participants. Three participants showed increased use of gestures for untrained verbs. Some participants showed change on a general assessment of comprehension.

The authors propose that GVT was an effective method for facilitating word retrieval in people with aphasia, with no difference seen between nouns and verbs. Gains were most prominent in people with phonological impairments but people with semantic difficulties still showed some gains. Gains in noun retrieval were most evident in people with Broca's aphasia. Gains in verb retrieval were most evident in people with Wernicke's aphasia. The participant who showed no improvements had the most severe semantic impairment and a severe limb apraxia.

Participants showed widespread spontaneous use of gesture but gesture was not being used as a strategy to facilitate word retrieval. Gains in gesture were not related to the severity of limb apraxia. The authors propose that GVT had increased participants' awareness of gesture as a potential communication method.

Study 15

Raymer, A.M., Ciampitti, M., Holliway, B., Singletary, F., Blonder, L.X., Ketterson, T., Anderson, S., Lehnen, J. Heilman, K.M. and Gonzalez, Rothi, L.J. (2007). Semantic–phonologic treatment for noun and verb retrieval impairments in aphasia. *Neuropsychological Rehabilitation, 17(2)*, 244–270.

Focus of therapy: Participants with semantic, phonological and mixed semantic–phonological deficits.

Target of therapy: Semantic–phonological.

Therapy approach: Reactivation.

Client details

Eight participants with aphasia were included in the study.

General information

Participants included two woman and six men, aged 38 to 81 years. Participants had experienced a unilateral left hemisphere CVA, with lesion sites varying across participants. They had between 10 and 18 years of education.

Overall pattern of language impairments and preservations

Of the eight participants, six presented with Broca's aphasia, one with Wernicke's aphasia and one with anomic aphasia. On screening, they had to demonstrate word-retrieval impairments (<75% accuracy) for both nouns and verbs, with no more than a moderate motor speech difficulty. Participants were assessed on a noun/verb battery investigating picture naming, sentence completion and spoken word-to-picture verification. Five individuals presented with semantic impairments for both nouns and verbs. Three individuals presented with mixed patterns of impairments for nouns and verbs.

Time post-onset

Participants ranged from 4 months to 120 months post-onset at the time of the study.

Therapy

The study investigated the use of semantic–phonologic treatment for word retrieval, comparing the effects for nouns and verbs. A multiple baseline design across participants and stimulus sets was used. Participants were tested during an extended baseline phase of eight to ten sessions, with daily probes during each treatment phase and at 1 month post-treatment. Naming of treated and untreated sets was assessed. Noun and verb training took place in separate phases, with order of treatment counterbalanced across participants. Training took place two to four times per week for a total of ten sessions, with a 1 month break between treatment phases. Pre-treatment and at the end of each treatment phase, participants were also tested on other language and communicative measures.

Task	Semantic–phonologic (SP) treatment
	1. Presentation of picture with model of target word, participant practised word × 3
	2. Presentation of four yes/no questions about semantic & phonological characteristics about item
	3. Participant produces target word × 3
	4. After 5 second pause, participant is asked to say the word again
Materials	Eighty black-and-white line drawings of 40 nouns and 40 verbs. All items that participants unable to name on two/three occasions. 20 nouns and 20 verbs for treatment. Twenty nouns and 20 verbs untrained. Sets balanced for baseline naming performance and syllable length.
Hierarchy	None
Feedback on error	If question answered incorrectly, repeated and given answer.
Feedback if correct	Not stated

After completing the protocol for all 20 words, the clinician reviewed all of the words for the participant to repeat again.

Outcome

Changes in naming proves were considered by looking at the C statistic z scores, sensitive to changes in the slope of performance across sessions, gain scores from baseline to the final four treatment sessions and effect sizes. Results were only considered significant if all three measures exceeded target levels. Five of the eight participants showed significant improvement for both trained nouns and verbs, with no significant difference in effect size across word class. There was no consistent evidence of improved retrieval of untrained sets. Of the five participants, three maintained the high levels of performance at maintenance for both nouns of verbs and two showed better maintenance of trained nouns compared to verbs. No clear changes were evident in the conversational measures for nouns or verbs, although a strong correlation was seen between improvement in verbs post-treatment and changes on the Communicative Effectiveness Index (Lomas *et al.*, 1989).

Semantic–phonological treatment was effective in improving the naming of trained nouns and verbs. More positive treatment responses were seen in individuals with mild to moderate naming impairments. The participant with the most severe naming impairments at baseline had the poorest outcome for trained words. The authors explore differences between the five participants who benefited from treatment and the three who did not show significant improvement. They conclude that semantic–phonological training may be less effective in participants with severe semantic impairments.

Other comments

The authors acknowledge that the low stable baseline resulted in large treatment effects for fairly modest gains in naming. They, suggest the move from none to some accurate responses can lead to changes noticeable to communication partners.

Study 16

Conroy, P., Sage, K. and Lambon Ralph, M.A. (2009c). Errorless and errorful therapy for verb and noun naming in aphasia. *Aphasiology, 23(11)*, 1311–1337.

Focus of therapy: Participants with semantic, phonological and mixed semantic–phonological deficits.

Target of therapy: Semantic–phonological.

Therapy approach: Reactivation.

Client details

The study included nine participants.

General information

The participants included six women and three men, aged between 42 and 84 years. They were all right-handed, monolingual English speakers. They had between 10 and 16 years of education and had worked in various occupations. Participants had had a CVA at least 6 months prior and had no other history of significant neurological illness. All participants had normal or corrected hearing and vision.

Overall pattern of language impairments and preservations

Of the nine participants, five were non-fluent, two presented with fluent anomic aphasia, one with fluent jargon and one with agrammatic aphasia. At screening, they had to score at least 75% correct on a word repetition task and between 10 and 90% correct on a test of noun and verb naming to be included in the study. Participants were assessed on a range of tests investigating naming, phonological processing, semantic processing, self monitoring, memory, executive and attention skills. Participants varied in the severity of their naming impairment, the extent to which semantic and/or phonological impairments contributed to their naming difficulties and the co-occurrence of cognitive deficits.

Time post-onset

Participants ranged from 7 to 136 months post-CVA at the time of the study.

Therapy

Therapy aimed to improve noun and verb retrieval, contrasting the effects of errorless and errorful learning. A multiple baseline design was used across three time periods (pre-therapy, 1 week and 5 weeks post-therapy) with performance on items treated with errorless therapy, items treated with errorful therapy and control items compared. Performance was analysed at both group and individual level. Participants received ten sessions of therapy (two sessions each week for 5 weeks). Errorless and errorful therapies were carried out concurrently with randomised order across sessions. During each session, there were ten naming attempts for each treated word.

Task	1. Errorless therapy	2. Errorful therapy
Materials	Three sets of 40 words (20 nouns and 20 verbs). Set A – errorless therapy, Set B – errorful therapy and Set C – control items. Sets matched for length, frequency and word class. All words were ones that participants had failed to name at baseline.	
Hierarchy	Picture plus written and spoken name given with a request to repeat twice initially, listen again, then three more times.	1. Picture plus broad semantic cues 2. Specific semantic cue 3. First grapheme and phoneme 4. Onset plus vowel in spoken/written form 5. Target word for repetition
Feedback on error	Given additional repetition	Move to next cue
Feedback if correct	Not stated	Not stated

As participants were able to repeat with a high degree of accuracy, it was assumed that they would be able to produce a correct response.

Outcome

In terms of accuracy of naming at group level, there was a main effect of word class with more correct nouns than verbs. There was a main effect of assessment time, with a significant difference between accuracy at 1 week and 5 weeks post-therapy. There was a borderline effect ($p=0.06$) of therapy type (errorless>errorful). At an individual level, all participants showed a significant improvement in the naming of treated items at both 1 week and 5 weeks post-therapy. All participants showed a decrease in naming accuracy at 5 weeks and this was significant for 5 participants. Naming of untreated items showed minimal change with the exception of one fluent participant who showed significant gains post-therapy as there were more single word responses. Only one participant showed a significant difference between the therapies. The participants with the most severe naming impairments showed greater gains for nouns compared to verbs.

In summary, therapy was effective in improving the naming of treated words, and nouns were produced more accurately than verbs. There was a trend for errorless therapy to more effective than errorful across the group. Functional gains were not considered.

Other comments

Some of the participants were also involved in the study of the effects of increasing and decreasing cues on noun and verb naming (Conroy *et al.*, 2009b). The authors discuss that, initially, all participants preferred errorless therapy. As therapy progressed, the more severe participants continued to like errorless but the less severe participants began to prefer error-ful as it provided support and a level of challenge without being so prescriptive. Errorless therapy was quicker to administer. Data from both of these studies was used in a study investigating the factors influencing therapy gain (Lambon Ralph *et al.*, 2010). A factor analysis showed gains after anomia therapy were related to a cognitive factor and a pho-nological factor. The cognitive factor combined assessment on tests of attention, executive functioning and visuo-spatial memory. The phonological factor comprised word reading and repetition. Pre-treatment naming ability also predicted therapy outcome.

Study 17

Conroy, P., Sage, K. and Lambon Ralph, M.A. (2009b). The effects of decreasing and increasing cue therapy on improving naming speed and accuracy for verbs and nouns in aphasia. *Aphasiology, 23(6)*, 707–730.

Focus of therapy: Participants with semantic, phonological and mixed semantic–phono-logical deficits.

Target of therapy: Semantic–phonological.

Therapy approach: Reactivation.

Client details

The study described seven participants.

General information

Participants included five women and two men, aged between 43 and 85 years. They were all right-handed, monolingual English speakers. They had between 10 and 16 years of education and had worked in various occupations. Participants had had a CVA at least 6 months prior and had no other history of significant neurological illness. All participants had normal or corrected hearing and vision.

Overall pattern of language impairments and preservations

Of the seven participants, two presented with fluent anomic aphasia, one with fluent jargon, three with non-fluent aphasia and one with non-fluent, agrammatic aphasia. At screening, they had to score at least 75% correct on a word repetition task and between 10 and 90% correct on a test of noun and verb naming to be included in the study. Participants were assessed on a range of tests investigating naming, phonological processing, semantic processing, self monitoring, memory, executive and attention skills. Participants varied in the severity of their naming impairment, the extent to which semantic and/or phonological impairments contributed to their naming difficulties and the co-occurrence of cognitive deficits.

Time post-onset

Participants ranged from 16 months to 65 months post-CVA.

Therapy

Therapy aimed to improve noun and verb retrieval, contrasting the effects of decreasing and increasing cue therapy. A multiple baseline design was used across three time periods (pre-therapy, 1 week and 5 weeks post-therapy) with performance on items treated with decreasing cue therapy, items treated with increasing cue therapy and control items compared. Performance was analysed at both group and individual level. Participants received ten sessions of therapy (two sessions each week for 5 weeks). Decreasing and increasing cue therapy were carried out concurrently with randomised order across sessions. During each session, there were ten naming attempts for each treated word.

Task	1. Decreasing cue therapy	2. Increasing cue therapy
Materials	Three sets of 40 words (20 nouns and 20 verbs). Set A – decreasing cue therapy, Set B – increasing cue therapy and Set C – control items. Sets matched for length, frequency and word class. All words were ones that participants had failed to name at baseline.	
Hierarchy	1. Picture plus written and spoken name given with a request to repeat twice initially, listen again, then three more times. 2. Picture plus a substantial grapheme and phoneme cue (CV in CVC and CVC in bisyllabic words) 3. Picture plus a minimal grapheme and phoneme cue (C in CVC words and CV for bisyllabic words) 4. Picture plus semantic cue in the form of brief definition of action and object 5. Picture only	1. Picture only 2. Picture plus semantic cue in the form of brief definition of action and object 3. Picture plus a minimal grapheme and phoneme cue (C in CVC words and CV for bisyllabic words) 4. Picture plus a substantial grapheme and phoneme cue (CV in CVC and CVC in bisyllabic words) 5. Picture plus written and spoken name given with a request to repeat initially twice, listen again, then three more times.
Feedback on error	Move to previous level	Not stated
Feedback if correct	Not stated	Not stated

As participants were able to repeat with a high degree of accuracy, it was assumed that they would produce a correct response within the cueing hierarchy. In decreasing cue therapy, cue level was changed across sessions dependent on the accuracy of first responses.

Outcome

In accuracy of naming at a group level, there was a main effect of word class with more correct nouns than verbs. There was no significant effect of therapy type and no significant difference between accuracy at 1 week and 5 weeks post-therapy. In terms of speed of retrieval at group level, there was no effect of therapy type but participants were significantly slower at naming items at the 5 week follow up. There was also a main effect of word class, with verbs named slower than nouns; the authors attribute this to the increased length of verbs.

At an individual level, all participants showed a significant improvement in the naming of treated items at both 1 week and 5 weeks post-therapy with no change in the naming of untreated items. Four participants showed a decrease in naming accuracy at five weeks post-therapy and this was significant for three participants. One participant showed a significant increase in naming accuracy at follow up. No individual showed a significant difference between the therapies. The authors suggest the extent of gains in naming may be related to baseline language performance (across a range of assessments) and performance on the Rey complex figure (an assessment of memory).

In summary, therapy was effective in improving the naming of treated words. Nouns were produced more accurately than verbs post-therapy and the noun advantage is considered to reflect a combination of increased gains during therapy and better maintenance. There was no difference between the two therapies in either naming accuracy or speed of retrieval. Functional gains of therapy were not considered.

Other comments

Some of the participants were also involved in the study of the effects of errorless and errorful learning on noun and verb naming (Conroy, *et al.*, 2009c). Decreasing cue therapy combines the success of errorless learning while maintaining effort and engagement in the task. The authors suggest that participants preferred decreasing cue therapy. Decreasing cue therapy was also quicker to administer but required more effort from the clinician in terms of monitoring performance and adapting the level of cues. Data from both of these studies was used in a study investigating the impact of language and cognitive status on therapy outcome following anomia therapy (Lambon Ralph *et al.*, 2010). A factor analysis showed gains after anomia therapy were related to a cognitive factor and a phonological factor. The cognitive factor combined assessment on tests of attention, executive functioning and visuo–spatial memory. The phonological factor comprised word reading and repetition. Factors were independent predictors of both immediate and longer term therapy gains. Pre-treatment naming ability also predicted therapy outcome.

13 Therapy for reading

Summary of reading studies

Reading therapies are a relatively recent development in aphasia despite the dyslexias providing the initial impetus for developments in cognitive neuropsychology in the 1960s and 1970s. While historically, for many clinicians working with people with aphasia, reading and writing impairments have taken a lower priority than the more visible deficits in spoken production, a greater focus is now apparent on reading difficulties, both in research and, we would say, in clinical practice. This is most likely contributed to by the use of computers as a therapy medium and most certainly motivated, at least to some extent, by client goals. Those studies reported in the literature focus primarily on pure alexia (letter-by-letter reading) and orthographic-to-phonological conversion, with the individual differences between clients resulting in slight differences in the choice, progression and outcome of therapy. Perhaps more so than in the previous chapters, the terminology used in reading studies is worthy of mention. Similar to the frequent synonymous use of the terms *aphasia* and *dysphasia, alexia* and *dyslexia* are often used interchangeably by some authors and considered to differentiate partial from total loss of reading abilities. Throughout this chapter, terms used by the respective authors have been retained with no inferences drawn regarding the authors' orientation. In addition, some authors refer to *functors* synonymously with *function words* and *pseudowords* instead of *nonwords* and we have consistently reported authors' terminology. The studies reviewed here are listed in Table 13.1.

The influence of the developmental literature is probably seen more in reading than in other processing domains. The development of normal reading skills and the management of developmental dyslexia have informed a number of studies reported in this chapter (for discussion of reading models in the acquisition of literacy, see Chall, 1983; Frith, 1986; Gough, 1996; Metsala & Ehri, 1998; Shankweiler & Liberman, 1989; Share & Stanovich, 1995). In this area, there are also more studies investigating the effects of treatment in languages other than English (e.g. DePartz (1986), French, Ablinger & Domahs (2009), German). Language differences are important to consider in the study of reading treatments. Differences in the transparency of the language, i.e. the extent to which there is a regular/consistent relationship between graphemes and phonemes may result in pre-morbid differences in reading strategy and differences in the presentation/incidence of particular types of dyslexia. It will certainly influence the choice and predicted outcome of treatment. For example, treatments targeting orthographic-to-phonological conversation will be less successful in languages which contain many irregular words e.g. English.

There are a large number of studies investigating the effects of treatment for pure alexia/letter-by-letter reading. In Chapter six, this was characterised as impairment to visual orthographic analysis or access to the orthographic input lexicon, although debate exists as to

Table 13.1 Summary of reading therapy studies reviewed here

Level of impairment	Therapy studies	Therapy tasks
Visual orthographic analysis (pure alexia/letter-by-letter reading)	Study 1: Arguin and Bub (1994 p. 246)	Computer presented therapy. • Same/different letter matching (speeded presentation) • Reading of pronounceable letter strings (speeded presentation)
	Study 2: Greenwald and Rothi (1998, p. 248)	• Spoken naming of written letters
	Study 3: Maher *et al.* (1998, p. 250)	• Semantic access strategy • Motor cross-cueing strategy (kinaesthetic input)
	Study 4: Lott *et al.* (1994, p. 252)	• Tactile–kinaesthetic letter naming • Tactile–kinaesthetic word reading
	Study 5: Lott and Friedman (1999, p. 254)	• Tactile–kinaesthetic letter naming • Speeded tactile–kinaesthetic letter-by-letter reading (single letters, letter strings and words)
	Study 6: Friedman and Lott (2000, p. 256)	Computer presented therapy. • Semantic categorisation of rapidly presented nouns • Oral reading of rapidly presented nouns • Oral reading of rapidly presented function words
	Study 7: Sage *et al.* (2005, p. 259)	• Whole-word recognition • Letter-by-letter reading (with kinaesthetic cue)
	Study 8: Ablinger and Domahs (2009, p. 262)	Computer presented therapy. • Auditory–visual verification task • Whole-word recognition (reading aloud)
Orthographic input lexicon (surface dyslexia)	Study 9: Coltheart and Byng (1989, p. 264)	• Reading of irregular words using picture and symbol mnemonics
	Study 10: Francis *et al.* (2001b, p. 266)	• Simultaneous oral spelling of irregular words • Simultaneous oral spelling of irregular words using client's own phonetic reading in a phrase with correct pronunciation

Orthographic input lexicon and access to semantics (surface dyslexia)	Study 11: Scott and Byng (1989, p. 270)	• Comprehension of homophones via computer presented sentence completion task. Homophonic and orthographically similar word foils.
Semantic system	Study 12: Byng (1988, p. 271)	• Picture to written word matching tasks for abstract words. • Dictionary work to generate synonyms for abstract words.
Orthographic-to-phonological conversion (phonological dyslexia and/or deep dyslexia)	Study 13: De Partz (1986, p. 273) Study 14: Nickels (1992, p. 275) Study 15: Berndt and Mitchum (1994, p. 277) Study 22: Stadie & Rilling (2006, p. 293)	All studies based on De Partz (1986) • Generation of code word for each letter • Segmentation of initial phoneme from code word • Production of phoneme on presentation of grapheme • Phoneme blending
	Study 16: Conway *et al.* (1998, p. 279)	• Phonological awareness using the Auditory Discrimination in Depth (ADD) programme)
	Study 17: Kendal *et al.* (1998, p. 282)	• Teaching of the 'c-rule' and the 'g-rule'
	Study 10 : Francis *et al.* (2001b, p. 266)	• Identifying letters • Linking letters to phonemes • Blending consonant clusters
	Study 18: Yampolsky and Waters (2002, p. 283)	• Grapheme–phoneme correspondences • Phoneme blending • Phonological awareness using the Wilson reading system
	Study 19: Friedman and Lott (2002, p. 285)	• Bigraph–phoneme correspondences
	Study 20: Kim and Beaudoins-Parsons (2007, p. 287)	• Bigraph–phoneme correspondences
Lexical semantic route (phonological and/or deep dyslexia)	Study 21: Friedman *et al.* (2002, p. 290)	• Paired associate learning • Stimulation (reading aloud)
	Study 22: Stadie and Rilling (2006, p. 293)	Computer presented therapy. • Lexical treatment (reading aloud following semantic or phonological primes)

whether it reflects a more general deficit in visual processing (Farah & Wallace, 1991). When considering treatment, key symptoms to consider are the failure to process letters in parallel, a significant length effect in reading aloud and extremely slow and laborious reading. Spelling and recognition of orally spelled words are superior to reading. Some people also present with deficits in letter identification resulting in problems with letter matching and naming; this restricts the usefulness of the letter-by-letter strategy.

Treatment choice for pure alexia has been governed partly by the presence of additional deficits in letter recognition and naming. In these cases, therapy has aimed to improve letter naming enabling more effective letter-by-letter reading, with some studies then trying to improve reading speed. Some studies have used kinaesthetic (e.g. motor cross-cueing, Maher *et al.* 1998) or tactile–kinaesthetic strategies (e.g. tracing onto hand, Lott, Friedman & Linebaugh, 1994) either as a cognitive-relay strategy or to stimulate visual recognition. These studies have resulted in improved reading accuracy across trained and untrained stimuli, with Lott and Friedman (1999) also demonstrating that the use of such a strategy does not necessarily reduce reading speed. Other studies have focused on repeated training in letter identification, matching and naming, with some incorporating speeded presentation (e.g. Arguin & Bub, 1994) to reduce response time. Many of these studies have used computer presentation, potentially enabling independent practice and making the need for intensive practice more viable.

An alternative approach has been to try and promote whole-word reading, i.e. reduce reliance on the letter-by-letter strategy. These approaches have been motivated by the fact that some letter-by-letter readers demonstrate access to lexical semantic knowledge when stimuli are presented briefly (typically 250 msec) and they are unable to use letter-by-letter analysis (Saffran & Coslett, 1998). Implicit semantic access/categorisation therapy resulted in no improvement for VT (Maher *et al.*, 1998) but was successful for RS (Friedman & Lott, 2000). RS showed item-specific gains in the reading of trained words, with subsequent experiments suggesting this was due to strengthening of lexical processing rather than the use of semantic reading. Again therapy was presented on computer with monitoring of performance via email and telephone. Sage, Hesketh and Lambon Ralph (2005) explicitly contrasted the effects of training for whole-word recognition and letter-by-letter reading, with both methods involving errorless learning. Errorless approaches were chosen as FD presented with severe alexia and it was thought that his frequent errors may interfere with learning. FD showed improvement in both treatments, although generalisation to untreated words was only seen after letter-by-letter reading. Despite this, the authors argue that the word therapy was more useful to him. Following word therapy, FD changed his reading strategy, with a reduction in letter-by-letter attempts and an emergence of symptoms characteristic of deep dyslexia. The authors suggest this shift was more useful to him when trying to read for meaning and may have been a consequence of the errorless training.

A limited number of studies have looked at the orthographic input lexicon, with only one study (Scott & Byng, 1989) looking at access to semantics from the lexicon. Targeting semantics via written input has also received little attention, although see Byng (1988). Those studies focusing on the orthographic input lexicon raise some of the same issues of generalisation seen in output phonology whereby therapy effects show a tendency to be item specific.

A number of studies have reported attempts to remediate the orthographic-to-phonological conversion route, a process impaired in both deep and phonological dyslexia. The first study reported by De Partz (1986) successfully re-educated a person in using grapheme-to-phoneme correspondence rules; SP, a young French client with a Wernicke-type aphasia, had intact lexical knowledge which mediated the process. Following therapy reading, accuracy significantly improved with the emergence of occasional errors due to the misapplication of rules. SP was thus taught some complex graphemes and grapheme contextual rules to facilitate the reading of some irregular words in French. Several other studies have replicated this approach, with successful re-teaching of individual grapheme-to-phoneme correspondence but more limited gains in reading due to difficulties with blending. LR (Berndt & Mitchum, 1994), an older man with global aphasia, had difficulties blending combinations of phonemes longer than two in length (e.g. CVC combinations), possibly due to an impairment in short-term memory. Blending was also difficult for TC (Nickels, 1992) although the length of intervention with TC was considerably shorter than De Partz's earlier client. The conversion of the initial grapheme-to-phoneme was, however, sufficient to improve the oral reading of high-imageability words, reduce the number of semantic errors in reading and aid spoken naming due to the production of a self-generated phonemic cue. Stadie and Rilling (2006) also replicate the De Partz (1986) approach but use words for the blending phase and present blending in a very systematic way via segmental and syllabic presentation on computer. Other studies, e.g. Yampolsky & Waters (2002), Conway *et al.* (1998) have combined a focus on grapheme-to-phoneme conversion with tasks targeting phonological awareness, e.g. phonological segmentation and blending, in approaches similar to those used for the treatment of developmental dyslexia.

Friedman and Lott (2002) attempted to address the area of blending phonemes by requiring their clients, LR and KT, to learn *bigraphs* (e.g. a VC or CV combination) rather than individual graphemes. They reported greater success with blending but the clients also needed longer periods of intervention. While the number of graphemes (letters or groups of letters standing for a single phoneme, e.g. C, T, TH, EA) in English is relatively limited, the number of bigraphs is very large. If there was generalisation to untrained but related bigraphs – for instance, learning that AT is /æt/ and EM is /ɛm/ might help a client to deduce the pronunciation of AM – this might not be a problem. Friedman and Lott (2002), however, found no evidence of improvement to bigraphs that were not treated. Kim and Beaudoin Parsons (2007) replicated the results of bigraph training with an additional client but also demonstrated that the client's reading improved for both high and low-imageability words beginning with a treated bigraph or a grapheme within a treated bigraph.

Studies focusing on orthographic conversion have required intensive training over a long period of time to facilitate relearning and this may be difficult in some clinical settings. Bigraph training may be even more time consuming due to the large number of correspondences to be trained. In reading aloud, treatment effects will be restricted to words with regular grapheme-to-phoneme correspondence and may result in overgeneralisation and the production of regularisation errors in irregular word reading. As previously highlighted, the use of such approaches may therefore be more beneficial in languages with transparent orthography. The treatment of orthographic-to-phonological conversion may also result in the reduction of semantic and visual errors, with the summation of information from both the lexical and non-lexical reading routes. There may also be improvements in spoken naming if the client's written naming is superior to oral naming and clients are encouraged to visualise name and then read aloud.

Other approaches to the treatment of deep and phonological dyslexia have attempted to strengthen lexical reading. Friedman *et al.* (2002) compare a reorganisation approach using paired associate learning with repeated oral reading (described as stimulation) with two clients. Within paired associate learning, hard to read functors and verbs were paired with easy to read homophones or near-homophones. Improvement was seen on the trained words with no improvement on control words. The study shows that a paired associate learning task can result in improved reading accuracy for trained words. The pairing of words with a homophone or near homophone was crucial for the high level of accuracy as improvement was less when words were repeatedly read aloud. Stadie and Rilling (2006) directly compared the effects of lexical and non-lexical training in a German speaker with deep dyslexia. Lexical treatment involved the reading of words following the presentation of either semantic or phonological primes and resulted in item-specific gains. The non-lexical treatment resulted in generalised gains in reading but took more sessions than the lexical treatment. The authors suggest that lexical treatment may be an alternative option for some clients and that there may be an additional benefit of working simultaneously on both lexical and non-lexical reading.

The majority of these studies have considered the effects of treatment in relation to the reading aloud of single words, with occasional studies looking at reading accuracy and speed at sentence level (e.g. Friedman & Lott, 2002) and at paragraph level (e.g. Ablinger & Domahs, 2009). There has been quite limited consideration of the impact on reading comprehension, particularly everyday reading. Client DL (Lott & Friedman, 1999) showed gains in sentence comprehension. Client PT (Kim & Beaudoin Parsons, 2007) showed improved reading comprehension of longer and more complex paragraphs following bigraph training, which the authors suggest would aid PT's understanding of everyday materials. There have also been some incidences of the clients reporting improvement in functional reading activities, e.g. MR (Greenwald & Rothi, 1998), LR (Friedman & Lott, 2002), FD (Sage *et al.*, 2005) and DL and his wife (Lott and Friedman, 1999). While these self reported improvements are positive, they should be interpreted with some caution when they are not accompanied by objective measures of performance. The relationship between reading aloud and reading comprehension and the impact of improved single-word reading on everyday reading activities still needs to be investigated further.

EVALUATIONS OF THERAPY STUDIES

Study 1

Arguin, M. and Bub, D.M. (1994) Pure alexia: Attempted rehabilitation and its implications for interpretation of the deficit. *Brain and Language, 47*, 233–268.

Focus of therapy: Pure alexia, letter-by-letter reading (visual orthographic analysis).

Therapy approach: Reactivation.

Client details

General information

DM was a right-handed, undergraduate student in engineering when he suffered from a rupture of an arteriovenous malformation in the left posterior cerebral artery. DM presented with a complete right homonymous hemianopia and memory difficulties.

Overall pattern of language impairments and preservations

DM presented with reading difficulties but no evidence of an impairment in other language functions. His reading aloud showed a marked length effect characteristic of letter-by-letter reading. The authors suggest, following detailed experimental investigation of his letter processing, that DM does not base his identification of letters on abstract orthographic representations (letter types) and that this incapacity prevents whole-word processing and forces letter-by-letter reading.

Time post-onset

DM was more than 2 years post-onset at the time of the study.

Therapy

Training aimed to re-establish processing of letters as abstract letter types and the integration of these letter types into high order orthographic units representing letter combinations. A series of experimental tasks were carried out at baseline, midway through training period one, and at the end of training periods one and two. Letter matching was carried out initially during a 6 day period and then reading of letter strings was carried out for 5 days. The length of treatment sessions is not stated. Training and experimental tasks were carried out on computer.

Task	**1. Same/different letter matching** Speeded same/different comparisons of upper- and lower-case letter pairs based on nominal identity. DM indicated whether the letters were the same.	**2. Direct reading of pronounceable letter strings** Speeded naming of letter strings.
Materials	Training set – half of alphabet. Other letters untrained. Sets contained equal number of vowels and consonants and letters where upper/lower case physically different. Letter strings mainly four letters generated by random juxtaposition of trigrams e.g. HUC + UCK = HUCK	
Hierarchy	Reduced response deadline (i.e. reaction time) as training progressed.	Reduced response deadline (i.e. reaction time) as training progressed.
Feedback on error	Not stated	Not stated
Feedback if correct	Not stated	Not stated

Outcome

The effects of training were monitored by a number of experimental diagnostic procedures: (1) letter matching including physical matching and nominal matching, (2) letter priming using neutral, physically identical and different/same letter primes, (3) reading of four letter strings with same case and cross-case presentation and (4) word reading with words of different length with same case and cross-case presentation. This section will present only the main conclusions from these experiments.

Following the two training procedures, DM showed major improvements in reading, with improved reading latency across tasks. He continued to use a letter-by-letter strategy. The difficulty with longer words remained but there was a trend for reduction in the length effect. There was limited evidence of the reinstatement of normal letter type encoding. Individual letters were processed more rapidly and this effect was not specific to trained letters. The authors suggest this was due to improvement to a general procedure transcoding letter shapes onto a representation of their identities, rather than facilitation of a particular set of ortho-graphic representations. DM's improved rate of letter identification is not attributed to an encoding of letter identities as abstract types as he still failed to show similar patterns of priming for physically identical and same/different letter primes. Following training proce-dure two, a set-specific benefit was apparent in letter string naming and word reading, with shorter reaction times for items made of letters from the trained set. The effect was main-tained in case alternated paradigms. The authors suggest training affected assembly of indi-vidual letter identities into intermediate representations of letter combinations e.g. bigrams, trigrams, rather than a general procedure contributing to the assembly process.

Other comments

The study is quite different to clinical treatment studies. The experimental paradigms were designed to test specific hypotheses about the nature of the impairment in pure alexia and the specific effects of treatment on apparently impaired processes.

Study 2

Greenwald, M. L. and Rothi, L. J. G. (1998). Lexical access via letter naming in a profoundly alexic and anomic patient: a treatment study. *Journal of the International Neuropsychologi-cal Society, 4*, 595–607.

Focus of therapy: Visual orthographic analysis.

Therapy approach: Cognitive-relay strategy using letter-by-letter reading.

Client details

General information

MR was a 72-year-old right-handed retired clerical worker who reported no developmental reading difficulties. She had a left CVA resulting in severe alexia with agraphia, a right homonymous hemianopia, anomia, some apraxia and Gertmann's syndrome. An MRI scan showed occipital lobe damage that extended to the temporal-parietal-occipital junction.

Overall pattern of language impairments and preservations

MR's language performance was consistent with an anomic aphasia characterised by fluent output, lexical retrieval difficulties, preserved repetition and relatively spared auditory com-prehension. Her anomia was considered to be due to both impaired semantics and access to phonology from semantics.

MR was unable to read aloud words or nonwords, or use a letter-by-letter strategy.

Successful attempts at naming letters and phonemes were probably due to chance. Severe naming difficulties contrasted with two preserved abilities: (1) an intact ability to name a word when a word was orally spelled to her (100% success) and (2) an ability to name environmental sounds (75% success). With respect to the former ability, her success in pronouncing both regular and exception words, nonwords and words of low imageability and frequency, suggested that her ability to encode letters and access phonology were intact via orally spelled words and that her problems related to an impaired ability to decode graphemic cues from the written form. She was unable to perform any pre-lexical or lexical tasks when words were written.

Time post-onset

MR was 13 months post-onset at the time of the study.

Therapy

Therapy aimed to teach reading using a letter-by-letter strategy of letter naming. Treatment was provided in two phases. During both of these phases, treatment was given twice each day, 5 days a week over 5 weeks (2½ weeks for each set of training items). The session involved approximately 15 minute treatment and 5–15 minutes probing behaviours. A multiple-baseline design across behaviours was used to examine the efficacy of therapy.

Task	Phase 1: Letter naming Shown a letter and asked to name.	Phase 2: Letter Identification Identification of letter from a large sample.
Materials	Two sets of eight letters. Each item trained four times each session. Order of items was randomised. Eighty-eight per cent success criterion over two consecutive sessions or 24 sessions before moving to Set 2.	Larger sample of letters.
Hierarchy	None	Additional practice with letters named incorrectly.
Feedback on error	Incorrect response acknowledged and client asked to finger trace the letter once or twice and re-attempt to name the letter. On second error, the incorrect response was again acknowledged and the clinician provided the letter name, traced the letter and provided a description of the shape of the letter. The client was asked to finger trace the letter and repeat the name three times.	
Feedback if correct	Positive response acknowledged and client asked to finger trace the letter while repeating the letter name three times.	

Outcome

During Phase 1, naming of the first set of letters improved significantly (although this was not robust from session to session). There was a significantly better naming performance with the second set of letters when these were introduced. During Phase 2, when both sets were treated together, significant improvement continued for both sets of letters. No generalisation was seen to oral reading of words containing untreated letters, or to oral naming of Arabic numerals or written symbols. MR reported some carryover of her success in therapy to daily life, being able to read (or attempt) functional signs and labels.

Improvement was maintained when tested 1 week post-therapy. At 6–12 months post-therapy, MR demonstrated a higher success rate with upper-case letters than lower-case letters, a possible influence of therapy, together with improved abilities in letter formation, again possibly due to tracing the written letter shapes during the period of intervention.

Other comments

MR is also reported in Greenwald, Raymer, Richardson and Rothi (1995), where her naming impairment is the focus of therapy. Greenwald and Rothi stress the value of assessing how orally spelled words are pronounced, an influential factor in deciding to use the spoken system in the therapy reported here.

Study 3

Maher, L. M., Clayton, M. C., Barrett, A. M., Schober-Peterson, D. and Rothi, L. J. G. (1998). Rehabilitation of a case of pure alexia: exploiting residual abilities. *Journal of the International Neuropsychological Society, 4*, 636–647.

Focus of therapy: Pure alexia (visual orthographic analysis).

Therapy approach: Reactivation (described by authors as 'restitutive') using a semantic access strategy. Cognitive-relay (described by authors as 'substitutive') using a motor cross-cueing strategy to reactivate access to letters.

Client details

General information

VT was a 43-year-old right-handed woman who had a CVA that resulted in alexia, a dense right homonymous hemianopia, dysarthria (described as 'confusion' with articulation) and some memory loss. An MRI scan showed a large left hemisphere occipital infarct, in the territory supplied by the posterior cerebral artery, and some cerebellar involvement. A second CVA had not resulted in further symptoms. VT had a university degree. Before her CVA, she had worked as a chemist and laboratory supervisor.

Overall pattern of language impairments and preservations

VT had a severe reading impairment in the presence of preserved written and spoken language production. A deficit was identified at the level of abstract letter identification, as seen by poor letter recognition and an inability to match letters and words of varying fonts, in the presence of retained ability to perceive letter stimuli. She had access to the orthographic input lexicon as seen in her ability to recognise orally spelled real words and nonwords. She was unable, however, to read these words aloud but could do so when she copied the target word onto her hand – that is, visually tracing the words and supporting this with head movement. This suggested a difficulty getting from the visual stimulus to the orthographic lexical store. Once a word and sentence were traced on her hand, she was able to access the semantic system without error. Writing was unimpaired. Immediately post-trauma, VT had successfully learned to read Braille to a proficient level and had later received speech and language therapy for her dysarthria.

Time post-onset

VT was 14 months post-onset prior to a period of speech and language therapy. This study commenced on discharge from that therapy period (length of time not stated).

Therapy

Therapy had two aims:

(1) To gain semantic access to a word through repeated exposure to the word.
(2) To read a word following a motor cue (pretending to copy the written word) with and without colour highlighting in the spaces between words.

Therapy consisted of three phases, each involving a different task, which were conducted sequentially. The first phase of therapy targeting semantic access was conducted over six sessions; the time period was not stated. The second phase (i.e. motor cross-cueing without colour spacing) was conducted four times per week over 4½ weeks, with each session lasting 1 hour. The third phase (i.e. motor cross-cueing with colour spacing) was provided in six sessions spread over 2 weeks. A control task design was used to monitor efficacy.

Task	1. Implicit semantic access strategy Make a semantic judgement on a written word presented for approximately 1 second	2. Motor cross-cueing Trace each letter of a word onto a hard surface and say the word as quickly as possible	3. Colour spacing with motor cross-cueing Trace each letter of a word onto a hard surface and say the word as quickly as possible
Materials	Four categories of 10 written words. 20 words in each treatment session with 2–5 trials for each word	100 six-word sentences and 100 five-word sentences. (from Yorkston & Beukelman, 1981). Organised into blocks of 10 sentences	Seven- and eight-word sentences organised into blocks of 10 sentences (from Yorkston & Beukleman, 1981). Spaces between words were highlighted by a colour
Hierarchy	None	None	None
Feedback	Immediate verbal feedback given on accuracy for 50% of items, with delayed verbal feedback (at end of block of items) for other 50%	Feedback provided on reading speed of each response	Feedback provided on reading speed of each response

Outcome

Treatment response was measured by changes in reading speed, with some visual inspection of the data. Following the first phase of therapy, VT made no improvement, remaining at chance in making semantic judgements. Following the second phase, VT's reading speed doubled, rising from approximately 20 words per minute (wpm) to 44.5 wpm. Generalisation was seen to non-treated sentences. Following the third task involving colour spacing, no additional gains were seen. Reading speed in Braille remained consistent throughout all phases.

Treatment benefits were, therefore, apparent following the motor cross-cueing strategy but not with the semantic strategy. These gains were not attributable simply to repeated practice, as seen by the generalisation to untreated items, or to generalised practice effects, as seen in the consistency of her performance reading Braille. The authors describe this strategy as a letter-by-letter strategy but with a motor element rather than a spoken naming one. Reading speed remained slower than pre-morbid performance but VT had regained her ability to read so long as she used the motor cross-cueing and took sufficient time.

Other comments

Maher *et al.* provide a detailed discussion on the visual analysis system, identifying the component processes and the mechanisms underlying different deficits that may underpin pure alexia. The motor cross-cueing strategy was developed from an earlier study by Lott *et al.* (1994), in which the therapy involved copying the letters onto the palm of the hand and providing the client with tactile as well as motor feedback.

Study 4

Lott, S., N., Friedman, R.B. and Linebaugh, C.W. (1994). Rationale and efficacy of a tactile–kinaesthetic treatment for alexia. *Aphasiology, 8,* 181–195.

Focus of therapy: Pure alexia, letter-by-letter reading (visual orthographic analysis).

Therapy approach: Cognitive-relay strategy to use letter-by-letter reading.

Client details

General information

TL was a 67-year-old, right-handed man. He was a college educated, retired printer. He had a cerebral haemorrhage. An initial CT scan showed a large left temporoparietal haematoma with compression of the adjacent left ventricle and minimal left to right midline shift. Three months post-onset, a scan showed clearing of the haematoma with residual damage to the left posterior temporal and lateral occipital lobes.

Overall pattern of language impairments and preservations

TL presented with fluent aphasia consistent with transcortical sensory aphasia, characterised by moderate anomia, good repetition, a mild comprehension deficit and a persistent severe alexia with some agraphia. TL had difficulty reading words aloud with a marked length effect. He attempted to read via a letter-by-letter strategy but was largely unsuccessful due to severely impaired letter naming. In reading aloud, he showed a part-of-speech effect in which nouns were read more accurately than adjectives and verbs and function words were most difficult. He was unable to read nonwords. He was able to spell words and recognise words that were orally spelled to him more accurately than he was able to read aloud and there was no part-of-speech effect in these modalities. Comprehension was also more accurate for spoken words and orally spelled words than written words. In writing, he had greater difficulty writing lower-case than upper-case letters due to a pre-morbid preference for upper-case. The authors attribute TL's difficulty to a pure alexia. He had poor letter naming precluding the use of a letter-by-letter strategy. His symptoms of phonological alexia (part-of-speech effects and poor nonword reading) were attributed to problems activating the orthography to phonology route via the visual modality.

Time post-onset

TL was 14 months post-onset at the start of the study.

Therapy

Therapy aimed to enable TL to read in a letter-by-letter strategy by using a tactile–kinaesthetic approach to train letter naming. A multiple-baseline design was used to compare performance at baseline, during sequential treatment phases and maintenance phase. Treatment progressed from Set 1 letters, Set 1 training words, Set 2 letters, Set 2 training words, Set 3 letters and Set 3 training words. Training continued until TL reached 88% letter naming and 90% accuracy for two consecutive sessions. There were three sets of untrained words that were never trained but were probed regularly. Treatment consisted of 1-hour therapy sessions held 3 times a week for a total of sixty sessions. At home, he was instructed to trace the letters/words ay least three times a day. He was also encouraged to use the copying strategy whenever he attempted to read.

Task	*Letter naming* Copy the letter onto the palm of his hand using a capped pen and then name the letter.	*Word accuracy* Copy the letter onto the palm of his hand, then name each letter of the word in sequence and finally say the word aloud.
Materials	Three sets of letters. Set 1 contained the letters TL was most accurate in naming. Sets 2 and 3 contained letters of moderate and low accuracy respectively. Two lists of ten words for each letter set, one for training and one untrained. Words were three to five letter, monosyllabic verbs. Word lists were matched for length, frequency, number of orthographic neighbours and letter occurrence. Words in later sets contained some letters carried over from previous sets.	
Hierarchy	a. Letters printed with arrows indicating how letter made b. Letters without arrows	No hierarchy
Feedback on error	Not stated	Not stated
Feedback if correct	Not stated	Not stated

Outcome

Criterion level performance was achieved once each stimulus set was trained. After all treatment phases, letter naming improved from 49% to mean 63% correct, trained word reading from 39% to mean 90% correct and untrained word reading from 41% to mean 81% correct on final two sessions. Accuracy at 1, 4 and 8 weeks post-treatment across all stimuli decreased but remained above baseline levels. Post-therapy, reading aloud improved with removal of the part-of-speech effect. Some generalisation was seen in oral sentence reading. TL's word reading was slower as using the tactile–kinaesthetic strategy took longer than his old strategy. There was no improvement on other language measures.

The use of the tactile–kinaesthetic strategy resulted in improvements in TL's reading aloud of trained and untrained words. The authors attribute the gains to treatment as TL showed no improvement on other language tasks and performance did not reach criterion until items were specifically trained. Reading accuracy declined during the 8 weeks post-treatment. The authors suggest this declining performance may have been avoided if criterion level performance was required across three or four consecutive sessions. Post-treatment, TL's better naming of letters resulted in a reduction of the symptoms of phonological alexia.

Other comments

The same treatment approach was used in Lott and Friedman (1999), with an additional stage of treatment focusing on speed.

Study 5

Lott, S.N. and Friedman, R.B. (1999).Can treatment for pure alexia improve letter-by-letter reading speed without sacrificing accuracy. *Brain and Language, 67,* 188–201.

Focus of therapy: Pure alexia, letter-by-letter reading, visual orthographic analysis.

Therapy approach: Cognitive-relay strategy to use letter-by-letter reading.

Client details

General information

DL was a 67-year-old, right-handed man with a PhD in public health. He had a left CVA. A CT scan showed a recent left posterior temporal-occipital infarct in addition to an old infarct in the right frontal parietal lobe and small lacune in the posterior right basal ganglia region. On testing, DL presented with no major cognitive impairments.

Overall pattern of language impairments and preservations

DL presented with moderate anomic aphasia. Naming was poor with the production of circumlocutions and semantic errors. Repetition and spelling were well preserved. Auditory comprehension was impaired for colours and body parts and at complex paragraph level. His written spelling and ability to recognise words that were orally spelled to him was better than his oral reading of the same words. Reading aloud showed a length effect but no effect of concreteness, regularity or part of speech. Nonword reading was at a similar level to real word reading. Reading was slow and was characterised by letter-by-letter reading. DL was poor at letter naming, pointing to letters named by the examiner, and at cross-case matching, particularly when pairs represented the same letter but differed in shape. He was, however, able to recognise letters as familiar symbols. The authors suggest DL has a severe pure alexia with poor letter identification and letter naming.

Time post-onset

DL was 4 months post-onset at the start of the study.

Therapy

Training consisted of two phases. Experiment 1 targeted DL's letter naming accuracy via a tactile–kinaesthetic treatment. Experiment 2 focused on improved reading speed via a speeded letter-by-letter reading treatment.

Experiment 1

A multiple-baseline design with baseline phase followed by sequential treatment phases was used to monitor the effects of training. Three sets of letters were treated, with training on the next set started when performance reached 90% accuracy on two consecutive probe tasks. DL received three, 1-hour training sessions per week. Training of all three sets was completed in eighteen sessions over a period of 2 months. Training sessions were supplemented by home practice.

Task	**Tactile–kinaesthetic letter naming** Copy the letter onto the palm of his hand using a capped pen and then name the letter.
Materials	Three sets of letters. Set 1 contained the letters DL was most accurate in naming. Sets 2 and 3 contained letters of moderate and low accuracy respectively.
Hierarchy	None
Feedback on error	Not stated
Feedback if correct	Not stated

Outcome of Experiment 1

After training the procedure for letters in Set 1, DL used the tactile–kinaesthetic method to name the untrained letters. Performance on all three sets of letters reached 90% accuracy criterion. Following treatment, DL's performance on naming letters in isolation, naming letters in non-pronounceable letter strings and in word reading improved. Using the tactile–kinaesthetic method resulted in slightly increased response times.

Experiment 2

A multiple-baseline design was used with treatment proceeding in stages: (1) speeded naming of letters in isolation, (2) speeded naming of letters in non-pronounceable letter strings and (3) letter-by-letter word reading. At each stage, training continued until DL's response time reached plateau, defined as twelve consecutive sessions without an appreciable decrease in time. All stimuli were tested within probe sessions. DL again received three, 1-hour treatment sessions each week supplemented by home practice. Individual letters were treated for fourteen sessions, letter strings for thirty-seven sessions and words for forty sessions. Training took place over a 9 month period.

Task	***Speeded tactile–kinaesthetic letter-by-letter reading*** Use tactile–kinaesthetic strategy to name letters as quickly and accurately as possible.
Materials	All letters of alphabet, 40 non-pronounceable letter strings of four to seven letters in length and 120 words of three to seven letters. Letter strings and words divided into a set for training (20 strings and 80 words) and an untrained set (20 strings and 40 words). Words in trained and untrained sets matched for letter length and frequency and contained pairs that were orthographically similar.
Hierarchy	a. Single letters b. Non-pronounceable letter strings c. Words
Feedback on error	Feedback on accuracy and average response time
Feedback if correct	Feedback on accuracy and average response time

Outcome of Experiment 2

Speeded naming of letters in isolation was stopped after fourteen treatment sessions as there was measurable improvement in DL's speed of naming individual letters. There was, however, also improvement in the speed of naming in letter strings and word reading, neither of which had been trained at this stage. DL's accuracy in naming letters improved. Accuracy in naming letters in letter strings remained the same but accuracy in word reading dropped. Speeded naming of letters in letter strings resulted in reduced mean letter naming time for trained and untrained letter strings and for words. Accuracy in naming letters in letter strings remained high and word reading accuracy returned to a level comparable to the start of treatment. Speeded letter-by-letter reading resulted in decreased mean reading time for both trained and untrained words with accuracy remaining high.

Outcome

Treatment resulted in improved reading of trained and untrained words, with both groups of words read faster and more accurately. Similar improvements were seen on another single-word reading test. At sentence level, DL's accuracy and speed improved. There was no change at paragraph level. There was minimal change on other language measures. On a questionnaire about reading, DL rated himself higher on 4/11 parameters, i.e. how frequently he read and how well he comprehended single words, sentences and paragraphs. DL's wife rated him higher on 9/11 parameters with additional gains in how much he enjoyed reading, how well he read aloud and how well he comprehended signs, labels and newspapers. In a final experiment, DL's reading performance when he was allowed to use strategy was compared to reading without the strategy. When he was not allowed to use the strategy, reading was slower and less accurate. Slower reading times when DL was not using the strategy were attributed to the increased time needed to decode each letter through the visual modality.

DL's reading of trained and untrained words improved with some generalisation to sentence level reading. DL and his wife reported improvement in several aspects of reading. Effects are likely to be due to treatment as minimal change was seen on tests of language processing. Initial speeded letter naming resulted in reduced word reading accuracy and the authors attribute this to the effects of guessing. The training of letter strings and words resulted in improved reading speed. Reading with the strategy was faster and more accurate than when he was not allowed to use it. The authors discuss the important role of treatment context due to the different cognitive processing involved in naming letters in isolation, in letter strings and words. The authors suggest that to read a whole word using the tactile–kinaesthetic approach, the reader needs to segment the word into letters, identify and name each letter, store the name of each letter in memory, keep track of the next letter and pull all the letter names together to read the word.

Other comments

The study uses the same initial treatment approach as Lott *et al.* (1994) but then develops it to include speeded reading. The study shows improved reading in terms of accuracy and speed and the client reported some functional gains.

Study 6

Friedman, R. B. and Lott, S. N. (2000) Rapid word identification in pure alexia is lexical but not semantic. *Brain and Language, 72*, 219–237.

Focus of therapy: Pure alexia, letter-by-letter reading (visual orthographic analysis).

Therapy approach: Reactivation.

Client details

General information

RS was a 46-year-old, left-handed man. He was a professor with a PhD in engineering. He underwent subtotal resection of a left occipital lobe, hemangiopericytoma. Subsequent surgery was performed to reduce oedema. He presented with a right hemianopia.

Overall pattern of language impairments and preservations

RS had no aphasia. In reading aloud, RS was more accurate and faster reading shorter words than longer words. There was no evidence of part-of-speech or regularity effects. His letter naming ability was intact, He read letter-by-letter but made 'educated guesses' after he had identified the first few letters of a word. His spelling and recognition of orally spelled words were superior to his reading. The authors suggest RS has a mild pure alexia.

Time post-onset

RS was 4 months post-onset at the start of the study.

Therapy

The paper describes a series of experimental treatment studies investigating whether RS could be trained to made use of semantic reading, possibly mediated via the right hemisphere. Each experiment and their results are set out below and the overall outcome then summarised.

Experiment 1

Experiment 1 investigated the effects of semantic categorisation of rapidly presented nouns. A multiple-baseline design consisting of a baseline, sequential treatment of three therapy sets and a maintenance phase was used to investigate the effects of therapy on trained and untrained words. Training on each therapy set continued until RS achieved 90% accuracy on the trained items on the probe test on two consecutive sessions. Therapy was administered via computer. Treatment was initially provided for 2 hours daily for 2 weeks. RS then carried out the therapy program at home at least three times per week for an additional 16 weeks. During this time, weekly probes were carried out and RS sent the file via email for scoring. Following the analysis of the results, RS was told whether to continue with the current set or proceed to the next set.

Task	*Categorisation of rapidly presented nouns* Stimulus word presented for 30 ms and RS asked to press one key if stimulus belonged to current category and press another key if it did not.
Materials	Three sets of words from different semantic categories: (1) occupations, (2) birds and (3) animals. Two lists of 20 words in each set, one list for training, 1 untrained. Each list contained ten members of category and ten distracter words which were matched to member word based on orthographic similarity, length, part of speech and frequency. Words presented in lower case.
Hierarchy	None
Feedback on error	Computer presented 'wrong' on screen
Feedback if correct	Computer presented 'right' on screen

Each set of trained words reached criterion level performance of 90% correct following training specific to that set. No set of control words reached criterion. There was some degree of improvement for the control words between baseline testing and completion of Set 1 words but there was no improvement following training of sets 2 and 3. In reading aloud, RS's length effect dramatically reduced but no part-of-speech effect emerged.

Experiments 2–4

Experiments 2–4 were carried out to determine whether RS learned to recognise particular visual patterns or to respond 'yes' to particular action words. The results of these experiments showed RS's categorisation of trained words was superior to that of untrained words regardless of case or font and that RS was processing word meaning during categorisation. The authors, therefore, suggest training improved RS's ability to successfully activate the abstract representations of trained words.

Experiment 5

Experiment 5 investigated the effects of oral reading of rapidly presented words. The authors predicted that oral reading training would be unsuccessful if treatment effects were due to semantic reading. A multiple-baseline design, consisting of a baseline phase and sequential treatment phases, was used to investigate effect on trained words. RS ran the training program on his home computer at least three times per week over a period of 22 weeks. Stimuli were probed once weekly over the phone. Training continued on each set until RS achieved 90% accuracy on two consecutive probes.

Task	**Oral reading of rapidly presented nouns** Words presented for 30 ms and RS asked to read aloud.
Materials	Untrained stimuli from Experiment 1
Hierarchy	None
Feedback on error	RS pressed a key and computer presented spoken word and RS decided whether he was correct.
Feedback if correct	RS pressed a key and computer presented spoken word and RS decided whether he was correct.

Contrary to prediction, RS learned the trained words to 90% accuracy once each set was specifically trained.

Experiment 6

Experiment 6 repeated the training paradigm used in Experiment 5 with functor words. It was predicted that success in Experiment 5 may still be a consequence of semantic reading as nouns are semantically rich and stimuli were presented in categories. Poorer performance on functors would be predicted if semantic reading was being used. Twenty functor words (10 trained and 10 untrained) were used. Pairs were matched for orthographic similarity, length of speech and frequency of occurrence. With treatment, RS reached 90% criterion for trained items over a period of nine sessions. There was some improvement in untrained functors but they did not reach criterion.

Experiment 7

Experiment 7 repeated the oral reading training with 20 nonwords (pseudowords). Following 47 weeks of training, three times a week, RS's reading of trained items never came close to criterion level.

Outcome

RS was able to recognise rapidly presented words when performing a categorisation task. RS was equally successful in orally reading rapidly presented nouns and function words. The authors suggest that reading via semantics was not crucial to the success of rapid word training. Functors were learned more rapidly that nouns, possibly due to word frequency. The authors attribute the effect of treatment to a strengthening of the link between visual analysis of trained written words and accessing orthographic representations within lexicon. No improvement was seen in the learning of nonwords. The authors suggest that RS could only strengthen links that already existed rather than create new ones. Following training, untrained words showed minimal improvement in accuracy. However, in reading aloud, speed of reading increased with a reduction in the length effect. The authors suggest RS was relying less on letter-by-letter reading and more on rapid whole-word processing.

Other comments

The treatment program was primarily carried out independently on the computer with monitoring via email and phone. The authors suggest the use of tele-treatment may play a greater role in rehabilitation in future.

Study 7

Sage, K., Hesketh, A. and Lambon Ralph, M.A. (2005) Using errorless learning to treat letter-by-letter reading: contrasting word versus letter-based therapy. *Neuropsychological Rehabilitation, 15(5)*, 619–642.

Focus of therapy: Pure alexia, letter-by-letter reading (visual orthographic analysis).

Therapy approach: Reactivation via errorless learning.

Client details

General information

FD was a 73-year-old man who had previously held a variety of jobs including a grocers shop and for a tyre company. FD had a series of neurological problems. He had two neurological vascular incidents which did not involve hospital admission, where a working left hemiparesis resolved with no apparent cognitive or communication difficulties. A further incident resulted in hospital admission with speech difficulties and memory loss. A CT scan showed an extensive haemorrhagic infarct in the left parietal and temporal lobes, with previous old infarcts in the right parietal and occipital regions. Following a carotid endocardectomy, he was readmitted to hospital with loss of vision. A further CT scan showed a left occipital haematoma and a fresh bleed in the occipital horn of the right lateral ventricle. At the time of his discharge from hospital, he had right visual field difficulties, some residual unsteadiness and persisting communication difficulties. The study took place sometime later. At the time of the study, he showed a generalised visual perception deficit resulting in problems with visual object recognition and space and position perception.

Overall pattern of language impairments and preservations

FD had good auditory comprehension when assessment was purely auditory e.g. synonym judgement. On spoken word-to-picture matching, he had some difficulties due to his difficulties with picture recognition. His spoken output was characterised by moderate word-finding difficulties with semantic errors in naming and in connected speech. Naming to definition was significantly better than picture naming but was outside the normal range. He had excellent repetition skills. FD showed some difficulty with both oral and written spelling with a significant length effect. He was able to write fluently at sentence level but produced a number of errors.

   FD had severely impaired reading skills and reading was his priority for intervention. He was able to do single-letter cross-case matching but made errors when five letter stimuli were used. He made some errors in letter naming in both lower and upper case. On a timed reading task, with words of varied length, his performance deteriorated as length increased, resulting in a reduction in accuracy and an increase in reading time. He was unable to read nonwords. On untimed reading tasks, FD read words letter-by-letter. Occasionally for highly familiar words, he gave an approximate definition without recognising the word. A previous study had shown that FD had some implicit lexical and semantic knowledge under brief presentation conditions. The authors conclude FD presents with letter-by-letter reading with good, although not perfect, letter processing. They suggest his peripheral dyslexia may be consistent with a general visual perceptual deficit.

Time post-onset

Time post-onset is not stated.

Therapy

The study compares two treatment methods; both methods involve errorless learning as the authors suggest FD's learning may be impeded by his frequent errors. Treatment one aimed to improve FD's ability to recognise whole words, with the prediction of item-specific learning. Treatment two aimed to improve the accuracy and speed of FD's letter-by-letter reading, with predicted generalisation to untreated words. Therapy took place via monitored daily practice with FD's family carrying out therapy. Each therapy phase took place over 7 weeks. A repeated baseline design was used to examine the effects on treated and control words 3 weeks pre-therapy, after each treatment phase and 4 months after the end of treatment.

During treatment one, the first procedure was used for the first 4 week period. FD only reached 53% correct so the procedure was changed. The second procedure was introduced for a further 3 weeks but the period of therapy was interrupted by medical problems and a hospital admission. During treatment two, there was little change in single-letter accuracy following a focus on single letters and three letter sequences during a 4 week period. Work on the treatment set took place over 3 weeks.

Task	Treatment 1: Whole-word recognition	Treatment 2: Letter-by-letter reading Present card with letter/sequence of letters. Helper traces letter on FD's palm whilst saying the letter.
Materials	Three lists of 30 words matched for frequency, length, imageability, familiarity and age of acquisition. Ten words in each set were chosen by FD (personal interest words). Sets contained 4 sets of triads where first three letters of word were the same. One list used for each treatment method. One control set.	
Hierarchy	a. Go through words, showing FD each card and telling him the word. The five present each word again, say the word and ask FD to repeat five times whilst looking at the card. b. Go through each card containing the word and the letter shape. Read the word and use FD's finger to draw around the shape, commenting on particular features e.g. double letters, length etc. Say the word and ask FD to repeat five times whilst looking at the card.	Prior to work on treatment set, work on single letters and three letter words. Work on treatment sets started with four letter sequences. a. Four letter sequences – all four letters traced and produced. Helper says word for repetition. b. Followed by FD being asked to say word (could remember from repetition) c. After five words as above. FD no longer able to use immediate recall. d. When consistent at step three. FD was asked to read aloud the letters before saying the word.
Feedback on error	Normally repetition resulted in a correct response i.e. errorless. If an error was produced, word repeated correctly five times.	If errors made in producing letters at step four, helper went back to step two.
Feedback if correct	Not stated	Not stated

Outcome

Following treatment one (whole-word recognition), there was significant improvement on treated items. No change was seen on other word sets. Improvement was maintained over second treatment period and at follow-up. Following treatment two (letter-by-letter), there was significant improvement on treated words and the control set which was maintained at follow-up. Improvement was evident in both the word triads and in the words of personal interest. There was no improvement in the accuracy of his letter identification. There was significant change in reading time across the four time periods, with times at baseline being significantly slower than all other periods but no difference between times after the different therapies or at follow-up. There were changes in reading strategy and error types as the study progressed. At baseline, overt letter-by-letter attempts were high with a large percentage of omission errors. Following word therapy, letter-by-letter attempts reduced for all three word sets and FD's use of letter-by-letter reading remained low even after letter therapy. Following therapy, no responses, and visual and semantic errors increased. FD reported an improvement in his ability to gauge the nature and content of some articles in magazines.

FD showed improvement on treated lists after word and letter therapy, with additional generalisation to untreated words after letter therapy. After whole-word therapy, FD altered his reading strategy from letter-by-letter reading to attempted whole-word recognition resulting in reduced reading time and errors consistent with deep dyslexia. The authors propose this shift in strategy was useful to him when trying to read for meaning and that the shift may be a result of the errorless learning paradigm. The authors suggest therapists should investigate letter recognition and implicit reading skills of pure alexic readers to determine the appropriate therapy.

Other comments

The study is a carefully controlled comparison of two different treatment methods for clients with letter-by-letter reading.

Study 8

Ablinger, I. and Domahs, F. (2009) Improved single-letter identification after whole-word training in pure alexia. *Neuropsychological Rehabilitation, 19(3)*, 340–363.

Focus of therapy: Pure alexia, letter-by-letter reading (visual orthographic analysis).

Therapy approach: Reactivation.

Client details

General information

KA was a native speaker of German who worked as an insurance agent. At the age of 64, he had an ischaemic infarct in the territory of the left middle and posterior cerebral artery. A CT scan showed a lesion extending from the posterior hippocampus to the medial part of the lingual and fusiform gyri of the left hemisphere. Neuropsychological assessment showed impaired performance in visuospatial memory span, spatial constructive abilities, visual perceptual processing and alertness. Selective attention was in the normal range and verbal working memory was just below average.

Overall pattern of language impairments and preservations

KA presented with a mild Wernicke's aphasia with moderate comprehension and word-finding difficulties. KA's reading was assessed in-depth. With unlimited time, he was able to detect pseudo-letters and discriminate letter strings. He was impaired in cross-case matching and in single-letter naming. Performance on lexical decision was also impaired. When presented with a time limit, there was no difference between his performance on words and nonwords. With a limited time presentation of 250 ms, there was an increase in false positive responses for nonwords. Performance was not influenced by frequency or imageability. Reading aloud was characterised by letter-by-letter reading, with a decrease in reading accuracy and increase in reading duration as word length increased. Reading errors consisted of no responses, neologisms and visually similar errors. The authors attribute KA's deficit to an impairment of single-letter identification combined with impaired letter integration.

Time post-onset

KA was 13.5 months post-onset at the time of the study.

Therapy

Therapy aimed to promote the parallel processing of graphemes in order to reduce KA's word reading duration and to monitor whether indirect improvements were seen in single-letter identification. A repeated baseline design was used to monitor the reading of training and control items and letter naming with assessments before, between and after training phases. Before and after therapy, performance on cross-case matching and in a text reading task was also assessed. Treatment consisted of forty, twice daily sessions on weekdays over a period of 4 weeks. Set A was treated during the first phase and Set B during the second phase. Reading training took place alongside regular language therapy which did not address written language. This addressed 'sophisticated semantic processing' at word and text level in spoken input.

Task	**1. Auditory–visual verification task** KA asked to decide whether a written word matched a preceding spoken word. Visual stimuli were of the target word, phonologically related word or unrelated word.	**2. Whole-word recognition** Target word presented and KA asked to read word aloud.
Materials	Fourteen difficult letters divided into 2 sets (sets A and B). 2 sets of 80, 4–7 letter, medium frequency nouns. Set A did not contain Set B letters and vice versa. Each set of 80 items divided into 40 trained and 40 control words. Sets matched for word frequency, syllable number, reading duration and accuracy. Stimuli presented in upper-case letters.	
Hierarchy	Initial exposure duration of 1000 ms decreasing over sessions to 800 ms.	First five sessions, word presented for 1300 ms and then 1000 ms for remaining eleven sessions.
Feedback on error	Not stated	Re-presentation of target word for reading. If still incorrect, target named by therapist and word presented again.
Feedback if correct	Not stated	Not stated

The auditory–visual verification task took place in the first four sessions to ensure famili-arity with training items. There were then sixteen sessions of whole-word recognition.

Outcome

After Phase 1, KA's overall word reading improved significantly in terms of both reading accuracy and mean reading duration. Significant improvement was seen on both trained and control words, but mean reading duration of trained items was significantly shorter than for control words. After Phase 2, numerical changes did not reach statistical significance as accuracy had already approached ceiling after Phase 1. After Phase 2, there was a difference between trained and control items. Following therapy, KA was still using a letter-by-letter strategy and despite an overall reduction in word duration, the length effect still persisted. Speed of letter naming improved significantly after the first phase, with improvement in both the treated difficult letters (Set A) and in untreated difficult letters (Set B). Numeri-cal improvement after the second phase did not reach statistical significance. Therapy did not change overall letter naming accuracy. At the end of therapy, there was a significant improvement in cross-case matching. Improvements were also seen in text reading. Text reading duration reduced and the proportion of words read accurately increased but perform-ance remained severely impaired in relation to control participants.

KA's word reading improved significantly in terms of speed and accuracy, with a parallel improvement in single-letter naming speed. Improvement was not specific to trained words or letters. The authors attribute the gains to a strengthening of the letter features needed for letter identification. The continued use of letter-by-letter reading and the presence of the length effect post-treatment is attributed to persisting difficulties at the level of orthographic integration. The authors acknowledge the possible contribution of the parallel language therapy but suggest the specific improvements in word reading cannot be related to non-specific oral therapy.

Other comments

The rationale for therapy is discussed in relation to interactive processing (Plaut *et al.*, 1996) where top-down influences support letter identification.

Study 9

Coltheart, M. and Byng, S. (1989). A treatment for surface dyslexia. In X. Seron and G. Deloche (Eds.), *Cognitive approaches in neuropsychological rehabilitation*. Hillsdale, NJ: Lawrence Erlbaum Associates.

Focus of therapy: Orthographic input lexicon (surface dyslexia).

Therapy approach: Reactivation.

Client details

General information

EE was a 40-year-old left-handed male postal worker who fell off a ladder. A CT scan showed an extensive haemorrhagic contusion of the right temporal lobe and a large subdural hae-matoma extending over the left temporal onto the left parietal lobe. A right temporoparietal craniotomy and evacuation of acute subdural haematoma and haemorrhagic contusions of the right temporal lobe was performed.

Overall pattern of language impairments and preservations

EE's spoken output was characterised by word-finding difficulties, with good auditory comprehension of single words. His reading of irregular words was significantly impaired compared with his reading of regular words, although the latter was impaired to some extent. His real word reading was characterised by regularisation errors. In a homophone matching task, EE showed a significant disadvantage for irregular words. Homophone confusions were also present in reading comprehension. The authors suggested that EE's pattern was consistent with surface dyslexia and that it reflected impairment at the level of visual word recognition (the orthographic input lexicon).

Time post-onset

Therapy commenced when EE was 6 months post-trauma.

Therapy

Therapy was designed to improve the reading of irregular words using a whole-word training approach. Therapy consisted of three phases, corresponding to three different tasks. Therapy in Phase 1 lasted for a total of 5 weeks. Each week the reading of the words without the mnemonic aids was tested. Therapy was carried out at home for 15 min each day, 2 weeks with Group 1 words and 2 weeks with Group 2 words. In Phase 2, therapy was carried out at home for a period of 1 week. Performance was re-tested immediately post-therapy and again at 4 weeks post-therapy. The duration of the third therapy phase was not stated. A multiple-baseline therapy design was used to demonstrate the efficacy of treatment.

Task	Phase 1: Reading of irregular words	Phase 2: Reading of words	Phase 3: Reading of words
	Written word presented alongside a picture mnemonic representing meaning	Written word presented with mnemonic symbol	Written word presented with mnemonic symbol
Materials	Twenty-four words containing two vowels + 'gh', e.g. 'cough'. Words divided into two groups of 12.	Fifty-four words which EE misread during pre-test. Pre-test 485 most frequent words in Kucera and Francis (1967) frequency counts. Mnemonic symbols drawn on word chosen by EE. Words divided into two groups of 27. Only one group of words treated.	101 words which EE misread during pre-test. Pre-test next 388 words in Kucera and Francis (1967) frequency counts. Mnemonic symbols drawn on word chosen by EE. Words divided into two groups. Only one group of words treated.
Hierarchy	None	No hierarchy	No hierarchy

Feedback on error	Not stated. Progress chart kept each day.	Not stated	Not stated
Feedback if correct	Not stated. Progress chart kept each day.	Not stated	Not stated

Outcome

A significant improvement for treated words followed Phase 1 of the therapy programme. Some improvement of untreated Group 2 words was seen following treatment of Group 1 words. Accurate performance for both groups of words was maintained 1 year post-therapy. As with the first phase, a significant improvement for both treated and untreated words followed Phases 2 and 3 of therapy, although reading of treated words was superior to that of untreated words.

In the second and third phases, EE's reading of the words was stable prior to treatment, leading the authors to suggest that improvement was not due to spontaneous recovery. There was significant improvement of treated words and improvement was maintained post-therapy, with some improvement of the reading of untreated words. The authors suggest that this non-specific treatment effect may be explained by a visual word recognition system based on distributed representations, as Hinton, McClelland and Rumelhart (1986) suggested.

Other comments

Coltheart and Byng provide a comprehensive discussion of the components of an item-specific model compared with a distributed-representation approach, emphasising the letter, word and semantic levels in the latter, and suggesting how a distributed-representation approach may underpin an explanation of the successful therapy reported here. EE's therapy is also summarised in Nickels (1995).

Study 10

Francis, D. R., Riddoch, M. J. and Humphreys, G. W. (2001b). Treating agnostic alexia complicated by additional impairments. *Neuropsychological Rehabilitation, 11*, 113–145.

Focus of therapy: Orthographic-to-phonological conversion and the orthographic input lexicon.

Therapy approach: Relearning.

Client details

General information

MGM was a 19-year-old man who sustained a head injury at the age of eight. An MRI scan highlighted damage to the occipital, frontal and temporal lobes (temporal lobe damage more pronounced on the right-hand side). Before the trauma, reading acquisition was unimpaired. MGM had shown signs of being ambidextrous.

Overall pattern of language impairments and preservations

MGM's aphasic symptoms had resolved at the time of the reported study, with an almost total alexia remaining, coupled with a severe impairment in visual processing, which was not due to poor visual acuity or visual field defects. A severe visual agnosia was present as seen by his better performance on naming real objects than line drawings, his improved performance with tactile input (as opposed to visual input), and his better response to verbal information that relied on information other than visual information. A profound apperceptive agnosia was also present, together with an impairment of stored knowledge for words and reduced verbal memory.

Reading was characterised by a limited ability to perceive letter shapes, either visually or via tactile input, in the presence of largely intact phonological processing skills (i.e. use of his sub-lexical reading route). Good phonological processing was seen in good auditory discrimination of nonwords, auditory rhyme judgements and phoneme segmentation.

Time post-onset

MGM was 11 years post-onset at the time of the study.

Therapy

Therapy had a number of aims:

(1) to teach identification of letters
(2) to re-teach letter–sound correspondences
(3) to resolve blending in words
(4) to teach irregular words using simultaneous oral spelling with the client's own phonetic reading.

Four separate interventions were carried out; the initial three addressed orthographic-to-phoneme conversion, while the final therapy targeted the orthographic input lexicon. The first therapy was given three times per week (4 hours a week) over a 9 month period. The second therapy commenced approximately half way through the first therapy at around 5 months. The third intervention was only carried out for one session. The final therapy was carried out over twelve sessions, which took place twice a week over 6 weeks. A repeated multiple-baseline design was used.

Therapies 1–3: Targeting orthographic-to-phoneme conversion

Task	1. Identification of letters	2. Re-teaching letter–sound correspondences	3. Phoneme blending on final consonant clusters
	Reinforcing the shape of letters and then naming.	Letter–sound association taught via relay. Client asked to: a. give the cue phrase for a letter b. then provide the sound of a letter.	Identify letters of a word and segment the final consonant blend.

Materials	Twenty high-frequency letters used. For each correct letter, required: letter with part missing, a mirror image and second correct letter and verbal mnemonic.	Six letters consistently incorrect by client. 4 letters given a lexical relay (residual word knowledge related to a letter). Two letters given a phrase linking letter name and sound.	Two lists of words: 22 final consonant blends (treated) and 22 initial consonant blends (control).

Hierarchy	a. Letter shape Reinforcement via:
	  i. correcting letters with part missing
	  ii. verbally describing the shape of letters
	  iii. discriminating letters from the mirror image
	  iv. delayed copying.
	b. Letter naming via mnemonics that incorporated a visual description and phonemic cue.
			a. Sound out letters in a word and blend to produce the word.
			b. Repeat sounding out word but omitting the final consonant
			c. Add the final consonant and say the word.

Feedback on error	Not stated.	Not stated.	Not stated.
Feedback if correct	Not stated.	Not stated.	Not stated.

Therapy 4: Targeting orthographic input lexicon

Methods 1 and 2 carried out simultaneously.

Task	Method 1: Simultaneous oral spelling of irregular words (based on Bryant & Bradley, 1985)	Method 2: Simultaneous oral spelling of irregular words using client's own phonetic reading (correct word and incorrect pronunciation or word placed in a rhyming/alliterative phrase)
Material	Twenty irregular words (high frequency, often function words) divided into two sets for the two methods. For the second method, a rhyming or alliterative phrase containing the client's own phonetic reading of the word and the correct pronunciation was devised, e.g. if 'be' is pronounced as /b ɛ /, then the phrase 'Ben BE good' might be generated to contrast /b ɛ / and /bi/.	

Hierarchy	a. Client identifies a word which is written down. b. Client names the word. c. Client writes the word while simultaneously naming each letter.	As for previous method but using the rhyming/alliterative phrase. The whole phrase is repeated instead of just the single name after the word is written down and then copied.
	d. Client names the word again and then repeats the procedure with the same word.	
Feedback on error	Not stated.	
Feedback if correct	Not stated.	

Outcome

Therapies 1–3

MGM's letter naming improved after the first stage. While this stage continued for 9 months, the authors reported marked improvement after 5 months of treatment, improving from near floor performance to 77–88% success. Only treated items improved. Generalisation was seen across fonts. MGM was also able to read words containing the treated letters, using a letter-by-letter strategy, despite no focus on words in therapy. After 6 weeks of the second therapy phase, MGM had learned the first four letters using the relay strategy and went on to learn the remaining two letters by the end of the following 9 weeks. By the end of the first 9 months, MGM was reading short words and sentences. After only one session of the third stage of therapy, MGM's reading of final cluster words increased from 14% (41% with self-correction) to 68% (91% with self-correction). His ability to read untreated words (i.e. initial clusters) immediately, without self-correction, also improved significantly (from 38% to 71%); however, when self-correction was considered, the overall rate of success with untreated words did not change. MGM's reading pattern was, at this stage, characteristic of surface dyslexia where words were read through sounding out each letter.

Therapy 4

Those words treated by the second method, using the phrase, were successfully learned, while those words using the initial method were not. Francis *et al.* propose that the success of therapy was due to the fact that the methods used bypassed the underlying deficit (i.e. the visual processing impairment) and capitalised on intact abilities (e.g. phonological processing skills). They further suggest that the fourth intervention linked with the previous therapies – that is, 'the verbal description of the letter shape was linked, via rhyme or phonetic similarity, to its name' (p.140). This contrasts with other studies in which a whole-word approach was used over a phonetic strategy. They argue that a cognitive neuropsychological assessment directly influenced the selection of therapeutic methods despite being counter-intuitive.

Other comments

Francis *et al.* provide a discussion of the influences of cognitive neuropsychology on intervention into reading disorders, raising many issues related to why and how therapy works. Strategies are drawn from the literature on reading acquisition.

Study 11

Scott, C. J. and Byng, S. (1989). Computer assisted remediation of a homophone comprehension disorder in surface dyslexia. *Aphasiology, 3*, 301–320.

Focus of therapy: Orthographic input lexicon and access from the orthographic input lexicon to the semantic system (surface dyslexia).

Therapy approach: Reactivation.

Client details

General information

JB was a 24-year-old student nurse who suffered a head injury. A CT scan showed an infarct in the left temporal lobe.

Overall pattern of language impairments and preservations

JB's comprehension during conversation was good, although some difficulties were present in understanding both spoken complex commands and inference. On formal testing, severe word-finding difficulties were evident with the production of some semantic errors. Reading was slow and laboured, with reading of single words characterised by sub-vocal rehearsal. JB was able to extract the gist of sentences and paragraphs. She showed a non-significant trend for better reading of regular words relative to irregular words. Error responses were regularisations and words that were visually and phonologically related to the target word. She was able to read nonwords when these involved consonant and vowel units but experienced difficulties when vowel digraphs were present. In a homophone matching task, JB also showed a non-significant advantage for regular words. When asked to define homophones, she was inconsistent and showed a frequency effect, more often providing a definition for the most frequent homophone. The authors suggested that JB had impaired access to the orthographic input lexicon, with a partial dissociation of the orthographic input lexicon from the semantic system and the phonological output lexicon. Reading comprehension occurred via the phonological form rather than the orthographic form. Writing was characterised by word-finding difficulties and numerous spelling errors. On testing, JB was significantly impaired in her writing of irregular words relative to regular words, although some retrieval of irregular forms did occur. Error responses were regularisations. Spelling of homophones was impaired. The authors suggest some partial access to the orthographic output lexicon, but partial dissociation of the output lexicon from the semantic system and use of the sub-lexical route to aid spelling. They conclude that JB shows many of the features of surface dyslexia and surface dysgraphia.

Time post-onset

Therapy commenced 8 months post-trauma.

Therapy

Therapy aimed to improve the comprehension of homophones by re-establishing the link from the orthographic input lexicon to the semantic system. Therapy consisted of twenty-nine sessions over 10 weeks. A control task therapy design was used to demonstrate the efficacy of therapy.

Task	*Homotrain* Computer presented sentence completion task. Sentence presented on screen with missing homophonic word. Six-word choices presented beneath.
Materials	Sentences containing 68 homophone pairs. Word choices: target, homophone pair, pseudo-homophone and three orthographically similar foils.
Hierarchy	None
Feedback on error	Visual feedback – word in red Negative tune Required to make another selection
Feedback if correct	Visual feedback – word in blue Short, cheerful tune Sentence reproduced at foot of screen. Homophone to be typed in. Bad noise if inappropriate letters pressed.

Outcome

JB made gradual and significant improvement during therapy. Comprehension of treated and untreated homophone sentences improved following therapy, although performance was superior for treated homophones. Significant improvement was seen in the ability to provide definitions for the treated and untreated homophones. No significant improvement was recorded in the ability to write homophones to dictation or in the ability to write irregular words to dictation.

Treatment resulted in significant improvement in homophone comprehension. There was no significant improvement in the writing of words, suggesting improvement was a consequence of treatment rather than spontaneous recovery. The authors suggested that significant improvement for treated items was a consequence of an item-specific improvement within the orthographic input lexicon. Improvement seen with the untreated homophones was considered to be a consequence of a general improvement in the functioning of the access route from the orthographic input lexicon to the semantic system. Generalisation to untreated items was only evident when sentence context was present. The lack of improvement in the ability to write even the treated homophones to dictation was thought to be a consequence of the word remaining on the screen during the therapy procedure, removing the need to encode the word in memory.

Other comments

JB's therapy is also described in Nickels (1995). Scott and Byng provide a discussion of their findings in relation to Behrmann's (1987) study of a person with surface dysgraphia, reviewed in Chapter 13.

Study 12

Byng, S. (1988). Sentence processing deficits: theory and therapy. *Cognitive Neuropsychology, 5,* 629–676.

Focus of therapy: Semantic system – written comprehension of abstract words.

Therapy approach: Reactivation.

Client details

General information

BRB was a 41-year-old man who had a left middle cerebral artery infarct. He had previously worked as a businessman.

Overall pattern of language impairments and preservations

BRB was initially diagnosed with moderate to severe expressive dysphasia and a mild receptive dysphasia characteristic of Broca's aphasia. Some articulatory difficulty was present on consonant clusters and polysyllabic words. At the time of the study, BRB had problems with the mapping of thematic roles in reversible and locative sentences (also treated), and was poor at spoken and written synonym judgements for abstract, but not concrete, words. He was unable to read nonwords, but could read function words and highly imageable words, making visual errors with low-imageability and low-frequency words. Reduced short-term memory matching span was also noted. Verbal output was characterised by few sentences and many single words, with a low proportion of closed-class items.

Time post-onset

This phase of therapy was begun 5 to 6 years post-onset, 6 months after a period of sentence therapy targeting mapping of thematic relations.

Therapy

Therapy aimed to improve the comprehension of abstract words. The therapy was introduced by the therapist and then continued at home. Therapy consisted of 4 weeks of practice, 1 week per phase. A cross-over therapy design was used to monitor the efficacy of this therapy and the sentence therapy.

Task	1. Picture–written word matching task	2. Synonym generation task 'Dictionary therapy'
	Written word presented with four accompanying pictures: target, semantic distracter, two unrelated distracters. Select the picture to go with the written word.	Using a dictionary to look at all the different meanings for each word, BRB made up his own one word synonym or synonyms for each item 'to best encapsulate the range of meanings'.
Materials	The 75 words of the Shallice and McGill Picture–word matching test, with concrete and abstract words each divided into 3 groups: (i) correct in both auditory and visual pre-therapy testing	The 75 words treated in the picture–word matching task.

	(ii) correct in one modality (iii) correct in neither modality. Each of these groups was then divided into 2, to provide different items for treatment phases 1 and 2	
Hierarchy	No hierarchy	No hierarchy
Feedback on error	BRB had to check the response against an answer sheet (answers given as the number of the picture to prevent rote learning)	Not stated
Feedback if correct	BRB had to check the response against an answer sheet (answers given as the number of the picture to prevent rote learning)	Not stated

Outcome

BRB's performance on task stimuli of the picture–word matching task increased to 100% correct. Improvement was item specific (treated items improved while untreated items did not) and task specific (performance on the same items in synonym judgements did not improve). Following the synonym generation task, performance on the synonym judgement task improved significantly. Improvement was, again, item specific but generalised to a word-to-picture matching task using the same items.

   BRB, therefore, improved in his understanding of the treated written abstract words. The authors proposed that this improvement was a consequence of the 'restoration' of some lexical entries that had been 'lost'. This improvement was, however, task specific (i.e. comprehension of the same items from a picture–word matching task was not demonstrated in a synonym judgement task). The second type of treatment (dictionary method) provided a richer set of meanings than the picture–word matching method. The dictionary method, therefore, enabled BRB to learn a specific set of word meanings which he was able to generalise to a different task. Improvement can be attributed to therapy, as there was stable performance before therapy. Functional improvements were not stated.

Other comments

The design of this study was very robust in ensuring that change was attributable to therapy and also in addressing maintenance of therapy effects. Therapy with BRB is also summarised in Byng and Coltheart (1986).

Study 13

De Partz, M.-P. (1986). Re-education of a deep dyslexic patient: rationale of the method and results. *Cognitive Neuropsychology*, 3, 149–177.

Focus of therapy: Orthographic-to-phonological conversion.

Therapy approach: Relearning.

Client details

General information

SP was a 31-year-old left-handed university-educated executive. He had a large intracerebral haematoma in the left parietotemporal lobe which was evacuated surgically. He was a native French speaker and therapy took place in this language. Before his illness, SP had read for at least 3 hours a day.

Overall pattern of language impairments and preservations

SP's spoken production was fluent and characterised by anomia, phonological and occasional semantic errors. He retained good repetition of letters and syllables, although some phonological difficulties were evident in word repetition. Auditory comprehension of single words was generally intact, although he had some difficulties in certain semantic fields (e.g. body parts). Reading performance was characterised by impaired reading of nonwords; content words were read more accurately than function words and nouns were better than verbs. Reading showed an effect of imageability but no effect of length, frequency or regularity. In written word-to-picture matching tests and odd-word-out tests, semantic, visual and derivational errors were produced. The authors considered SP's pattern to be consistent with deep dyslexia.

Time post-onset

Therapy commenced when SP was 3 months post-onset.

Therapy

Therapy aimed to re-teach grapheme-to-phoneme correspondence and consisted of three stages. Stages 1 and 2 involved 9 months of intensive therapy. Stage 3 consisted of an additional sixty-five therapy sessions, with the overall period of therapy totalling approximately 1 year. A multiple-baseline therapy design was used to measure efficacy.

Stage 1: Simple grapheme reading reconstruction

Task	1. Generate code word for individual letters	2. Phoneme segmentation	3. Phoneme blending
	Letter of alphabet linked with lexical relay code word. Say code word in response to letter.	Segment initial phoneme from code words and say phoneme.	Sound out letters and blend to produce nonwords, then words.
Materials	Code words generated by client.	Code words as for Task 1	Written words. Simple three or four letter monosyllabic nonwords and regular real words.
Hierarchy	No hierarchy	a) Phoneme produced via code word b) Phoneme produced in response to letter	Initial use of nonwords to prevent use of a semantic strategy
Feedback on error	Not applicable	If incorrect phoneme produced – return to code word	Not stated

Stage 2: Complex grapheme reading reconstruction

Therapy targeted groups of letters that corresponded to one phoneme in French or that presented few pronunciation ambiguities. The code words for this stage were content words that were homophones (or near-homophones) or words which contained the targeted letter sequences. The steps of therapy were as above.

Stage 3: Learning grapheme contextual rules

Therapy involved the client being trained to apply three grapheme contextual rules. Error analysis had identified the three specific conversion rules sensitive to context that were causing most of his errors. Each of these rules was explained to the client and he was trained in their use in reading aloud and pointing out tasks. Nonwords and abstract words were used to prevent the use of a semantic strategy.

Outcome

At the end of Stages 1 and 2, SP was able to transcode letters into their corresponding phonemes. SP's reading aloud significantly improved and the discrepancy between words and nonwords was eliminated. The majority of the remaining reading errors were a consequence of the misapplication of grapheme-to-phoneme rules. Following the third stage of therapy, errors in reading aloud were reduced to 2%, while processing of letters and tasks involving reading comprehension were performed without error. Therapy resulted in SP being able to read aloud, albeit slowly. The authors propose that the improvement resulted from reorganisation of the impaired grapheme-to-phoneme process by using spared lexical knowledge as a relay between graphemes and their pronunciation.

Other comments

The author notes that the re-training of orthographic-to-phonological rules permitted the correct reading of only a relatively small proportion of the French lexicon, due to the many orthographical irregularities in French. De Partz suggests that this patient seems to be simultaneously using a combination of grapheme–phoneme codes and reading via direct access to meaning.

With respect to client suitability, the client reported here was fluent and able to repeat. This may limit the use of this therapy with non-fluent clients. The client further demonstrated a mnemonic capacity in memorising the different associations. The results also followed extensive therapeutic input that required high motivation and resource availability. His youthfulness may also have been a contributing factor in sustaining motivation.

A replication of this therapy procedure is discussed in Nickels (1992) and the therapy is summarised in Nickels (1995). The approach also forms the non-lexical treatment in the Stadie and Rilling (2006) study.

Study 14

Nickels, L. A. (1992). The autocue? Self-generated phonemic cues in the treatment of a disorder of reading and naming. *Cognitive Neuropsychology, 9*, 155–182.

Focus of therapy: Orthographic-to-phonological conversion to improve spoken naming.

Therapy approach: Relearning of orthographic-to-phonological conversion rules. Cognitive-relay strategy to read aloud a visualised word to help spoken naming.

Client details

General information

TC was a right-handed male businessman. He had a left CVA when 43 years old, resulting in a global aphasia, right-sided weakness and right-sided sensory impairment. A CT scan showed a substantial left middle cerebral artery infarct. Five months post-onset, TC's perceptual, visuo–spatial and non-verbal reasoning skills were considered to be intact.

Overall pattern of language impairments and preservations

TC's speech was fluent with word-finding difficulties. He used a combination of speech, writing, drawing and gesturing of key words to communicate. He was able to write some high-imageability words. His auditory comprehension in conversation was functional, but on testing he made errors in single-word and sentence comprehension. His written comprehension of single words and sentences was also impaired but better than that of his auditory comprehension. TC was unable to read or write nonwords. His reading aloud was characterised by semantic errors and showed an imageability effect. The author proposes that TC had deep dyslexia, with additional deficits in the sub-lexical writing route and in accessing semantics from the auditory input lexicon.

Time post-onset

TC was 16–18 months post-onset when therapy commenced.

Therapy

Therapy aimed to teach grapheme-to-phoneme correspondence to improve reading aloud. As TC's written naming was superior to his spoken naming, it was hoped that he would be able to use 'visualised' written word forms to generate spoken forms. Therapy consisted of two 15–30 min sessions per week for 10 weeks. Some additional home exercises were carried out. A multiple-baseline therapy design was used.

Task	1. Generate relay word (or code word) Letter of alphabet linked with relay word. Say relay word in response to letter.	2. Phoneme segmentation Segment initial phoneme from relay words and say phoneme.	3. Phoneme blending Sound out letters and blend to produce nonwords, then words.
Materials	Relay words generated by TC. Relay words had the letter in its most frequent pronunciation.	Relay words	Written words. Simple three or four letter monosyllabic nonwords and regular real words.
Hierarchy	No hierarchy	a. Phoneme produced via relay word b. Phoneme produced in response to letter	Initially nonwords, words introduced to reduce difficulty.

Feedback on error	Not applicable	Not stated	Not stated
Feedback if correct	Not applicable	Not stated	Not stated

TC was unable to blend phonemes, which required the therapy programme to be changed. The final phase of therapy required TC to silently associate the initial letter of the target word with the relay word, sound out the initial phoneme and then produce the target word. If unable to produce the target word, TC was encouraged to think about the meaning of the word and to sound out additional letters. At this stage, it was discussed with TC that he could try and visualise words and then use this strategy to produce them in speech.

Outcome

A significant improvement was found in the reading of real words. Spoken naming also improved significantly and approximated to written naming performance. TC remained unable to read nonwords and there was no effect of regularity in reading or naming. Improvement in the reading of real words was maintained 5 months post-therapy. TC's reading aloud and spoken naming therefore improved post-therapy. No other significant changes were evident. TC's improvement was considered to be a consequence of therapy. As TC remained unable to read nonwords, however, and there was no regularity effect in reading, these improvements cannot be a consequence of the use of grapheme-to-phoneme correspondences. The author hypothesised that TC visualised the initial letters and converted them to phonemes. These acted as self-generated phonemic cues.

Other comments

While this study drew on the therapy procedure described by De Partz (1986), reviewed earlier, Nickels highlights the different outcomes obtained for different clients. The client reported by Nickels was unable to blend phonemes together, a factor that would appear to be predictive of the success seen with client SP, reported by De Partz (1986). The treatment was nevertheless successful, showing how similar therapy protocols impact on different processes. TC's therapy is also summarised in Nickels (1995).

Study 15

Berndt, R. S. and Mitchum, C. C. (1994). Approaches to the rehabilitation of 'phonological assembly': elaborating the model of non-lexical reading. In G. Humphreys and M. J. Riddoch (Eds.), *Cognitive neuropsychology and cognitive rehabilitation*. London: Lawrence Erlbaum Associates.

Focus of therapy: Orthographic-to-phonological conversion.

Therapy approach: Relearning.

Client details

General information

LR was a 50-year-old female university professor who had a CVA, resulting in aphasia, dyslexia, dysgraphia and dyscalculia.

Overall pattern of language impairments and preservations

LR's overall pattern of language impairment was characterised by poor auditory comprehension, naming, repetition and sentence construction difficulties in spontaneous speech. She had retained non-linguistic cognitive abilities but impaired immediate verbal memory. On assessments of reading, LR showed poor nonword reading, better reading of high-imageability words than low-imageability words but no effect of regularity. Semantic errors in reading were evident. The authors suggested that LR's pattern was consistent with deep dyslexia. Pre-therapy assessment of the components of phonological assembly showed some problems in grapheme parsing, grapheme–phoneme association and blending. Although capable of parsing and blending lexical units, LR showed no appreciation that spoken words could be analysed into their component sounds.

Time post-onset

LR was 9 years post-onset when therapy commenced.

Therapy

Therapy focused on improving orthographic-to-phonological associations to place constraints on the lexical reading process, thereby reducing semantic and visual reading errors. Therapy did not aim to encourage LR to sound out every word. No details regarding the frequency or duration of therapy for the first and second tasks were given. A total of 17 hours was required to achieve production of an isolated phoneme in response to a written letter in the third task. Twelve sessions of therapy were reported for the final task. Task three of the therapy programme was modelled on De Partz (1986). A multiple-baseline therapy design was used to monitor efficacy.

Task	1. Phonological segmentation Sound segments produced. LR to manipulate colour tokens to represent sequence.	2. Written letter segmentation Precise details of task not stated.	3. Grapheme/ phoneme associations Produce phoneme in response to written letter.	4. Phoneme blending Blending of two phoneme combinations.
Materials	Colour-coded tokens. Combinations of up to three sounds.	Written words	Eighteen consonant graphemes, five vowels	
Hierarchy	a. Discrete segments b. Blended segments	None	a. See letter and generate code word b. Segment first sound from code word. c. Learn to produce sound in response to letter	1. C + V combinations 2. V + C combinations
Feedback on error	Not stated	Not stated	Not stated	Not stated
Feedback if correct	Not stated	Not stated	Not stated	Not stated

Outcome

In Task 1, LR performed well when component phonemes were produced separately. The task was abandoned at the blending stage as LR resisted the idea that words could be decomposed. Despite this, following Task 1, LR's letter sounding had improved. Following the use of written words in Task 2, LR was able to segment the initial sounds from spoken words without difficulty. Following Task 3, LR was able to produce single phonemes in response to a presented grapheme. Although she was able to produce more of the component sounds of nonwords, she was not able to produce all three sound segments due to her inability to blend. Following blending therapy, LR was able to blend C + V, but she experienced increased difficulty with V + C, combinations. Voice onset time was a feature often implicated in errors. No improvement was seen in blending three-phoneme combinations. Following therapy, therefore, there was no significant improvement in LR's ability to read nonwords. There was, however, a significant improvement in the reading of high-imageability words. A non-significant improvement was noted in the reading of regular words with a corresponding decrease in the reading of irregular words. Semantic errors declined as predicted, but there was an increase in errors with visual and/or phonological similarity to the target. Therapy did not result in an improvement in nonword reading but did result in an improvement in the reading of high-imageability words. The authors suggested that LR was attempting to use sub-lexical information to support her reading. This had, however, more complicated effects on her reading than the authors had predicted. The effect on phoneme blending of deficits in phonetic control and short-term memory are discussed.

Other comments

This paper replicates the therapy procedure described in De Partz (1986). The authors elaborate on the processes involved in the non-lexical reading route and how these aspects can be assessed. They highlight the need to assess short-term memory deficits when considering this type of therapy.

Study 16

Conway, T. W., Heilman, P., Rothi, L. J. G., Alexander, A. W., Adair, J., Crosson, B. A. and Heilman, K. M. (1998). Treatment of a case of phonological alexia with agraphia using the Auditory Discrimination in Depth (ADD) program. *Journal of the International Neuropsychological Society, 4*, 608–620.

Focus of therapy: Orthographic-to-phoneme conversion.

Therapy approach: Reactivation of the non-lexical reading route via motor–articulatory feedback.

Client details

General information

GK was a 50-year-old ambidextrous man who worked as a systems analyst up until his CVA. An MRI scan showed an infarct of the posterior two-thirds of the temporal lobe, as well as parts of the inferior parietal and occipital lobes. This had resulted in aphasia, alexia, agraphia, limb apraxia and visual field problems.

Overall pattern of language impairments and preservations

At the time of the study, GK's pattern of aphasia was consistent with conduction aphasia where auditory comprehension and lexical retrieval were within normal limits, repetition was impaired and phonological errors, with conduite d'approche, were evident in speech production. Reading difficulties also remained as reading was slow and there was a lexicality effect (nonwords were more difficult than real words) but no effect of regularity or semantic errors. This was consistent with a phonological dyslexia where problems arose from impairment in orthographic-to-phonological conversion. Spelling was impaired and also showed lexicality effects.

Time post-onset

GK was 15 months post-onset when therapy commenced.

Therapy

Therapy aimed to improve phonological awareness to increase access to the sub-lexical route to reading and writing. The Auditory Discrimination in Depth (ADD) program (Lindamood & Lindamood, 1975) was adopted as set out in the manual. Four stages were carried out sequentially. The first stage required 15.75 treatment hours, the second stage 12.25 hours, the third stage 22.2 hours and the final stage a further 50.9 hours, giving a total of 101.1 hours. A multiple baseline across behaviours design with multiple probing was used to monitor treatment effects.

Outcome

GK improved following all treatment stages. Phonological awareness on single-syllable words improved, although this was not maintained 2 months later. He showed significant improvement in identifying phoneme changes on multisyllable nonwords, which was maintained. Reading of nonwords improved and was maintained, as did reading of real words, and other reading skills such as word attack (non-lexical reading). Some skills returned, however, to pre-therapy levels (e.g. passage comprehension). At follow-up, word identification had continued to improve. Spelling improved significantly and this was maintained. The spelling of irregular words, used as a control measure, did not change over the study period.

   This study used a phonological awareness approach (i.e. non-lexical) and resulted in changes to both non-lexical and lexical reading, and spelling. The improvement in real word reading was possibly linked to the gains made in word attack skills. Conway *et al.* propose that evidence for improvement being directly attributable to therapy is seen in the pattern of change with each therapy stage. While no direct evidence is offered to support the influence of the motor–articulatory training, the authors believed it to be a critical component of their therapy approach.

Other comments

Conway *et al.* acknowledge that GK had a mild phonological alexia and do not suggest that the case offers evidence for success in moderate or severe cases. Replicating this study with more severe cases than GK, as well as with other forms of dyslexia, is recommended by the authors. Stages 1 and 2 of the programme are repeated with an additional client (Kendall *et al.*, 2006). The client had non-fluent aphasia, alexia, agraphia and apraxia of speech. Extensive phonological training (74 hours) resulted in minimal gains in nonword reading and phonological processing and no gains in real word reading. The authors suggest that phonological therapies are not likely to be successful if a minimal level of pre-therapy phonological sequence knowledge does not exist.

Task	1. Oral awareness training	2. Simple nonword training	3. Complex nonword–word training	4. Multisyllable nonword–word training
Task	Multisensory training in oral awareness.	Repetition and identification of phonemes in simple nonwords.	Repetition and identification of phonemes in complex nonwords.	Repetition and identification of phonemes in multisyllable nonwords and text.
Materials	Line drawings of the mouth and articulators (mouth pictures), phonemes, graphemes and verbal labels for 11 consonant groups and four vowel groups. Mirror.	Use of all materials from Stage 1. Chains of 10 nonsense segments (e.g. /ip/, /ap/, /a/, /pap/) – V, VC, CV, CVC. Coloured wooden blocks. Plastic tiles of graphemes, handwritten spellings, printed words.	As for Stage 2 but using CCV, VCC, CVCC, CCVC, CCVCC nonwords, and simple phonic rules.	As for Stage 2 but using up to five syllable stimuli, passages and suffixes and prefixes.
Hierarchy	a. Client to look at own mouth in mirror, produce a phoneme and decide main articulators involved, e.g. tongue, lips. b. Determine presence of voicing (noisy or quiet) through feeling throat. c. Verbal label attached. d. Client asked to identify phonemes contrasting in features, e.g. voice. e. Client shown three mouth pictures and asked to decide most appropriate for each phoneme.	a. Stage 1 integrated. b. Client to repeat a nonword. c. Mouth pictures sequenced to indicate phonemes in nonword (hand mirror used). d. Second new nonword introduced differing by one phoneme. d. Client to repeat both while tapping each mouth picture in sequence of phonemes for each word. e. Original sequence of mouth pictures changed to reflect difference between 2 nonwords. f. When 90–100% accurate, mouth pictures replaced with blocks. Reading and spelling introduced at this stage.	a. As for Stage 2. b. Selection of phonics rules introduced.	a. As for Stage 2. b. Selection of prefixes and suffixes introduced.
	Not stated	Rigorous questioning approach used to get client to identify error.	As for Stage 2	As for Stage 2
Feedback if correct	Not stated	Not stated	Not stated	Not stated

Study 17

Kendall, D. L., McNeil, M. R. and Small, S. L. (1998). Rule-based treatment for acquired phonological dyslexia. *Aphasiology, 12*, 587–600.

Focus of therapy: Orthographic-to-phonological conversion.

Therapy approach: Relearning.

Client details

General information

WT was a 42-year-old right-handed nurse anaesthetist. She was struck by lightning at the age of 25 which resulted in a global aphasia. An MRI scan at age 39 showed involvement of the left middle cerebral artery, left frontotemporal cortex and left basal ganglia.

Overall pattern of language impairments and preservations

WT had mild auditory comprehension and spoken production deficits; her production was characterised by a reduced rate and lowered information content. Reading comprehension was lower for paragraphs than single words. More errors were seen in her reading aloud, where she omitted whole words and made both morphological errors (omitting and adding affixes) and errors with low-frequency words. Oral reading of nonwords was poor. Repetition of nonwords was higher but still impaired. Kendall *et al.* propose that WT has an impairment of the sub-lexical reading route (phonological dyslexia).

Time post-onset

Therapy commenced when WT was 18 years post-onset.

Therapy

Therapy was designed to teach two of the seven grapheme-to-phoneme correspondence rules – the 'c-rule' and the 'g-rule'.[1] Six treatment sessions were given on the use of the 'c-rule' and then five on the 'g-rule' over a 6 week period. Extensive baseline and maintenance probing occurred. Sessions lasted approximately 2 hours; the first hour was used for assessment and probing, while treatment was provided during the second hour. A multiple-baseline across behaviours design was used alongside generalisation probes.

Task	Teaching 'c-rule' and 'g-rule'
	Presented with multiple examples of nonwords where each rule is applied and asked to say the word then write the word (when picture removed). Instruction on pronunciation given.
Materials	Sixty words per rule (four conditions) – ten simple real words (one syllable, high concreteness, frequency, imagery and meaningfulness), 20 simple nonwords, ten difficult real words (two–three syllable nouns, low concreteness, low imageability) and 20 difficult real words. Each word was presented three times per session (total 180 items per session).

Hierarchy	None
Feedback on error	Feedback on verbal response:
	1. Phonetic cue given 2. Real word (rhyming word) given ('it sounds like . . .') 3. Repetition of nonword
	Feedback on written response not stated.
Feedback if correct	Not stated

Outcome

Following therapy for the 'c-rule', WT's performance increased 'beyond baseline levels and variability on magnitude and/or slope' on each of the four word lists. No statistics were reported. Generalisation occurred to the 'g-rule' during this phase. This was explained as WT applying a strategy to the 'g-rule' that had been derived from learning the 'c-rule'. Following treatment of the second rule, further improvement was present when ceiling performance had not already been reached. Generalised improvement was seen on other testing. Maintenance was present for both rules.

Kendall *et al.* hypothesise that WT had inefficient use of her sub-lexical route and that treatment was aimed at impaired grapheme–phoneme rule usage. Following therapy, Kendall *et al.* comment that it is unclear whether the deficit was to do with the actual rule and its efficient implementation or due to a processing resource allocation deficit, although they propose the former.

Other comments

A lack of statistical information raises some concerns about the robustness of the data.

Study 18

Yampolsky, S. and Waters, G. (2002). Treatment of single-word oral reading in an individual with deep dyslexia. *Aphasiology, 16*, 455–471.

Focus of therapy: Orthographic-to-phonological conversion.

Therapy approach: Relearning.

Client details

General information

MO was a 23-year-old right-handed woman who had a left frontoparietal craniotomy for a ruptured arteriovenous malformation. Large tissue loss involved the frontal, parietal and temporal lobes. MO had recently graduated from high school at the time of the rupture and enjoyed reading.

Overall pattern of language impairments and preservations

MO had unimpaired visual analysis and functional access to semantic representations but impaired comprehension of abstract and derived words. A severe impairment was present in reading aloud single words and she was unable to apply orthographic-to-phonological conversion rules, blend unfamiliar letter strings or read nonwords, suggesting both an impaired lexical and sub-lexical route. Frequency and imageability effects were present, along with phonological and semantic errors. Yampolsky and Waters classified MO as having deep dyslexia.

Time post-onset

MO was 3 years post-onset at the time of the study.

Therapy

Therapy aimed to establish sub-lexical reading ability by relearning orthographic-to-phonological correspondences and blending using real words. Therapy was given three times per week over a 12-week period. Sessions were 2 hours in length. A multiple-baseline across behaviours design, with treatment and generalisation probes, was used.

Task	**Phonological awareness and blending activities:** phoneme naming, manipulation of graphemes/phonemes in words and reading aloud.
Material	The Wilson Reading Scheme (12 levels of increasing difficulty based on six syllable types of CVC words).
Hierarchy	Each session divided into four parts: a. Client presented with cards of single letters and asked to say the corresponding phoneme. b. Presented with single-letter cards placed into CVC words, client asked to blend the sounds and say the words, tapping out each sound and dragging her finger under each letter while sounding out the words. Following correct response, CVC words are altered by changing one phoneme at a time. c. Presented with cards with the full written CVC word, client asked to read aloud the words, again dragging her finger under each phoneme while sounding out the words. d. Client independently reads a list of 12 words using phonemes treated so far.
Feedback on error	Clinician cues client by modelling correct phoneme with example word (e.g./ p/ as in pig).
Feedback if correct	Not stated. In word tasks, clinician manipulates phoneme when correct to alter CVC word.

Outcome

MO's oral reading accuracy of treated words increased from baseline levels of as low as 30% to between 65 and 90% accuracy, suggesting that MO did re-acquire blending skills for CVC words. This is in contrast to other studies (e.g. Matthews, 1991; Mitchum & Berndt, 1991; Nickels, 1992). Generalisation to untreated words within the programme was seen. No improvement was seen on control items, suggesting item-specific improvement, or on other language tests, supporting improvement being due to therapy.

Yampolsky and Waters state that generalisation seen in the study may have been a consequence of the overlap of consonants across tasks. The lack of generalisation to control words may also be influenced by the fact that these words were not matched to the treated sets. Furthermore, while therapy only used real words, it may be argued that MO only used her lexical route. The authors argue, however, that her improved nonword reading is evidence of MO's use of her non-lexical route. Functional gains in reading were also reported.

MO also demonstrated a significant decrease in semantic errors in reading, leading Yampolsky and Waters to claim evidence in support of the 'summation hypothesis' account of word retrieval (Hillis & Caramazza, 1995) where phonological (sub-lexical) and lexical semantic information combine to produce a response in reading aloud. Naming also showed a non-significant improvement, suggesting that the phonological gains involved in using her GPC system may have assisted spoken production through increased phonological information.

Other comments

Yampolsky and Waters comment on MO's co-existing apraxia of speech, suggesting the need for therapy in this area but also highlighting the interaction with any future improvements in oral reading abilities.

Study 19

Friedman, R. B. and Lott, S. N. (2002). Successful blending in a phonological reading treatment for deep dyslexia. *Aphasiology, 16*, 355–372.

Focus of therapy: Orthographic-to-phonological conversion.

Therapy approach: Cognitive-relay strategy of learning a new method of decoding words.

Client details

Two clients were reported in this paper.

General information

LR was a 40-year-old man who had worked as a bus supervisor and a model prior to a CVA. A CT scan showed an infarct in the left frontotemporal region and compression of the lateral ventricle. KT was a 20-year-old right-handed woman who had a CVA following a motor vehicle accident at the age of 15. She had completed 9 years of education at this time. A CT scan showed an infarct in the territory of the left middle cerebral artery with some further frontal and lateral involvement.

Overall pattern of language impairments and preservations

LR had a mild-to-moderate non-fluent aphasia. Auditory comprehension was good for single words and up to four-stage commands, but was impaired beyond this level. Spoken production was only good for automatic sequences and impaired in all other output tasks. Length effects were seen in repetition. Oral reading was impaired at the single-word and sentence level, although comprehension was retained for single words. Writing was also impaired beyond short high-frequency words. Overall, LR's reading impairment was characterised by an inability to read or spell nonwords, semantic errors, and a trend for part-of-speech and concreteness effects, suggesting deep dyslexia.

KT also presented with a non-fluent aphasia but was able to produce longer phrases and sentences. Auditory comprehension was impaired only for complex information. Spoken production was characterised by impairment in confrontation naming, and semantic and phonological errors in repetition of three and more syllable words. Oral reading was impaired on all measures, while comprehension of single words was retained. Writing of single words was impaired. Like LR, KT's reading pattern was consistent with a diagnosis of deep dyslexia, as seen in her semantic errors, a part-of-speech trend, difficulties reading nonwords and a trend towards a concreteness effect.

Time post-onset

LR was 2 years post-onset at the time of the study and KT was 5 years post-onset.

Therapy

Therapy taught bigraph–phoneme correspondences.[2] LR attended three hundred and fifty-five treatment sessions over a 31-month period. KT attended therapy for one hundred and fourteen sessions over a 15-month period. Three 1-hour sessions took place each week for both clients. A multiple-baseline design was used to monitor efficacy.

Task	Teaching bigraph–phoneme correspondence	
Materials	Three sets of stimuli, each containing CV and VC bigraphs for a group of phonemes and a set of training words. All bigraphs were paired with a relay word that began with the bigraph, e.g., 'it' with 'Italy'. Bigraphs were written on flashcards with the picture and the written name of the relay word on the back of the card. Words were written on one side with the card with the bigraphs on the reverse.	
Hierarchy	**Training bigraphs** a. Client learns relay word for each bigraph. b. Client produces only target sounds of relay word when shown bigraph. 90% success criterion for 2 consecutive probe tests.	**Training words** a. Client produces CV bigraph b. Client produces VC bigraph c. Client combines these into the words by repeating them in rapid succession ('blending').
Feedback on error	An explicit response cueing hierarchy was applied: a. Show relay word and picture b. Sentence completion cue c. Sentence completion plus visual articulatory placement cue	An explicit response cueing hierarchy was applied: a. Show bigraphs b. Remind use of relay word c. Remind about repeating in rapid succession

d. Sentence completion plus phonemic cue e. The word is modelled f. Target sound is modelled.	d. The bigraphs and 'blending' word is modelled e. The word is modelled.

Outcome

Both LR and KT learned the bigraphs; LR increased his success from 0% to 95%, while KT increased from 6% to 97%. No generalisation occurred from trained bigraphs to untrained bigraphs; this was an expected finding. Before the words were introduced, however, generalisation was seen to words containing those trained bigraphs. When words were introduced, LR's success with these increased from 1% to 82%, while KT improved from 8% to 84%. Generalisation was seen from trained to untrained words which contained the trained bigraphs, while no generalisation was seen to words containing untrained bigraphs.

The impact on reading, including functional activities, was recorded for LR; on self-report, improvement was noted on such activities as reading frequency, oral reading, and understanding newspapers and books. Reading speed was also reported to improve 'dramatically'. This information was not available for the second client.

While Friedman and Lott interpret their findings in relation to dual- and single-route models of reading, and an underlying impairment in phonological processing, they present the mechanism of training bigraph–phoneme (or bigraph–syllable) correspondences as 'creating specific pairings' that are memorised and stored separate to lexical information, and then activated on-line when required. While this is similar to grapheme–phoneme correspondences, the difference lies in the ease with which the bigraphs can be blended when combined into words for reading. Evidence of children's greater ease with syllable blending is used to motivate the therapeutic approach. The lowered co-articulatory demands of syllable blending and the requirement of only deleting a pause when blending bigraphs/syllables are reasons offered for why this approach provides an easier alternative to blending a series of isolated consonants.

The authors clearly state that the approach does not attempt to retrain normal or previous processes of reading or remediate the underlying phonological processing difficulties. Instead, it offers 'a new means of decoding words' that circumvents impaired processes.

Other comments

The length of intervention time, three hundred and thirty-five and one hundred and fourteen sessions respectively for the two clients, was extensive, with probable implications for provision of services. The approach is replicated in Kim and Beaudoin Parsons (2007).

Study 20

Kim, M. and Beaudoin Parsons, D. (2007) Training phonological reading in deep alexia; does it improve reading words with low imageability? *Clinical Linguistics and Phonetics, 21(5)*, 321–351.

Focus of therapy: Orthographic-to-phonological conversion (Deep Dyslexia).

Therapy approach: Reactivation.

Client details

General information

PT was a 51-year-old, right-handed, monolingual English speaker. He was educated to degree level and worked as an army pilot. He had a left middle cerebral artery lesion. A CT scan showed a large area of decreased attenuation in the left temporo-parietal lobe. On testing, he had a mild impairment of attention with spared performance on other non-linguistic, cognitive tasks.

Overall pattern of language impairments and preservations

PT's language performance was consistent with a moderate Broca's aphasia although he showed significant difficulties in auditory comprehension. His speech was halting with significant word-finding difficulties. He was able to produce a range of syntactic structures but sentences were frequently ungrammatical. He had a moderate apraxia of speech. PT was able to perform auditory rhyme judgements showing that his auditory input processing, segmentation skills and phonological short-term memory were intact. Written rhyme judgement was impaired. Word reading was impaired with an imageability and part-of-speech effect; his reading of functors was significantly impaired compared to nouns, adjectives and verbs. The part-of-speech effect disappeared when words were controlled for imageability. Errors were primarily omissions (no responses) with some visual–phonological errors and a small proportion of semantic, morphological, perseverative and unclassifiable errors. PT's nonword reading was severely impaired. At paragraph level, when requested to read aloud, PT scanned each sentence silently and then read aloud, paraphrasing the sentence based on the words he had recognised. There were a large number of both content and function word errors; these were mainly omissions. Despite his inability to read aloud, he was sometimes able to get the gist of the story. Reading comprehension accuracy reduced as the length and complexity of paragraphs increased. The authors conclude PT's reading profile is consistent with deep dyslexia.

Time post-onset

PT was 31 months post-onset at the time of the study.

Therapy

The study used bigraph-syllable training adapted from Friedman and Lott (2002). The study investigated whether therapy would result in improvements in the low reading of low-imageability words and paragraph reading. A single subject, repeated baseline design was used. Two baseline probes were carried out and then treatment was applied sequentially to three sets of stimuli. Within each treatment set, CV bigraphs were trained one consonant at a time to 90% accuracy over two consecutive sessions; VC bigraphs were then trained to the same level before the introduction of CVC words. At the beginning of each session, the bigraphs in the current training set were assessed with weekly probes of training and control words. Treatment consisted of two sessions per week. Initially sessions were 1–1.5 hours but once

PT was familiar with treatment, sessions length reduced to around 45 minutes. Training required seventy sessions over a period of 8 months. At the time of the study, PT was also receiving clinical therapy sessions twice a week for 50 minutes per session. Therapy focused on auditory comprehension, word retrieval, sentence production, number processing, pronouns and calendar use.

Task	Teaching bigraph–phoneme correspondence	
Materials	Three sets of stimuli, each containing CV and VC bigraphs for a group of phonemes and a set of training words. Set 1 consisted of 25 CV bigraphs, 14 VC bigraphs, 25 training words and ten control words. Set 2 consisted of 25 CV bigraphs, 18 VC bigraphs, 25 training words and ten control words. Set 3 consisted of 20 CV bigraphs, 14 VC bigraphs, 20 training words and eight control words.	
Hierarchy	*Training bigraphs* a. Client learns relay word for each bigraph b. Client produces only target sounds of relay word when shown bigraph 90% success criterion for two consecutive probe tests	*Training words* a. Client produces CV bigraph b. Client produces VC bigraph c. Client combines these into the words by repeating them in rapid succession ('blending')
Feedback on error	An explicit response cueing hierarchy was applied: a. Show relay word and picture b. Sentence completion cue c. Sentence completion plus visual articulatory placement cue d. Sentence completion plus phonemic cue e. The word is modelled f. Target sound is modelled	An explicit response cueing hierarchy was applied: a. Show bigraphs b. Remind use of relay word c. Remind about repeating in rapid succession d. The bigraphs and 'blending' word is modelled e. The word is modelled
Feedback if correct	Not stated	Not stated

Outcome

PT met the 90% accuracy criteria for all of the trained bigraphs once treatment was applied. PT's reading of CV bigraphs in all sets and VC bigraphs in Sets 1 and 2 improved significantly. The treatment effect for Set 3 bigraphs did not reach significance as baseline performance improved. PT's reading of trained words in Sets 2 and 3 did not improve significantly, probably due to high baseline performance. There was significant generalisation to his reading of untrained words, containing treated bigraphs, in Sets 1 and 2. Change for Set 3 did not reach significance.

On tests of single-word reading, his reading of high-imageability words remained high. There was a significant increase in his reading of low-imageability words. Analysis of reading accuracy showed improvement was due to significant change on words beginning with a trained bigraph (including both those with matching and different vowel pronunciations) and words beginning with a single grapheme contained in a trained bigraph. Reading accuracy for words which did not start with a trained bigraph or grapheme did not change. At paragraph level, accuracy of reading aloud increased for both high and low-imageability words with a reduction in omission errors. PT's reading comprehension also improved significantly. Therapy in the clinical sessions resulted in modest improvement in his naming, auditory comprehension and number skills with no change in sentence production and calendar skills.

Treatment was effective in facilitating the reading of trained bigraphs with limited evidence of generalisation to untrained bigraphs. Reading accuracy for trained words was quite high at baseline. Training resulted in improvement but this did not reach significance. There was significant improvement in the untrained words containing treated bigraphs. Improvements were seen in single-word reading in words which began with a trained bigraph or grapheme. The authors attribute the gains to PT being able to sound out a string of graphemes via the phonological route resulting in cueing of word reading for low-imageability words. Gains at paragraph level were also seen. The authors suggest that his improved reading comprehension of longer and more complex paragraphs would help PT to process daily reading materials. The gains in reading are specifically related to the trained skills and the authors suggest that, as a consequence of this, improvement is unlikely to be due to his concurrent clinical therapy.

Other comments

The authors describe some of the inherent limitations of grapheme–phoneme conversion training e.g. overgeneralisation. They acknowledge that bigraph-syllable treatment is much more time consuming than grapheme–phoneme treatment due to the large number of correspondences to be trained. They suggest, however, that bigraph treatment may be justified when an individual finds it difficult to blend and may be more effective for improving reading for low-imageability words.

Study 21

Friedman, R.B., Sample, D.M. and Lott, S.N. (2002) The role of level of representation in the use of paired associate learning for rehabilitation of alexia. *Neuropsychologia, 40,* 223–234.

Focus of therapy: Orthographic-to-phonological conversion (Phonological Dyslexia), Lexical semantic route.

Therapy approach: Paired associate learning reorganisation. Reactivation (referred to as stimulation in study).

Client details

General information

HN was a 48-year-old woman who worked as a government administrator. She was educated to degree level and had completed some master's level coursework. Following surgery, she had a pulmonary embolism and subsequent left CVA. A CT scan showed a large low density lesion in the left hemisphere consistent with an infarct in the distribution of the left internal carotid artery. DN was a 67-year-old man who worked as a lawyer. Just prior to a left CVA, DN had had surgery for an aortic valve replacement. A CT scan following stroke revealed left cerebella, left frontoparietal, left temporal and small left occipital infarcts and small right basal ganglion infarct. Tests of cognitive function indicated no cognitive impairments for either HN or DN.

Overall pattern of language impairments and preservations

HN presented with good verbal expression of automatic sequences and preserved word repetition. DN presented with moderate–severe non-fluent aphasia with limited verbal expression. He was able to repeat single words. Both clients were unable to repeat nonwords. On confrontation naming, performance was at 50% accuracy for both HN and DN. Extensive assessment of their reading skills was carried out and they presented with very similar patterns of performance. They presented with difficulties in letter naming and identification, although there were able to make decisions on lower-/upper-case letter matches and distinguish letters from their mirror images. Reading aloud was characterised by a part-of-speech effect (nouns and adjectives read more accurately than verbs and functors) and concreteness effect. Performance was significantly influenced by regularity and length. Errors were primarily unrelated errors, with some orthographic errors and a small percentage of morphological and semantic errors. HN and DN were unable to read nonwords. In reading comprehension, HN and DN presented with minimal difficulties in single-word comprehension. They had increased difficulty in comprehension as length and complexity increased with severe impairments at paragraph level. HN required significantly more reading time than DN. Both HN and DN presented with severe difficulties in written spelling and were unable to recognise words or nonwords spelled orally to them. The authors conclude HN and DN present with phonological dyslexia, although recognise that the presence of some semantic errors place them both in the 'fuzzy area' between deep and phonological dyslexia if these disorders are considered points on a continuum.

Time post-onset

HN was 4 years and DN was 2 years post-onset at the time of the study.

Therapy

Therapy consisted of two phases: paired associate learning and stimulation. The paired associate learning paired a word that was difficult to read with a homophone or near homophone that was high in semantic content and easy to read. Stimulation consisted of the repeated presentation of the target word for reading. A multiple baseline was used with an initial baseline across three data points, repeated probing of target words in each sessions and other words each week and evaluation of change over the therapy period using a time series data analysis. During Phase 1, paired associate learning, three word sets were treated sequentially, with progression to the next set when criterion of 90% accuracy in two consecutive sessions was reached. If no progress was made for twelve consecutive sessions, treatment was terminated. Clients were given cards to practise at home.

Task	Phase 1: Paired associate learning	Phase 2: Stimulation
	Target word shown to client for reading. If unable to read, presentation of target alongside picture/word of homophone or near homophone.	Target word shown to client for reading. If unable to read, presentation of target word embedded in sentence.
Materials	Functors/verbs the client was unable to read on at least 2 baselines (82 for HN, 78 for DN). 3 sets of 20 words used in Phase 1. 2 sets paired with homophones. 1 set paired with near-homophones. Control words (22 for HN, 18 for DN) subsequently treated in Phase 2.	
Hierarchy	No hierarchy	No hierarchy
Feedback on error	If unable to read target word shown homophone and is asked to read. If unable to read homophone, therapist reads aloud homophone and target and client asked to repeat.	If unable to read target, word presented in a sentence. If client still unable to read word, given a model for repetition.
Feedback if correct	Not stated	Not stated

Outcome

Following Phase 1, HN and DN learned to read the target words with greater than 90% accuracy as assessed by the daily probes. HN required twenty-five sessions over 3 months. DN required seventy sessions over 15 months although there was a 9 month break due to medical issues. A time series data analysis showed significant changes on all three sets for both HN and DN. HN learned targets using homophones and near-homophones equally well. DN demonstrated more difficulty learning targets paired with near-homophones. There was no improvement on the untrained control words.

In Phase 2, untrained control words were treated using stimulation. Both HN and DN showed significant improvement in reading these target words post-therapy but neither obtained the high level of performance reached in the previous phase. HN required thirty-eight sessions to achieve 58% accuracy. DN achieved 57% accuracy after thirty-three sessions and therapy was terminated as there had been change for twelve sessions. Following Phase 2, the words were then treated using the paired associate learning method. HN required an additional ten sessions and DN required twenty-three sessions to achieve 90% accuracy. Following therapy, there was no change in reading comprehension. HN reported improvements in her ability to read and understand single words, signs and labels. DN reported no changes.

The study shows that a paired associate learning task can result in improved reading accuracy for trained words. The pairing of words with a homophone or near homophone was crucial for the high level of accuracy as improvement after stimulation therapy was less. Paired associate learning was designed to reorganise function by relying on the intact semantic route rather than impaired non-lexical route.

Other comments

The authors discuss the use of paired associate learning in aphasia treatment. They propose that (a) if two items are at the same level of representation, repairing is likely to be more successful than if items are across different levels of representation and (b) pairings that remain intact across levels of representation can be chained together to build new pairings or new routes to correct responses.

Study 22

Stadie, N. and Rilling, E. (2006) Evaluation of lexically and nonlexically based reading treatment in a deep dyslexic. *Cognitive Neuropsychology, 23(4)*, 643–672.

Focus of therapy: Orthographic-to-phonological conversion (Deep Dyslexia), Lexical semantic route – graphemic input lexicon, semantic system and phonological output lexicon (Deep Dyslexia).

Therapy approach: Lexical treatment reactivation. Non-lexical treatment relearning.

Client details

General information

MG was a 53-year-old, right-handed German monolingual woman. She had 10 years of education and worked as a specialist shop assistant. She had a left hemisphere stroke due to Takayasu-arteritis. A CT scan showed an ischaemic area in the left basal ganglia. Further investigations showed complete occlusion of the left and stenosis of the right carotid artery, which probably resulted in diffuse cortical hypoperfusion. She had right-sided sensory deficits, right hemiplegia, right facial paresis and a diminished attention span in addition to aphasia. She had no difficulties with object recognition.

Overall pattern of language impairments and preservations

No information is given about MG's communication. On testing, her semantic processing with picture based material was intact. Her spoken and written comprehension of words in picture matching and synonym tasks was mildly impaired, with no significant difference between modalities. Spoken naming of nouns and verbs was impaired with the production of semantic errors and a significant frequency effect. Written naming was significantly worse than spoken naming but again performance was characterised by semantic errors and a frequency effect. An in-depth assessment of MG's reading was carried out. MG had some difficulty with single-letter naming but made no errors in cross-case matching and was able to discriminate between visually similar words. Her lexical decision was impaired. MG had relatively accurate real word reading, with accuracy determined by frequency. Reading errors consisted of semantic, semantic–visual, visual–phonological, morphological and function word errors. She had more difficulty reading irregular words but produced no regularisation errors. She presented with a severe impairment in nonword reading and was unable to blend words that were orally spelled to her as letter sounds. She showed impairments in rhyme judgement and in pseudo-homophone words/nonwords. The authors conclude MG's reading was characteristic of deep dyslexia. Her inability to read nonwords was attributed to a mild impairment in grapheme-to-phoneme conversion and an inability to blend. Her difficulties in lexical reading were a combination of difficulties at the orthographic input lexicon, partial access to the semantic system and additional deficits in the phonological output lexicon.

Time post-onset

MG was 2 years post-onset at the time of the study.

Therapy

The study compares two treatments for deep dyslexia, one focusing on non-lexical processing and one focusing on strengthening the lexical route to improve lexical access. An additional set of items was trained using both methods. The lexically based intervention used either semantic or phonological priming to activate the related target word. The authors predicted a significant improvement in reading performance, with improvement in both trained and untrained words due to a general decrease of threshold and increased strength of connections within the processing system. A significant improvement in both trained and untrained words was also predicted following non-lexical treatment. A greater treatment effect was predicted for items trained with the lexically based procedure than the non-lexical treatment and for items trained using both methods. A cross-over item-specific design with control tasks was used with assessments before, between and after intervention phases. Lexical treatment was carried out for ten sessions with up to 20 items trained each session and probes within sessions to govern the items which continued to receive training. Non-lexical treatment was carried out for nineteen sessions (first step, five sessions; second step, six sessions; and third step, eight sessions). Treatment sessions were 45–60 minutes duration and took place three times per week.

Task	Treatment 1: Lexical treatment	Treatment 2: Non-lexical treatment
	Computer presents prime word. MG asked to read target word aloud.	Procedure as DePartz (1986) except only words used in blending phase and blending treated systematically via segmental and syllabic presentation.
Materials	Total of 192 items divided into four sets: Set 1 for lexical treatment, Set 2 for non-lexical treatment, Set three for combined treatment and Set 4 a control set. Each set consisted of 24 content and 24 function words. Items controlled and varied for written frequency. Set of prime words for lexical treatment:phonological primes for function words and semantic primes for content words.	
Hierarchy	No hierarchy.	a. Training of grapheme–word associations b. Training of grapheme-to-phoneme associations c. Blending – sequential presentation of each grapheme of target word with lines for missing graphemes. Syllabic and segmental blending presented block-wise, varying order in each session.

Feedback on error	a. Repetition of complete trial b. If second incorrect response, prime word presented in spoken form followed by written target. c. If third incorrect response, therapist read target word aloud.	a. If incorrect association, client reminded of corresponding association word and encouraged to lengthen phoneme. b. If incorrect blending, repetition of phonemes in isolation and then encouraged to blend. If still incorrect, blending until correct.
Feedback if correct	Positive feedback from therapist.	Not stated.

Outcome

Following the lexical treatment, reading accuracy increased significantly for trained items with no change for untrained items. MG's reading performance on a functionally related lexical decision task improved slightly but not significantly. There was no change in performance on the unrelated control tasks. Pre-therapy, reading of content words was better than function words; this advantage disappeared post-therapy with similar performance across sets as the function words benefited most from treatment. Following the non-lexical treatment, reading accuracy improved significantly for both content and function words, with a significant improvement in the untrained items but non-significant gains in the reading of trained words. There was also a significant improvement in nonword reading, indicating a generalised learning effect. There was no change in unrelated control tasks. In a follow-up assessment 10 weeks after treatment, there was no change in reading performance, indicating gains had been maintained. Words treated during both phases did not show significantly more improvement than words treated during one phase.

Lexical treatment resulted in item-specific gains for trained words. In contrast to the authors' predictions, there was no generalisation to untrained words. The non-lexical treatment resulted in improved reading accuracy with generalisation to untrained words and nonword reading. Functional reading performance is not discussed. The authors conclude the lexical based treatment was effective and that improvement was seen following less sessions than non-lexical treatment. Both semantic and phonological priming was effective as both content words and function words improved. The authors propose it is unclear whether improvement resulted from reading the word aloud or the primes but suggest that MG perceived the prime. The non-lexical treatment was also effective with improvement seen in fewer sessions than previously reported. The authors suggest this may be due to the structured way in which blending was treated via the computer program. The lack of significant benefit for the combination set was attributed to the serial nature of the two treatments.

Other comments

The authors discuss assessment and treatment in relation to the summation hypothesis (Hillis & Caramazza, 1991, 1995) and the interaction between lexical and non-lexical reading routes. There is very minimal discussion as to why the predicted generalisation to untrained words was not seen following the lexical treatment.

Notes

1 The 'c-rule': when c comes just before a, o or u, it is produced as /k/; at other times, it is produced as /s/. The 'g-rule': when g comes at the end of words or just before a, o or u, it is produced as /g/; at other times, it is produced as /dʒ/.
2 To teach 'pat', the bigraphs 'pa'–/pæ/ and 'at'–/æt/ would be taught. This is in contrast to other grapheme–phoneme correspondence approaches, which have taught phonemes in isolation: 'p'–/pə/, 'a'–/æ/ and 't'–/tə/.

14 Therapy for writing

Summary of writing studies

If reading therapy has not fallen within the traditional domain of aphasia rehabilitation, writing has done so even less. Clinical priorities, resource constraints and possibly even expertise have meant that less attention has been directed to impairments of writing. The importance of writing, however, for everyday functional tasks, e.g. writing notes, shopping lists, emails etc., the growth in digital communication more generally, and the potential to use writing as an alternative means of communication has led to a surge in published studies in recent years. These studies, listed in Table 14.1, have demonstrated therapy can improve writing skills. Similar to the discussion of terminology in the preceding chapter, the terms *agraphia* and *dysgraphia* to denote writing impairments are often used interchangeably and will be used according to the authors cited. Over the last decade, Beeson and colleagues have published a number of studies investigating the use of the same therapy technique (Copy and Recall Treatment; CART). While the same therapy technique is used, the studies vary in relation to the client type and setting and so are included separately. In a further group study, Beeson, Rising and Volk (2003) investigated those who benefited from this treatment approach; this study is not included as a separate review but the results are discussed in this summary.

Therapy for writing comprises two main approaches: first, therapy targeting the lexical writing route and, secondly, therapy targeting the sub-lexical writing route. Decisions regarding which type of therapy is used are based on the relative sparing/impairment of each route, other retained abilities and the impact that remediation of a route would have on the client's spelling. For example, therapy that re-teaches phoneme-to-grapheme correspondences has a more beneficial impact for a regular language, such as Italian, than for English, a language with very irregular spelling. Writing therapy has been introduced following the recovery of spoken language (Luzzatti, Colombo, Frustaci & Vitolo, 2000) and to provide clients who have minimal speech with an alternative means of communication (e.g. Robson, Pring, Marshall, Morrison & Chiat, 1998, Clausen & Beeson, 2003). Therapy targeting communicative writing is generally used with clients with severe impairments of both writing and speech. It is assumed that writing may be more amenable to treatment and that training a small set of written words will make a significant difference to the person's functional communication. Often clients are at floor on writing assessments although may produce the initial letters of words. These communicative writing studies work on the lexical route, with a focus on the reactivation or relearning of a small set of words via repetitive practice.

Therapy for the lexical route has consisted of both reactivation techniques and the use of relay strategies. Reactivation techniques (e.g. Deloche, Dordan & Kremin, 1993; Beeson, 1999, Rapp & Kane, 2002) involve training clients to write words via repetitive practice. Words are copied or written to dictation via a number of different cues (e.g. anagrams, first

Table 14.1 Summary of writing therapy studies reviewed here

Level of impairment	Therapy studies	Therapy tasks
Semantic system (Deep dysgraphia)	Study 1: Hatfield (1983, p. 301)	• Writing to dictation of function words via linking with homophonic or pseudohomophonic content word.
Phonological-to-graphemic conversion (Deep dysgraphia)	Study 1: Hatfield (1983, p. 301) Study 2 : De Partz *et al.* (1992, p. 304)	• Teaching of spelling rules
Phonological-to-graphemic conversion (Phonological dysgraphia)	Study 3: Luzzatti *et al.* (2000, p. 307)	• Phonological segmentation of words • Teaching of phoneme-to-grapheme correspondence for single and syllabic phonemes • Identifying phonological contexts where words are likely to be irregular
	Study 9 in Chapter 11: Hillis and Caramazza (1994, p. 319)	• Teaching of phonological to orthographic rules (a) pointing to letter when given phoneme (b) thinking of a word beginning with a phoneme (c) associating word with phoneme (d) writing the word
Phonological-to-graphemic conversion and orthographic output lexicon (Partial impairment to sub-lexical and lexical route)	Study 4: Beeson *et al.* (2000, p. 309)	• Use of sound letter correspondence to work out spellings • Self-monitoring of errors • Electronic speller to provide possible alternatives
Semantic system and orthographic output lexicon (Deep dysgraphia)	Study 5: Pavan Kumar & Humphreys (2008, p. 311)	• Repeated copying followed by recall of the word
Semantic system and orthographic output lexicon	Study 6: Schmalzl & Nickels (2006, p. 313)	• Copying followed by recall of the word with or without mnemonics. Mnemonics semantically linked to word and highlight shape of defective letters.
Access to orthographic output lexicon (Surface dysgraphia)	Study 7: Behrmann (1987, p. 315)	• Training of homophones via link with pictures depicting meaning. • Written word-to-picture matching followed by writing of words.
Orthographic output lexicon	Study 1: Hatfield (1983) (p. 301)	• Writing to dictation of words with different vowel spellings. Link group of words to a key word with the same spelling.
	Study 8 in Chapter 11: Hillis (1989, p. 317)	• Written naming using a cueing hierarchy
	Study 2 : De Partz *et al.* (1992, p. 304)	• Writing words using pictured object representing meaning which is presented alongside word/ embedded within word.

	Study 8: Deloche *et al.* (1993, p. 317)	Computer presented therapy.

Study 8: Deloche *et al.* (1993, p. 317)

Computer presented therapy.

- Orthographic cues to facilitate the writing of words
- Anagram of written name
- First syllable

Study 9: Robson *et al.* (1998, p. 319)

Picture therapy phase
- Writing word form following:

(a) Identification of initial grapheme
(b) Anagram sorting
(c) Delayed copying
(d) Generalisation therapy
(e) Writing words to convey information in picture description, list and communicative tasks.

Message therapy
- Writing words to convey complex message in response to the presentation of everyday problems

Study 10: Beeson (1999, p. 323)
- Anagram sorting followed by repeated copying and recall of the word
- Repeated copying followed by recall of the word
- Writing treated words to convey information within a conversation

Study 11: Beeson *et al.* (2002, p. 325)
- Anagram sorting followed by repeated copying and recall of the word
- Repeated copying followed by recall of the word

Study 12: Clausen and Beeson (2003, p. 328)
- Repeated copying followed by recall of the word
- Writing treated words in structured conversation in group setting

Study 13: Rapp and Kane (2002, p. 331)
- Writing to dictation – hear word, repeat it and attempt to spell

Orthographic output lexicon and graphemic output buffer

Study 14: Raymer *et al.* (2003, p. 333)
- Copy and recall therapy (with progressive number of letters covered before recall of whole word)

Graphemic output buffer

Study 15: Mortley *et al.* (2001, p. 335)

Computer presented therapy to facilitate writing via good oral spelling

- Writing words to dictation via letter-by-letter transcoding
- Using a dictionary to find a word once the first few letters have been written
- Writing sentences to dictation using letter-by-letter strategy
- Adaptive word processor that provides choice of words with given letters

Study 13: Rapp and Kane (2002, p. 331)
- Writing to dictation – hear word, repeat it and attempt to spell

Study 16: Sage and Ellis (2006, p. 337)
- Pairwise comparison of target with correct and incorrect spelling
- Insert missing letters – filling in missing letters of word with reference to target
- Word search grids

Study 17: Panton and Marshall (2008, p. 339)
- Writing to dictation – spelling words to dictation, copy and recall
- Strategic note-writing skills

letter cues). An exception is the study described by Sage and Ellis (2006) which uses techniques which do not require the client to write the word; instead errorless techniques involving insertion of missing letters, pairwise comparison of target word/errors and word searches are utilised. Therapy has generally resulted in item-specific learning, with improvements seen in the writing of the treated words but no improvement in the writing of untreated words. Improvement has been considered to result from changes within the orthographic output lexicon. Therapy may be more effective where the semantic system supports access to the word within the lexicon, either by using semantically linked mnemonics (Schmalzl & Nickels, 2006) or by treating high imageability words with more robust semantic representations (Pavan Kumar & Humphreys, 2008). There may also be some generalisation to words which share the same beginnings or endings of treated words due to improved part-word knowledge (Raymer, Cudworth & Haley, 2003).

Therapy for the lexical route has resulted in some generalisation to untreated words when the client has had impairments within the graphemic output buffer. Clients RSB (Rapp & Kane, 2002) and JRE (Rapp, 2005) had additional impairments at buffer level and showed some generalisation to untreated words. This generalised improvement was considered to reflect changes to processes within the buffer, such as scanning speed or the speed of conversion between letters and their written shape. Ray (reported in Panton & Marshall, 2008) had a primary impairment at the level of the graphemic output buffer. He also showed improvement in untreated words post-therapy, with a shift in the location of the errors, suggesting the graphemic buffer was operating more effectively. Gains in the writing of untreated words were not, however, maintained at 3 months follow-up. In all clients, gains in treated words exceeded gains in untreated words; this could be a consequence of additional deficits at a lexical level or stronger lexical representations maintaining activation within the buffer.

Various relay strategies have been used to improve lexical spelling with different patterns of generalisation. In Hatfield's (1983) study, the clients were encouraged to link difficult words with words they could spell. Therapy resulted in item-specific improvement. The spelling of irregular words in Behrmann's (1987) study was improved by linking the word's spelling with a pictorial image. Some generalisation was seen in the spelling of other words, possibly due to an increased ability to detect errors. Client MF (Mortley, Enderby & Petheram, 2001) was taught to use his better oral spelling to aid his written spelling; this strategy enabled him to write all words and sentences.

Therapy for the sub-lexical writing route (De Partz, Seron & Van der Linden, 1992; Luzzatti *et al.*, 2000) has involved the teaching of phoneme-to-grapheme correspondences. Improvement is seen in both treated and untreated regular words as clients learn conversion rules which they can then apply to any word they can say. Clients are then taught specific rules to enable the spelling of some irregular words. Beeson, Rewega, Vail and Rapcsak (2000) promotes the use of both the lexical and sub-lexical spelling routes, with the clients using sound to letter correspondence to spell the word, and then using lexical knowledge to determine whether it is correct and attempt self-correction. This problem-solving approach aims to give the clients strategies for resolving spelling difficulties and may be appropriate for clients with less severe writing difficulties.

In studies targeting both the sub-lexical and lexical writing routes, improvement has generally resulted from repetitive tasks carried out over a long period. For example, client RMM (Robson *et al.* 1998) learned about 60 words in fifty-nine, 45 minute sessions. As a consequence, direct therapy is often supported by self-directed work or work on a computer, with the clinician monitoring progress across sessions. The use of a computer may improve motivation for some people with aphasia, with the spell check facility to verify the accuracy of spelling providing an added benefit (although there is currently limited evidence of this from the literature). When writing has improved in constrained tasks, there is some evidence that clients need to be encouraged to use their writing within conversation (Beeson *et al.*, 2002) and will only use writing functionally if it can be done quickly (Mortley *et al.*, 2001). Clausen and Beeson (2003) used a group to facilitate the use of written words in conversation and highlight the need to treat words which can be used to initiate conversation e.g. 'NAME?', as well as words which are the response to such questions. A group setting may also be helpful to increase a person's awareness of and acceptance of writing as a form of communication.

Beeson *et al.* (2003) report the effects of CART therapy for eight clients with severe aphasia. Four of the clients showed strong positive effects of treatment, one showed minimal effects and the remaining three clients showed some progress but failed to reach criterion on the treated words. Individual responses to treatment were analysed to determine the factors that influenced treatment outcome. The study suggests a number of factors which influence who benefits from communicative writing therapy, i.e those clients demonstrating (1) improved spelling of target words within a single session, (2) consistent accurate completion of homework, (3) relatively preserved semantic system, (4) ability to discern words from nonwords, (5) preserved non-verbal problem-solving ability and (6) increased motivation in therapy due to communicative need. While there is some support for these factors from comparison of individual cases, it is currently difficult to substantiate their impact and whether therapy will be ineffective or less effective for clients who do not have these characteristics.

Within the writing studies, improvement has been considered in relation to the accuracy of the written words, comparing pre- and post-therapy performance. In studies focusing on communicative writing, a more relevant measure could be recognisable responses; responses may be communicative even if they are not 100% accurate. Panton and Marshall (2008) provide an excellent example of where therapy is driven by the client's functional goal of being able to take notes and where improvement is considered directly in relation to this goal.

EVALUATIONS OF THERAPY STUDIES

Study 1

Hatfield, F. (1983). Aspects of acquired dysgraphia and implications for re-education. In C. Code and D. J. Muller (Eds.). *Aphasia therapy*. London: Edward Arnold.

Focus of therapy: Semantic system (deep dysgraphia) and orthographic output lexicon (surface dysgraphia).

Therapy approach: Cognitive relay strategy to improve access to words within the semantic system. Reactivation within the orthographic output lexicon.

Client details

The study involved four clients.

General information

BB was a 43-year-old male grocery wholesaler. He had an embolic CVA resulting in a right hemiparesis. DE was a 26-year-old male assistant store keeper in a pharmaceutical firm. He had a traumatic neck injury (left internal carotid artery occlusion) resulting in left frontal and temporal damage and a right hemiparesis. PW was a 72-year-old male local government officer. A CVA resulted in a right hemiparesis with a CT scan showing damage to the frontal, parietal and temporal lobes. TP was a 51-year-old female senior radiographer who suffered a sub-arachnoid haemorrhage affecting the left temporo-occipital region. This resulted in a transient hemiparesis and a permanent right homonymous hemianopia. All four clients were reasonably proficient spellers before their cerebral incident.

Overall pattern of language impairments and preservations

BB, DE and PW all presented with Broca's type speech and a pattern of reading consistent with deep dyslexia. TP presented with a fluent aphasia with severe anomia and impaired comprehension. TP had received regular therapy for writing before the study. When assessed on their ability to write words to dictation, BB, PW and DE performed better when writing content words relative to function words and they were unable to write nonwords. Their spelling of regular and irregular words did not differ significantly. They produced visual, semantic and derivational errors in writing. The author proposes that BB, DE and PW had a deep dysgraphia with a severe impairment of the sub-lexical spelling route (phoneme-to-grapheme conversion) and a partial sparing of the lexical semantic route. TP's writing was more preserved relative to the other clients. Her spelling of regular words was superior to her spelling of irregular words and she was able to write nonwords. TP's performance was characterised by the production of orthographically plausible errors, homophone errors and letter-by-letter writing. The author proposes that TP presented with surface dysgraphia.

Time post-onset

When therapy commenced, BB was 2 years, DE was 10 years, PW was 15 years and TP was 1 year post-onset.

Therapy

Therapy had two aims:

(1) Semantic system: to improve the ability to spell function words by linking them to homophonic (or pseudohomophonic) content words.
(2) Orthographic output lexicon: to facilitate the acquisition of complex spelling rules and the spelling of homophones.

No information was given on the frequency or intensity of therapy. Sessions were supported by home practice consisting of sentence completion tasks. The paper only discusses progress on the therapy task; no single-case study design was used to demonstrate efficacy.

Task	**Semantic system** Writing to dictation of function words using homophonic content words.	**Orthographic output lexicon** 1. Re-teaching of double consonant rule via explanation. 2. Writing to dictation of words with different vowel spellings. Grouping of words in which vowels spelled in the same way. Groups linked to one key word which was reliably spelled by subject.
Materials	Seven locational prepositions Six auxiliaries Five pronouns Function words paired with a homophonic content 'link' word which was selected by subject. e.g. 'on' paired with 'Don'.	Three groups of words which involve different ways of spelling vowels. e.g. /aɪ/ as in pain and pine /i/ as in meat and meet.
Hierarchy	a. Association of link word with target word b. Dictation of link word with picture support c. Writing of link word d. Dictation of sentence including function word e. Writing of function word under link word f. Dictation of sentence for the writing of the function word	a. Sorting words into groups. b. Memorising key word and group.
Feedback on error	Not stated	Not stated
Feedback if correct	Not stated	Not stated

Outcome

Following three sessions, BB, PW and DE – the clients with deep dysgraphia – were able to use the prior writing of the link word to facilitate the correct spelling of the function word. By the end of the therapy programme, they were able to use the strategy silently to facilitate the spelling of function words. The author reported some improvement in the ability to write function words but reassessment data were difficult to interpret due to the omission of some words from the tests. Very limited reassessment data were available for TP following the therapy targeting the orthographic input lexicon.

Other comments

The author claimed a satisfactory outcome from the therapy for deep dysgraphia with some improvement in the ability to write function words. It is, however, difficult to determine the success of both therapies due to the limited reassessment data reported. Further information is necessary to evaluate the specific versus non-specific effects of treatment. The therapy protocol for deep dysgraphia is sufficiently detailed to allow replication, while the reporting of the therapy for surface dysgraphia does not permit replication.

Study 2

De Partz, M.-P., Seron, X. and Van der Linden, M. (1992). Re-education of a surface dysgraphia with a visual imagery strategy. *Cognitive Neuropsychology, 9*, 369–401.

Focus of therapy: Phonological-to-graphemic conversion (orthographic output lexicon).

Therapy approach: Relearning of graphemic contextual rules to improve the non-lexical spelling route. Cognitive relay strategy to improve the writing of irregular words via the orthographic output lexicon.

Client details

General information

LP was a 24-year-old, right-handed male nursing student.[1] He contracted encephalitis which required a lobectomy of the left temporal point and suction of the lower left frontal lobe. Surgery resulted in a right hemiparesis and mild right hemispatial neglect. LP presented with cognitive difficulties characteristic of frontal lobe damage and impaired visual and verbal memory.

Overall pattern of language impairments and preservations

LP presented with good functional comprehension, although he did make some semantic errors on single-word comprehension tasks. His speech was characterised by word-finding difficulties, circumlocutions and semantic errors. Repetition and automatic speech production were intact. Reading performance was characterised by relatively intact reading of nonwords, with no effect of frequency, length or regularity in the reading of words. LP was, however, impaired in his ability to understand homophones, his detection of regularisation errors and in visual lexical decision. The authors suggest that LP has a pre-semantic reading deficit in the orthographic input lexicon resulting in a reliance on the sub-lexical reading route. It was proposed that meaning was accessed via access to the phonological form and processing via the auditory route.

   Writing performance was characterised by relatively well-preserved writing of nonwords. Writing of words showed a marked frequency effect, a trend for improved performance in the writing of regular words compared with irregular and ambiguous words and poor writing of homophones. The authors suggest that LP presents with a surface dysgraphia due to an impaired lexical route for writing alongside a relatively well-preserved sub-lexical route. Consistency of errors in the writing of irregular and ambiguous words was considered to reflect a loss of orthographic representations rather than an access difficulty.

Time post-onset

Therapy was commenced when LP was around 1 year post-onset.

Therapy

Therapy had two aims:

(1) to maximise the use of the non-lexical writing route via the teaching of context-sensitive graphemic rules (Phase 1)
(2) to improve the writing of irregular and ambiguous words using a visual imagery strategy (Phase 2).

A multiple-baseline therapy design was used to examine the efficacy of therapy. Therapy consisted of two phases.

Phase 1

Phase 1 of therapy consisted of three sessions per week for 6 months.

Task	Re-teaching of context-sensitive graphemic rules Rules presented and explained. Use of rule in various written tasks e.g. writing to dictation, sentence and text completion.
Materials	Five rules frequently used in French selected for training following an analysis of LP's errors.
Hierarchy	Each rule introduced and practised separately and then practised together.
Feedback on error	Rule explained Correct form presented to be read and copied.
Feedback if correct	Not stated

Phase 2

Therapy for Phase 2 consisted of four stages corresponding to a different task. During Stage 1, the learning of imagery was carried out three times a week for 2 weeks. Stages 2 and 3 each involved three sessions per week for 3 months. The recall of spellings taught during Stages 2 and 3 were assessed 1 day, 4 days and 15 days after the initial therapy session. Stage 4 also consisted of 3 months of therapy.

Task	1. Learning of imagery	2. Learning of written words with embedded visual image	3. Training of self-imagery	4. Transfer to spontaneous writing
	Generating images in response to pictures and words and drawing/ describing those images	Writing the word with its embedded image	Comparing the effects of therapist or patient-generated images	Detecting trained words and their derivations in spontaneous production and producing them with their drawings

Materials	240 words previously mis-spelled by LP. Each treated word was given a semantically related image which was embedded within the part of the word which had been mis-spelled. 120 words used in Stage (Task) 2: 60 treated, 60 untreated words. Groups were matched for frequency. One hundred and twenty words used in Stage (Task) 3: 30 untreated, 30 with patient image, 30 with therapist image, 30 trained using classic didactic verbal learning.			
Hierarchy	a. Direct visualisation – form an image with visual support b. Indirect visualisation – form an image from name of object	a. Copy the word with the embedded visual image b. Delayed copying of word and image (10 sec) c. Produce word and image in response to spoken word	As Task 2	None
Feedback on error	Not applicable	If word produced incorrectly in b or c, returned to copying.	As Task 2	Not stated
Feedback if correct	Not applicable	Not stated	Not stated	Not stated

Outcome

Following Phase 1, there was a reduction in the errors made on words requiring the taught rules. Some new errors also emerged as a consequence of the misapplication of those rules. There was no change in LP's ability to write irregular and ambiguous words following Phase 1. Following Tasks 2 and 3 in Phase 2, LP's writing of the treated words using visual imagery improved. There was also some improvement in his writing of the untreated words. The writing of words treated using a traditional didactic verbal learning method did not improve. There was no significant difference between those words treated using therapist-generated images and those treated using patient-generated images. Performance was stable 1 year after therapy.

   Both phases of therapy resulted in significant improvement in LP's writing ability, which the authors argued was not due to spontaneous recovery. LP's performance had been stable before therapy. Phase 1 resulted in no change in LP's ability to write irregular and ambiguous words. The improvements seen in Phase 2 were significantly greater for the treated words than the untreated words and no improvements were seen following didactic verbal learning. Improvements were maintained 1 year post-therapy.

Other comments

With rigorous initial assessment and reassessment data presented, this study permits a thorough evaluation of a therapy that resulted in significant and long-term gains.

Study 3

Luzzatti, C., Colombo, C., Frustaci, M. and Vitolo, F. (2000). Rehabilitation of spelling along the sub-word-level routine. *Neuropsychological Rehabilitation, 10*, 249–278.

Focus of therapy: Phonological-to-graphemic conversion.

Therapy approach: Relearning.

Client details

Two clients are described in the study.

General information

RO was a 48-year-old man who had a cerebral abscess in the left hemisphere. He had 8 years of schooling and had worked as an administrator. DR was a 33-year-old man who worked as a dental technician. He had a cerebral haemorrhage following the rupture of an aneurysm of the left internal carotid artery.

Overall pattern of language impairments and preservations

RO had a Broca's aphasia. He presented with a moderate comprehension deficit and non-fluent agrammatic speech with word-finding difficulties. His reading was characteristic of phonological dyslexia. He was unable to write any words accurately and could only write about 60% of single letters. The authors suggest that RO had an impairment to the sub-lexical writing routine. He also had additional difficulties with acoustic-to-phonological conversion. DR also presented with a Broca's aphasia, with agrammatic speech and reading characteristic of phonological dyslexia. On formal assessment of his writing, he produced around 25% correct responses for regular words with particular difficulties with words requiring syllabic translation or containing voiced consonants or nasals. His writing of irregular words was less accurate than his writing of regular words. The authors suggest that DR has a mixed writing impairment involving both the lexical and non-lexical routes, with most accurate writing of regular words with one phoneme to one letter correspondence.

Time post-onset

RO was 3 years 9 months and DR was 10 years post-onset at the time of the study.

Therapy

Therapy aimed to improve phonological segmentation and phonological-to-graphemic conversion. As Italian is predominantly a regular language, improvement to phoneme-to-grapheme conversion would permit the accurate writing of the majority of words. Following the learning of regular conversion rules, the clients were taught to identify phonological contexts where irregularities were likely to occur. The clients' writing was assessed before, at regular intervals during and after therapy. A multiple-baseline therapy design was used. Clients had to reach 90% accurate performance at each therapy stage before proceeding to the next stage. Three to four treatment sessions were carried out each week. RO's treatment extended over a 15 month period with DR's treatment extending over 12 months.

	1. Segmentation of words into syllables and syllables into phones (continuant phones)	2. Writing of single phonemes and words to dictation (continuant phones)	3. Segmentation of words into syllables and syllables into phones (plosive phones)	4. Writing of single phonemes and words to dictation (plosive phones)	5. Introduction of syllabic and complex conversion rules
Task	Presentation of words with prolongation of phones to aid segmentation.	Client retrieves name of letter and then writes down.	Presentation of words for segmentation.	Client retrieves name of letter and then writes down.	Introduce rules for the transcription of syllabic conversion and phonemes written via a single letter.
Materials	Words containing continuant consonant phonemes /f v s z r l m n/ and five vowels	Words containing nine continuant consonant phonemes /f v s z r l m n/ and five vowels	Words containing the phonemes /p b t d/	Words containing the phonemes /p b t d/	Words containing the phonemes /k g ʃ tʃ dʒ kw ts dz/

Hierarchy	a. Segmentation into syllables
	  i. Bisyllabic words with alternating consonants
	  ii. Words with three or more syllables
	  iii. Nonwords
	b. Segmentation into phones
	  i. Words of increasing length
	  ii. Words with clusters
	  iii. Words with doubled consonants
		a. Bisyllabic words and nonword with CV structure
		b. Words with three syllables
		c. Words with four syllables
		d. Words with consonant clusters
		e. Words with doubled consonants
			a. 1:1 phoneme-to-grapheme conversion
			b. CV syllables with plosive onset
				None	Not stated

Feedback on error	Not stated	Remind client of common word containing the letter	Not stated	Not stated	Not stated
Feedback if correct	Not stated	Not stated	Not stated	Not stated	Not stated

Following Phase 5 of therapy, the clients learned to identify phonological contexts when words were likely to be irregular so they could check the orthography.

Outcome

Both clients progressed through each stage of the programme, reaching the 90% accuracy criterion. At the end of therapy, RO showed appropriate use of one-to-one and syllabic phoneme-to-grapheme conversion. He was able to write 90% of regular words and 50% of irregular words; his errors writing irregular words were regularisation errors. The gains were mirrored in his reading performance, with improved reading of function words, abstract nouns and nonwords. His spontaneous speech remained unchanged. Writing performance was maintained 18 months after therapy. At the end of therapy, DR showed near-normal performance in writing, making errors only on words with non-univocal spellings. His writing performance was maintained 6 months after therapy.

Both clients showed significant gains in writing that can be attributed to therapy. The clients were a long time post-onset and showed improvements that were specific to the phase of therapy. Performance resulted in the improvement of all words and was maintained following the end of therapy. No information is given about whether the clients were using their new writing skills in functional settings.

Other comments

With rigorous initial assessment and reassessment data presented, this study permits a thorough evaluation of the therapy with the reported clients. The study considers the need to treat prerequisite phonological segmentation skills before direct teaching of phonological-to-graphemic rules. The outcomes of such a therapy technique in English would be more limited.

Study 4

Beeson, P.M., Rewega, M.A., Vail, S. and Rapcsak, S.Z. (2000) Problem-solving approach to agraphia treatment: Interactive use of lexical and sub-lexical spelling routes. *Aphasiology*, *14*, 551–556.

Focus of therapy: Phonological-to-graphemic conversion and orthographic output lexicon. Improve interaction between lexical and sub-lexical spelling routes.

Therapy approach: Relearning and cognitive relay.

Client details

Two clients are discussed in the study.

General information

SV was a 44-year-old, right-handed woman. She had two Bachelor's degrees and a master's degree and had worked as a computer programmer. She was also an amateur writer of fiction. She had aphasia as a consequence of a left hemisphere stroke. An MRI scan showed a left hemisphere infarct involving the temporal lobe, insula and frontal operculum. The second client, SW, was a 42-year-old, right-handed man with a high school education. He previously managed an equipment rental company. He had a traumatic brain injury from a car accident, resulting in aphasia and memory difficulties. An MRI scan after surgery showed damage to the left anterior temporal lobe and a separate lesion in the region of the left basal ganglia.

Overall pattern of language impairments and preservations

SV had a mild anomic aphasia. She made no errors in single-word reading. She scored 83% correct in writing to dictation including self-corrections. She made more errors on irregular words with phonologically implausible errors showing some knowledge of the word form, phonologically plausible errors and partial responses. She scored 67% correct on nonword spelling, with most errors involving vowels. Her extended writing was slow and effortful with spelling errors and occasional errors of lexical selection. She wanted to resume her writing of fiction. SW also presented with anomic aphasia, with significant word-finding difficulties. In written naming, he made one error. In writing to dictation, he scored around 50% with predominantly phonologically plausible errors. He found it more difficult to write low imageability words compared to words of high imageability. He also scored at around 50% on nonwords, with errors in vowel selection.

The authors propose that both clients had some damage to both lexical and sub-lexical spelling routes with partial information from routes. Both made errors which included attempts at semantic spelling that reflected partial knowledge of the word form as well as errors which showed reliance on phoneme-to-grapheme conversion.

Time post-onset

SV was 4 years and SW was 14 months post-onset at the time of the study.

Therapy

Therapy aimed to promote a problem-solving approach to develop strategies for resolving spelling difficulties. SV was seen bi-weekly for 10 months. SW was seen weekly for 10 weeks. Both received homework practice. A control task design was used to monitor efficacy.

Task	**Problem-solving approach**
	When spelling difficulties occurred, a problem-solving approach progressed through the following steps:
	1. Try to write it as it sounds
	2. Decide if the spelling is correct
	3. If incorrect, try and correct it
	4. Use the electronic speller to check it or to find the correct spelling
	5. Make a list of the words that were hard.
Materials	Samples of client's own writing. SV – creative writing. SW – daily journal. SV had a list of key words that helped her retrieve the corresponding letters for each phoneme.
Hierarchy	None
Feedback on error	See task description
Feedback if correct	Not stated

Outcome

During the period of therapy, clinical observation and SV's self report suggested that the creative aspects of writing were easier. After 10 months, SV showed a significant reduction in errors in writing to dictation. When errors were made, there was an increase in phonologically plausible errors compared to pre-therapy performance. There was no change in digit span performance (control measure). The authors propose that SV's improvement reflected improved access to lexical representations, with partial spellings (gained by using sound letter correspondences) triggering retrieval in the orthographic output lexicon. After 10 weeks, SW made significantly less errors in writing to dictation, also producing a large number of self-corrections. His uncorrected errors were phonologically implausible mis-spellings. There was no change in his confrontation naming or reading aloud (control tasks). It is suggested that SW first tried to retrieve the word from the lexicon and if this failed, he used the sub-lexical route, repeating the word as he tried to write each letter. There was a notable increase in the number of successful self-corrections.

Both participants show interactive use of partially damaged lexical and sub-lexical spelling routes to resolve spelling errors. Therapy to promote a problem-solving approach resulted in significant gains in single-word writing. The authors propose that this approach may not be suitable for clients with more severe writing difficulties.

Other comments

As with other writing studies, therapy is heavily reliant on home practice; the number of therapy sessions was quite limited. There were some limitations in the assessment measures, with only a single baseline of writing to dictation and no information about the speed of writing or systematic examination of extended writing. The study gives useful insights from one of the participants about the strategies she was using while spelling.

Study 5

Pavan Kumar, V. and Humphreys, G.W. (2008) The role of semantic knowledge in relearning spellings: Evidence from deep dysgraphia. *Aphasiology, 22(5)*, 489–504.

Focus of therapy: Semantic system and orthographic output lexicon (deep dysgraphia).

Therapy approach: Reactivation.

Client details

General information

PH was a 30-year-old, right-handed man who had recently qualified with a law degree. PH had a left hemisphere stroke, resulting in right hemiplegia and mild signs of frontal behaviour. An MRI scan showed a large left inferior frontal lesion that extended posteriorly to the anterior and superior temporal lobe. PH's pre-morbid functioning was reportedly normal.

Overall pattern of language impairments and preservations

PH presented with a non-fluent, agrammatic aphasia with speech limited to auto-utterances. His spoken naming was impaired, with 'no' responses, semantic and phonological errors.

Performance on word-to-picture matching, synonym judgement and the three picture version of Pyramids and Palm Trees were all impaired. His reading was characteristic of deep dyslexia, with difficulty reading nonwords, regular and irregular words and the production of semantic errors. Writing was severely impaired and characteristic of deep dysgraphia. He was able to spell some short words accurately but no longer words. He was able to generate the first one or two letters in the word. He was unable to write nonwords. In writing, he made semantic and orthographic errors. He was able to copy words accurately. Delayed copying was also reasonably good, but he showed an advantage for high imagery (imageabilty) words. The authors propose PH had a semantic deficit.

Time post-onset

PH was 3 years post-onset at the time of the study.

Therapy

The study was designed to investigate the effect of imageability (described as the contrast between high and low imagery) on the learning of written word spellings. The authors propose that, if the orthographic output lexicon is independent of the semantic system, there should be equally good learning of high imagery compared to low imagery words. If semantic knowledge maintains the representation within the orthographic lexicon, there may be better learning of high imagery words. A repeated baseline design was used to monitor efficacy. Each set of treated words was practised for 2 weeks at home. Set 1 was given in week 1, Set 2 in week 3 and Set 3 in week 4, with Set 1 phased out. Homework tasks were done each day. Maintenance was assessed between 4–6 weeks post-practice.

Task	Homework task
	1. Take one word at a time 2. Copy ten times 3. Turn over the page and write the word again
Materials	Thirty treated nouns divided into 15 high imagery words and 15 low imagery words). 30 untreated words. Treated nouns divided in three sets: set 1 – 10 × HI, Set 2 – 10 × LI, Set 3 – 5 × HI and 5 × LI. Sets matched for frequency and length. Untreated set not matched (shorter & higher frequency).
Hierarchy	None
Feedback on error	Not applicable
Feedback if correct	Not applicable

Outcome

At initial baseline, PG was unable to write any of the words. Following practice, he learned to write the treated words. During training, there was no significant difference between the high and low imagery words. However, 3 weeks post-training, there was a significant difference, with performance on low imagery words deteriorating. There was no improvement in the writing of untreated words. The functional outcome of therapy is not considered.

PH was able to learn both the high imagery and low imagery words, with no generalisation to untreated words. The authors suggest this is a consequence of the restoration or learning of item-specific representations in the lexicon. There was, however, differential maintenance of high and low imagery words. This suggests that the semantic system supports the lexical representation and can provide longer term reinforcement of learning.

Other comments

The study replicates copying methods used in other writing therapy studies but shows that long-term learning is better for words with more robust semantic representations.

Study 6

Schmalzl, L. and Nickels, L. (2006) Treatment of irregular word spelling in acquired dysgraphia: Selective benefit from visual mnemonics. *Neuropsychological Rehabilitation, 16(1)*, 1–37.

Focus of therapy: Semantic system and access to the orthographic output lexicon.

Therapy approach: Reactivation and cognitive relay.

Client details

General information

FME was a 62-year-old woman. She had 12 years education and had been working as a nurse. She contracted viral herpes encephalitis 20 years prior to the study. A CT scan conducted at the time of the infection showed left temporal damage. Neuropsychological assessment revealed significant memory difficulties and reduced performance in both verbal and non-verbal IQ compared to pre-morbid estimates of intellectual functioning.

Overall pattern of language impairments and preservations

FME presented with fluent speech with significant word-finding difficulties. She reported difficulties with spelling and with comprehension of written text if she could not read it aloud. Comprehension of both spoken and written words was impaired, with additional deficits in lexical decision. Mild difficulties were seen in reading aloud and repetition. Spoken naming was significantly better than written naming but both were impaired compared to controls. Spoken naming was significantly affected by word frequency and errors were predominantly semantic and phonologically related errors. Written naming was significantly affected by length and errors were a mixture of semantic, orthographic and phonologically plausible errors. Writing to dictation was impaired but was significantly better than written naming of the same items. Writing to dictation was significantly affected by imageability and frequency. Writing of nonwords was impaired and was affected by length. FME's homophone spelling was impaired relative to reading and oral definition; homophone confusion errors were present in both definition of written words and writing to dictation.

The authors conclude that FME has damage to multiple components of both sub-lexical and lexical routes of reading and of spelling, with spelling more severely impaired. The authors suggest impairments in the phonological input and orthographic input lexicons, damage to the semantic system, a deficit in accessing the orthographic output lexicon with an over-reliance on the sub-lexical route if she was unable to retrieve the word's representation, and a possible deficit in the graphemic output buffer. Evidence for each of these difficulties is presented in detail.

Time post-onset

FME was 20 years post-onset at the time of the study.

Therapy

Therapy was directed towards relearning spellings of high-frequency, irregular words by strengthening specific orthographic representations. The efficacy of using mnemonics incorporating visual imagery for supporting learning was investigated. Visual mnemonic cues were semantically related to the word and linked to letter shape.

A multiple-baseline, cross-over design was used to determine the relative benefits of a copying treatment with and without visual mnemonics. Reading and spelling of irregular words was tested on seven occasions: three pre-treatment baselines at 12, 8 and 4 weeks prior to therapy, two post-treatment baselines (one after each therapy phase), and two follow-up tests at 4 and 12 weeks after the second therapy phase. At the start of each session, pre-tests were carried out on the treated set and respective repeated set. Each of the treatment phases was conducted over a period of 4 weeks with two sessions per week. Home practice was carried out between treatment sessions.

Task	Treatment task	Home practice
	a. Listen to the word b. Study the correct spelling of the word on the flashcard c. Copy the word d. Write the word from memory after a 5 second delay e. Recall the image associated to the word (for mnemonic treatment only).	a. Study the correct spelling of the word on the flashcard b. Copy the word c. Remove flashcard and write the word from memory after a 5 second delay d. Check spelling e. If correct, move onto next flashcard. If not, repeat the procedure until spelling of word after 5 second delay is correct.
Materials	Two hundred high-frequency irregular words divided into four sets of 50 words matched for frequency, length and error rate in both reading and writing. Set 1 – treatment set without mnemonics. Set 2 – treatment set with mnemonics. Set 3 – repeated set for treatment without mnemonics. Set 4 – repeated set for treatment with mnemonics. Treatment stimuli were presented on flashcards. For Set 1, flashcard contained correct spelling of word in lower case. For Set 2, flashcard contained correct spelling of word with mnemonic cue that was linked semantically to word and emphasised letter shape of defective letters.	
Hierarchy	See task description	See task description

Feedback on error	Repeat procedure until correct after delay	Repeat procedure until correct after delay
Feedback if correct	Move to next item	Move to next item

Outcome

Compared to the final pre-treatment baseline, there was no improvement on the 200 word set following treatment without mnemonics. There was no significant improvement on any set of items, including those treated in Phase 1. Significant improvement was seen following treatment with mnemonics and, although there was some decline post-therapy, performance remained significantly better than baseline at the 1 month and 3 month follow-ups. During treatment Phase 2, there was significant improvement on the items treated with mnemonics, with no change on the repeated items. No change was seen in FME's ability to read, define or spell homophones, with a similar proportion of homophone confusion errors in definition and spelling. Post-therapy when spelling homophones, there was an increase in orthographic errors and a corresponding reduction in phonologically plausible errors suggesting a reduced reliance on the sub-lexical route.

Therapy without mnemonics, i.e. repeated copying, resulted in no change in written production; this contrasts with previous studies (e.g. Beeson, 1999) which have reported improvement following this type of therapy. The authors suggest that this may either be a consequence of her memory difficulties and the need to reduce the interval between copying and recall or her semantic difficulties. Therapy with mnemonics resulted in significant improvement in the writing of the treated words. This improvement is attributed to activation of the semantic representations which then supported access to specific representations in the orthographic output lexicon. Improvement is likely to be a consequence of therapy as FME was many years post-onset and effects are specific to treated items. The study does not consider whether therapy resulted in any functional benefits in writing.

Other comments

The authors discuss the effectiveness of using visual imagery as a mnemonic aid for learning verbal material in individuals with significant memory impairment. The study is an excellent example of hypothesis testing during assessment when the client presents with multiple impairments.

Study 7

Behrmann, M. (1987). The rites of righting writing: homophone remediation and acquired dysgraphia. *Cognitive Neuropsychology, 4*, 365–384.

Focus of therapy: Access to orthographic output lexicon (surface dysgraphia).

Therapy approach: Reactivation.

Client details

General information

CCM was a 53-year-old high school educated woman who had an infarct in the middle cerebral artery in the left temperoparietal region. She had no hemiplegia or hemianopia. CCM was bilingual in English and Afrikaans.

Overall pattern of language impairments and preservations

CCM presented with conduction aphasia. She had impaired repetition in the presence of fluent verbal output. Sentence comprehension was relatively preserved. Reading performance was characterised by intact lexical decision, well-preserved nonword reading, and equivalent reading of regular and irregular words. Writing performance was characterised by well-preserved writing of nonwords and regular words but impaired writing of irregular words and homophones. Writing of irregular words involved the production of phonologically plausible errors. Neither imageability, word class or length affected performance in either writing or reading. The authors suggest that CCM has an impaired lexical writing route with a well-preserved sub-lexical route and therefore described her as having an acquired surface dysgraphia.

Time post-onset

Therapy commenced when CCM was 10 months post-onset.

Therapy

Therapy aimed to retrain the lexical spelling route via the training of homophone pairs. Therapy consisted of weekly sessions over a period of 6 weeks, with additional home practice. A combination of an item-specific and control task design was used to investigate the efficacy of therapy.

Task	**Writing of homophone pairs** Writing of homophones paired with pictorial representation of meaning. Meaning used to promote correct spelling.
Materials	Fifty homophone pairs of which either one or both homophones were written incorrectly in assessment. Eight pairs treated per session.
Hierarchy	a. Homophones introduced with pictorial representation b. Written forms contrasted c. Written word-to-picture matching d. Writing of homophones with pictorial support e. Writing of homophones to dictation
Feedback on error	Not stated
Feedback if correct	Not stated

Home practice consisted of forced choice word-to-picture matching, written homophone naming to pictures and sentence completion tasks.

Outcome

Significant improvement was recorded in the writing of treated homophones. This was maintained 8 weeks post-therapy. There was no significant improvement in the writing of untreated homophones, suggesting no generalisation. Significant improvement was also seen in the writing of irregular words. CCM's performance in sentence comprehension and in digit span did not change.

Therapy resulted in improvements in homophone and irregular word spelling. These were attributed to therapy, as CCM was not in the period of spontaneous recovery; a stable baseline in homophone writing was evident before therapy and no change in performance was recorded on control tasks. The authors proposed that the specific improvements in treated homophones and untreated irregular words were the consequence of a partial reinstatement of lexical spelling and the use of a visual check mechanism which detected spelling errors.

Other comments

A list of the homophones used in treatment are included in the paper. This study shows improvement in some of the observed characteristics of surface dysgraphia.

Study 8

Deloche, G., Dordan, M. and Kremin, H. (1993). Rehabilitation of confrontation naming in aphasia: relations between oral and written modalities. *Aphasiology, 7*, 201–216.

Focus of therapy: Access to the orthographic output lexicon (surface dysgraphia) in order to improve spoken naming.

Therapy approach: Reactivation.

Client details

Two clients were examined in the study.

General information

RB was a 28-year-old woman who had worked as a secretary before she had a meningeal haemorrhage resulting from a burst aneurysm of the left sylvian bifurcation. GC was a 50-year-old right-handed woman who had a meningeal haemorrhage due to disruption of an aneurysm of the left sylvian territory. A CT scan showed hypodensity in the posterior part of the insula and rolandic area extending to the frontal region.

Overall pattern of language impairments and preservations

RB presented with fluent, informative speech with occasional word-finding difficulties. Spoken and written comprehension were well preserved, along with oral reading and repetition. Writing to dictation was impaired, with errors consistent with surface dysgraphia. In assessments of confrontation naming, RB scored 79% correct in oral naming, with errors predominantly verbal paraphasias, and 73% correct in written naming. Errors in written naming were predominantly morpholexical errors or plausible transcriptions of phonological form. The authors suggest that RB was deriving written word forms from transcription of spoken word form by the application of phonological-to-graphemic conversion rules.

GC presented with conduction aphasia. Spontaneous speech was characterised by word-finding difficulties with phonemic and semantic errors and circumlocutions. Written comprehension was preserved in the presence of impaired auditory comprehension. Oral reading of words was preserved, while impairment was seen in nonword reading. Repetition was also impaired. In assessments of confrontation naming, GC scored 42% correct in written naming and 35% correct in oral naming. Both oral and written naming were characterised by no responses and semantic and morpholexical errors. The authors suggest that oral naming may be derived from the orthographic word form, as GC often used a finger spelling strategy.

Time post-onset

Therapy was commenced when RB was 10 months post-onset and when GC was 12 years post-onset.

Therapy

Therapy aimed to improve written naming and monitor the effects on spoken naming. Therapy consisted of twenty-five sessions over 6 weeks. Within each session, five blocks of 16 items were presented, one for each condition. Conditions were rotated across blocks in each session. A repeated baseline design was used to monitor changes in naming on three occasions before therapy, immediately after therapy and then 1 year later.

Task	**Presentation of a picture for written naming** Picture presented on computer (with a variety of different cues) and client types response.
Materials	120 items from written naming were divided into two groups – 80 items for therapy and 40 used as control items. Groups were matched for number correct/incorrect. **Five presentation conditions** A: Cue presented on screen alongside picture • For RB: Open ended sentence as semantic cue • For GC: Anagram of written name B: Cue presented on screen alongside picture • For RB: Anagram of written name • For GC: First syllable of written name A': As A but with feedback (see below) B': As B but with feedback (see below) C: No cue
Hierarchy	Not stated
Feedback on error	In A' and B', an auditory warning was given on first error. On second error, letter in error appeared on screen for copying.
Feedback if correct	Not stated

Outcome

RB showed a significant facilitation of written naming with anagrams compared to when no cue was given. No significant facilitation occurred with semantic cues. Overall, a significant improvement was seen in written and oral naming of both treated and control items when compared with pre-therapy. Untreated oral naming improved significantly more than treated written naming. Written naming was characterised by a reduction in semantic, morphological and homophonic errors. Improvement was maintained 1 year post-therapy.

GC showed no difference between control cues, anagrams and first syllable cues. Overall, a significant improvement was present in oral and written naming of treated items. A significant improvement in written naming of control items was also seen, but no generalisation occurred to oral naming of untreated items. Improvements were maintained 1 year post-therapy.The authors suggest that RB's improvement in oral naming was a consequence of increased speed of processing and the reduction of semantic errors. They further suggested that therapy also helped RB to relearn phoneme-to-grapheme conversion, resulting in improvements in both the treated and control items, and that the results provide evidence that RB was using phonemic information to support written naming.

GC's improvement was attributed to the use of morpholexical cues to aid written naming. It is not considered how the use of these cues facilitated the improvement in the writing of control items. The authors suggested that the lack of a significant improvement in the oral naming of untreated items was a consequence of GC failing to reach a threshold of performance in written naming. For both clients, improvements were unlikely to be a consequence of spontaneous recovery due to stable baseline performance pre-therapy and the time post-onset.

Other comments

Changes were seen in the written naming of both clients that can be attributed to therapy. The control items in presentation condition C were written in every session, so changes in the production of these may not necessarily indicate the use of a strategy.

Study 9

Robson, J., Pring, T., Marshall, J., Morrison, S. and Chiat, S. (1998). Written communication in undifferentiated jargon aphasia: a therapy study. *International Journal of Language and Communication Disorders, 33*, 305–328.

Focus of therapy: Orthographic output lexicon.

Therapy approach: Reactivation.

Client details

General information

RMM was a 75-year-old highly educated woman who had a left CVA, resulting in damage to the left temporoparietal region. She had initial right hemiplegia and right homonymous hemianopia.

Overall pattern of language impairment and preservations

RMM's speech was fluently produced, undifferentiated jargon. She had minimal awareness regarding spoken output and no signs of self-monitoring. Auditory comprehension was relatively well preserved. Writing was produced with considerable effort, and frequent attempts at single words suggested some evidence of monitoring written output. She was able to copy single words and sort anagrams. In a delayed copying task, she showed a significant advantage for words relative to nonwords (particularly for longer items). The authors proposed that this was a consequence of RMM having partial access to preserved orthographic information.

Time post-onset

Therapy was commenced when RMM was 18 months post-onset.

Therapy

Therapy aimed to establish a small written word vocabulary and to transfer this to functional use. Therapy consisted of three phases with the following aims.

> Phase 1: To increase access to stored orthographic representations.
> Phase 2: To build on the success made in Phase 1 and encourage the functional use of the words.
> Phase 3: To enable RMM to associate single written words with complex messages.
> In each session, tasks were selected depending on RMM's performance.

Phase 1: Picture therapy

This phase of therapy consisted of fourteen, 45-min sessions over a period of 5 weeks.

Task	1. **Reflect on knowledge of word forms**	2. **Retrieval of lexical form** Writing words in response to picture stimuli.
Materials	Seventy-four words within six semantic categories. Words were paired by a semantic link. Pairs were split, resulting in two sets of 37 words. Sets were matched for length and frequency. One set was treated, one set was untreated.	
Hierarchy	a. Identification of initial grapheme b. Sorting pictures into those with long/short words	a. Anagram sorting with letter tiles b. Delayed copying c. Writing words unaided
Feedback on error	Not stated	Provision of cues to aid production e.g. first letter, number of letters. Discussion of incorrect. Correct form presented.
Feedback if correct	Not stated	Correct responses reinforced

Phase 2: Replication and generalisation therapy

This phase of therapy consisted of fifteen, 45-min sessions. Three sessions were devoted to replication of Phase 1. Six sessions were devoted to generalisation therapy. Six sessions were split.

Task	1. Generalisation therapy Use of written words in response to a variety of cues. Production of written word communicatively.	2. Replication therapy Tasks as in Phase 1.
Materials	Eighteen items from treated set in Phase 1. Items which were produced correctly either with no cue or with a first letter cue.	Eighteen items in untreated sets. Semantic pair to items treated in generalisation therapy.
Hierarchy	a. Writing words to picture pairs b. Complex picture description c. Writing words to verbal description d. Writing words to conversational cue e. Map task – writing in landmarks f. Holiday list – writing items to be packed Description of day out	a. Reflect on knowledge of words b. Retrieval of word forms
Feedback on error	Provision of cues as in Phase 1. Communicative attempts reinforced.	Provision of cues to aid production e.g. first letter, number of letters. Discussion of incorrect. Correct form presented.
Feedback if correct	Correct responses reinforced.	Correct responses reinforced.

Phase 3: Message therapy phase, with revision of previous phases

This phase consisted of a total of thirty sessions. Five sessions were conducted with Set A items, sixteen sessions with Set B items and nine sessions with Set C items.

Task	1. Replication therapy Tasks as in Phase 1.	2. Message therapy Convey a variety of concepts and messages using single written words.
Materials	Set A: 18 words from generalisation therapy in Phase 2 three sets of new words from five semantic categories. Set B and C both received picture therapy. Set D were used as control items.	Set B items. Eighteen new words initially treated using picture therapy.

Hierarchy	a. Reflect on knowledge of words b. Retrieval of word forms	a. Matching written synonyms and then copying the target b. Selecting a written phrase and then copying the target c. Selection of target from semantically related words d. Written picture naming in response to message e. Select written word from two messages and copy target f. Select picture from two messages and write name g. Write target word from two messages
Feedback on error	Provision of cues to aid production e.g. first letter, number of letters. Discussion of incorrect. Correct form presented.	Provision of cues as in Phase 1. Communicative attempts reinforced.
Feedback if correct	Correct responses reinforced.	Correct responses reinforced.

Outcome

Following Phase 1, written picture naming improved from 0 to 14/74 correct with an additional set of items that were produced correctly following an initial letter cue. A significant difference was seen between treated and untreated items. There was a decline in accuracy 6 weeks post-therapy but a significant improvement was still present compared with pretherapy. There was no change in RMM's insight into her speech, and no functional use of writing.

Following Phase 2, RMM's written naming of treated items improved, and improvement was more rapid than in Phase 1. Generalisation therapy resulted in an increased use of written words demonstrated through a communicative questionnaire task. Improvement was noted in both the items treated in generalisation therapy and those treated only using picture therapy. RMM remained reluctant to use writing outside of therapy sessions.

As in previous phases, therapy resulted in improved picture naming for treated items, following Phase 3, with some decline 6 weeks post-therapy. Following message therapy, RMM's ability to write a word to convey a simple message improved. Improvement was seen in both the words treated using message therapy and those treated only using picture therapy. Friends reported RMM using treated written words within everyday communication. RMM was also attempting to use words not treated in therapy to communicate.

Therapy resulted in item-specific improvements in the writing of single words. The authors proposed that this improvement was a consequence of improved access to lexical orthographic representations of the words. As therapy progressed, the ease with which these representations were accessed improved. Functional use of writing did not emerge without specific targeting in therapy. Phase 3 seemed to result in functional writing as it showed that writing could be used to convey information not present in the original stimulus. Benefits of generalisation and message therapy were not item specific, with therapy resulting in communication at a functional level. The authors suggested that the functional use of writing was not a consequence of an improvement in RMM's self-monitoring but reflected the communicative value of the treated words.

Other comments

This comprehensive study provides a detailed account of how to treat writing in order to improve the communicative abilities of a client with limited speech. The stimuli used in the therapy study are included in the paper. Following specific improvements in the writing of single words, an explicit stage of therapy to encourage communicative use was required.

Study 10

Beeson, P.M. (1999) Treating acquired writing impairment: strengthening graphemic representations. *Aphasiology, 13,* 767–785.

Focus of therapy: Orthographic output lexicon.

Therapy approach: Reactivation.

Client details

General information

ST was a 75-year-old man who had a large left temporo-occipital-parietal stroke following a left carotid endarterectomy. He had a mild right hemiparesis and right hemianopia. He was degree educated and was a retired toolmaker in the automotive industry. ST was multilingual, describing Polish and Yiddish as his first languages. He had learned German and English later but had been proficient in English for 40 years prior to the stroke.

Overall pattern of language impairments and preservations

ST presented with a Wernicke's aphasia. His spontaneous speech was characterised by fluent, stereotyped utterances lacking semantic content. His speech was supplemented by the use of gesture and drawing. He was unable to name pictures or to repeat or read words aloud. His comprehension of high-frequency nouns and simple commands was relatively intact but he had moderate to severe difficulties understanding phrases and complex sentences. He was unable to write words either in written naming or writing to dictation. His written naming was characterised by the production of the first letter. In writing to dictation, he mainly wrote phonologically implausible nonwords. He was able to copy words accurately but only wrote the first few letters of the word following a delay. He also had difficulties transcoding letter across case. The author suggests that ST's writing impairment was a consequence of a significant degradation of orthographic representations in the lexicon with additional difficulties in the graphemic output buffer and with allographic conversion. He showed no evidence of using phonological-to-graphemic correspondences in writing.

Time post-onset

ST was 4 years post-onset at the start of the study.

Therapy

Therapy was designed to improve ST's single-word writing and maximise the use of writing in daily communication. Therapy consisted of four phases: two phases of therapy accompanied by home practice and two home programmes. Phase 1 consisted of ten twice-weekly sessions supplemented by home practice. Phase 2 consisted of clinician-directed homework with the exchange of sheets each week. ACT therapy was used in the therapy sessions with CART therapy used at home. Phase 3 consisted of eight once-weekly sessions supplemented by home practice. Phase 4 consisted of 6 weeks of self-directed homework. A multiple-baseline design was used to monitor progress on the trained items. During the period of therapy, ST was also attending a weekly aphasia group.

Task	1. Anagram and copy treatment (ACT) ACT used in therapy sessions. Arrange the letters of the word in the correct order, copy the word repeatedly and then write the word from memory.	2. Copy and recall treatment (CART) Clinician-directed home program. Look at picture and then repeatedly copy the word. Self-test pages to recall word without model.	3. Conversational communicative writing ACT therapy for new words and CART therapy for all treated words. Use of conversational exchanges to prompt the use of the trained words.	4. Self-directed home program Client chooses words from an illustrated dictionary. Words repeatedly copied.
Materials	Twelve nouns and five verbs	Ten nouns and ten verbs	Twenty functionally useful nouns	Forty self-directed words
Hierarchy	a. Anagrams with target letters b. Anagrams with target letters and two foils	None	None	None
Feedback on error	In anagram task, therapist arranged the letters. If errors in recall, returned to anagram tasks.	Not applicable	As in Phase 1.	Not stated
Feedback if correct	Not stated	Not applicable	Not stated	Not stated

Outcome

Following Phase 1, ST met the 80% criterion for the treated words. No improvement was seen in his spelling of untrained words. Following Phase 2, continued item-specific improvement was evident with the maintenance of the words trained in Phase 1 and learning of the words used in Phase 2. ST was not using the words in conversation. After Phase 3, ST continued to meet criterion for the trained words. Within conversational probes, he was able to provide some appropriate written words. An increased use of written single words and some multi-word responses was also noted at home and in the aphasia group. Following Phase 4, ST was able to make recognisable or correct responses for half of the self-selected words.

Overall, treatment resulted in significant item-specific learning in the production of the trained words. Improvement was maintained over a long period and resulted in the use of writing in conversation following the pragmatic training. No improvement was seen in the writing of untrained words or the spoken production of either trained or untrained words. Therapy was successful in enabling ST to learn a small number of words and use them to aid his communication. The authors suggest that therapy resulted in the strengthening of the orthographic representations of the trained words. The study stresses the importance of using home practice alongside and subsequent to clinician-directed therapy.

Other comments

The study shows the potential for self-directed therapy exercises that minimise clinician involvement. The client's writing shows improvement following therapy but it is not clear whether the anagram component is necessary (considering the gains seen in Phase 4). The study stresses the importance of using a small number of words in the treatment set.

Study 11

Beeson, P.M., Hirsch, F.M. and Rewega, M.A. (2002) Successful single-word writing treatment: Experimental analyses of four cases. *Aphasiology, 16(4/5/6)*, 473–491.

Focus of therapy: Orthographic output lexicon.

Therapy approach: Reactivation.

Client details

The study involved four clients.

General information

FD was a 55-year-old, right-handed man with 14 years education. He was in the air force and then retired to work as an insurance salesman and cashier. A CT scan showed a non-haemorrhagic infarct in the distribution of the left middle cerebral artery and complete occlusion of the internal carotid artery. AD was a 57-year-old, left-handed man with 12 years education who worked as a bar and restaurant manager. He had a complete left internal carotid artery occlusion leading to an acute ischaemic infarct in the left middle cerebral artery territory with damage to the left temporal lobe, left medial basal ganglia and the head of the caudate nucleus. LG was a 41-year-old, right-handed man with 12 years education who was a communication supervisor for emergency medical services. A CT scan showed a large ischaemic infarct in the left middle cerebral artery distribution. ED was a 39-year-old, left-handed man who was a general manager in a store and had 14 years education. ED had surgery for an arteriovenous malformation which resulted in a haemor-rhagic stroke. All clients had a right hemiparesis.

Overall pattern of language impairments and preservations

FD presented with a global aphasia. His spoken output was characterised by stereotyped utterances which were supplemented by facial expression and a few gestures. He was using a communication book to convey basic information but was not using writing to communicate. His writing was extremely limited in both written naming and writing to dictation. His written comprehension was also severely impaired and he was unable to read aloud. He was able to identify real words in a written lexical decision task but also accepted nonwords as words. In contrast to his language skills, he had preserved non-verbal problem-solving skills.

AD presented with global aphasia and apraxia of speech. His spoken output consisted of perseverative utterances. He communicated using gestures and drawing. Writing attempts were generally unsuccessful but occasionally showed some partial knowledge of words. In written naming and writing to dictation, his writing was very limited and he became frustrated. He was able to copy single words reasonably accurately. His written comprehension and reading aloud were severely impaired. On non-verbal cognitive testing, he demonstrated well-preserved conceptual semantic knowledge, visual memory and problem-solving skills.

LG presented with Broca's aphasia characterised by stereotyped utterances and some single words. He communicated via gesture. His auditory comprehension was moderately impaired. On written assessment, he produced 25% words correctly with errors including implausible nonwords and unrelated words. Visual lexical decision was close to normal. Access to conceptual semantic information and written comprehension were impaired but were relative strengths. He also showed normal problem-solving skills.

ED's verbal output was characteristic of anomic aphasia with the use of simplified grammatical structure and evidence of word-finding difficulties. When unable to produce words, he occasionally wrote the first letter of a word. ED wanted to work on writing so he could compose emails. ED's written naming and writing to dictation were impaired. He attempted to write the first letters which were correct about half of the time. He was able to verbally name pictures and repeat words but showed no ability to use phoneme-to-grapheme conversion. His written comprehension was within normal limits and he was mildly impaired on visual lexical decision.

All clients, therefore, presented with severe difficulties in both spoken and written output with minimal ability to write single words.

Time post-onset

FD was 2 years, AD was 18 months, LG was 1 year, and ED was 5 years post-stroke at the time of the study.

Therapy

Therapy aimed to teach each client a core set of single words and maximise the use of writing in daily communication in clients with limited speech. AD, LG and EG had twice-weekly sessions whereas FD had a session once weekly. Clients also did homework practice 6 days a week. Therapy duration varied between clients and was dependent on how quickly clients reached criterion on each set of words (80% correct over 2 weeks). During therapy, all participants were also attending a weekly aphasia group. A single subject, multiple-baseline design was used to monitor the effect of treatment on sets of words which were introduced sequentially. FD and AD received ACT therapy in sessions with a homework programme of CART. LG and ED received only homework based CART therapy.

Task	1. Anagram and copy treatment (ACT)	2. Copy and recall treatment (CART)
	ACT used in therapy sessions. Arrange the letters of the word in the correct order, copy the word repeatedly and then write the word from memory.	Clinician-directed home program. Look at picture and then repeatedly copy the word. Self-test pages to recall word without model.
Materials	Words selected by participants for their functional significance. Included mainly common nouns as well some verbs and proper nouns. Minimum of 20 words (4 sets of five words) for each participant. Treatment sets for AD & ED extended to seven.	
Hierarchy	a. Anagrams with target letters b. Anagrams with target letters and two foils	None
Feedback on error	In anagram task, therapist arranged the letters. If errors in recall, returned to anagram tasks.	Not applicable
Feedback if correct	Not stated	Not applicable

Outcome

Prior to therapy, FD was unable to spell any of the target words correctly. He showed rapid improvements when the target words were treated and after 9 weeks, had reached criterion for four sets (20 words). He showed no improvement on written naming or writing to dictation of untrained words. FD began to copy words from his communication book to portray his message and also initiated the learning of other words, e.g. the name of his physician, as he began to use written communication to supplement his very limited speech.

AD received ACT and CART therapy for four sets of words and reached criterion after nineteen sessions. Subsequent CART only therapy targeted three additional sets of words. During probe sessions for the new words, it was noticed that AD was developing very specific associations between words and their pictured representations so multiple exemplars for the target words were introduced. Post-therapy, there was no change in accuracy of written naming or writing to dictation of untrained items. Clinical observation showed increased use of writing in both individual and group sessions with some access to partial word knowledge as it wrote the first letters. AD continued to practise new words using the CART procedure.

LG received only CART therapy and worked on seven words in each set. Baseline performance was stable with LG learning words fairly rapidly when targeted. Following twenty-three sessions, he was close to criterion on the fourth set of words and another three sets of six words were then targeted. These reached criterion after seven sessions. LG therefore learned 46 words. He showed no improvement on untrained words in assessment. However, he showed a notable increase in attempts to spell untrained words in group sessions and was able to produce the initial portion of words and spell some words accurately. The authors propose this anecdotal evidence suggests some general improvement in LG's access to graphemic representations.

ED also received only homework based CART therapy. Over 9 weeks, ED learned 20 words. He showed no improvement in the writing of untrained words but did start to use emails. In emails, he copied the spellings for untrained words and sought help from family. His emails were agrammatic but meaningful. In conversation, he used writing more often and this sometimes cued his retrieval of a spoken word.

Pre-therapy, participants showed minimal ability to write words but all participants showed gains in the writing of treated words. Gains are attributed to a strengthening of specific graphemic representations. Improvement was item-specific; there was no generalisation to untrained items but the authors propose that, in each case, there were functional gains in writing. All participants showed increased use of writing as a means of communication. Both LG and ED showed gains in writing demonstrating that CART alone can be a successful treatment. LG who learned most words had the strongest semantic skills prior to therapy. AD showed some difficulty accessing the semantic representations of items and required the introduction of multiple exemplars of target pictures. The authors hypothesise a well-preserved semantic system may be needed for the clients to use the words functionally.

Other comments

The authors suggest that the clients would have benefited from additional conversational writing tasks as described in Beeson (1999). They also suggest that CART homework therapy should continue over an extended period of therapy to build up a large corpus of words. This study shows that CART can be used successfully without ACT and that self-directed practice can result in writing gains. Beeson *et al.* (2003) provides an overall summary of the impact of CART and the factors impacting on therapy success. Beeson *et al.* (2003) suggested that CART may be an appropriate treatment programme for facilitating verbal naming and recommended combining treatment with verbal repetition to stimulate oral language. Harris Wright *et al.* (2008) investigated the impact of a modified version of CART including verbal and written production on oral naming. Both participants showed some gains in verbal naming for treated items over the course of treatment. One participant showed maintenance of the gains with some generalisation to untreated items. One participant showed no maintenance and no generalisation. The authors suggest the study provides some evidence that treatment in one modality may benefit performance in another. The different patterns of improvement were attributed to different underlying deficits in writing.

Study 12

Clausen, N. and Beeson, P.M (2003) Conversational use of writing in severe aphasia: A group treatment approach. *Aphasiology, 17(6/7)*, 625–644.

Focus of therapy: Orthographic output lexicon.

Therapy approach: Reactivation of written words. Use of written words as compensatory strategy.

Client details

The study involved four clients.

General information

SL was a 66-year-old, right-handed man with 20 years education. DR was a 72-year-old, right-handed woman with 16 years education. WD was a 68-year-old, left-handed man with 16 years education. AD was a 61-year-old, left-handed man with 12 years education. All were reported to have been competent communicators with normal written spelling abilities prior to the stroke. The clients had large left perisylvian lesions that affected both anterior and posterior language regions resulting in aphasia and right hemiparesis. All were using their left hand for writing post-stroke.

Overall pattern of language impairments and preservations

The clients all presented with severe Broca's aphasia. Spoken language was severely impaired and previous treatment directed at spoken production had been largely unsuccessful. All clients performed outside the normal range on the Pyramids and Palm Trees Test, with AD just outside normal limits, SL and DR having mild impairments, and WD having the most severe impairment and performing at chance. WD also presented with significant difficulties on non-verbal problem-solving. SL, DR and AD all had impaired visual lexical decision whereas WD was within normal limits. The authors report no background information about their writing abilities. All clients had previously received CART therapy and had responded with item-specific gains.

Time post-onset

SL was 8 years, DR and WD were 6 years and AD was 7 years post-onset at the time of the study.

Therapy

Therapy aimed to promote the use of drilled written words as an alternative to speech in structured conversation. Therapy consisted of two parts: (1) drill spelling of personal vocabulary using CART and (2) conversation coaching using scripts to elicit trained words. Therapy consisted of one, 1 hour individual session and one, 1 hour group session each week. Homework practice was carried out 6 days per week. A multiple-baseline design was used to measure efficacy with probes pre-therapy, weekly during therapy and 1 month post-therapy (although homework practice continued). Transfer of skills into conversation was tested two to five times per client in a 1:1 conversation with an unfamiliar conversation partner; this was done once the person had mastered a set of words within the group setting.

Task	Individual sessions: Copy and recall treatment	Individual sessions: Conversational communicative writing	Homework: Copy and recall treatment (CART)	Group sessions: Conversation coaching
	Picture presented with a verbal cue. Model of the word presented for copying × 3. Examples of written word removed. Drawing presented with verbal cue and participant asked to recall the word.	Use of conversational exchanges to prompt the use of the trained words.	Look at picture and then copy the word × 20. Self-test pages to recall word without mode.	Structured conversation to train pragmatic use of written words.
Materials	Sets of five functionally useful words including question word e.g. 'NAME?'. Words centred on biographical information, family, hobbies/interest, favourite foods etc. Not controlled for length, frequency, regularity or class. Two sets of words worked on at a time. Total number of sets varied between clients (five–eight in total).			Themed conversation topics to elicit personal vocabulary. No pictorial stimuli.
Hierarchy	None	None	None	None
Feedback on error	If errors in recall, return to copying.	If participant did not write response, additional prompts or direct instruction given.	Not applicable	If participant did not correctly recall a target item, verbal model given and person asked to write. If word spelt incorrectly, model provided for copying.
Feedback if correct	Not stated	Not stated.	Not applicable	Not stated

Outcome

Overall, all clients improved in their ability to write the treated vocabulary in the one-to-one and group sessions. All clients were using some of the words in the conversational probes with the unfamiliar communication partner but performance lagged behind the use of the words in the group setting. AD showed the greatest ease in his use of the written words in conversation and also produced some non-trained words during conversational exchanges. It is suggested that this may be due to AD having the greatest need to communicate with unfamiliar people. WD had a significant semantic impairment and the authors attribute his increased tendency to write incorrect words and to perseverate on written responses to his semantic difficulties. The authors propose that the group setting was an appropriate context for facilitating written communication. Despite the weekly repetition of discussion topics, the authors report the group atmosphere was conversational and genuine.

Other comments

The data is difficult to interpret as words written to dictation in the group were scored as correct and only accurate spellings were considered. Some clients produced communicative but not fully accurate responses and it would have been helpful to consider these when evaluating the functional use of writing. The study discusses the psychosocial support within the group and that the group setting also served to 'normalise' the use of writing as an alternative means of communication. The study provides a framework for eliciting writing within conversation. However, the authors comment that communication partners varied in the extent to which they could elicit the written words and thus conversation partner training may be needed. The value of including question words in therapy to gain information from other people is highlighted.

Study 13

Rapp, B. and Kane, A. (2002). Remediation of deficits affecting different components of the spelling process. *Aphasiology, 16*, 439–454.

Focus of therapy: Orthographic output lexicon and graphemic output buffer.

Therapy approach: Reactivation.

Client details

Two clients are described in the study.

General information

MMD was a right-handed woman who had a CVA at the age of 65. A CT scan showed left posterior parietal and temporal lesions. She was high school educated and worked in a clerical position until retirement. Pre-morbidly, she was an avid reader and a good speller. RSB was a 58-year-old right-handed man. He had a CVA subsequent to an aortic valve replacement resulting in damage to the left anterior parietal region. He had a PhD and worked in toxicology research. He was bilingual in English and Spanish and had no pre-morbid spelling difficulties.

Overall pattern of language impairments and preservations

Both clients presented with retained single-word comprehension and good comprehension within conversation. They had mild to moderate naming difficulties. In writing, they were able to do cross-case transcoding, indicating an intact ability for retrieving and producing letter shapes. Both MMD and RSB presented with impaired writing to dictation. MMD's writing was characterised by a frequency effect and she produced a high percentage (44%) of phonologically plausible errors. RSB's writing was characterised by a length effect. His errors were phonologically implausible nonwords involving single-letter deletions and substitutions. The authors propose that MMD's writing reflected impairment to the orthographic output lexicon, whereas RSB's impairment was at the level of the graphemic buffer.

Time post-onset

MMD was 2½ years post-onset and RSB was 4 years post-onset at the time of the study.

Therapy

Therapy aimed to improve single-word spelling and to monitor the effect of treatment on untreated words. Treatment was discontinued when the clients reached a stable performance of less than 5% of errors. MMD received twenty-five sessions of therapy (with a gap half way through) and RSB had a total of sixteen sessions. No information was given on the frequency of sessions. An item-specific treatment design was used to contrast improvement on the trained words (those receiving therapy), repeated items (those written each session without feedback) and control items.

Task	**Writing to dictation** Hear word, repeat it and attempt to spell.
Materials	One set of ten treated words matched for frequency/length with two other sets (the repeated and control items).
Hierarchy	None
Feedback on error	Shown correct spelling of word with therapist saying the letters aloud. Client studies word and then given another chance to spell the word correctly.
Feedback if correct	Shown correct spelling of word with therapist saying the letters aloud. Client studies word.

Outcome

For both clients, no difference was seen in the error rates across the three sets of words and across the two pre-therapy baselines. Following therapy, MMB showed more accurate writing of the treated words, as shown by a significant reduction in letter errors. Her writing of the treated words was significantly better than that of the repeated items, although these also significantly improved. No change was seen in her writing of the control words. At follow-up (20 weeks post-therapy), the error rate for both the treated and repeated items increased but there was still a significant effect of therapy for the treated items. RSB showed significant improvement in his writing of the treated, repeated and control words. Improvement for the treated items was significantly greater than for the other sets. At follow-up, his error rate on all three sets remained unchanged.

   Therapy resulted in significant improvement in the writing of the treated words for both clients, but different patterns of generalisation and maintenance were seen. MMB showed no generalised learning and gains were not maintained at follow-up. RSB showed generalisation to control items and writing of all items was maintained at post-therapy levels. No functional outcomes of therapy were discussed. The authors suggest that therapy for MMB resulted in a strengthening of word representation within the lexicon. For RSB, the authors suggest that there was a strengthening of the orthographic representation (making the representation more resistant to buffer damage) and improvement to the buffering process (e.g. scanning speed, speed of letter-to-shape conversion).

Other comments

The number of items within the word sets is small. Despite this, many sessions were required to improve the spelling of the treated words. Although significant improvement was seen on reassessment, the evaluation of efficacy and measuring generalisation was limited due to the small number of items in the treated, repeated and control sets. RSB and MMD are also described in Rapp (2005) with an additional client, JRE. JRE had an impairment within the graphemic output buffer. Rapp (2005) reports treatment for 20–30 item word sets. Results for MMB and RSB are replicated, with MMB showing item-specific effects and RSB showing some generalised improvements. JRE also shows generalised improvement but, for both RSB and JRE, gains on treated items were significantly better than improvement on other word sets.

Study 14

Raymer, A.M, Cudworth, C. and Haley, M.A. (2003) Spelling treatment for an individual with dysgraphia: Analysis of generalisation to untrained words. *Aphasiology, 17(6/7)*, 607–624.

Focus of therapy: Orthographic output lexicon and graphemic output buffer.

Therapy approach: Reactivation.

Client details

General information

NM was a 61-year-old man. He had a twelfth grade education and was retired after careers in the military and as a refrigeration instructor. He had a left hemisphere stroke following carotid endarterectomy resulting in aphasia and paresis of the right lower limb. A CT scan showed a left lesion extending from the inferior occipital cortex to the superior primary motor cortex but sparing perisylvian cortex.

Overall pattern of language impairments and preservations

NM had minimal residual verbal language difficulties and could engage in extended, meaningful conversation. He was within normal limits for verbal language and reading on standardised aphasia tests. He reported difficulties spelling words, writing sentences to dictation and in spontaneous writing. He was able to copy and could transpose from upper to lower case. His spelling to dictation was impaired for words and nonwords. There was no significant difference between written and oral spelling. There was a tendency to spell four–five letter words better than seven–eight letter words but this was not significant. There was, however, a significantly larger percentage of letters correct in the short words. Errors were predominantly incomplete spelling attempts with correct spelling of the initial part of the word but failure to recall the final part. Other spelling errors consisted of letter deletions, transpositions, insertions, substitutions, occasional no response errors, orthographically similar words and unrecognisable mis-spellings. Nonword spelling errors were similar to those for words. NM spelled significantly more high-frequency words than low frequency words. There was no significant effect of regularity. The authors attribute NM's spelling difficulty to disruption in the orthographic output lexicon and the graphemic output buffer.

Time post-onset

NM was 2 years post-onset at the time of the study.

Therapy

Therapy aimed to improve spelling and to establish whether training improves the orthographic output lexicon or graphemic output buffer by monitoring generalisation to untrained words which are either related or unrelated to trained words. A multiple-baseline design was used to monitor progress on trained and untrained words, with two sets of words treated sequentially. Training of Set 2 commenced when Set 1 reached 80% accuracy over two consecutive probes. Therapy consisted of two, 90 minute sessions per week over the course of 3 months, with daily homework practice.

Task	Copy and recall therapy
	a. Copy written word
	b. Clinician covers first two letters and NM recalls and writes first two letters and then copies rest of the word
	c. Clinician covers two additional letters and NM recalls covered letters and then copies rest of the word
	d. Continue until NM can recall complete spelling
Materials	Two sets of items for training. Four sets of untrained items, Two for each training set, one sharing beginning three–four letters and one sharing end letters. Each set consisted of ten, two syllable words (five–nine letters) mono-morphemic words. Sets matched for length.
Hierarchy	See task description
Feedback on error	Repetition of prior step
Feedback if correct	Proceed to next step

Homework consisted of copying each training word, 3 times a day.

Outcome

Prior to training, spelling performance was low and stable. When Set 1 was introduced, performance on trained words improved significantly following eight training sessions. During training for Set 1, untrained Set 2 words showed some improvement but this was not significant. Following training for Set 2, spelling accuracy improved to 100% correct within four treatment sessions. During Set 1 training, significant improvement was seen on two untrained sets, one of which had no spelling similarity to trained words. During Set 2 training, NM showed significant improvement on a set of related words but not for a set of unrelated words. Over the course of therapy, there was a statistically significant improvement on the unrelated nonwords but not on the related nonwords. Post-therapy, NM gained an average of 79.2% beginning spellings and 31.1% ending spellings, a difference that was significant. He significantly improved his spelling accuracy for untrained part-word spellings with an improvement in the untrained endings of words. Improvement was seen in the writing sub-tests (writing to dictation and picture description) of standardised tests. On completion of training, NM continued his spelling practice with personally relevant words.

Following a modified CART, NM demonstrated significant improvement on trained words. There was a complex pattern of improvement on untrained words and the authors conclude this reflects an interaction of training effects influencing both the orthographic output lexicon and the graphemic output buffer. Prior to therapy, it was predicted that changes in spelling knowledge within the lexicon would improve trained items but also parts of untrained words with similar spellings. This generalisation was seen with improved part-word spelling of word endings. Training effects from improvement in the graphemic output buffer were predicted to result in generalised spelling improvements across all stimuli, with more significant gains at the start of words. Word beginnings were spelled more accurately than word endings but improvements in the accuracy of untrained words did not reach significance for all sets. There is very limited consideration of functional gains in writing.

Other comments

The study uses an adapted version of copy and recall therapy (Beeson, 1999). The study again reinforces the value of independent practice.

Study 15

Mortley, J., Enderby, P. and Petheram, B. (2001). Using a computer to improve functional writing in a patient with severe dysgraphia. *Aphasiology, 15*, 443–461.

Focus of therapy: Graphemic output buffer.

Therapy approach: Cognitive relay.

Client details

General information

MF was a 67-year-old man who was a retired civil servant. He had a left CVA resulting in multiple infarcts.

Overall pattern of language impairments and preservations

MF had retained auditory and written comprehension. His spontaneous speech was characterised by high-level word-finding problems. He presented with severe writing difficulties and was unable to use a dictionary or word processor to compensate for these difficulties. On formal testing, he was able to do mirror reversal and cross-case matching but had some problems with letter naming, letter sounding and matching spoken to written letters. He was unable to write either words or nonwords to dictation or write words within written naming. His errors consisted of a random array of letters. He was aware of his errors but was unable to correct them. His oral spelling of words was superior to his written spelling. The authors propose that MF had intact lexical knowledge for shorter words at least but that his writing may reflect a multi-level impairment involving the graphemic output buffer.

Time post-onset

MF was 18 months post-onset when writing therapy began.

Therapy

Therapy was designed to use MF's good oral spelling to aid his written spelling by encouraging him to say the word, spell the word orally letter by letter and then write the word letter by letter. Therapy ran for a period of 6 months with the use of a computer to administer the tasks. Therapist input was restricted to an hour a week for the first month and then one session every 2–3 weeks. No information was given regarding the amount of time MF spent on the computer. A control task design was used. Before the introduction of the strategy, therapy was carried out to develop prerequisite skills: writing single letters to dictation, increasing his awareness of his ability to orally spell words and knowledge of the computer keyboard.

	1. Writing words to dictation	2. Introduction of dictionary	3. Sentence-based writing tasks	4. Functional writing tasks
Task	Hear word, spell the word aloud and then write down each letter	Start writing the words and then use the dictionary to find the rest of the word	Using the strategy to write sentences	Use of an adaptive word processor which provides a list of possible words
Materials	Various words of increasing length	Various words	Various sentences of increasing length	
Hierarchy	a. Write down word spoken by therapist b. Write down three letter words spoken by therapist c. Write down four letter words on computer d. Write down five letter words on computer e. Write down words of six or more letters on computer	a. Written picture naming b. Solving of definitions	a. Identification of the individual words within a sentence b. Write sentences spoken by therapist c. Sentence copying on computer d. Writing sentences on computer to describe a composite picture	a. Write a diary b. Encourage regular correspondence using computer
Feedback on error	Therapist gives next letter or computer gives a choice of letter	Not stated	Not stated	Not stated
Feedback if correct	Not stated	Not stated	Not stated	Not stated

Outcome

During the period of therapy, MF demonstrated the ability to write single words of increasing length, write sentences of increasing length and use these newly acquired writing skills in functional tasks. He also learned to use a dictionary and an adaptive word processor to aid his spelling of longer words. When reassessed using pen and paper, he showed significant improvement in all written tasks. No changes were seen in tasks unrelated to therapy (e.g. digit span, sentence comprehension and letter sounding). Eight weeks after therapy, MF's written spelling performance was maintained and continued to improve. Only following the introduction of the adaptive word processor did writing become quick and easy enough to be of functional benefit.

The introduction of the therapy strategy which encouraged MF's reliance on his oral spelling resulted in a significant improvement in the writing of treated and untreated words in isolation, sentences and connected writing. Improvement was likely to be a consequence of therapy, as no change was seen on control tasks.

Other comments

The therapy tasks used in the study was similar to that reported in a study by Pound (1996). The computer allowed intensive work with minimal input from the therapist, with significant and impressive gains in the client's writing ability. The paper discusses the relationship between oral and written spelling.

Study 16

Sage, K. and Ellis, A.W. (2006) Using orthographic neighbours to treat a case of graphemic buffer disorder. *Aphasiology, 20(9/10/11)*, 851–870.

Focus of therapy: Graphemic output buffer.

Therapy approach: Reactivation.

Client details

General information

BH was a 68-year-old woman. She had previously worked as a clothing inspector in a factory. She had a CVA resulting in a mild right sided hemiparesis. An MRI scan showed a widespread region of ischaemic damage extending throughout fronto-temporal, parietal and occipital regions of the left hemisphere and a small region in the occipital lobe of the right hemisphere.

Overall pattern of language impairments and preservations

BH presented with good auditory and written comprehension and excellent spoken output, including normal naming and sentence production skills. Her reading aloud of single words was good but she had some difficulty with nonword reading. Her written output was severely impaired. A full description of BH's spelling skills is reported in an earlier study (Sage & Ellis,

2004). BH showed a similar pattern of difficulty in writing to dictation and in oral spelling. In both, there was a significant effect of length and errors included substitutions, additions, omissions, movement and compounds e.g. reign – RIANG. Spelling accuracy was also significantly affected by age of acquisition, imageability, frequency and the size of the orthographic neighbourhood. Nonword spelling was significantly more impaired than word spelling but was also affected by length with a similar pattern of errors. The authors propose that the pattern is consistent with graphemic buffer disorder.

Time post-onset

BH was 3 years post-onset at the time of the study.

Therapy

The paper describes two priming experiments and a therapy study. Only the therapy study is described here. The paper looks at the influence of orthographic neighbours on spelling; an orthographic neighbour is a word generated by changing one letter in the target word. The priming experiments showed BH was able to write words more accurately when they had been primed using orthographic neighbours than when no primes had been given and that there was more priming from word neighbours than nonword neighbours. Therapy investigated the impact of an errorless learning approach on spelling, contrasting the impact of providing direct treatment for the words and providing therapy for orthographic neighbours of the target word. A multiple-baseline therapy design was used to investigate the effect of therapy on three word sets. Performance was contrasted during two baselines, 1 week and 6 weeks post-therapy. Therapy took place in two, 1 hour sessions over a period of 2 weeks.

Task	1. Pairwise comparison	2. Insert missing letters	3. Wordsearch grids
	Target word at top. Compare to two versions of target: one correct/one incorrect. BH identified correctly spelled word, identified where the other word was mis-spelled and corrected.	Target word at top. Same target presented several times with two letters missing each time. BH had to fill in missing letter with reference to correct target.	Target words listed below word gird. Within grid, words presented in either horizontal, vertical or diagonal plane. BH had to search for and ring target words.
Materials	Forty-five target words that BH had misspelled twice. Divided into three sets of 15 matched for combined frequency and neighbourhood size. Words in Set 1 received direct therapy (via three tasks). Words in Set 2 received no therapy. Words in Set 3 did not receive therapy but one neighbour of each word did receive therapy (via three tasks).		
Hierarchy	None	None	None
Feedback on error	Not stated	Not stated	Not stated
Feedback if correct	Not stated	Not stated	Not stated

Therapy was designed to promote errorless learning and BH made very few errors across therapy programme.

Outcome

Spelling accuracy was considered in terms of whole target words correct and letter accuracy. Both analyses revealed similar patterns. Therapy resulted in a significant improvement for the direct treatment set (trained words) that was maintained at 6 weeks follow-up. The untreated control set did not improve. There was an improvement in the indirect set (neighbour word received therapy) which was not significant immediately post-therapy but reached significance at follow-up.

The study shows that errorless therapy can result in significant improvement in the writing of trained items. The authors propose that direct training of words is most effective and that improvement is a consequence of directly strengthening activation between the orthographic output lexicon and the buffer. Some improvement was seen following the training of orthographic neighbours due to top down support from the lexicon to the letter units at the buffer level. The authors do not propose using this technique to treat words but suggest that generalisation to orthographic neighbours may be seen post-therapy.

Other comments

The therapy technique described in this study differs from many reported in the literature as it does not involve writing the words. The authors conclude therapy should focus directly on words to be trained.

Study 17

Panton, A. and Marshall, J. (2008) Improving spelling and everyday writing after a CVA: A single-case therapy study. *Aphasiology, 22(2)*, 164–183.

Focus of therapy: Graphemic output buffer.

Therapy approach: Reactivation and cognitive relay.

Client details

General information

Ray was a 57-year-old, right-handed man who had a left middle cerebral artery infarct resulting in aphasia and right hemiparesis. He was educated to master's level and worked as a further education lecturer and political councillor. His first language was English but he also spoke French and Spanish. He was using his non-preferred left hand for writing.

Overall pattern of language impairments and preservations

Ray's speech, although grammatical, was hesitant with word-finding difficulties and phonological errors. He had good auditory and written comprehension at sentence level, minimal difficulties understanding conversation and could read lengthy work documents. His primary concern was his writing and he wanted to be able to take notes e.g. in meetings. In written naming and writing to dictation, he produced recognisable attempts at target words with errors involving letter deletions, transpositions, additions and substitutions. The majority of errors occurred in word medial position and there was a clear influence of length in both word and nonword spelling. Ray found a novel task exploring his note-taking ability extremely demanding. Very few words were correct or reflected recognisable attempts. Most words were aborted. Despite these difficulties, there was evidence of him using some strategies, e.g. focusing on key words, abbreviations.

The authors propose that Ray's difficulties are consistent with a buffer level impairment. His recognisable attempts and limited evidence of frequency and imageability effects suggested the words were being retrieved from the orthographic output lexicon.

Time post-onset

Ray was 1 year post-stroke at the time of the study.

Therapy

Therapy aimed to improve Ray's note-taking abilities via a dual approach of increasing the capacity of his buffer and facilitating a strategic approach. Therapy consisted of twelve, 1-hour sessions over 6 weeks with independent worksheets between sessions. A multiple-baseline with control task design was used to monitor efficacy. Performance on writing to dictation of treated and untreated words and on the novel, note-writing task was considered.

Task	*Writing to dictation of target words* a. Spell each word to dictation b. Spell each word letter-by-letter dictation c. Copy each word d. Show the word partially obscured and then recall the full spelling	*Strategic note-writing skills* Listen to a recorded phone message and a short news story dictated by the therapist. Client was encouraged to write down key points using abbreviations, symbols and relevant punctuation.
Materials	Thirty treated, work-related words (mean length of 9.9 letters). Thirty untreated words matched for frequency and word length to treated words.	Recorded phone messages and short news stories.
Hierarchy	See task description.	None
Feedback on error	Not stated. At each stage, client was encouraged to monitor the accuracy of his spelling.	Not stated
Feedback if correct	Not stated	Examination of notes to highlight strategies used.

Worksheets involved copying words, anagram sorting and filling in missing letters in the target words.

Outcome

There was a significant improvement in the writing of the practised words, and improvement was maintained 3 months post-therapy. Performance on unpractised words also significantly improved immediately post-therapy but was not maintained at follow-up. Ray also showed some improvement in the writing to dictation of nonwords post-therapy and at maintenance but this did not reach significance. Ray's remaining errors in writing to dictation were letter deletions, substitutions, additions and transpositions, but errors occurred later in the word than pre-therapy. In the note-taking task, Ray conveyed significantly more elements of the messages/story. He produced more whole words, including both practised and unpractised words. He also produced more close approximations to words. Post-therapy, Ray applied more strategies, e.g. grouping of words, use of symbols/punctuation and strategic word substitutions. There was no change in performance on the control tasks.

Therapy resulted in significant gains in the writing of the practised words and his note-taking abilities. Some gains were also seen on the writing of unpractised words and nonwords, with a shift in the location of errors. The authors attribute some of the gains to improvement within the buffer. However, practised words were significantly better than unpractised words, suggesting some item-specific gains. The authors suggest these gains reflect better access to orthographic forms in the lexicon and that this may have been a secondary impairment not identified at assessment.

Other comments

The study comments on the importance of considering 'life-goals' at the outset and using these to direct assessment and therapy, potentially combining work on the impairment with strategic adaptation.

Note

1 Although two clients were examined in the study, only one is discussed here.

15 Cognitive neuropsychology and aphasia in context

While the contribution of cognitive neuropsychology *per se* is still a much debated area (see Harley, 2004), as is its role in aphasia intervention (see Laine & Martin, 2012, and the ensuing forum in *Aphasiology*), there is clear consensus that cognitive neuropsychology has significantly progressed our understanding of aphasia and the ways in which we approach clinical practice (e.g. Whitworth, Webster & Howard, 2012). The cognitive neuropsychological architecture, while undeniably still not fully understood, provides us with a testable model for how single words are processed, around which principles and tools have developed to isolate and then monitor these processes over time. This relationship between theory and practice is clearly a reciprocal one. Nickels *et al.* (2010) state that 'the key aim of cognitive neuropsychology should be characterized as the use of data from the investigation and treatment of individuals with cognitive disorders to develop, evaluate, and extend theories of normal cognition' (p.539), with findings from work with people with aphasia directly informing further theoretical developments.

Since the first edition of this book, there have been relatively few developments in assessment, possibly due to earlier tools, such as the PALPA, continuing to be widely used; the systematic attention to theory in these earlier assessments withstanding the test of time. The development of the CAT has perhaps been the most notable addition to the assessment arena, providing a comprehensive yet efficient battery of tasks to inform further assessment decisions, and facilitating the iterative hypothesis testing process in a clinically viable manner. Assessing a breadth of language processes, while also including tools for considering non-linguistic neuropsychological impairment and the impact of aphasia on communication in daily life, the CAT has encouraged a holistic assessment of the person while retaining the thoroughness in testing the language processing system, and allowing an initial profile of strengths and weakness to then inform further diagnostic assessment. There has been more notable refinement of our methods for investigating the outcome of intervention, both in single case methodology and in systematically replicating our methods in case series. These methods have not only enabled us to scrutinise our outcomes better but also increased confidence in planning and selecting therapy approaches. This is reflected in the steady and continued growth in the therapy literature where reports of both novel approaches and more in-depth exploration of our existing approaches are seen.

In this volume, we have described how a cognitive neuropsychological model can be used to identify the nature of the impairments and the retained abilities in single-word processing of people with aphasia, and we have presented a range of different kinds of therapy that have been shown to be effective in reasonably well-designed studies that use a cognitive neuropsychological perspective in designing and evaluating therapy for specific disorders. We make no claims to this being an exhaustive review of the literature. Nor have we reported only perfect therapy designs. Many of the studies that have been reviewed did not meet all the desired criteria, although we have aimed to be true to broad principles. The coverage of these studies in the literature is also patchy. For instance, there are many studies of therapy for disorders of word retrieval and, as we have seen, there is now real sophistication in the accounts of how therapy in this area might work and the levels of deficit for which particular approaches might be suitable (Nickels, 2002b). In contrast, there remain a small number of studies of therapy for difficulties in language comprehension – possibly, as we noted, because such difficulties are not often seen to be the most disabling aspect of chronic aphasia.

While we believe that the studies reviewed in Part 3 provide the best current evidence base for developing and designing therapy in clinical practice, there is no guarantee that the therapy approaches we have described are the best possible methods; new methods and new understanding will come. Our understanding of aphasic language impairments, of specific therapy techniques, and of the ways in which therapies work has improved immeasurably over the last 30 years. We acknowledge, however, that this knowledge is still often sketchy and fragmentary. As clinicians, we have an obligation to do what we can with the knowledge available to us. Basso (2003) emphasises: 'What is done should always be the best that can be done with reference to current knowledge. The more knowledge we have, the better we should do, but we cannot wait for the ultimate truth to act' (p. 263).

Implications of cognitive neuropsychology for clinical practice

With the majority of the therapy studies reported in the literature having focused on spoken word retrieval and therapy for anomia, it is probably in this area that our knowledge is currently most robust. We now have considerable evidence for the successful reactivation of links between semantics and the phonological output lexicon through a variety of semantic and phonological tasks (see Chapters 11 and 12). This has come with an appreciation that many of the tasks used activate word meaning and word form simultaneously; as a result the relationship between the nature of the therapy tasks and the level of the impairment is not transparent. Semantic tasks have, for example, been used successfully with people with lexical impairments, while phonological tasks have been used with people with semantic, lexical and post-lexical impairments. The literature also highlights an absence of evidence for differential therapy effects across these tasks or with different types of learning paradigms, e.g. errorless or errorful (see Chapter 11). Equally, we have found that when we apply therapies developed for nouns to verbs, verbs respond in similar ways to nouns on semantic and phonological tasks, despite the differences between the two word classes (see Chapter 12). With verbs, as with nouns, the improvements are also usually item specific.

Therapies for written word retrieval that draw on similar tasks to those above are also relatively independent of the underlying deficit (e.g. written naming following a variety of cues, anagram sorting and copying) (see Chapter 14). Significant gains in treated items are seen although, unlike spoken production, the number of words treated and the degree of improvement have often been quite limited.

Therapy for single-word spoken comprehension has perhaps progressed to a lesser degree due to the little attention it has received (see Chapter 10). The cognitive neuropsychological model has, none-the-less, facilitated therapy being targeted in a more focused way, targeting, for example, impairments at the levels of phonological analysis, spoken word recognition and access to the meaning of spoken words. Therapy for reading has equally focused on tasks and strategies targeting orthographic analysis, visual word recognition and accessing the meaning of written words, with significant improvement seen (see Chapter 13).

Of crucial importance, however, is our understanding of therapy effects and how they generalise to other items and to other contexts. Through close monitoring of outcomes, we know, for instance, that the majority of therapy studies targeting access to spoken words have found item-specific improvement, irrespective of whether the approach used has involved phonological cues, orthographic cues or word repetition. In a smaller group of clients, generalisation to untreated items has been found and we believe that understanding how, why and for whom generalisation occurs is likely to be a focus for the future (see Best *et al.*, 2013, for an overview of generalisation in anomia). Best *et al.* (2013) argue that clients with semantic difficulties and accessing the word form are least likely to show generalisation to untreated items following cueing therapies for word retrieval while generalisation is more likely with clients with post-lexical deficits. This supports Franklin *et al.*'s (2002) study where generalisation was seen in the presence of a phonological assembly deficit, although this could not be replicated in studies by Waldron and colleagues (Waldron *et al.*, 2011a, 2011b). There is, however, some evidence that people who have semantic deficits do show generalisation to the naming of untreated words when therapy involves semantic tasks and the tasks focus explicitly on differences between items (Nickels and Best 1996b; Kiran and Thompson 2003). Where strategies are developed, improvement is more likely for both treated and untreated stimuli. Some generalisation to untreated words in written word retrieval has also been reported (e.g. Rapp and Kane 2002) following therapy with more peripheral impairments, e.g. in the graphemic output buffer (e.g. Rapp and Kane 2002), mirroring Franklin *et al.*'s (2002) study targeting the phonological output buffer. Generalisation of therapy effects in auditory comprehension show similar patterns, with therapy targeting peripheral processes (e.g. Morris *et al.*, 1996) more likely to result in improvement in both treated and untreated words than therapies which operate at a lexical level where improvement has been found to be item specific.

From a clinical perspective, the dominant finding of improvement due to reactivation being item specific leads to the need for clinicians, with the client and family, to choose personally relevant words for therapy to maximise the functional impact for the client (e.g. Hillis, 1998; McKelvey *et al.*, 2010) across all domains, e.g. spoken word retrieval to everyday speaking, written word retrieval to everyday writing and single-word reading to functional reading (see Renvall, Nickels & Davidson, 2013a, 2013b, for insightful discussions on sourcing functional and personally relevant items and topics for therapy). Renvall, Nickels & Davidson (2013a) also draw attention to the high frequency of other word categories, such as adjectives, adverbs and pronouns, in addition to nouns and verbs, to promote even greater representation of words in therapy that are used most frequently in everyday life.

Aside from personally relevant and high frequency functional items, however, there is a real issue: how do we ensure that skills learned in therapy have an impact on the real-life, day-to-day communication of a person with aphasia? Are the words learned in the clinic used in real-life situations? Is it the case that only skills learned in 'real-life situations' result in real-life improvement? While we are not aware of evidence to support this latter question, clinicians will agree that aphasia therapy rests on an implicit belief that gains seen in therapy will ultimately contribute to more effective communication. Even though therapy frequently involves eliciting highly non-contextualised linguistic or cognitive behaviours, there is a conviction that these provide a foundation for the skills that a client will require in daily life (see Carragher, Conroy, Sage & Wilkinson, 2012, for a review of this literature, particularly with regard to conversation). A number of studies have looked at word retrieval in tasks used in clinic and conversational contexts and found promising signs of generalisation or change.

Herbert *et al.* (2008), for example, explicitly targeted a specific set of items in both naming and communicative contexts and showed that scores on picture naming were related to word-retrieval measures in conversation, a finding supported by others (Hickin *et al.*, 2006; Green-wood *et al.*, 2010; Best *et al.*, 2011). Best, Greenwood, Grassly and Hickin (2008) also found improved participation in everyday activities and interaction following therapy for spoken word retrieval. Boo and Rose (2011), in their study aimed at improving access to verbs, found improved informativeness in conversation overall, demonstrating impact beyond the constrained task to communication in context.

Other studies have addressed the impact of therapy by combining approaches where the theoretically motivated treatment is used in conjunction with more functional activities, e.g. using a combination of individually delivered Copy and Recall Treatment (CART) for written production and group therapy where structured conversations directly facilitate the use of the target words (Clausen & Beeson, 2003). Panton and Marshall (2008) also used a combined therapy approach which focused on the underlying impairment and on the development of strategies to explicitly improve note taking in the client's workplace, attributing the success of therapy to both the attention to the impairment and to the functional aspiration. Robson *et al.* (1998), after finding no generalisation to written word forms in a communicative context, subsequently focused their therapy on the functional nature of the task and demonstrated improvement following this. Robson *et al.* viewed their initial therapy phase, focused only on the impairment, as necessary but not sufficient; therapy focusing on 'generalisation' or communicative contexts was also needed. What immediately emerges here as a dilemma for clinicians and researchers alike is the question of measurement and how to assess generalisation in more naturalistic contexts. This is exemplified in the study by Herbert *et al.* (2003) (see Chapter 11) where lexical therapy which targeted a specific set of items was combined with communicative use of those items, described by the authors as 'a lexical approach with an interactional approach' (2003, p. 1178). In order to measure outcome both at the single-word level and in a more communicative context, a finding seen in five of their six clients, novel assessments were developed, with varying levels of sensitivity, to capture the use of nouns in everyday communication along with a questionnaire of client's views. The dilemma of measuring across contexts is a clear challenge for the future.

Therapy in a broader context

We have, from the outset, acknowledged the broader communication environment as fundamental to planning and delivering intervention. While developments in studies motivated by cognitive neuropsychology provide us with some guiding principles for therapy, there are numerous other factors that impact on the therapy process. These affect both the course and the outcome of therapy, and need to be taken into account. A number of these are linked to principles of neuroplasticity (see Pulvermuller & Berthier, 2008) although not all. While it is not the intention of this final chapter to provide a comprehensive discussion of all factors that might impact on aphasia therapy (see Raymer *et al.*, 2008, for a comprehensive discussion of many of these), some of the factors we wish to draw attention to are set out below.

Dosage and intensity of therapy

The quantity of therapy a client has, both in terms of total hours and the intensity in which it is delivered, is a significant consideration (e.g. Bhogal, Teasell & Speechley, 2003; Basso, 2005; Cherney *et al.*, 2008). A meta-analysis of aphasia therapy found that 2 or more hours of treatment per week resulted in greater change than treatment delivered in lower dosage across a longer period (Robey, 1998). As Somerville (1974) pointed out, far too many treatment studies involve therapy given in 'homeopathic doses'. We would only anticipate significant improvement with enough therapy, but often very little treatment is available to people with aphasia both in the UK and in other countries (Enderby & Petheram, 2002; Katz *et al.*, 2000). Some of the studies reviewed in Part 3 do, however, show specific targeted improvements with relatively little intervention (in terms of therapist time), giving grounds for optimism. In other areas of aphasia therapy, particular approaches recommend specific schedules of intensity. An example of this is Constraint Induced Language Therapy (CILT), a therapy aiming to constrain other forms of communication in favour of verbal output, where Pulvermüller *et al.* (2001) recommend 3 hours per day for 10 days. We would advocate high productivity wherever possible to stimulate access to language processes and optimise the time spent in therapeutic interaction.

Medium of delivery

Therapy can be 'delivered' in many different ways: in one-to-one sessions with a trained therapist, in groups, as home practice, with a computer, by working with a friend, family member or volunteer, or remotely by telephone or over the internet. Each of these has different advantages and drawbacks, but the variety of methods, used creatively, offer some means of ensuring that people with aphasia can get a reasonable amount of treatment. The use of technology and computers is seen across the therapy domains, but perhaps more so in word retrieval (e.g. Best *et al.*, 1997) and in reading (e.g. Arguin & Bub, 1994). Computers, the internet and 'apps' running on tablets will, we are sure, become increasingly used as a way of delivering more intensive practice with treatment tasks. Currently there are a variety of computer-based programmes available commercially (see e.g. Aphasia Software Finder, http://www.aphasiatavistocktrust.org); we note that almost none of these have any direct evidence of their effectiveness, which is disappointing. In contrast, Cherney and colleagues' careful development of treatment programmes delivered by a computerised 'avatar' therapist, gathering data on treatment effectiveness, offers a model of a disciplined way of delivering therapy through computers (Cherney, 2010; Lee, Fowler, Rodney, Cherney & Small, 2010).

Motivation

Therapy will probably be most effective, and certainly most useful, if the person with aphasia is involved as a motivated, active participant, aiming towards goals that make sense in their real lives (e.g. Hillis, 1998). As a corollary of this, therapy usually needs to have 'face validity'; it needs to appear to be directed towards real-life goals. So, for example, although De Partz (1986) may be correct to emphasise that relearning grapheme-to-phoneme correspondences for reading should first be practised with nonwords, some people with aphasia may reject this approach because their aim is to relearn how to read real words. The social imperative or salience of therapy, defined by Raymer *et al.* (2008) as 'the perceived value or relevance of the experience to the participant' (p. S267), is closely associated with motivational levels and should be considered alongside language processing goals; salience will not only promote engagement in therapy but is considered a crucial variable influencing outcome of therapy (see Raymer *et al.*, 2008, for more complete discussion).

Neurological stability

Neurological changes in the early periods of spontaneous recovery are important determinants of outcome. The early period after the onset of aphasia is a time of rapid and confusing change, of multiple therapies and of huge social adjustment to a changed social role. Therapy during this period may have to be rather differently organised to build upon and enhance the neurological changes (Huber, Springer & Willmes, 1993; Robey, 1998; Holland & Fridriksson, 2001). Notwithstanding evidence of improvement in aphasia in the very early period post-stroke as a result of treatment (e.g. Godecke, Hird, Laylor, Rai & Phillips, 2011), it is no accident that most of the studies reviewed in Part 3 are from clients in the post-acute stage (with the notable exception of Grayson *et al.*, 1997). Practically, it is much easier to demonstrate specific therapy effects when the results are not clouded by rapid changes in many domains, but this is also a period when people with aphasia may be ready to put substantial effort into systematic language therapy.

Other non-language functions

Non-linguistic cognitive abilities and disabilities may be important determinants of therapy outcomes (Helm-Estabrooks, 2002). These may include semantic and episodic memory (Swinburn *et al.*, 2005), non-verbal reasoning ability (Bailey, Powell & Clark, 1981), attention (Lapointe & Erickson, 1991; Laures, Odell & Coe, 2003), executive problem solving difficulties (Lambon Ralph, Snell, Fillingham, Conroy and Sage, 2010) and ability to learn (Ferguson, 1999; Fillingham, Hodgson, Sage & Lambon Ralph, 2003). Lambon Ralph *et al.* (2010) have shown that performance on tests of cognition is one of the predictors, with language, for improvement following therapy for word retrieval. There is already some evidence that has found, by targeting the co-occurring cognitive deficits, improvement is seen on primarily linguistic activities (e.g. Coelho, 2005; Salis, 2012). In addition, many people with aphasia are (not surprisingly) depressed following a stroke (Huff, Ruhrmann & Sitzer, 2001; Kauhanen *et al.*, 2000) and this may affect their ability to benefit from treatment. Current knowledge of the impact of these factors remains fragmentary (see Basso, 2003), however, with a growing awareness of their importance, they are likely to be considered to a greater level in future studies.

The therapeutic relationship/contribution of the therapist

While many of the components of therapy can be specified and monitored (e.g. therapy goals, target items), the therapy process itself involves subtle and probably highly important interactions between the client and therapist at many different levels (Byng & Black, 1995). Just as therapists differ immensely in their therapy 'style', we suspect that there are some therapists who are better at making their clients better, as accounts of aphasia and its therapy often attest (see, for example, Hale, 2002). The interaction between the attributes and skills of the therapist and the therapy itself are less tangible, and therefore less measureable, but should be considered a critical part of the therapeutic process.

There are, clearly, multiple factors affecting therapy outcomes which almost certainly interact. Teasing them apart and determining their importance will be a complex process, but is a process that is essential for deciding on the right (i.e. optimally effective in addressing their real-life goals) therapy methods for individual people with aphasia, and for deciding how services should be organised.

Further insights from neurology

At the neurological level, how and why therapy might work is an important issue (e.g. Musso *et al.*, 1999). It is now clear that behavioural change and neurological change are related; functional changes are reflected at a structural level (e.g. Rijntjes & Weiller, 2002; Saur, Lange, Baumgaertner *et al.*, 2006). There is an extensive and interesting literature in this area, but as far as we are aware, there are no findings to date that constrain or inform the practice of aphasia therapy. There are also some very interesting preliminary findings on how techniques that seek to modify cell connectivity by external electromagnetic stimulation in particular areas might change the recovery from aphasia, or the ability of people with aphasia to benefit from treatment. Several forms of non-invasive brain stimulation have been examined as a means to change brain function and thereby promote neuroplasticity (Webster, Celnik & Cohen, 2006; Plow, Carey, Nudo & Pascual-Leone, 2009). The techniques most commonly used in stroke rehabilitation include repetitive transcranial magnetic stimulation (rTMS) and anodal or cathodal transcranial direct current stimulation (tDCS), delivered to the ipsilesional, or contralesional hemisphere. The aim is to either increase ipsilesional excitability or decrease contralesional excitability.

Following stroke, the functional improvement from non-invasive brain stimulation methods alone is, however, reported to be only 10% to 30% and is short-lasting (Hummel & Cohen, 2006; Talelli & Rothwell, 2006; Webster *et al.*, 2006). In the search for more effective and longer-lasting interventions, the combination of rehabilitation and brain stimulation does seem reasonable. Animal studies, for instance, have shown that the combination of peripheral and central stimulation enhances synaptic plasticity more than central stimulation alone (Fritsch *et al.*, 2010). Brain stimulation, while not a complete therapy in itself, does show promise as an adjunct to other therapies and may magnify therapeutic outcomes. Particular focus has rested on tDCS as it is portable, non-expensive, safe (lower risk of seizures than TMS) and involves a relatively simple set-up. These features make tDCS a putative candidate for home treatment as an add-on to behavioural training or even as a substitutive therapy for pharmacological treatments. The small number of aphasia studies that have applied TMS or tDCS to investigate its therapeutic effects—primarily on speech production—have obtained mixed, albeit mostly positive, results. For example, to examine whether right hemisphere activation in aphasia is correlating with the recovery process, more recent studies have focused on facilitating the left or inhibiting the right inferior frontal gyrus, to test whether short term improvements in language can be observed (Baker, Rorden & Fridriksson, 2010; Fridriksson, Richardson, Baker & Rorden, 2011; Weiduschat *et al.*, 2011). In addition, several reports (Vines, Norton & Schlaug, 2011, Medina *et al.*, 2012) have described therapies that specifically engage or stimulate the homologous right hemisphere regions, primarily in patients who have extensive left hemisphere brain damage which might have the potential to facilitate the language recovery process beyond the limitations of natural recovery.

Using these non-invasive methods in clinical practice could bring enormous gains for the treatment of aphasia. See Aphasiology (Special Issue, Volume 26, 2012) for a review of this exciting new field of neuromodulation through primarily non-invasive cortical stimulation techniques to enhance recovery and supplement the effects of aphasia rehabilitation (Holland & Crinion, 2012).

Refining the therapy process through cognitive neuropsychology

While keeping these factors affecting the outcomes of therapy in mind, there are, we believe, some very important advantages in adopting a cognitive neuropsychological approach to treatment. As our earlier discussion highlighted, of primary importance is that, when based on good assessment, this approach is framed by knowledge of the client's strengths and weaknesses in language processing. This gives the therapist the specific knowledge to allow him or her to develop therapy that builds upon and develops the strengths, and that addresses (or avoids) the impaired processes. Secondly, development of therapy for single clients, or for a small series of clients, means that the content and form of the therapy needs to be described very precisely. This has meant that the content of therapy, as well as its aims and intended mechanisms of change, can be brought into the realm of enquiry. This is in radical contrast to the large-scale group studies of aphasia therapy where a variety of different techniques (never described in any detail – because it would be impossible to do so) are used with a very heterogeneous group of people with aphasia. The problem in these instances is that, even where the therapy is found to be effective, it is impossible for anyone else to use the same (effective) therapy due to it not being described in any detail (Howard, 1986). It is only when therapy is described in, using Coltheart's (1983) term, 'cookbook detail' that we can build from studies that show therapy to be effective. This difficulty is not, however, a problem with RCTs themselves. It is possible to design and conduct therapy experiments with clearly defined and replicable 'treatment proto-cols' and with clearly defined and appropriate outcome measures.

Furthermore, cognitive neuropsychological studies invariably, by the nature of the approach, use *targeted* therapy aiming to cause improvement in *specific* language functions. The result is that outcome measures can assess improvement in just those tasks (or just those items) where therapy is intended to produce an effect; they may, as we have seen, be con-trasted with tasks or items where effects of treatment are not anticipated. The result is that therapy can be given a 'fair' test: did it result in improvement in just those tasks (or items) where improvement was anticipated?

Finally, these studies allow us to begin to think about *why* therapy works – what is the underlying mechanism resulting in behavioural change? In most cases, therapy studies clearly state why it is that the therapy tasks *should* result in the changes anticipated. It is much rarer though to find clear and specific evidence that these truly *are* the mechanisms; even where a therapy can be shown to be effective, it is not always clear that it is effective for the reasons supposed. To refer again to the example with word-retrieval impairments, 'semantic therapy' has been seen as improving semantic representations, and lexical/pho-nological therapy as improving access to lexical representations for output. This is because these correspond to the clients' identified underlying deficits, and they were what were tar-geted in therapy. Howard's (2000) argument, however, that the available evidence supports the view that both sets of therapy methods, despite their superficial differences, were effec-tive for the same reason, i.e. they paired semantic and phonological word representations and strengthened the links between them, challenges this view. Which of these perspectives is correct is unclear; importantly, though, adopting a cognitive neuropsychological perspective makes debates about such issues possible.

In more practical terms, adopting a cognitive neuropsychological approach requires the therapist to think clearly about three things. First, on the basis of the assessment results, the clinician must identify *why* performance in language tasks is breaking down. Secondly, in the process of treatment, the therapist needs to be clear *why* doing a particular task should result in change. Third, the clinician should be able to answer the question: *why* would improve-ment in this task make a difference to the participant's real-life communication. In short, it provides the therapist with the theoretical and practical framework to be able to live up to Schuell, Jenkins and Jimenez-Pabon's (1964) exhortation that 'A good therapist should never be taken unawares by the question, 'Why are you doing this?'' (p. 333).

The future of cognitive neuropsychology and aphasia

When the first edition of this volume was published, we set out two ways in which we thought studies of aphasia therapy should develop over the next few years. While these continue to challenge us, we have a few more to add. The first of these was the need to continue to refine and develop our knowledge of how the effectiveness of particular therapy methods relates to the client's pattern of aphasia. Over the last 30 years, we have made enormous strides in our ability to identify levels of breakdown within motivated and theoretically explicit models of language processing. The result is a much improved ability to identify both impaired processes and intact processes. The second challenge was to then decide what therapy approach to adopt with a client. There are, crudely, two possible approaches that we outlined. The first approach is to base the decision on some theoretical or logical understanding of how the therapy works and who it is appropriate for. There are a number of examples of this. For instance, Nickels' 'autocue' therapy (self-generated phonemic cues for word retrieval) is, she argues, appropriate for clients who (i) benefit from phonemic cues and (ii) know about the initial letter of words that they cannot produce in written form. Similarly, Miceli, Armitrano, Capasso and Caramazza (1996) believe that their 'lexical therapy' is appropriate for clients with post-semantic impairments in word retrieval. The difficulty here is that these beliefs about how specific therapies work may turn out to be wrong. As we have discussed, Howard (2000) argues that the evidence suggests that both 'semantic' and 'lexical' (or 'phonological') therapies for word retrieval may work in the same way and for the same types of clients through pairing meanings with phonological forms. Whether this argument is correct is, for the moment, immaterial. The point is that how therapies operate can only really be determined empirically by proper hypothesis testing. In particular, it requires applying a therapy both to those for whom it is believed to be appropriate and those for whom it is not (see Nettleton and Lesser, 1991).

The second perhaps more productive approach to this, however, is probably, as we have seen in some of the studies reported here, to conduct studies that compare the degree of improvement for different kinds of clients with one kind of treatment. When a case series approach is adopted, each participant can be analysed as a single case, making it possible to use homogeneity tests to examine if there are significant differences among the participants in the size of the treatment effects (Howard, 2003). Where there are differences, these can be related to the forms of deficit (see Best *et al.*, 2002) or the severity of the deficit (see (Conroy *et al.*, 2009a, 2009b). By continuing to conduct studies involving more than one client, we exploit the diversity among clients and building our theoretical understanding of how and why people with aphasia respond in different ways to treatment approaches, progressing our understanding of both the approaches and aphasia.

Furthermore, we need studies that compare the effectiveness of different therapies for one client. Most of the studies we have reviewed consider only one treatment approach. When the participant shows improvement, this is obviously a gratifying result, but we do not know if another approach might not have been more effective. Studies of this kind can, therefore, provide critical information about the optimum therapy methods. Moreover, the comparison of different therapy methods can, in the light of knowledge of the participant's underlying deficits, provide critical information about how the treatments are having their effects. To date, a few studies that have adopted this kind of approach (e.g. Hickin *et al.*, 2002; Hillis & Caramazza, 1994; Howard, 2000; Springer, Glindemann, Huber & Willmes, 1991) have shown that this can be productive. Equally, other studies (e.g. Boo & Rose, 2011; Raymer & Ellsworth, 2002) comparing different methods have shown very limited difference in terms of therapy effect within and across participants.

There are, however, a number of further challenges to build on the foundations set over the last 30 or so years. We need to further explore the diversity across severity of aphasia and those with multiple deficits or co-occurring cognitive deficits, often seen as less suitable for a cognitive neuropsychological approach, in order to both extend our knowledge and our impact. We have already begun to examine treatment effects beyond the training tasks themselves, looking to other tasks and contexts, in particular the realm of real-life communication. Exploring the relationship between single words, connected speech and interactive communication presents clear challenges for us all, not just at a cognitive or linguistic level but in relation to clients' and families' own assessment of the impact of our therapy approaches on real-life communication. We consider it axiomatic that the aim of all therapies with people with aphasia is to improve their functioning in the real, social world, to enable them to cope with barriers to participation and fulfilment. In that sense, the therapy methods are embedded in a 'social model' (Byng, Pound & Parr, 2000). These aims can often be addressed through improving language abilities, and it is to this end that the studies in this book are addressed. There is no contradiction between functional, social aims and therapy directed at reducing impairments. In music, one practises scales not because a performance consists of playing scales, but because doing this develops skills that result in better performance. The same applies to therapy directly targeting impaired components of language.

As Basso (2003) argues, we, as therapists, have a responsibility to use the best available knowledge about aphasia and about aphasia therapy in our treatment with people with aphasia. Like Basso, we have argued that the best existing knowledge base is drawn from our understanding of the cognitive neuropsychology of language, and so it is from that field that we have drawn our principles. As Oliver Zangwill (1947) wrote, almost 70 years ago, 'No method of treatment is better than the principles on which it is based, and the search for principles should concern us no less than the immediate clinical situation' (p. 7).

Glossary

Allographic realisation   spatial representations of letters in their different allographic forms (e.g. upper and lower case)

Allographs   a variant form of a grapheme (e.g. 'a' or 'A')

Anomia   delays and failures in word retrieval

Articulatory programming   the conversion of phonemes into neuromuscular commands

Auditory phonological analysis   identifies speech sounds by analysing the string of sounds heard

Brain reorganisation strategies   strategies that aim to encourage alternative parts of the brain to take over the impaired language function

Circumlocution   error responses that indicate access to some intact semantic information in the absence of a phonological representation, e.g. NAIL → 'you bang it into wood'

Cognitive relay strategies   strategies that seek an alternative route or means of performing the language function; that is, use intact components of the language system to achieve the impaired function through indirect means

Compensation strategies   strategies that attempt to maximise the use of retained language and communication behaviours, without focusing on the impaired functions

Conduite d'approche   repeated phonological errors produced during spoken word production; repeated attempts often result in a closer approximation to the target word. Often present due to difficulties with phonological assembly

CT   computerised tomography (also known as computerised axial tomography, or a CAT scan) is a sophisticated radiographic diagnostic technique that produces computerised images of the brain (or body), enabling areas of damage to be identified

CVA   cerebrovascular accident, or stroke, which occurs when there is a rupture or occlusion of a blood vessel in the brain resulting in damage to the surrounding tissue

Direct lexical route for reading   the route involved in reading aloud via a lexical but not semantic route

Direct lexical route for writing   the route involved in writing to dictation via a lexical but not semantic route

Graphemic output buffer   storage of abstract graphemic representations (i.e. case not specified)

Graphemic output lexicon   a store of the spelling of familiar words or written word forms

Graphic-to-motor realisation   translation of allographs to motor patterns

Homophones   words with same phonology but a different meaning (e.g. sail–sale, two–too–to)

Morphological errors   error responses that share at least the root morpheme with the target word but have errors in addition, deletion or substitution of prefixed or suffixed morphemes (e.g. DISCORD → 'concorde', UNREALITY → 'real')

MRI   magnetic resonance imaging scan is a diagnostic technique that uses magnetic fields and computer technology to produce detailed images of the brain (or body); it is more detailed than computerised tomography

Neologisms nonword error responses that do not share sufficient phonemes to be classified as phonological errors

Orthographic input lexicon a store of visual word recognition units; accesses written word forms by recognising the word as a familiar one

Orthographic output lexicon a store of the spelling of familiar words or written word forms

Orthographic-to-phonological conversion (non-lexical reading route) reading aloud via sub-word level orthographic-to-phonological correspondences. It involves the 'sounding out' of graphemes

Phoneme-to-grapheme conversion (non-lexical writing route) writing via the segmentation of a word into phonemes and then translation of the phonemes into graphemes

Phonemic cueing provision of a phonological cue to facilitate production of a word, either by providing a single phoneme (usually the initial) or progressively more phonological information

Phonological assembly the generation of a metrically specified phoneme string for production

Phonological errors error responses that are similar to the target in phonological form. A common criterion for phonological similarity is that at least 50% of the phonemes in the stimulus occur in the error response in approximately the same order

Phonological input lexicon a store of auditory word recognition units; accesses auditory word forms by recognising the word as a familiar one

Phonologically plausible errors errors in reading or writing that are an appropriate production for the phonology of the word

Phonological output lexicon a store of spoken word forms; provides access to spoken word forms

Reactivation approaches therapy that aims to reactivate access to impaired language and processing

Relearning approaches therapy that aims to re-teach impaired language procedures or knowledge

Semantic cueing provision of semantic information to facilitate production of a word

Semantic errors error responses that are semantically related to the target (e.g. NAIL → 'screw')

Semantic lexical route for reading the route involved in the reading aloud of words via access to their meaning

Semantic lexical route for writing the route involved in the writing of words via access to their meaning

Semantic system a store of word meanings

Substitution strategies strategies that encourage the adoption of an external prosthesis to promote communication

Visual errors reading errors that are similar to the target in orthographic form

Visual orthographic analysis identifies letters and codes the position of letters within a word. May be involved in the parsing of letters into graphemes

Visual and semantic errors errors that are both visually and semantically related to the target

Word form deafness a deficit in the phonological input lexicon

Word meaning deafness a deficit in accessing the semantic system from the phonological input lexicon

Word sound deafness a deficit in auditory phonological analysis

References

Ablinger, I. & Domahs, F. (2009). Improved single-letter identification after whole word training in pure alexia. *Neuropsychological Rehabilitation, 19(3),* 340–363.

Abou El-Ella, M. Y., Alloush, T. K., El-Shobary, A. M., El-Dien Hafez, N. G., Abed El-Halimo A. I. & El-Rouby, I. M. (2013). Modification and standardisation of Arabic version of the Comprehensive Aphasia Test. *Aphasiology, 27(5),* 599–614.

Adlam, A. R., Patterson, K., Bozeat, S. & Hodges, J. R. (2010). The Cambridge Semantic Memory Test Battery: detection of semantic deficits in semantic dementia and Alzheimer's disease. *Neurocase: The Neural Basis of Cognition, 16(3),* 193–207.

Albert, M., Sparks, R. & Helm, N. A. (1973). Melodic intonation therapy for aphasia. *Archives of Neurology, 29,* 130–131.

Albert, M. L., Goodglass, H., Helm, N. A., Rubens, A. B. & Alexander, M. P. (1981). *Clinical aspects of dysphasia.* Vienna: Springer-Verlag.

Allport, D. A. (1985). Distributed memory, modular systems and dysphasia. In S. K. Newman & R. Epstein (Eds.), *Current perspectives on dysphasia.* Edinburgh: Churchill Livingstone.

Allport, D. A. & Funnell, E. (1981). Components of the mental lexicon. *Philosophical Transactions of the Royal Society of London, B295,* 397–410.

Arguin, M. & Bub, D. N. (1994). Pure alexia: attempted rehabilitation and its implications for interpretation of the deficit. *Brain and Language, 47,* 233–268.

Baayen, R. H., Piepenbrock, R. & Gulikers, L. (1995). *The CELEX lexical database (Release 2)* [CD-Rom]. Philadelphia, PA: Linguistic Data Consortium, University of Pennsylvania.

Bachy-Langedock, N. & De Partz, M. P. (1989). Co-ordination of two re-organization therapies in a deep dyslexic patient with oral naming disorders. In X. Seron & G. Deloche (Eds.), *Cognitive approaches in neuropsychological rehabilitation.* Hillsdale, New Jersey: Lawrence Erlbaum Associates.

Badecker, W., Hillis, A. E. & Caramazza, A. (1990). Lexical morphology and its role in the writing process: evidence from a case of acquired dysgraphia. *Cognition, 35,* 205–244.

Bailey, S., Powell, G. E. & Clark, E. (1981). A note on intelligence and recovery from aphasia; the relationship between Raven's matrices scores and change on the Schuell aphasia test. *British Journal of Communication Disorders, 16,* 193–203.

Bak, T. & Hodges, J. R. (2003). Kissing and dancing – a test to distinguish the lexical and conceptual contributions to noun/verb and action/object dissociation. Preliminary results in patients with frontotemporal dementia. *Journal of Neurolinguistics, 16,* 169–181.

Baker, J. M., Rorden, C. & Fridriksson, J. (2010). Using transcranial direct-current stimulation to treat stroke patients with aphasia. *Stroke, 41,* 1229–1236.

Barry, C., Morrison, C. M. & Ellis, A. W. (1997). Naming the Snodgrass and Vanderwart pictures. Effects of age of acquisition, frequency and name agreement. *Quarterly Journal of Experimental Psychology: Human Experimental Psychology, 50,* 560–585.

Basso, A. (1989). Spontaneous recovery and language rehabilitation. In X. Seron & G. Deloche (Eds.), *Cognitive approaches in neuropsychological rehabilitation.* Hillsdale, New Jersey: Lawrence Erlbaum Associates.

Basso, A. (2003). *Aphasia and its therapy*. Oxford: Oxford University Press.

Basso, A. (2005). How intensive/prolonged should be an intensive/prolonged treatment be? *Aphasiology, 19 (10/11)*, 975–984.

Basso, A. & Marangolo, P. (2000). Cognitive neuropsychological rehabilitation: the emperor's new clothes? *Neuropsychological Rehabilitation, 10(3)*, 219–229.

Bastiaanse, R., Bosje, M. & Franssen, M. (1996). Deficit-oriented treatment of word-finding problems; another replication. *Aphasiology, 10*, 363–383.

Bastiaanse, R., Bosje, M. & Visch-Brink, E. (1995). *Psycholinguistische Testbatterij voor de Taalverwerking van Afasien Patienten*. London: Psychology Press.

Bastiaanse, R., Edwards, S. & Rispens, J. (2002). *The Verb and Sentence Test (VAST)*. London: Thames Valley Test Publishers.

Bastiaanse, R., Nijober, S. & Taconis, M. (1993). The auditory language comprehension programme: a description and case study. *European Journal of Disorders of Communication, 12*, 415–433.

Beauvois, M. F. & Derouesne, J. (1981). Lexical or orthographic agraphia. *Brain, 104*, 21–49.

Beeson, P. (1999). Treating acquired writing impairment: strengthening graphemic representations. *Aphasiology, 13(9–11)*, 767–785.

Beeson, P., Hirsch, F. M. & Rewega, M. A. (2002). Successful single-word writing treatment: experimental analyses of four cases. *Aphasiology, 16(4–6)*, 473–491.

Beeson, P., Rewega, M. A., Vail, S. & Rapcsak, S. Z. (2000). Problem-solving approach to agraphia treatment: interactive use of lexical and sublexical spelling routes. *Aphasiology, 14(5–6)*, 551–565.

Beeson, P., Rising, K. & Volk, J. (2003). Writing treatment for severe aphasia: who benefits? *Journal of Speech, Language and Hearing Research, 46*, 1038–1060.

Beeson, P. & Robey, R. R. (2006). Evaluating single subject treatment research: lessons learned from the aphasia literature. *Neuropsychological Review, 16*, 161–169.

Behrmann, M. (1987). The rites of righting writing: homophone remediation in acquired dysgraphia. *Cognitive Neuropsychology, 4*, 365–384.

Behrmann, M. & Bub, D. (1982). Surface dyslexia and dysgraphia – dual routes, single lexicon. *Cognitive Neuropsychology, 9*, 209–251.

Behrmann, M. & Byng, S. (1992). A cognitive approach to neurorehabilitation of acquired language disorders. In D. I. Margolin (Ed.), *Cognitive Neuropsychology in Clinical Practice*. Oxford: Oxford University Press.

Behrmann, M. & Lieberthal, T. (1989). Category-specific treatment of a lexical–semantic deficit: a single case study of global aphasia. *British Journal of Disorders of Communication, 24*, 281–299.

Belin, P., Van Eeckhout, P., Zilbovicius, M., Remy, P., Francois, C., Guillaume, S., Chain, F., Rancurel, G. & Samson, Y. (1996). Recovery from non-fluent aphasia after melodic intonation therapy: a PET study. *Neurology, 47*, 1504–1511.

Berndt, R. S., Haendiges, A. N., Burton, M. & Mitchum, C. C. (2002). Grammatical class and imageability in aphasic word production: their effects are independent. *Journal of Neurolinguistics, 15*, 353–371.

Berndt, R. S., Haendiges, A. N., Mitchum, C. C. & Sandson, J. (1997). Verb retrieval in aphasia: II. Relationship to sentence processing. *Brain and Language, 56*, 107–137.

Berndt, R. S. & Mitchum, C. C. (1994). Approaches to the rehabilitation of 'phonological assembly': elaborating the model of non-lexical reading. In G. Humphreys & M. J. Riddoch (Eds.), *Cognitive neuropsychology and cognitive rehabilitation*. London: Lawrence Erlbaum Associates.

Best, W. (1995). A reverse length effect in dysphasic naming: when elephant is easier than ant. *Cortex, 31*, 637–652.

Best, W., Greenwood, A., Grassly, J. & Hickin, J. (2008). Bridging the gap: can impairment based therapy for anomia have an impact at the psychosocial level? *International Journal of Language & Communication Disorders, 43(4)*, 390–407.

Best, W., Greenwood, A., Grassly, J., Hickin, J., Herbert, R. & Howard, D. (2013). Aphasia rehabilitation: does generalisation from anomia therapy occur and is it predictable? A case series study. *Cortex, 49(9)*, 2345–2357.

Best, W., Herbert, R., Hickin, J., Osborne, F. & Howard, D. (2002). Phonological and orthographic facilitation of word-retrieval in aphasia: immediate and delayed effects. *Aphasiology, 16* (1/2), 151–168.

Best, W., Howard, D., Bruce, C. & Gatehouse, C. (1997). Cueing the words: a single case study of treatments for anomia. *Neuropsychological Rehabilitation, 7(2)*, 105–141.

Bhogal, S. K., Teasell, R. & Speechley, M. (2003). Intensity of aphasia therapy, impact on recovery. *Stroke, 34,* 987–992.

Bigland, S. & Speake, J. (1992). *Semantic links.* Northumberland: STASS Publications.

Bird, H., Franklin, S. & Howard, D. (2002). 'Little words' – not really: function and content words in normal and aphasic speech. *Journal of Neurolinguistics, 15,* 209–237.

Bird, H., Howard, D. & Franklin, S. (2000). Why is a verb like an inanimate object? Grammatical category and semantic category deficits. *Brain and Language, 72,* 246–309.

Bird, H., Howard, D. & Franklin, S. (2003). Verbs and nouns: the importance of being imageable. *Journal of Neurolinguistics, 16(2–3),* 113–149.

Boo, M. & Rose, M. L. (2011). The efficacy of repetition, semantic, and gesture treatments for verb retrieval and use in Broca's aphasia. *Aphasiology, 25 (2),* 154–175.

Booth, S. & Perkins, L. (1999). The use of conversation analysis to guide individualised advice to carers and evaluate change in aphasia: a case study. *Aphasiology, 13,* 283–303.

Booth, S. & Swabey, D. (1999). Group training in communication skills for carers of adults with aphasia. *International Journal of Language and Communication Disorders, 34,* 291–309.

Boutard, C. (2001). The contribution of computers to dysphasia and dyslexia therapy. *ANAE-Approche Neuropsychologique Des Apprentissages Chez L Enfant, 13 (2–3),* 141–143.

Boyle, M. (2010). Semantic Feature Analysis treatment for aphasic word retrieval impairments: what's in a name? *Topics in Stroke Rehabilitation, 17 (6),* 411–422.

Boyle, M. & Coelho, C. A. (1995). Application of a semantic feature analysis as a treatment for aphasic dysnomia. *American Journal of Speech and Language Pathology, 4,* 94–98.

Brady, M. C., Kelly, H., Godwin, J. & Enderby, P. (2012). Speech and language therapy for aphasia following stroke. *Cochrane Database of Systematic Reviews* (Vol. Issue 5. Art. No: CD000425).

Breedin, S. D., Saffran, E. M. & Coslett, H. B. (1994). Reversal of concreteness effect in a patient with semantic dementia. *Cognitive Neuropsychology, 11,* 617–660.

Brodeur, M. B., Dionne-Dostie, E., Montreuil, T. & Lepage, M. (2010). The Bank of Standardized Stimuli (BOSS), a new set of 480 normative photos of objects to be used as visual stimuli in cognitive research. *PLoS ONE, 5(5),* (e10773).

Bruce, C. & Howard, D. (1987). Computer generated phonemic cueing: an effective aid for naming in aphasia. *British Journal of Disorders of Communication, 22,* 191–201.

Brumfitt, S. (1993). Losing your sense of self: what aphasia can do. *Aphasiology, 7,* 569–575.

Bryant, P. E. & Bradley, L. (1985). *Children's reading problems: psychology and education.* Oxford: Blackwell.

Bub, D., Cancelliere, A. & Kertesz, A. (1985). Whole-word and analytic translation of spelling to sound in a non-semantic reader. In K. Patterson, J. Marshall & M. Coltheart (Eds.), *Surface dyslexia: neuropsychological and cognitive studies of phonological reading.* London: LEA.

Bub, D. & Kertesz, A. (1982). Deep agraphia. *Brain and Language, 17,* 146–165.

Byng, S. (1988). Sentence processing deficits: theory and therapy. *Cognitive Neuropsychology, 5,* 629–676.

Byng, S. & Black, M. (1995). What makes a therapy? Some parameters of therapeutic intervention in aphasia. *European Journal of Disorders of Communication, 30,* 303–316.

Byng, S. & Coltheart, M. (1986). Aphasia therapy research: methodological requirements and illustrative results. In R. Hjelmquist & L. B. Nilsson (Eds.), *Communication and handicap.* Amsterdam: Elsevier.

Byng, S., Pound, C. & Parr, S. (2000). Living with aphasia: a framework for therapy interventions. In I. Papathanasiou (Ed.), *Acquired neurological communication disorders: a clinical perspective.* London: Whurr.

Capitani, E., Laiacona, M., Mahon, B. & Caramazza, A. (2003). What are the facts of semantic category-specific deficits? A critical review of the clinical evidence. *Cognitive Neuropsychology, 20*, 213–261.

Caplan, D. & Bub, D. (1990). Psycholinguistic assessment of aphasia. Paper presented at the American Speech and Hearing Association Conference, Seattle, WA.

Caplan, D., Vanier, M. & Baker, C. (1986). A case study of reproduction aphasia. 1: word production. *Cognitive Neuropsychology, 3(1)*, 99–128.

Caramazza, A. (1986). On drawing inferences about the structure of normal cognitive systems from the analysis of patterns of impaired performance: the case for single patient studies. *Brain and Cognition, 5*, 41–66.

Caramazza, A. (1989). Cognitive neuropsychology and rehabilitation: an unfulfilled promise? In X. Seron & G. Deloche (Eds.), *Cognitive Approaches in Neuropsychological Rehabilitation* (pp. 383–398). Hillsdale, New Jersey: Lawrence Erlbaum Associates.

Caramazza, A. & Hillis, A. E. (1990). Where do semantic errors come from? *Cortex, 26*, 95–122.

Caramazza, A. & Mahon, B. (2003). The organization of conceptual knowledge: the evidence from category-specific semantic deficits. *Trends in Cognitive Sciences, 7*, 354–361.

Castro, S. L., Caló, S. & Gomes, I. (2007). *PALPA-P – Provas de Avaliação da Linguagem e da Afasia em Português*. Hove: Erlbaum.

Chall, J. S. (1983). *Stages of reading development*. New York: McGraw-Hill.

Chapey, R. (1981). Divergent semantic intervention. In R. Chapey (Ed.), *Language intervention strategies in adult aphasia*. Baltimore: Williams & Wilkins.

Chapey, R. (1981). *Language intervention strategies in adult aphasia*. Baltimore, MD.: Williams & Wilkins.

Chapey, R., Duchan, J., Elman, R. J., Garcia, L. J., Kagan, A., Lyon, J. & Simmons-Mackie, N. (2008). Life-participation approach to aphasia: a statement of values for the future. In R. Chapey (Ed.), *Language intervention strategies in aphasia and related neurogenic communication disorders* (5th edn, pp. 278–289). Philadelphia: Lippincott, Williams and Wilkins.

Cherney, L. R. (2010). Oral Reading for Language in Aphasia (ORLA): evaluating the efficacy of computer-delivered therapy in chronic nonfluent aphasia. *Topics in Stroke Rehabilitation, 17(6)*, 423–431.

Cherney, L. R., Patterson, J.P., Raymer, A., Frymark, T. & Schooling, T. (2008). Evidence-based systematic review: effects of intensity of treatment and constraint-induced language therapy for individuals with stroke-induced aphasia. *Journal of Speech Language and Hearing Research, 51(5)*, 1282–1299.

Clark, E. (1993). *The lexicon in acquistion*. Cambridge: Cambridge University Press.

Clausen, N. S. & Beeson, P. M. (2003). Conversational use of writing in severe aphasia: a group treatment approach. *Aphasiology, 17*, 625–644.

Code, C. & Herrmann, M. (2003). The relevance of emotional and psychosocial factors in aphasia to rehabilitation. *Neuropsychological Rehabilitation, 13(1–2)*, 109–132.

Coelho, C. A. (2005). Direct attention training as a treatment of reading impairment in aphasia. *Aphasiology, 19(3/4/5)*, 275–283.

Coelho, C. A., McHugh, R. E. & Boyle, M. (2000). Semantic feature analysis as a treatment for aphasic dysnomia. *Aphasiology, 14*, 133–142.

Cole-Virtue, J. & Nickels, L. (2004). Why cabbage and not carrot? An investigation of factors affecting performance on spoken word to picture matching. *Aphasiology, 18*, 153–179.

Coltheart, M. (1980a). Deep dyslexia: a right hemisphere hypothesis. In M. Coltheart, K. Patterson & J. C. Marshall (Eds.), *Deep dyslexia*. London: Routledge.

Coltheart, M. (1980b). The semantic error: types and theories. In M. Coltheart, K. E. Patterson & J. C. Marshall (Eds.), *Deep dyslexia*. London: Routledge and Kegan Paul.

Coltheart, M. (1981). The MRC psycholinguistic database. *Quarterly Journal of Experimental Psychology, 33(A)*, 497–505.

Coltheart, M. & Byng, S. (1989). A treatment for surface dyslexia. In X. Seron & G. Deloche (Eds.), *Cognitive approaches in neuropsychological remediation*. New York: Lawrence Erlbaum Associates.

Coltheart, M., Langdon, R. & Haller, M. (1996). Computational cognitive neuropsychology and reading. In B. Dodd, L. Worrall & R. Campbell (Eds.), *Models of language: illuminations from impairment*. London: Whurr Publishers.

Coltheart, M., Rastle, K., Perry, C., Langdon, R. & Ziegler, W. (2001). DRC: a dual route cascaded model of visual word recognition and reading aloud. *Psychological Review, 108*, 204–256.

Conroy, P., Sage, K. & Lambon Ralph, M. A. (2006). Towards theory-driven therapies for aphasic verb impairments: a review of current theory and practice. *Aphasiology, 20(12)*, 1159–1185.

Conroy, P., Sage, K. & Lambon Ralph, M. A. (2009a). A comparison of word versus sentence cues as therapy for verb naming in aphasia. *Aphasiology, 23(4)*, 462–482.

Conroy, P., Sage, K. & Lambon Ralph, M. A. (2009b). The effects of decreasing and increasing cue therapy on improving naming speed and accuracy for verbs and nouns in aphasia. *Aphasiology, 23(6)*, 707–730.

Conroy, P., Sage, K. & Lambon Ralph, M. A. (2009c). Errorless and errorful therapy for verb and noun naming in aphasia. *Aphasiology, 23(11)*, 1311–1337.

Conway, T. W., Heilman, P., Rothi, L. J. G., Alexander, A. W., Adair, J., Crosson, B. A. & Heilman, K. M. (1998). Treatment of a case of phonological alexia with agraphia using the Auditory Discrimination in Depth (ADD) Program. *Journal of the International Neuropsychological Society, 4(6)*, 608–620.

Crawford, J. R., Garthwaite, P. H. & Porter, S. (2010). Point and interval estimates of effect sizes for case-controls design in neuropsychology: rationale, methods, implementations, and proposed reporting standards. *Cognitive Neuropsychology, 27(3)*, 245–260.

Cruice, M., Worrall, L. & Hickson, L. M. H. (200). Quality of life measurement in speech pathology and audiology. *Asia Pacific Journal of Speech, Language and Hearing, 5(1)*, 1–20.

Cubelli, R., Foresti, A. & Consolini, T. (1988). Re-education strategies in conduction aphasia. *Journal of Communication Disorders, 21(3)*, 239–249.

Cunningham, R. (1998). Counselling someone with severe aphasia: an explorative case study. *Disability and Rehabilitation, 20(9)*, 346–354.

Cutler, A. (1981). The reliability of speech error data. *Linguistics, 19*, 561–582.

De Haan, E. H. F. (2001). Face perception and recognition. In B. Rapp (Ed.), *The handbook of cognitive neuropsychology: what deficits reveal about the human mind*. Philadelphia: Psychology Press.

De Partz, M., Seron, X. & Van der Linden, M. (1992). Re-education of a surface dysgraphia with a visual imagery strategy. *Cognitive Neuropsychology, 9*, 369–401.

De Partz, M. P. (1986). Re-education of a deep dyslexic patient: rationale of the method and results. *Cognitive Neuropsychology, 3*, 149–177.

DeDe, G., Parris, D. & Waters, G. (2003). Teaching self-cues: a treatment approach for verbal naming. *Aphasiology, 17(5)*, 465–480.

Dell, G. S., Nozari, N. & Oppenhiem, G. M. (in press). Word production: behavioural and computational considerations. *Oxford Handbook of Language*. Oxford: Oxford University Press.

Dell, G. S., Schwartz, M. F., Martin, N., Saffran, E. & Gagnon, D. A. (1997). Lexical access in aphasic and nonaphasic speakers. *Psychological Review, 104*, 801–838.

Deloche, G., Dordan, M. & Kremins, H. (1993). Rehabilitation of confrontation naming in aphasia: Relations between oral and written modalities. *Aphasiology, 7*, 201–216.

Destreri, N. D., Farina, E., Alberoni, M., Pomati, S., Nichelli, P. & Mariani, C. (2000). Selective uppercase dysgraphia with loss of visual imagery of letter forms: a window on the organization of graphomotor patterns. *Brain and Language, 71*, 353–372.

Druks, J. & Masterson, J. (2000). *An object and action naming battery*. London: Taylor & Francis.

Edwards, S. & Tucker, K. (2006). Verb retrieval in fluent aphasia: a clinical study. *Aphasiology, 20(7)*, 644–675.

Edwards, S., Tucker, K. & McCann, C. (2004). The contribution of verb retrieval to sentence construction: a clinical study. *Brain and Language, 91*, 78–79.

Ellis, A. W., Flude, B. M. & Young, A. W. (1987). 'Neglect dyslexia' and the early visual processing of letters in words. *Cognitive Neuropsychology, 4*, 439–464.

Ellis, A. W. & Morrison, C. M. (1998). Real age-of-acquisition effects in lexical retrieval. *Journal of Experimental Psychology: Learning, Memory and Cognition*, 24, 515–523.

Enderby, P. & Petheram, B. (2002). Has aphasia therapy been swallowed up? *Clinical Rehabilitation*, *16*, 604–608.

Farah, M. J. (1990). *Visual agnosia: disorders of object recognition and what they tell us about normal vision*. Cambridge, MA: MIT Press.

Farah, M. J. & Wallace, M. (1991). Pure alexia as a visual impairment: a reconsideration. *Cognitive Neuropsychology, 8*, 313–334.

Faroqi-Shah, Y. & Thompson, C. K. (2012). Approaches to treatment of agrammatism. In R. Bastiaanse & C. K. Thompson (Eds.), *Perspectives on agrammatism*. Hove, East Sussex: Psychology Press.

Ferguson, A. (1999). Learning in aphasia therapy: it's not so much what you do, but how you do it! *Aphasiology, 13*, 125–132.

Fillingham, J. K., Hodgson, C., Sage, K. & Lambon Ralph, M. A. (2003). The application of errorless learning to aphasic disorders: a review of theory and practice. *Neuropsychological Rehabilitation, 13*, 337–363.

Fillingham, J. K., Sage, K. & Lambon Ralph, M. A. (2005). Further explorations and an overview of errorless and errorful therapy for aphasic word-finding difficulties: the number of naming attempts during therapy affects outcome. *Aphasiology, 19(7)*, 597–614.

Fillingham, J. K., Sage, K. & Lambon Ralph, M. A. (2006). The treatment of anomia using errorless learning. *Neuropsychological Rehabilitation, 16(2)*, 129–154.

Fink, R. B., Martin, N., Schwartz, M. F., Saffran, E. M. & Myers, J. L. (1992). Facilitation of verb retrieval skills in aphasia: a comparison of two approaches. *Clinical Aphasiology, 21*, 263–275.

Foygel, D. & Dell, G. S. (2000). Models of impaired lexical access in speech production. *Journal of Memory and Language, 43*, 182–216.

Francis, D. R., Clark, N. & Humphreys, G. W. (2002). Circumlocution-induced naming (CIN): a treatment for effecting generalisation in anomia? *Aphasiology, 16(3)*, 243–259.

Francis, D. R., Riddoch, M. J. & Humphreys, G. W. (2001a). Cognitive rehabilitation of word meaning deafness. *Aphasiology, 15(8)*, 749–766.

Francis, D. R., Riddoch, M. J. & Humphreys, G. W. (2001b). Treating agnosic alexia complicated by additional impairments. *Neuropsychological Rehabilitation, 11(2)*, 113–145.

Franklin, S. (1989). Dissociations in auditory word comprehension; evidence from nine fluent aphasic patients. *Aphasiology, 3(3)*, 189–207.

Franklin, S. (1995). Designing single case treatment studies for aphasic patients. *Neuropsychological Rehabilitation, 7*, 401–418.

Franklin, S., Buerk, F. & Howard, D. (2002). Generalised improvement in speech production for a subject with reproduction conduction aphasia. *Aphasiology*, 16, 1087–1114.

Franklin, S., Howard, D. & Patterson, K. (1995). Abstract word anomia. *Cognitive Neuropsychology*, 12 (549–566).

Franklin, S., Howard, D. & Patterson, K. E. (1994). Abstract word meaning deafness. *Cognitive Neuropsychology, 11*, 1–34.

Franklin, S., Turner, J., Lambon Ralph, M. A., Morris, J. & Bailey, P. J. (1996). A distinctive case of word meaning deafness? *Cognitive Neuropsychology, 13(8)*, 1139–1162.

Franklin, S., Turner, J. M. & Ellis, A. W. (1992). *The ADA Comprehension Battery*. London: Action for Dysphasic Adults.

Fridriksson, J., Richardson, J. D., Baker, J. M. & Rorden, C. (2011). Transcranial direct current stimulation improves naming reaction time in fluent aphasia: a double-blind, sham-controlled study. *Stroke, 42*, 819–821.

Friedman, R. B. & Lott, S. N. (1996). Phonologic treatment for deep dyslexia using bigraphs instead of graphemes. *Brain and Language, 55(1)*, 116–119.

Friedman, R. B. & Lott, S. N. (2000). Rapid word identification in pure alexia is lexical but not semantic. *Brain and Language, 72*, 219–237.

Friedman, R. B. & Lott, S. N. (2002). Successful blending in a phonological reading treatment for deep alexia. *Aphasiology, 16(3)*, 355–372.

Friedman, R. B., Sample, D. M. & Lott, S. N. (2002). The role of level of representation in the use of paired associate learning for rehabilitation of alexia. *Neuropsychologia, 40 (2)*, 223–234.

Frith, U. (1986). A developmental framework for developmental dyslexia. *Annals of Dyslexia, 36*, 69–81.

Fritsch, B., Reis, J., Martinowich, K., Schambra, H. M., Ji, Y., Cohen, L. G. *et al.* (2010). Direct current stimulation promotes BDNF-dependent synaptic plasticity: potential implications for motor learning. *Neuron, 66*, 198–204.

Fujibayashi, M., Nagatsuka, N., Yoshida, T., Howard, D., Franklin, S. & Whitworth, A. (2004). *SALA shitsugoshou kensa: Sophia Analysis of Language in Aphasia*. Sophia University, Tokyo.

Funnell, E. (1983). Phonological processes in reading: new evidence from acquired dyslexia. *British Journal of Psychology, 74*, 159–180.

Funnell, E. (1987). Morphological errors in acquired dyslexia: a case of mistaken identity. *Quarterly Journal of Experimental Psychology, 39A*, 497–538.

Gernsbacher, M. A. (1984). Resolving 20 years of inconsistent interactions beyween lexical familiarity and orthography, concreteness and polysemy. *Journal of Experimental Psychology: General, 113*, 256.

Gielewski, E. J. (1989). Acoustic analysis and auditory retraining in the remediation of sensory aphasia. In C. Code & D. Muller (Eds.), *Aphasia Therapy. Second Edition*. London: Whurr Publishers Ltd.

Gonzalez Rothi, L. J., Musson, N., Rosenbek, J. & Sapienza, C. M. (2008). Neuroplasticity and rehabilitation research for speech, language and swallowing disorders. *Journal of Speech, Language and Hearing Research, 51*, 222–224.

Goodglass, H. & Kaplan, E. (*1983*). *The assessment of aphasia and related disorders (second edition)*. Philadelphia: Lea and Febiger.

Goodglass, H., Kaplan, E. & Barresi, B. (2001). *Boston Diagnostic Aphasia Examination (third edition)*. Philadephia: Lippincott, Williams and Wilkins.

Goodglass, H., Kaplan, E. & Weintraub, S. (2001). *The Boston Naming Test*. Philadelphia: Lippincott, Williams & Wilkins.

Goral, M. & Kempler, D. (2009). Training verb production in communicative context: evidence from a person with chronic non-fluent aphasia. *Aphasiology, 23(12)*, 1383–1397.

Gough, P. B. (1996). How children learn to read and why they fail. *Annals of Dyslexia, 46*, 3–20.

Grant, D. A. & Berg, E. A. (1993). *Wisconsin Card Sorting Test*. New York: Psychological Assessment Resources Inc.

Grayson, E., Hilton, R. & Franklin, S. E. (1997). Early intervention in a case of jargon aphasia: efficacy of language comprehension therapy. *European Journal of Disorders of Communication, 32*, 257–276.

Green, G. (1982). Assessment and treatment of the adult with severe aphasia: aiming for functional generalisation. *Australian Journal of Human Communication Disorders, 10*, 11–23.

Greener, J., Enderby, P. & Whurr, R. (1999). Speech and language therapy for aphasia following stroke. *Cochrane Database of Systematic Reviews* (Vol. Issue 4. Art. No.: CD000425.).

Greenwald, M. L., Raymer, A. M., Richardson, M. E. & Rothi, L. J. G. (1995). Contrasting treatments for severe impairments of picture naming. *Neuropsychological Rehabilitation, 5*, 17–49.

Greenwald, M. L. & Rothi, L. J. G. (1998). Lexical access via letter naming in a profoundly alexic and anomic patient: a treatment study. *Journal of the International Neuropsychological Society, 4(6)*, 595–607.

Greenwood, A., Grassly, J., Hickin, J. & Best, W. (2010). Phonological and orthographic cueing therapy: a case of generalised improvement. *Aphasiology, 24(9)*, 991–1016.

Hall, D. A. & Riddoch, M. J. (1997). Word meaning deafness: spelling words that are not understood. *Cognitive Neuropsychology, 14*, 1131–1164.

Harley, T. (2004). Does cognitive neuropsychology have a future? *Cognitive Neuropsychology, 21*, 3–16.

Hatfield, F. & Patterson, K. (1983). Phonological spelling. *Quarterly Journal of Experimental Psychology, 35A*, 451–468.

Hatfield, F. & Shewell, C. (1983). Some applications of linguistics to aphasia therapy. In C. Code & D. J. Muller (Eds.), *Aphasia therapy*. London: Edward Arnold.

Hatfield, F. M. (1983). Aspects of acquired dysgraphia and implications for remediation. In C. Code & D. J. Muller (Eds.), *Aphasia therapy*. London: Arnold.

Helm-Estabrooks, N. (2002). Cognition and aphasia: a discussion and a study. *Journal of Communication Disorders*, 35, 171–186.

Helm-Estabrooks, N., Fitzpatrick, P. M. R. & Baresi, B. (1982). Visual action therapy for global aphasics. *Journal of Speech and Hearing Disorders*, 47, 385–389.

Herbert, R., Best, W., Hickin, J., Howard, D. & Osbourne, F. (2003). Combining lexical and interactional approaches to therapy for word finding deficits in aphasia. *Aphasiology*, 17(12), 1163–1186.

Herbert, R., Hickin, J., Howard, D., Osbourne, F. & Best, W. (2008). Do picture-naming tests provide a valid assessment of lexical retrieval in conversation in aphasia? *Aphasiology*, 22(2), 184–203.

Hersch, D. (1998). Beyond the 'plateau': discharge dilemmas in chronic aphasia. *Aphasiology*, 12, 207–243.

Hickin, J., Best, W., Herbert, R., Howard, D. & Osbourne, F. (2002). Phonological therapy for word-finding difficulties: a re-evaluation. *Aphasiology*, 16, 981–999.

Hillis, A. E. (1989). Efficacy and generalisation of treatment for aphasic naming errors. *Archives of Physical Medicine and Rehabilitation*, 70, 632–636.

Hillis, A. E. (1993). The role of models of language processing in rehabilitation of language impairments. *Aphasiology*, 7, 5–26.

Hillis, A. E. (1998). Treatment of naming disorders: new issues regarding old therapies. *Journal of the International Neuropsychological Society*, 4, 648–660.

Hillis, A. E. & Caramazza, A. (1991). Mechanisms for accessing lexical representations for output: evidence from a category-specific semantic deficit. *Brain and Language*, 40, 106–144.

Hillis, A. E. & Caramazza, A. (1994). Theories of lexical processing and rehabilitation of lexical deficits. In M. J. Riddoch & G. E. Humphreys (Eds.), *Cognitive neuropsychology and cognitive rehabilitation*. London: Lawrence Erlbaum Associates.

Hillis, A. E. & Caramazza, A. (1995). Converging evidence for the interaction of semantic and phonological information in accessing lexical representations for spoken output. *Cognitive Neuropsychology*, 12, 187–227.

Hillis, A. E., Rapp, B., Romani, C. & Caramazza, A. (1990). Selective impairment of semantics in lexical processing. *Cognitive Neuropsychology*, 7(3), 191–243.

Hinton, G. E., McClelland, J. L. & Rumelhart, D. E. (1986). Distributed representations. In D. E. Rumelhart & J. L. McClelland (Eds.), *Parallel Distributed Processing*. London: Bradford Books.

Hodges, J. R., Patterson, K., Oxbury, S. & Funnell, E. (1992). Semantic dementia – progressive fluent aphasia with temporal lobe atrophy. *Brain*, 115, 1783–1806.

Holland, A. (2007). Counselling/coaching in chronic aphasia: getting on with life. *Topics in Language Disorders*, 27(4), 339–350.

Holland, A. & Fridriksson, J. (2001). Aphasia management during the early phases of recovery following stroke. *American Journal of Speech–Language Pathology*, 10(1), 19–28.

Holland, A. L. (1982). Observing functional communication of aphasic adults. *Journal of Speech and Hearing Disorders*, 47, 50–56.

Holland, R. & Crinion, J. (2012). Can tDCS enhance treatment of aphasia after stroke? *Aphasiology*, 26(9), 1169–1191.

Horton, S. & Byng, S. (2002). 'Semantic therapy' in day to day clinical practice: perspectives on diagnosis and therapy related to semantic impairments in aphasia. In A. E. Hillis (Ed.), *The handbook of language disorders: integrating cognitive neuropsychology, neurology and rehabilitation*. London: Psychology Press.

Howard, D. (1985). The semantic organisation of the lexicon: evidence from aphasia. Unpublished PhD Thesis, University of London.

Howard, D. (1986). Beyond randomised controlled trials; the case for effective case studies of the effects of treatment in aphasia. *British Journal of Communication Disorders*, 21, 89–102.

Howard, D. (1995). Lexical anomia: or the case of the missing lexical entries. *Quarterly Journal of Experimental Psychology, 48*, 999–1023.

Howard, D. (2000). Cognitive neuropsychology and aphasia therapy: the case of word retrieval. In I. Papathanasiou (Ed.), *Acquired neurogenic communication disorders*. London: Whurr Publishers.

Howard, D. (2003). Single cases, group studies and case series in aphasia therapy. In I. Papathanasiou & R. De Bleser (Eds.), *The sciences of aphasia: from therapy to theory*. Oxford: Pergamon Press.

Howard, D. & Franklin, S. (1988). *Missing the meaning*. Cambridge, MA: MIT Press.

Howard, D. & Harding, D. (1998). Self-cueing of word retrieval by a woman with aphasia: why a letter board works. *Aphasiology, 12*, 399–420.

Howard, D. & Hatfield, F. M. (1987). *Aphasia therapy: historical and contemporary issues*. London: Lawrence Erlbaum Associates.

Howard, D. & Nickels, L. (2005). Separating input and output phonology: semantic, phonological and orthographic effects in short term memory impairment. Cognitive *Neuropsychology, 22*, 42–77.

Howard, D. & Orchard-Lisle, V. (1984). On the origin of semantic errors in naming: evidence from a case of global aphasia. *Cognitive Neuropsychology, 1*, 163–190.

Howard, D. & Patterson, K. (1989). Models for therapy. In X. Seron & G. Deloche (Eds.), *Cognitive approaches in neuropsychological rehabilitation*. Hillsdale, NJ: Lawrence Erlbaum Associates.

Howard, D., Patterson, K., Franklin, S., Orchard-Lisle, V. & Morton, J. (1985a). The facilitation of picture naming in aphasia. *Cognitive Neuropsychology, 2*, 49–80.

Howard, D., Patterson, K., Franklin, S., Orchard-Lisle, V. & Morton, J. (1985b). Treatment of word retrieval deficits in aphasia: a comparison of two therapy methods. *Brain, 108*, 817–829.

Howard, D. & Patterson, K. E. (1992). *The Pyramids and Palm Trees Test*. Bury St. Edmunds: Thames Valley Test Corporation.

Howard, D., Swinburn, K. & Porter, G. (2010). Putting the CAT out: what the Comprehensive Aphasia Test has to offer. *Aphasiology, 24(1)*, 56–74.

Howard, D., Best, W. & Nickels, L. (submitted). Optimising the design of intervention studies: critiques and ways forward.

Huber, W., Springer, L. & Willmes, K. (1993). Approaches to aphasia therapy in Aachen. In A. Holland & F. Forbes (Eds.), *Aphasia treatment: world perspectives*. San Diego, CA: Singular Publishing Group.

Huff, W., Ruhrmann, S. & Sitzer, M. (2001). Post-stroke depression: diagnosis and therapy. *Fortschritte der Neurologie Psychiatrie, 69*, 581–591.

Hummel, F. C. & Cohen, L. G. (2006). Non-invasive brain stimulation: a new strategy to improve neurorehabilitation after stroke?. *Lancet Neurology, 5*, 708–712.

Humphreys, G. W. & Riddoch, M. J. (1987). *To see but not to see; a case study of visual agnosia*. London: LEA.

Jones, E. V. (1989). A year in the life of EVJ and PC. Paper presented at the British Aphasiology Society, Cambridge.

Kagan, A., Simmons-Mackie, N., Rowland, A., Huijbregts, M., Shumway, E., McEwen, S., Sharp, S. (2008). Counting what counts: a framework for capturing real-life outcomes of aphasia intervention. *Aphasiology, 22(3)*, 258–280.

Kaplan, E., Goodglass, G. & Weintraub, S. (2001). *The Boston Naming Test*. Maryland: Lippincott, Williams and Wilkins.

Katz, R., Hallowell, B., Code, C., Armstrong, E., Roberts, P., Pound, C. & Katz, L. (2000). A multinational comparison of aphasia management practices. *International Journal of Language & Communication Disorders, 35*, 303–314.

Katz, R. C. (2010). Computers in the treatment of chronic aphasia. *Semin Speech Lang, 31(1)*, 34–41.

Kauhanen, M. L., Korpelainen, J. T., Hiltunnen, P., Maata, R., Mononen, H., Brusin, E., Myllyla, V. V. (2000). Aphasia, depression and non-verbal cognitive impairment in ischaemic stroke. *Cerebrovascular Diseases, 10*, 455–461.

Kay, J. & Ellis, A. W. (1987). A cognitive neuropsychological case study of anomia: implications for psychological models of word retrieval. *Brain, 110*, 613–629.

Kay, J., Lesser, R. & Coltheart, M. (1992). *PALPA: Psycholinguistic Assessments of Language Processing in Aphasia.* Hove: Lawrence Erlbaum Associates.

Kelly, H., Brady, M. C. & Enderby, P. (2010). Speech and language therapy for aphasia following stroke. *Cochrane Database of Systematic Reviews* (Vol. Issue 5. Art. No.: CD000425).

Kempler, D. & Goral, M. (2011). A comparison of drill- and communication-based treatment for aphasia. *Aphasiology, 25(6),* 563–599.

Kendall, D. L., McNeil, M. R. & Small, S. L. (1998). Rule-based treatment for acquired phonological dyslexia. *Aphasiology, 12(7–8),* 587–600.

Kim, M. & Beaudoin-Parsons, D. (2007). Training phonological reading in deep alexia: does it improve reading words with low imageability? *Clinical Linguistics & Phonetics, 21(5),* 321–351.

Kiran, S. & Thompson, C. K. (2003). The role of semantic complexity in treatment of naming deficits: training semantic categories in fluent aphasia by controlling exemplar typicality. *Journal of Speech, Language and Hearing Research, 46,* 608–622.

Kucera, H. & Francis, W. N. (1967). *A computational analysis of present day American English.* Providence, RI: Brown University Press.

Laine, M. & Martin, N. (2012). Cognitive neuropsychology has been, is and will be significant to aphasiology. *Aphasiology, 26(11),* 1362–1376.

Lambon Ralph, M. A., Graham, K. S., Ellis, A. W. & Hodges, J. R. (1998). Naming in semantic dementia – what matters? *Neuropsychologia, 36,* 775–784.

Lambon Ralph, M. A. & Howard, D. (2000). Gogi aphasia or semantic dementia? Simulating and assessing poor verbal comprehension in a case of progressive fluent aphasia. *Cognitive Neuropsychology, 17,* 437–465.

Lambon Ralph, M. A., Snell, C., Fillingham, J. K., Conroy, P. & Sage, K. (2010). Predicting the outcome of anomia therapy for people with aphasia post CVA: both language and cognitive status are key predictors. *Neuropsychological Rehabilitation, 20(2),* 289–305.

Lapointe, L. L. & Erickson, R. J. (1991). Auditory vigilance during divided task attention in aphasic individuals. *Aphasiology, 5,* 511–520.

Le Dorze, G., Boulay, N., Gaudrea, J. & Brassard, C. (1994). The contrasting effects of a semantic versus a formal semantic technique for the facilitation of naming in a case of anomia. *Aphasiology, 8,* 127–141.

Lee, J., Fowler, R., Rodney, D., Cherney, L. R. & Small, S. L. (2010). IMITATE: an intensive computer-based treatment for aphasia based on action observation and imitation. *Aphasiology, 24(4).*

Leonard, C., Rochon, E. & Laird, L. (2008). Treating naming impairments in aphasia: findings from a phonological components analysis treatment. *Aphasiology, 22(9),* 923–947.

Lesser, R. (1990). Superior oral to written spelling – evidence for separate buffers. *Cognitive Neuropsychology, 7,* 347–366.

Lesser, R. & Milroy, L. (1993). Linguistics and aphasia; *Psycholinguistic and pragmatic aspects of intervention.* London: Longman.

Lesser, R. & Perkins, L. (1999). *Cognitive neuropsychology and conversation analysis in aphasia: an introductory case-book.* London: Whurr Publishers.

Levelt, W. J. M., Roelofs, A. & Meyer, A. S. (1999). A theory of lexical access in speech production. *Behavioral and Brain Sciences, 22,* 1–45.

Lindamood, C. H. & Lindamood, P. C. (1975). *Auditory discrimination in depth.* Allen, Texas: DLM Teaching Resources.

Lomas, J., Pickard, L., Bester, S., Elbard, H., Finlayson, A. & Zoghaib, C. (1989). The communicative effectiveness index: development and psychometric evaluation of a functional communication measure for adult aphasia. *Journal of Speech and Hearing Disorders, 54,* 113–124.

Lott, S. N. & Friedman, R. B. (1999). Can treatment for pure alexia improve letter-by-letter reading speed without sacrificing accuracy. *Brain and Language, 67,* 188–201.

Lott, S. N., Friedmann, R. B. & Linebaugh, C. W. (1994). Rationale and efficacy of a tactile–kinesthetic treatment for alexia. *Aphasiology, 8(2),* 181–195.

Lowell, S., Beeson, P. & Holland, A. (1995). The efficacy of semantic cueing procedures on naming performance of adults with aphasia. *American Journal of Speech–Language Pathology, 4,* 99–104.

Luce, P. A. & Large, N. R. (2001). Phonotactics, density and entropy in spoken word recognition. *Language and Cognitive Processes, 16*, 565–581.

Luce, P. A., Pisoni, D. B. & Goldinger, S. D. (1990). Similarity neighbourhoods of spoken words. In G. Altmann (Ed.), *Cognitive models of speech processing; psycholinguistic and computation perspectives*. Cambridge, MA: MIT Press.

Ludlow, C. L., Hoit, J., Kent, R., Ramig, L. O., Shrivastav, R., Strand, E., Sapienza, C. M. (2008). Translating principles of neural plasticity into research on speech motor control recovery and rehabilitation. *Journal of Speech, Language and Hearing Research, 51*, 240–258.

Luria, A. R. (1970). *Traumatic aphasia*. The Hague: Mouton.

Luzzatti, C., Colombo, C., Frustaci, M. & Vitolo, F. (2000). Rehabilitation of spelling along the sub-word-level routine. *Neuropsychological Rehabilitation, 10(3)*, 249–278.

Maher, L. M., Ckayton, M. C., Barrett, A. M., Schober-Peterson, D. & Rothi, L. J. G. (1998). Rehabilitation of a case or pure alexia: Exploiting residual abilities. *Journal of the International Neuropsychological Society, 4(6)*, 595–607.

Maneta, A., Marshall, J. & Lindsay, J. (2001). Direct and indirect therapy for word sound deafness. *International Journal of Language & Communication Disorders, 36(1)*, 91–106.

Marcel, A. J. & Patterson, K. (1978). Word recognition and production: reciprocity in clinical and normal studies. In J. Requin (Ed.), *Attention and performance VII*. Hillsdale, NJ: Lawrence Erlbaum Associates.

Marcotte, K. & Ansaldo, A. I. (2010). The neural correlates of semantic feature analysis in chronic aphasia: discordant patterns according to the etiology. *Seminars in Speech and Language, 31(1)*, 52–63.

Marshall, J. (1999). Doing something about a verb impairment: two therapy approaches. In S. Byng, K. Swinburn & C. Pound (Eds.), *The aphasia therapy file*. Hove: Psychology Press.

Marshall, J. (2013). Disorders of sentence processing in aphasia. In I. Papathanasiou, P. Coppens & C. Potagas (Eds.), *Aphasia and related neurogenic communication disorders*. Burlington, MA: Jones and Bartlett Learning.

Marshall, J., Chiat, S., Robson, J. & Pring, T. (1996). Calling a salad a federation: an investigation of semantic jargon. 2: Verbs. *Journal of Neurolinguistics, 9*, 251–260.

Marshall, J., Pound, C., White-Thompson, M. & Pring, T. (1990). The use of picture/word matching to assist word retrieval in aphasic patients. *Aphasiology, 4*, 185–195.

Marshall, J., Pring, T. & Chiat, S. (1998). Verb retrieval and sentence production in aphasia. *Brain and Language, 63(2)*, 159–183.

Marshall, J. C. & Newcombe, F. (1966). Syntactic and semantic errors in paralexia. *Neuropsychologia, 4*, 169–176.

Marshall, J. C. & Newcombe, F. (1973). Patterns of paralexia: a psycholinguistic approach. *Journal of Psycholinguistic Research, 2*, 175–199.

Marslen-Wilson, W. (1987). Functional parallelism in spoken word recognition. *Cognition, 25*, 71–102.

Martin, N., Dell, G. S., Saffran, E. & Schwartz, M. F. (1994). Origins of paraphasias in deep dysphasia – testing the consequences of a decay impairment to an interactive spreading activation model of lexical retrieval. *Brain and Language, 47*, 609–660.

Martin, N., Thompson, C. & Worrall, L. (2007). *Contemporary approaches to aphasia rehabilitation: consideration of the impairment and its consequences*. Plural Publishing Inc.

Matthews, C. (1991). Serial processing and the 'phonetic route'. Lessons learned in the functional reorganisation of deep dyslexia. *Journal of Communication Disorders, 24*, 21–39.

Matzig, S., Druks, J., Masterson, J. & Vigliocco, G. (2009). Noun and verb differences in picture naming: past studies and new evidence. *Cortex, 45*, 738–758.

McCann, C. & Doleman, J. (2011). Verb retrieval in nonfluent aphasia: a replication of Edwards & Tucker, 2006. *Journal of Neurolinguistics, 24(2)*, 237–248.

McCann, R. S. & Besner, D. (1987). Reading pseudohomophones – implications for models of pronunciation assembly and the locus of word frequency effects in naming. *Journal of Experimental Psychology: Human Perception and Performance, 13*, 14–24.

McCann, R. S., Besner, D. & Davelaar, E. (1988). Word recognition and identification – do word frequency effects reflect lexical access. *Journal of Experimental Psychology: Human Perception and Performance, 14*, 693–706.

McKenna, P. (1998). *The category-specific names test*. Hove, UK: Psychology Press.

McKenna, P. & Warrington, E. K. (1983). *The graded naming test*. Berkshire: NFER-Nelson.

Medina, J., Norise, C., Faseyitan, O., Coslett, H. B., Turkeltaub, P. E. & Hamilton, R. H. (2012). Finding the right words: transcranial magnetic stimulation improves discourse productivity in nonfluent aphasia after stroke. *Aphasiology, 26(9)*, 1153–1168.

Metsala, J. & Ehri, L. (1998). *Word recognition in beginning reading*. Hillsdale, NJ: LEA.

Miceli, G., Amitrano, A., Capasso, R. & Caramazza, A. (1996). The treatment of anomia resulting from output lexical damage: analysis of two cases. *Brain and Language, 52*, 150–174.

Miceli, G., Silveri, M. C. & Caramazza, A. (1985). Cognitive analysis of a case of pure dysgraphia. *Brain and Language, 25*, 187–212.

Miceli, G., Silveri, M. C. & Caramazza, A. (1987). The role of the phoneme-to-grapheme conversion system and of the graphemic output buffer in writing. In M. Coltheart, G. Sartori & R. Job (Eds.), *The cognitive neuropsychology of language*. London: LEA Ltd.

Mitchum, C. C. & Berndt, R. (1991). Diagnosis and treatment of the non-lexical route in acquired dyslexia: an illustration of the cognitive neuropsychological approach. *Journal of Neurolinguistics, 6*, 103–137.

Mitchum, C. C. & Berndt, R. S. (1994). Verb retrieval and sentence construction: effects of targeted intervention. In M. J. Riddoch & G. W. Humphreys (Eds.), *Cognitive neuropsychology and cognitive rehabilitation*. East Sussex: Lawrence Erlbaum Associates.

Mitchum, C. C. & Berndt, R. S. (1995). The cognitive neuropsychological approach to treatment of language disorders. *Neuropsychological Rehabilitation, 5(1–2)*, 1–16.

Mitchum, C. C. & Berndt, R. S. (2001). Cognitive neuropsychological approaches to diagnosing and treating language disorders: production and comprehension of sentences. In R. Chapey (Ed.), *Language intervention strategies in aphasia and related neurogenic communication disorders* (pp. 551–571). Baltimore, MD: Williams and Wilkins.

Monsell, S. (1987). On the relation between lexical input and output pathways. In D. A. Allport, D. MacKay, W. Prinz & E. Scheerer (Eds.), *Language perception and production: common processes in listening, speaking, reading and writing*. London: Academic Press.

Morris, J. & Franklin, S. (1995). Assessment and remediation of a speech discrimination deficit in a dysphasic patient. In M. Perkins & S. Howard (Eds.), *Case studies in clinical linguistics*. London: Whurr.

Morris, J. & Franklin, S. (2012). Investigating the effect of a semantic therapy on comprehension in aphasia. *Aphasiology, 26(12)*, 1461–1480.

Morris, J., Franklin, S., Ellis, A. W., Turner, J. E. & Bailey, P. J. (1996). Remediating a speech perception deficit in an aphasic patient. *Aphasiology, 10(2)*, 137–158.

Morris, J., Webster, J., Whitworth, A. & Howard, D. (2009). Newcastle University aphasia therapy resources: auditory processing. University of Newcastle upon Tyne.

Mortley, J., Enderby, P. & Petheram, B. (2001). Using a computer to improve functional writing in a patient with severe dysgraphia. *Aphasiology, 15(5)*, 443–461.

Morton, J. (1969). The interaction of information in word recognition. *Psychological Review, 76*, 165–178.

Morton, J. (1979b). Facilitation in word recognition: Experiments causing change in the logogen model. In P. Kolers, M. Wrolstad & H. Bouma (Eds.), *Processing of visible language*. New York: Plenum Press.

Morton, J. (1979a). Word recognition. In J. Morton & J. C. Marshall (Eds.), *Psycholinguistics (Vol. 2)*. London: Elek.

Morton, J. & Patterson, K. E. (1980). A new attempt at an interpretation, or, an attempt at a new interpretation. In M. Coltheart, K. E. Patterson & J. C. Marshall (Eds.), *Deep dyslexia*. London: Routledge and Kegan Paul.

Moss, A. & Nicholas, M. (2006). Language rehabilitation in chronic aphasia and time postonset: a review of single-subject data. *Stroke, 37*(*12*), 3043–3051.

Musso, M., Weiller, C., Kiebel, S., Muller, S. P., Bulau, P. & Rijintjes, M. (1999). Training induced brain plasticity in aphasia. *Brain, 122*, 1781–1790.

Nettleton, J. & Lesser, R. (1991). Therapy for naming difficulties in aphasia: application of a cognitive neuropsychological model. *Journal of Neurolinguistics, 6*, 139–157.

Newcombe, F. & Marshall, J. (1980). Response monitoring and response blocking in deep dyslexia. In M. Coltheart, K. Patterson & J. C. Marshall (Eds.), *Deep dyslexia*. London: Routledge and Kegan Paul.

Newcombe, F., Oldfield, R. C., Ratcliff, G. G. & Wingfield, A. (1971). Recognition and naming of object–drawings by men with focal brain wounds. *Journal of Neurology, Neurosurgery and Psychiatry, 34*, 329–340.

Nicholas, L. E. & Brookshire, R. H. (1993). A system of quantifying the informativeness and efficiency of the connected speech of adults with aphasia. *Journal of Speech and Hearing Research, 36*, 338–350.

Nickels, L. (1992). The autocue? Self generated phonemic cues in the treatment of a disorder of reading and naming. *Cognitive Neuropsychology, 9*, 155–182.

Nickels, L. (1995). Reading too little into reading – strategies in the rehabilitation of acquired dyslexia. *European Journal of Disorders of Communication, 30*(*1*), 37–50.

Nickels, L. (2001). Spoken word production. In B. Rapp (Ed.), *The handbook of cognitive neuropsychology: what deficits reveal about the human mind*. Philadelphia: Psychology Press.

Nickels, L. (2002a). Improving word finding: practice makes (closer to) perfect? *Aphasiology, 16*, 1047–1060.

Nickels, L. (2002b). Therapy for naming disorders: revisiting, revising and reviewing. *Aphasiology, 16*, 935–980.

Nickels, L. (2008). The hypothesis testing approach to the assessment of language. In B. Stemmer & H. A. Whitaker (Eds.), *Handbook of the neuroscience of language*. Oxford, UK: Elsevier.

Nickels, L. & Best, W. (1996). Therapy for naming disorders (Part II): specifics, surprises and suggestions. *Aphasiology, 10*(*2*), 109–136.

Nickels, L. & Howard, D. (1994). A frequent occurrence? Factors affecting the production of semantic errors in aphasic naming. *Cognitive Neuropsychology, 11*(*3*), 289–320.

Nickels, L. & Howard, D. (1995a). Aphasic naming – what matters? *Neuropsychologia, 33*, 1281–1303.

Nickels, L. & Howard, D. (1995b). Phonological errors in aphasic naming – comprehension, monitoring and lexicality. *Cortex, 31*, 209–237.

Nickels, L. & Howard, D. (2000). When the words won't come: relating impairments and models of spoken word production. In L. R. Wheeldon (Ed.), *Aspects of language production*. Hove, UK: Psychology Press.

Nickels, L. & Howard, D. (2004). Dissociating effects of number of phonemes, number of syllables and syllabic complexity on word production in aphasia; it's the number of phonemes that counts. *Cognitive Neuropsychology, 21*, 57–78.

Nickels, L., Kohnen, S. & Biedermann, B. (2010). An untapped resource: treatment as a tool for revealing the nature of cognitive processes. *Cognitive Neuropsychology, 27*(*7*), 539–562.

Nozari, N. K., A.K., Dell, G. S. & Schwartz, M. F. (2010). Naming and repetition in aphasia: steps, routes and frequency effects. *Journal of Memory and Language, 63*, 541–559.

Oppenhiem, G. M., Dell, G. S. & Schwartz, M. F. (2010). The dark side of incremental learning: a model of cumulative semantic interference during lexical access in speech production. *Cognition, 114*(*2*), 227–252.

Panton, A. & Marshall, J. (2008). Improving spelling and everyday writing after a CVA: a single-case therapy study. *Aphasiology, 22*(*2*), 164–183.

Parkin, A. J. (2001). The structure and mechanisms of memory. In B. Rapp (Ed.), *The handbook of cognitive neuropsychology: what deficits reveal about the human mind*. Philadelphia, PA: Psychology Press.

Patterson, K., Purell, C. & Morton, J. (1983). The facilitation of word retrieval in aphasia. In C. Code & D. J. Muller (Eds.), *Aphasia therapy* London: Edward Arnold.

Patterson, K. & Wilson, B. (1990). A rose is a rose or a nose – a deficit in initial letter identification. *Cognitive Neuropsychology, 7*, 447–477.

Patterson, K. E. (1978). Phonemic dyslexia: errors of meaning and the meaning of errors. *Quarterly Journal of Experimental Psychology, 30*, 587–601.

Patterson, K. E. (1979). What is right with 'deep' dyslexic patients? *Brain and Language, 8*, 111–129.

Patterson, K. E. & Kay, J. (1982). Letter-by-letter reading: psychological descriptions of a neurological syndrome. *Quarterly Journal of Experimental Psychology, 34A*, 411–441.

Patterson, K. E. & Marcel, A. J. (1977). Aphasia, dyslexia and the phonological coding of written words. *Quarterly Journal of Experimental Psychology, 29*, 307–318.

Patterson, K. E. & Shewell, C. (1987). Speak and spell: dissociations and word-class effects. In M. Coltheart, R. Job & G. Sartori (Eds.), *The cognitive neuropsychology of language*. Hillsdale, NJ: Lawrence Erlbaum.

Patterson, K. E. & Wilson, B. (1990). A rose is a rose or a nose – a deficit in initial letter identification. *Cognitive Neuropsychology, 7*, 447–477.

Patterson, K. E. & Wing, A. M. (1989). Processes in handwriting – a case for case. *Cognitive Neuropsychology, 6*, 1–23.

Pavan Kumar, V. & Humphreys, G. (2008). The role of semantic knowledge in relearning spellings: evidence from deep dysgraphia. *Aphasiology, 22(5)*, 489–504.

Plaut, D. C. (1999). A connectionist approach to word reading and acquired dyslexia: extension to sequential processing. *Cognitive Science, 23*, 543–568.

Plaut, D. C., McClelland, J. L., Siedenberg, M. & Patterson, K. (1996). Understanding normal and impaired word reading: computational principles in quasi-regular domains. *Psychological Review, 103*, 56–115.

Plaut, D. C. & Shallice, T. (1993). Deep dyslexia: a case study in connectionist neuropsychology. *Cognitive Neuropsychology, 10*, 377–500.

Plow, E. B., Carey, J. R., Nudo, R. J. & Pascual-Leone, A. (2009). Invasive cortical stimulation to promote recovery of function after stroke: a critical appraisal. *Stroke, 40*, 1926–1931.

Pound, C. (1996). Writing remediation using preserved oral spelling: a case for separate output buffers. *Aphasiology, 10*, 283–296.

Pound, C., Parr, S., Lindsay, J. & Woolf, C. (2000). *Beyond aphasia: therapies for living with communication disability*. Oxon: Speechmark Publishing Limited.

Price, C. J. (2001). Functional-imaging studies of the 19(th) century neurological model of language. *Revue Neurologique, 157*, 833–836.

Price, C. J. (2012). A review and synthesis of the first 20 years of PET and fMRI studies of heard speech, spoken language and reading. *NeuroImage, 62(2)*, 816–847.

Price, C. J., Gorno-Tempini, M. L., Graham, K. S., Biggio, N., Mecelli, A., Patterson, K. & Noppeney, U. (2003). Normal and pathological reading: converging data from lesion and impairment studies. *NeuroImage, 20*, S20–S41.

Pring, T., Hamilton, A., Harwood, A. & MacBride, L. (1993). Generalization of naming after picture/word matching tasks: only items appearing in therapy benefit. *Aphasiology, 7 (4)*, 383–394.

Pulvermuller, F. & Berthier, M. L. (2008). Aphasia therapy on a neuroscience basis. *Aphasiology, 22(6)*, 563–599.

Rapp, B. (2005). The relationship between treatment outcomes and the underlying cognitive deficit: evidence from the remediation of acquired dysgraphia. *Aphasiology, 19(10/11)*, 994–1008.

Rapp, B. & Goldrick, M. (2000). Discreteness and interactivity in spoken word production. *Psychological Review, 107*, 460–499.

Rapp, B. & Kane, A. (2002). Remediation of deficits affecting different components of the spelling process. *Aphasiology, 16(4–6)*, 439–454.

Raymer, A., Beeson, P., Holland, A., Kendall, D. L., *et al.* (2008). Translational research in aphasia:

from neuroscience to neurorehabilitation. *Journal of Speech, Language and Hearing Research (51)*, S259–S275.

Raymer, A. M., Ciampitti, M., Holliway, B., Singletary, F., Blonder, L. X., Ketterson, T., Gonzalez Rothi, L. J. (2007). Semantic–phonologic treatment for noun and verb retrieval impairments in aphasia. *Neuropsychological Rehabilitation, 17(2)*, 244–270.

Raymer, A. M., Cudworth, C. & Haley, M. A. (2003). Spelling treatment for an individual with dysgraphia: analysis of generalisation to untrained words. *Aphasiology, 17(6–7)*, 607–624.

Raymer, A. M. & Ellsworth, T. A. (2002). Response to contrasting verb retrieval treatments: a case study. *Aphasiology, 16(10–11)*, 1031–1045.

Raymer, A. M., Singletary, F., Rodriguez, A., Ciampitti, M., Heilman, K. M. & Rothi, L. J. G. (2006). Effects of gesture plus verbal treatment for noun and verb retrieval in aphasia. *Journal of the International Neuropsychological Society, 12(6)*, 867–882.

Renvall, K., Nickels, L. & Davidson, B. (2013a). Functionally relevant items in the treatment of aphasia (Part 1): challenges for current practice. *Aphasiology, 27*, 636–650.

Renvall, K., Nickels, L. & Davidson, B. (2013b). Functionally relevant items in the treatment of aphasia (part II): further perspectives and specific tools. *Aphasiology, 27*, 651–677.

Riddoch & Humphreys. (1993). *The Birmingham Object Recognition Battery*. Hove: Lawrence Erlbaum Associates.

Riddoch, M. J. & Humphreys, G. (2001). Object recognition. In B. Rapp (Ed.), *The handbook of cognitive neuropscyhology: what deficits reveal about the human mind*. Philadephia, PA: Psychology Press.

Riddoch, M. J. & Humphreys, G. W. (1986). Neurological impairments of object constancy: the effects of orientation and size disparities. *Cognitive Neuropsychology, 3*, 207–224.

Rijintjes, M. & Weiller, C. (2002). Recovery of motor and language abilities after stroke: the contribution of functional imaging. *Progress in Neurobiology, 66*, 109–122.

Robey, R. R. (1998). A meta-analysis of clinical outcomes in the treatment of aphasia. *Journal of Speech, Language and Hearing Research, 41*, 172–187.

Robson, J., Marshall, J., Pring, T. & Chiat, S. (1998). Phonological naming therapy in jargon aphasia: positive but paradoxical effects. *Journal of the International Neuropsychological Society, 4*, 675–686.

Robson, J., Pring, P., Marshall, J., Morrison, S. & Chiat, S. (1998). Written communication in undifferentiated jargon aphasia: a therapy study. *International Journal of Language and Communication Disorders, 33*, 305–329.

Rodriguez, A. D., Raymer, A. M. & Gonzalez Rothi, L. J. (2006). Effects of gesture + verbal and semantic–phonologic treatments for verb retrieval in aphasia. *Aphasiology, 20(2/3/4)*, 286–297.

Rogers, T. T., Lambon Ralph, M. A., Garrard, P., Bozeat, S., McClelland, J. L., Hodges, J. R. & Patterson, K. (2004). Structure and deterioration of semantic memory: a neuropsychological and computational investigation. *Psychological Review, 111(1)*, 205–234.

Romani, C. & Calabrese, A. (2000). Syllabic constraints in the phonological errors of an aphasic patient. *Brain and Language, 64*, 83–121.

Rose, M. & Douglas, J. (2008). Treating a semantic word production deficit in aphasia with verbal and gesture methods. *Aphasiology, 22(1)*, 20–41.

Rose, M. & Sussmilch, G. (2008). The effects of semantic and gesture treatments on verb retrieval and verb use in aphasia. *Aphasiology, 22(7&8)*, 691–706.

Rosenbek, J. (2001). Darley and apraxia of speech in adults. *Aphasiology, 15(3)*, 261–273.

Rossion, B. & Pourtois, G. (2004). Revisiting Snodgrass and Vanderwart's object set: the role of surface detail in basic-level object recognition. *Perception, 33*, 217–236.

Ruml, W. & Caramazza, A. (2000). An evaluation of a computational model of lexical access: comment on Dell *et al.* (1997). *Psychological Review, 107*, 609–634.

Sacchett, C. & Humphreys, G. (1992). Calling a squirrel a squirrel but a canoe a wigwam: a category specific deficit for artefactual objects and body parts. *Cognitive Neuropsychology, 9*, 73–86.

Saffran, E. & Coslett, H. B. (1998). Implicit vs. letter by letter reading in pure alexia: a tale of two systems. *Cognitive Neuropsychology, 7*, 1–20.

Sage, K. & Ellis, A. W. (2004). Lexical effects in a case of graphemic output buffer. *Cognitive Neuropsychology*, *21*, 381–400.

Sage, K. & Ellis, A. W. (2006). Using orthographic neighbours to treat a case of graphemic buffer disorder. *Aphasiology*, *20(9/10/11)*, 851–870.

Sage, K., Hesketh, A. & Lambon Ralph, M. A. (2005). Using errorless learning to treat letter-by-letter reading: contrasting word versus letter-based therapy. *Neuropsychological Rehabilitation*, *15(5)*, 619–642.

Sage, K., Snell, C. & Ralph, M. A. L. (2011). How intensive does anomia therapy for people with aphasia need to be? *Neuropsychological Rehabilitation*, *21(1)*, 26–41.

Salis, C. (2012). Short-term memory treatment: patterns of learning and generalisation to sentence comprehension in a person with aphasia. *Neuropsychological Rehabilitation*, *22(3)*, 428–448.

Schmalzl, L. & Nickels, L. (2006). Treatment of irregular word spelling in acquired dysgraphia: selective benefit from visual mnemonics. *Neuropsychological Rehabilitation*, *16(1)*, 1–37.

Schneider, S. L. & Thompson, C. K. (2003). Verb production in agrammatic aphasia: the influence of semantic class and argument structure properties on generalisation. *Aphasiology*, *17(3)*, 213–241.

Schuell, H. M., Jenkins, J. J. & Jimenez-Pabon, E. (1964). *Aphasia in adults: diagnosis, prognosis and treatment*. New York: Harper & Row.

Schwartz, M. F. & Dell, G. S. (2010). Case series investigations in cognitive neuropsychology. *Cognitive Neuropsychology*, *27(6)*, 477–494.

Schwartz, M. F., Dell, G. S., Martin, N. & Saffran, E. (1994). Normal and aphasic naming in an interactive spreading activation model. *Brain and Language*, *47*, 391–394.

Schwartz, M. F., Saffran, E. & Marin, O. S. M. (1980). Fractionating the reading process in dementia: evidence for word-specific print-to-sound associations. In M. Coltheart, K. E. Patterson & J. C. Marshall (Eds.), *Deep dyslexia*. London: Routledge and Kegan Paul.

Scott, C. J. & Byng, S. (1989). Computer assisted remediation of a homophone comprehension disorder in surface dyslexia. *Aphasiology*, *3*, 301–320.

Semenza, C. & Zettin, M. (1988). Generating proper names: a case of selective inability. *Cognitive Neuropsychology*, 5, 711–721.

Seron, X. (1984). Reeducation strategies in neuropsychology: cognitive and pragmatic approaches. In F. Rose (Ed.), *Advances in Neurology, vol 442: Progress in aphasiology*. New York: Raven Press.

Shallice, T. (1981). Phonological agraphia and the lexical route in writing. *Brain*, *104*, 413–429.

Shallice, T. (1988). *From neuropsychology to mental structure*. Cambridge: Cambridge University Press.

Shallice, T. & Warrington, E. K. (1977). Auditory verbal short term memory impairment and conduction aphasia. *Brain and Language*, *4*, 479–491.

Shallice, T. & Warrington, E. K. (1977). The possible role of selective attention in acquired dyslexia. *Neuropsychologia*, *15*, 31–41.

Shankweiler, D. & Liberman, I. Y. (1989). *Phonology and reading disability: solving the reading puzzle*. Ann Arbor: University of Michigan Press.

Share, D. L. & Stanovich, K. E. (1995). Cognitive processes in early reading development: a model of acquisition and individual differences. *Issues in Education: Contributions from Educational Psychology*, *1*, 1–57.

Siedenberg, M. & McClelland, J. L. (1989). A distributed developmental model of word recognition and naming. *Psychological Review*, *96*, 523–568.

Simmons-Mackie, N. & Kagan, A. (2007). Application of the ICF in aphasia. *Seminars in Speech and Language*, *28*, 244–253.

Simmons-Mackie, N., Raymer, A., Armstrong, E., Holland, A. & Cherney, L. R. (2010). Communication partner training in aphasia: a systematic review. *Archives of Physical Medicine and Rehabilitation*, *91(12)*, 1814–1837.

Snodgrass, J. G. & Vanderwart, M. (1980). A standardised set of 260 pictures: norms for name agreement, image agreement, familiarity and visual complexity. *Journal of Experimental Psychology: Human Learning and Memory*, *6(2)*, 174–215.

Spencer, K. A., Doyle, P. J., McNeil, M. R., Wamburgh, J. L., Park, G. & Carroll, B. (2000). Examining the facilitative effects of rhyme in a patient with output lexicon damage. *Aphasiology, 14*, 567–584.

Spreen, O. & Benton, A. L. (1977). *Neurosensory Center Comprehensive Examination for Aphasia (NCCEA)*. Victoria, BC: University of Victoria, Neuropsychology Laboratory.

Stadie, N. & Rilling, E. (2006). Evaluation of lexically and nonlexically based reading treatment in a deep dyslexic. *Cognitive Neuropsychology, 23(4)*, 643–672.

Swinburn, K. & Byng, S. (2006). *The communication disability profile*. London: Connect.

Swinburn, K., Porter, G. & Howard, D. (2004). *The Comprehensive Aphasia Test*. Hove: Psychology Press.

Talelli, P. & Rothwell, J. (2006). Does brain stimulation after stroke have a future? *Current Opinion in Neurology, 19*, 543–550.

Tate, R. L., S., M., Perdices, M., Togher, L. & Schultz, R. (2008). Rating the methodological quality of single-subject designs and *n*-of-1 trials: introducing the Single-Case Experimental Design (SCED) Scale. *Neuropsychological Rehabilitation, 18(4)*, 385–401.

Tessier, C., Weill-Chounlamountry, A., Michelot, N. & Pradat-Diehl, P. (2007). Rehabilitation of word deafness due to auditory analysis disorder. *Brain Injury, 21(11)*, 1165–1174.

Thompson, C. & Faroqi-Shah, Y. (2002). Models of sentence production. In A. E. Hillis (Ed.), *The handbook of adult language disorders: integrating cognitive neuropsychology, neurology, and rehabilitation*. Hove, East Sussex: Psychology Press.

Thompson, C. K. (2006). Single subject controlled experiments in aphasia: the science and the state of the science. *Journal of Communication Disorders, 39*, 266–291.

Thompson, C. K. (2011). *Northwestern Assessment of Verbs and Sentences*. Evanston, Illinois: Northwestern University.

Thompson, C. K., Shapiro, L. P., Kiran, S. & Sobecks, J. (2003). The role of syntactic complexity in treatment of sentence deficits in agrammatic aphasia: the complexity account of treatment efficacy (CATE). *Journal of Speech, Language and Hearing Research, 46*, 591–607.

Turner, S. & Whitworth, A. (2006a). Clinicians' perceptions of candidacy for conversation partner training in aphasia: how do we select candidates for therapy and do we get it right? *Aphasiology, 20(7)*, 616–643.

Turner, S. & Whitworth, A. (2006b). Conversational partner training programmes in aphasia: a review of key themes and participants' roles. *Aphasiology, 20(6)*, 483–510.

Tyler, L. K., Moss, H. E., Durrant-Peatfield, M. R. & Levy, J. P. (2000). Conceptual structure and the structure of concepts: a distributed account of category-specific defcits. *Brain and Language, 75*, 195–231.

Vallar, G. & Shallice, T. (1992). *Neuropsychological impairments of short term memory*. Oxford: Oxford University Press.

Valle, F. & Cuetos, F. (1995). *Evaluacio'n del Procesamiento Linguistico en la Afasia*. London: Psychology Press.

Vigliocco, G., Vinson, D. P., Druks, J., Barber, H. & Cappa, S. F. (2011). Nouns and verbs in the brain: a review of behavioural, electrophysiological, neuropsychological and imaging studies. *Neuroscience and Biobehavioural Reviews, 35*, 407–426.

Vines, B. W., Norton, A. C. & Schlaug, G. (2011). Non-invasive brain stimulation enhances the effects of melodic intonation therapy. *Front Psychology, 2*, 230.

Visch-Brink, E., de Smet, H. J., Vandenborre, D. & Marien, P. (in press). CAT-NL, nederlandse bewerking van K Swinburn, G Porter, D Howard (2004). *Comprehensive Aphasia Test*. Hove-New York: Psychology Press. Amsterdam: Pearson Assessment and Information.

Waldron, H., Whitworth, A. & Howard, D. (2011b). Comparing monitoring and production based approaches to the treatment of phonological assembly difficulties in aphasia. *Aphasiology, 25(10)*, 1153–1173.

Waldron, H., Whitworth, A. & Howard, D. (2011a). Therapy for phonological assembly difficulties: a case series. *Aphasiology, 25(4)*, 434–455.

Wambaugh, J. L., Cameron, R., Kalinyak-Fliszar, M., Nessler, C. & Wright, S. (2004). Retrieval of action names in aphasia: effects of two cueing treatments. *Aphasiology, 18(11)*, 979–1004.

Wambaugh, J. L., Doyle, P. J., Martinez, A. L. & Kalinyak-Fliszar, M. (2002). Effects of two lexical retrieval cueing treatments on action naming in aphasia. *Journal of Rehabilitation Research and Development, 39(4)*, 455–466.

Wambaugh, J. L. & Ferguson, M. (2007). Application of semantic feature analysis to retrieval of action names in aphasia. *Journal of Rehabilitation Research and Development, 44(3)*, 381–394. doi: 10.1682/jrrd.2006.05.0038

Warrington, E. K. (1975). The selective impairment of semantic memory. *Quarterly Journal of Experimental Psychology, 27*, 635–657.

Warrington, E. K. (1981). Concrete word dyslexia. *Brain, 103*, 99–112.

Warrington, E. K. (1996). *The Camden Memory Tests*. Hove: Psychology Press.

Warrington, E. K. & James, M. (1991). *The Visual Object and Space Perception Battery*. Bury St. Edmunds: Thames Valley Test Company.

Warrington, E. K. & Shallice, T. (1980). Word-form dyslexia. *Brain, 100*, 99–112.

Warrington, E. K. & Shallice, T. (1984). Category specific semantic impairments. *Brain, 107*, 829–854.

Webster, B. R., Celnik, P. A. & Cohen, L. G. (2006). Non-invasive brain stimulation in stroke rehabilitation. *Neurorehabilitation, 3*, 474–481.

Webster, B. R., Celnik, P. A. & Cohen, L. G. (2006). Non-invasive brain stimulation in stroke rehabilitation. *Neurorehabilitation, 3*, 474–481.

Webster, J. & Bird, H. (2000). *VAN: The Verb and Noun Test*. Northumberland: STASS Publications.

Webster, J. & Gordon, B. (2009). Contrasting therapy effects for verb and sentence processing difficulties: a discussion of what worked and why. *Aphasiology, 23(10)*, 1231–1251.

Webster, J., Morris, J. & Franklin, S. (2005). Effects of therapy targeted at verb retrieval and the realisation of the predicate argument structure: a case study. *Aphasiology, 19(8)*, 748–764.

Webster, J., Morris, J., Whitworth, A. & Howard, D. (2009). *Newcastle University Aphasia Therapy Resources: Sentence Processing*. University of Newcastle upon Tyne.

Webster, J. & Whitworth, A. (2012). Treating verbs in aphasia: exploring the impact of therapy at the single word and sentence levels. *International Journal of Language & Communication Disorders, 47(6)*, 619–636.

Weekes, B., Davies, R., Parris, B. & Robinson, G. (2003). Age of acquisition effects on spelling in surface dysgraphia. *Aphasiology, 17*, 563–584.

Weiduschat, N., Thiel, A., Rubi-Fessen, I., Hartmann, A., Kessler, J., Merl, P. & al., e. (2011). Effects of repetitive transcranial magnetic stimulation in aphasic stroke: a randomized controlled pilot study. *Stroke, 42*, 409–415.

Wertz, R. T. (1999). The role of theory in aphasia therapy: art or science? In D. T. Stuss, G. Winocur & I. H. Robertson (Eds.), *Cognitive neurorehabilitation* (pp. 265–278) Cambridge: Cambridge University Press.

Westbury, C. (2007). The Alberta Language Function Assessment Battery from http://www.psych. ualberta.ca/~westburylab/downloads/alfab.download.html

Whitworth, A. (1994). Thematic Role Assignment in Word Retrieval Deficits in Aphasia: Unpublished PhD thesis, University of Newcastle upon Tyne.

Whitworth, A., Webster, J. & Howard, D. (2012). Clinical aphasiology and CNP: a pragmatic alliance. Commentary on Laine and Martin, 'Cognitive neuropsychology has been, is and will be significant to aphasiology. *Aphasiology, 26(11)*, 1386–1390.

Whitworth, A., Webster, J. & Morris, J. (in press, 2014). Acquired aphasia. In L. Cummings (Ed.), *Cambridge handbook of communication disorders*. Cambridge: Cambridge University Press.

Willmes, K. (1990). Statistical methods for a single case study approach to aphasia therapy research. *Aphasiology, 4*, 415–436.

Wilson, B. & Patterson, K. (1990). Rehabilitation for cognitive impairment. Does cognitive psychology apply? *Applied Cognitive Psychology, 4*, 247–260.

Wilson, B. A., Cockburn, J. & Halligan, P. W. (1987). *Behavioural Inattention Test (BIT)*. Bury St Edmonds, UK: Thames Valley Test Company.

Worrall, L., Brown, K., Cruice, M., Davidson, B., Hersh, D., Howe, T. & Sherratt, S. (2010). The evidence for a life-coaching approach to aphasia. *Aphasiology, 24(4)*, 497–514.

Yampolsky, S. & Waters, G. (2002). Treatment of single word oral reading in an individual with deep dyslexia. *Aphasiology, 16(4–6)*, 455–471.

Yorkston, K. M. & Beukelman, D. R. (1981). *The Assessment of Intelligibility of Dysarthric Speech*. Austin, TX: Pro–Ed.

Zangwill, O. L. (1947). Psychology, speech therapy and rehabilitation. *Speech, 11*, 4–8.

Author index

Subject index

ACT therapy *see* anagram and copy treatment
A-FROM model (Aphasia Framework for Outcome Measurement) 90
ADA Comprehension Battery 29
adjectives 15
age of acquisition of vocabulary 12–13
agraphia 297; *see also* dysgraphia
Alberta Language Function Assessment Battery 24
alexia 241; *see also* dyslexia
allographic realisation 65, **352**; assessment 77–8; deficit 70
allographs 65, **352**
anagram and copy treatment 299*t*, 324, 327
anatomical modularity 6
anomia 46–7, **352**; *see also* word retrieval
aphasia *see* terminology
Aphasia Software Finder 346
apperceptive visual agnosias 81, 82
articulation difficulties 41
articulatory programming 38, 41, **352**
assessment 21; assessment batteries 23–4; auditory comprehension of spoken words 22, 28; cognitive neuropsychological perspective 91; hypothesis testing 21; number of test items 22–3; object and picture recognition 82–5; observations of communication 21–2; reading 55–64; refining level of assessment 22; selectivity of tests 21; spoken word production 22, 41–8; written word production (spelling) 71–9
associative agnosias 81, 82
attentional dyslexia 52*t*
auditory comprehension of spoken words 26*f*; assessments 22, 28–37; auditory phonological analysis 25, 26–7, 29–31; case studies 31, 32–3, 34, 37; deficits 26–8; implications for clinical practice 344; model 25; phonological input lexicon 27, 31–3; phonological input-to-output conversion 25; semantic system (comprehension) 28, 34–7; word meaning deafness 27, 33–4; word types 29
auditory comprehension therapy: compensation

strategies 105–7, 112–14; computer use 108; evaluations of therapy studies 103–20; implications for clinical practice 343, 344; phonological input lexicon 109–12; reactivation approaches 103–6, 107–20; semantic system (comprehension) 114–20; summary of studies 100–2, 101*t*; word meaning deafness 109–14;
auditory phonological analysis 18*t*, 25, **352**; assessment 29–31; case study 31; deficit 25, 26–7; therapy studies 103–12

bigraph training 245
blending 245
Boston Naming Test (BNT) 43
brain reorganisation strategies 92, **352**
brain stimulation 348

CART therapy *see* Copy and Recall Treatment
case series approach 4, 93–4, 127–8, 350
case studies: auditory comprehension of spoken words 31, 32–3, 34, 37; auditory phonological analysis 31; graphemic output buffer 77; object and picture recognition 82; orthographic output lexicon 74, 76; orthographic-to-phonological conversion (non-lexical reading route) 63, 64; phonological assembly 48; phonological input lexicon 32–3; phonological output lexicon 46–7, 61; phonological-to-graphemic conversion 74, 79; reading 58, 61, 63, 64; semantic system (comprehension) 37, 63; semantic system (production) 37, 74; spoken word production 37, 46–7, 48; written word production (spelling) 74, 76, 77, 79
CAT *see* Comprehensive Aphasia Test
category effects 28
CELEX database 12
central dyslexias 53–4*t*
cerebrovascular accidents (CVA) 348, **352**
'charm' effects 94, 96
CILT (Constraint Induced Language Therapy) 346

reading 50*f*; assessments 55–64; case
studies 58, 61, 63, 64; deficits 51–5,
58–60; direct lexical route 51, **352**; error
types 56; model 49, 50–1; orthographic
input lexicon 54–5, 58–60; orthographic-
to-phonological conversion 55, 63, 64;
phonological assembly in 51; semantic
lexical route 49, 50, **353**; semantic
system 55, 62–3; semantic system
(access) 60–1; sub-lexical route 15, 18,
50–1, **353**; visual orthographic analysis 51–4,
57–8; word types 56
reading therapy: cognitive relay strategies
248–56, 275–7, 285–7; computer use 241,
244, 247, 257–9, 270–1, 293–5; evaluations
of therapy studies 246–96; implications
for clinical practice 343; orthographic
input lexicon 244; orthographic-to-
phonological conversion (non-lexical reading
route) 244–5, 266–70, 273–95; reactivation
approaches 246–8, 250–2, 257–66, 270–3,
279–81, 288–95; relearning approaches
266–70, 273–9, 282–5, 293–5; summary of
studies 241–6, 242–3*t*
relearning approaches 89, 92, **353**; reading
therapy 266–70, 273–9, 282–5, 293–5;
writing therapy 307–11
repeated baseline studies 93*t*

SANDAL–SCANDAL–SMANDAL paradox 11
semantic cueing **353**
semantic dementia 13
semantic errors 16, **353**
semantic feature analysis therapy 126, 130
semantic lexical route: for reading 49, 50, **353**;
for writing 66, **353**
semantic representations 18*t*
semantic system 25, 80, **353**; access from
orthographic input lexicon 60–1; access from
. phonological input lexicon (*see* word meaning
deafness)
semantic system (comprehension) 25,
49; assessment 34–7, 62–3; auditory
comprehension therapy 114–20; case
studies 37, 63; deficits 28, 55
semantic system (production) 38, 65;
assessment 44–5, 72–4; case studies 37, 74;
deficits 39, 40; noun retrieval and production
therapy 128–68; writing therapy 301–4,
311–15
SFA therapy *see* semantic feature analysis
therapy
single-case study designs 93, 93*t*
spelling *see* writing therapy; written word
production (spelling)
spoken word comprehension *see* auditory
comprehension of spoken words

spoken word production: articulation/speech 41;
articulatory programming 38, 41, **352**;
assessments 22, 41–8; case studies 37,
46–7, 48; deficits 39, 40–1; error types 42;
model 38; phonological assembly 41, 47–8;
phonological output lexicon 40–1, 45–7;
semantic system (production) 39, 40, 44–5;
spoken naming 39*f*; spoken naming with
reading and repetition 40*f*; word retrieval
43–4; word types 42
spontaneous recovery 94
strokes 348, **352**
structural descriptions 80; assessment 84;
deficits 81
substitution strategies 92, **353**
subtractivity 6
surface dysgraphia 15, 69*t*, 76, 301–6, 315–19
surface dyslexia 3, 53*t*, 61, 264–6, 270–3

tDCS *see* transcranial direct current stimulation
terminology 241, 297, x
tests: number of items 22–3; selectivity of 21
theoretical models 4; assumptions 5–6;
auditory comprehension of spoken
words 25; competing models 7–9; language-
processing model for single words 4–6, 5*f*,
342–3; logogen model 4, 5*f*; Martin/Dell
models 7–8; reading 49, 50–1; spoken word
production 38; triangle model 8, 9; written
word production (spelling) 65–6, 67
therapeutic relationships 347
therapy 89–90, 343; approaches and aims 92,
92*t*; case series approach 4, 93–4, 127–8,
350; cognitive domain and mechanisms of
change 91–4; cognitive neuropsychological
perspective 89, 91, 348–51; compensatory
strategies 89, 92, **352**; dosage and intensity of
therapy 345–6; evaluations framework 97,
98–9*t*; the future 350–1; holistic context
90–1, 345–7; medium of delivery 346;
motivation 346; neurological stability 347;
other non-language functions 347;
restoration, relearning, retraining 89; salience
of therapy 346; single-case study designs 93,
93*t*; targeted therapy 349; therapeutic
relationships 347; *see also* auditory
comprehension therapy; noun retrieval and
production therapy; reading therapy; therapy
studies design; verb retrieval and production
therapy; writing therapy
therapy studies design 94; baseline phase 95–6;
data analysis phase 96–7; effectiveness 94;
hypothesis setting phase 95; key
principles 94–7; pre-therapy phase 95;
selection phase 95; therapy phase 96
transcranial direct current stimulation
(tDCS) 348